Feeling History

Feeling History

Lucan, Stoicism, and the Poetics of Passion

Francesca D'Alessandro Behr

The Ohio State University Press
Columbus

Copyright ©2007 by The Ohio State University.
All rights reserved.

Library of Congress Cataloging-in-Publication Data
D'Alessandro Behr, Francesca.
  Feeling history : Lucan, stoicism, and the poetics of passion / Francesca D'Alessandro Behr.
     p. cm.
  Includes bibliographical references and index.
  ISBN-13: 978-0-8142-1043-7 (cloth : alk. paper)
  ISBN-10: 0-8142-1043-0 (cloth : alk. paper)
  ISBN-13: 978-0-8142-9123-8 (cd-rom)
  ISBN-10: 0-8142-9123-6 (cd-rom)
  1. Lucan, 39-65. Pharsalia. I. Title.
  PA6480.D38 2007
  873'.01—dc22
                                         2006022721
  Paper (ISBN: 978-0-8142-5718-0)

Cover design by Jay Bastian
Typeset in Adobe Garamond

Aᴵ ᴍɪᴇɪ ɢᴇɴɪᴛᴏʀɪ
("ᴄᴏᴍᴇ è ꜰɪɢʟɪᴏ ᴜɴ ꜰʀᴜᴛᴛᴏ, ʟᴏʀᴏ . . . ʟᴀ ᴘɪᴀɴᴛᴀ ᴛᴜᴛᴛᴀ ɪɴᴛᴇʀᴀ")

Contents

	List of Abbreviations	ix
	Acknowledgments	xiii
	Introduction	1
Chapter 1	Lucan's Apostrophes as a Rejoinder to Virgil's Apostrophes in the *Aeneid*	16
Chapter 2	Addressing Negative Characters: The Didactic Nature of Apostrophe in the *Bellum Civile*	33
Chapter 3	Addressing Pompey: Lucan's Mimesis as Cognitively Useful Poetry and Apostrophe as a Stoic Trope	76
Chapter 4	Addressing the Emotions: Lucan's Narrator and the Character Cato in the *Bellum Civile*	113
Conclusion	Powerful Voices	162
Appendix	Stoic Inhumanity? A Philosophical Appraisal of Practical Pursuits and the Passions	171
	Notes	179
	Bibliography	231
	Index Locorum	255
	General Index	257

List of Abbreviations

Classical Authors and Works

Aeschylus [A.]
   Pr. (*Prometheus Victus*)
Apollonius of Rhodes [A.R.]
Aristotle [Arist.]
   E.E. (*Ethica Eudemia*)
   E.N. (*Ethica Nicomachea*)
   Po. (*Poetica*)
   Rh. (*Rhetorica*)
Caesar
   Bellum Civile (*B.C.*)
Cicero [Cic.]
   Acad. (*Academica*)
   Att. (*Epistula ad Atticum*)
   Cat. (*Orationes in Catilinam*)
   De orat. (*De oratore*)
   Fin. (*De finibus*)
   Off. (*De officiis*)
   Orat. (*Orator*)
   Parad. (*Paradoxa Stoicorum*)
   Tusc. (*Tusculanae disputationes*)
Diogenes Laertius [D.L.]
Epictetus [Epict.]
   Diss. (*Dissertationes*)
Euripides [Eur.]
   Alc. (*Alcestis*)
Galen
   De plac. (*De placitis Hippocratis et Platonis*)
Horace [Hor.]
   A.P. (*Ars Poetica*)
   C. (*Carmina*)
Isidorus [Isid.]
   Etym. (*Etymologiae*)

Josephus [J]
  B.J. (*Bellum Judaicum*)
Gorgias [Gorg.]
  Hel. (*Helena*)
Lactantius [Lact.]
  Inst. (*Institutiones divinae*)
Livy [Liv.]
Longinus [Long.]
  Subl. (*De sublimitate*)
Lucan [Luc.]
  BC (*Bellum Civile*)
Ovid [Ov.]
  Met. (*Metamorphoses*)
Plato [Pl.]
  Symp. (*Symposium*)
  R. (*Respublica*)
Plautus
  Am. (*Amphitruo*)
Plutarch [Plu.]
  Ant. (*Marcus Antonius*)
  Art. (*Artoxerxes*)
  Caes. (*Julius Caesar*)
  De Fort. Rom. (*De fortuna Romanorum*)
  Glor. Ath. (*Bellone an pace clariores fuerint Athenienses*)
  Moralia
  Pomp. (*Pompeius*)
  Rom. (*Romulus*)
  Virt. Mor. (*De virtute morali*)
Proclus [Procl.]
  In R. (*In Platonis Rempublicam commentarii*)
Quintilian [Quint.]
Sallust [Sall.]
  C. (*Catilina*)
Seneca [Sen.]
  Ag. (*Agamemnon*)
  Ben. (*De beneficiis*)
  Brev. vit. (*De brevitate vitae*)
  Clem. (*De clementia*)
  Cons. Marc. (*Ad Marciam de consolatione*)

Const. (*De constantia sapientis*)
Ep. (*Epistulae*)
Med. (*Medea*)
Prov. (*De providentia*)
Q.N. (*Quaestiones naturales*)
Tranq. (*De tranquillitate animi*)
Vit. beat. (*De vita beata*)
Sextus Empiricus [Sext.]
   M. (*Adversus mathematicos*)
Sophocles [S.]
   Tr. (*Trachiniae*)
Stobaeus, Johannes [Stob.]
Suetonius [Suet.]
   Jul. (*Divus Julius*)
   Luc. (*De vita Lucani*)
Tacitus [Tac.]
   Ann. (*Annales*)
Thucydides [Th.]
Velleius [Vell.]
Virgil [Virg.]
   Aen. (*Aeneid*)
   G. (*Georgics*)
Xenophon [Xen.]
   Mem. (*Memorabilia*)

Frequently Cited Works

AJP	*American Journal of Philology*
ANRW	Temporini, H. and W. Haase (ed.) 1981. *Aufstieg und Niedergang der römischen Welt*. Berlin and New York: deGruyter
BC	Housman, A. E. (ed.) 1926. *M. Annaei Lucani Belli Civilis Libri Decem*. Oxford: Blackwell
BICS	*Bulletin of the Institute of Classical Studies, London*
C&M	*Classica et Mediaevalia*
CA	*Classical Antiquity*
CJ	*Classical Journal*
CP	*Classical Philology*

EK	Edelstein, L., and I. G. Kidd (eds.) 1989. *Posidonius: The Fragments.* Cambridge: Cambridge University Press
FGrH	Jacoby, F. (ed.) 1923–1958. *Die Fragmente der griechischen Historiker.* Berlin and Leiden
HSCP	*Harvard Studies in Classical Philology*
LS	Long, A. A., and D. N. Sedley (eds.) 1987. *The Hellenistic Philosophers.* Cambridge: Cambridge University Press
OCD	Hornblower, S., and A. Spawforth (eds.) 1996. *The Oxford Classical Dictionary.* Oxford: Oxford University Press
PMG	Campbell, D. (ed.) 1991. *Poetarum Melicorum Graecorum Fragmenta,* Cambridge, Mass.: Harvard University Press
REL	*Revue des études latines*
SVF	Von Armin, H. F. (ed.) 1903–1924. *Stoicorum Veterum Fragmenta.* Leipzig: Teubner
TAPhA	*Transactions of the American Philological Association*

Acknowledgments

This book is a development of my doctoral dissertation and of a paper which I wrote the very first year of graduate school at the State University of New York at Buffalo during a seminar on Lucan. I remain indebted to those who participated in that seminar: that includes fellow students Alan, Paul, Jerry, and Professor Martha Malamud, who first taught me to appreciate Lucan's world and who put up with my idiosyncratic English.

I am grateful to all the SUNY Buffalo crew, especially Susan Cole, Jack Peradotto, Steve Dyson, Ted Peña, and Brad Ault, who, in different ways, helped me to love snowy Buffalo and classical antiquity.

This book (like every real book, I believe) was a collaborative project. I thank all my friends and colleagues who have patiently discussed it with me or read versions of it. I thank Casey Dué Hackney for her insights on Greek tragedy and lamentation; Richard Armstrong, who believed in the book from the beginning and read it several times; Mario Inglese, for his knowledge in theory; James Houlihan, who struggled with my English and was generous in praise; and Mark Zimmermann, who granted a reduction of my course load for the academic year 2004–2005. I thank the University of Houston for a grant to defray the costs of publication. Also, a special thank you goes to John Bernard, who read the typescript with great attention and edited it with great skill.

This book owes its birth—and other thanks—to Eugene O'Connor, my editor at The Ohio State University Press, and to the anonymous readers who contributed to the clarity and depth of its argument.

My text of Lucan's *Bellum Civile* follows A. E. Housman's edition; I am thankful to Cornell University Press for granting me permission to use Jane Wilson Joyce's translation of Lucan's *Pharsalia* (copyright © 1993 by Cornell University Press), reprinted by permission of the publisher. A longer version of chapter 1 first appeared in *Arethusa* 38.2 Spring 2005. Copyright © 2005 by The Johns Hopkins University Press. All translations from foreign languages are my own unless otherwise noted. All Latin outside the footnotes is translated save where my discussion so closely paraphrases the original as to render a translation redundant.

I dedicate this work to my parents, Giuliana Gualdi and Luigi D'Alessandro, who have taught me what is really worthy to be known and even across the ocean have been encouraging and supportive.

Finally, I am grateful for the love, support, and understanding of my husband, Thomas, and of my sons, Gervin and John-Paul. To them, too, goes a heartfelt "grazie."

Introduction

> From Archaeology
> One moral at least may be drawn
> To wit, that all
> Our school text-books lie
> What they call History
> Is nothing to vaunt of
> Being made as it is
> By the criminal in us:
> Goodness is timeless.
> (W. H. Auden, *Collected Poems* 1976)

It has been said that an author's ideological traces are apparent not only in the text's open and direct evaluations but also in its silences, in what it subtracts from open view.[1] In this book, I am interested in exploring how in Lucan's *Bellum Civile* the narrator, fearing these silences, uses the rhetorical space of apostrophe to express the poet's concerns about poetic limitations and potentialities. In Greek, apostrophe means a "turning away from." In the ancient sources it designates a declaimer's "turning away" from his presentation of facts and from the jury to address either the defendant or some absent entity (e.g., Quint. 4.1.63–70; 9.3.24). More generally, and especially in poetry, apostrophe designates the textual space in which the narrator talks directly to his characters.

The strength of apostrophe resides in the emotional intensity which the trope contributes to the text. In his treatise on sublimity, Longinus describes how, in one of his orations, Demosthenes defends his political choices through an appeal to the champions of Marathon (*Sub.* 16.2 quoting *De corona* 208). According to Longinus, with this rhetorical strategy Demosthenes persuades the judges and fills the hearts of all those present with renewed commitment to fight against enemies of the fatherland such as Philip. With a compelling approach he helps his listeners to realize that the glory of the past can (and should) be renewed in the present:

> When however, as though suddenly inspired by heaven and as if frenzied by the God of Prophecy, he [Demosthenes] utters his famous oath about the champions of Greece, "It cannot be that you were wrong; I swear it by those

who at Marathon stood in the forefront of the danger." Then you feel that by employing the single figure of adjuration [*to omotikon skêma*]—which here I have called apostrophe—he has deified his ancestors. He brings home the thought that we ought to swear by those who have thus nobly died as we swear by gods, and he fills the mind of the judges with the high spirit of those who there bore the brunt of the danger, and he has transformed the natural course of the argument into transcendent sublimity and passion and that secure belief which rests upon strange and prodigious oaths. He instills into the minds of his hearers the conviction—which acts as a medicine and an antidote—that they should, uplifted by these eulogies, feel no less proud of the fight against Philip than of the triumph at Marathon and Salamis. By all these means he carries his hearers clean away with him through the employment of a single figure. (*Subl.* 16.2, tr. W. Rhys Roberts)

In this book, I will show how Lucan's narrator acts like Demosthenes. Employing the hypnotic power of rhetoric, he moves the feelings of the readers and at the same time ensures that they do not lose themselves in the emotional surge. By addressing specific characters in his poem, he not only clarifies the analogies between past and present, but also tries to persuade his readers about the necessity to conduct themselves in a certain way.[2] The turning of discourse acutely reminds us of what is specific about apostrophe: to make its point by troping not the meaning of a word but on the circuit or situation of communication itself. The turning of discourse from the third person to the second corresponds to a shift from objective to subjective narration. As Edward Corbett has suggested, apostrophe is a figure of pathos "calculated to work directly on the emotions," and its most evident result is to guide the response of the listener.[3] Lucan's stylistic choices and his rhetorical circuits construct a powerful "drama of positions" in which the author conceives himself as a concerned, passionate, and knowledgeable teacher and us, his readers, as pupils who will learn a great deal in the process of being persuaded by the peformance.[4]

In one sense, looking at apostrophe may seem to be a relatively circumscribed critical enterprise. Yet, an attentive analysis of selected apostrophes from the *Bellum Civile* let us reach far and touch on unexpectedly broad critical horizons. It allows us to confront issues that are at the core of Lucan's vivid and disquieting imagination: does he believe in poetry's capacity to render one's point of view and to communicate it effectively? What is the role of interpellation in relationship to identification? What is the aim of the emotional urgency communicated by the narrator, and how does it square with his philosophical and didactic stance? What is the most important task of the aesthetic enterprise? In the end, this book should not simply be a study of direct address in Lucan's *Bellum Civile,* but rather an inquiry into the ethical implications of Lucan's adoption of a pervasively eloquent poetic persona. Lucan's long-acknowledged political engagement[5] must be connected with his philosophical and aesthetic stance which is powerfully revealed in apostrophe valued for its peculiar capacity to forge a link between narrator and audience, to bring characters to life as *dramatis personae* in order to trigger a reaction in the theater of the audience's mind.

The book will articulate this inquiry in the following manner. In chapter 1, I consider Lucan's use of apostrophes as a rejoinder to Virgil's apostrophes in the *Aeneid.* The ultimate effect of Virgil's apostrophe is debated. Elizabeth Block sees in Virgil's apostrophe the narrator's sympathy toward the victims of a war which he hates and does not believe legitimate. Gian Biagio Conte, however, finds a narrator who breaks the emotional engagement with the defeated created by empathy.[6] The treatment of apostrophe is intrinsically linked to the issue of representing grief as well as that of closure or narrative coherence; it reveals how the narrator comments on the suffering caused by Aeneas' war in Latium.[7] Does Virgil's use of apostrophe tend to justify the war's suffering, thereby helping the reader to approve of Aeneas' mission? Or does it rather reveal the injustice of Aeneas' project? It is crucial to keep in mind that when events are presented in a text, as Mieke Bal warns, they are always given from within a certain vision. This phenomenon is classified by Bal as focalization.[8] In fiction as well as in nonfiction a narrator might be expressing his own vision or that of another.[9] He can speak with his own voice while inhabiting the point of view of Jupiter or Turnus. Whose vision does Virgil's narrator embrace and support in his apostrophes? A narratological approach to this topic facilitates the task of assessing the *Aeneid*'s degree of polyphony; specifically it shows how through a rhetoric of voice and silence, Virgil ultimately produces a carefully controlled work with a unified viewpoint to which dissenting voices are carefully subordinated.[10]

In the *Aeneid* Virgil tries to preserve the fiction of his mimesis by allowing all characters—enemies included—to express their point of view. He also avoids interposing himself too often in the narrated events by restricting his use of apostrophe. Homer, for the most part, is reluctant to intrude in his text in the first or second person: above all, he directs sympathetic apostrophe to vulnerable and loyal characters (e.g., Patroclos) in the attempt to encourage the audience to share his emotional response to them.[11] It seems that under special circumstances Virgil, too, thinks that it is essential to sympathize with his characters through direct intervention, or to offer unequivocal elucidation about the meaning of an incident.[12] For the latter purpose, in certain apostrophes he tries to explain to the reader how an episodic hardship occurring in the plot (e.g., the death of a young soldier) can be understood and accepted in light of a broader perspective guaranteed by the narrator's omniscience. Similarly, the beautiful images employed by Virgil in death scenes (e.g., Dido 4.700–705; Euryalus 9.433–37; Gorgithion 10.781–82; Lausus 10.789–93) or the memorialization of the victims in the Italian landscape (e.g., Caieta 7.1–4; Misenus 6.229–35; Palinurus 6.377–83) foster the audience's reconciliation with human pain.[13]

The *Aeneid* ascribes to politics the power of fashioning human history into a linear narrative, with Jupiter as the guarantor of its ultimate goodness.[14] I will argue that in the narrator's statements—and half-statements—in apostrophe Virgil tries to control and perspectivize this teleological approach. At times he wants to resist it, but overall he seems to embrace it. In turn, the attitude which Virgil reveals in direct address is crucial to understanding Lucan's apostrophes. In his obsessive interventions into the text, as well as in his grotesque images, Lucan rejects the narrative closure created by Virgil's aestheticized deaths. In his ironic and gory narration, he discards the peaceful closure offered by Virgil's beautiful scenes; he reveals the unspeakable truth and ugliness of a world in which the good man is often brutally at a loss. In Lucan's poem, the epic dream of victory as the ever present companion of excellence is revealed as a mystifying lie, and the philosophical *virtus* of the defeated Cato is offered as a more truthful if less glamorous alternative to traditional success. Besides the repudiation of the subjective style, two features underline the distance between the *Bellum Civile* and the *Aeneid*: the rejection of a providential view of history (with Jupiter assuring the victory of the better party) and the corollary celebration of the defeated as the morally superior agent. Lucan condemns as fake Virgil's endorsement of the gods who sponsor Aeneas and, in due course, Caesarism. The narrator's main ambition is to uncover the ideological deceptions of traditional Roman epic, specifically its epic tendency to identify justice with beautiful victory. His frequent apostrophes—like Apollonius of Rhodes' numerous open comments, *aitia,* and use of the present tense in the *Argonautica*—reveal the poet's resolution to talk about himself and his present political concerns.[15] These apostrophes function as unmistakable signposts and provide a basic mapping which will orient the reader on the complex path toward the correct understanding of the poem.

Chapter 2 turns to Lucan's addresses to negative characters and his didactic use of apostrophe. Reading the *Bellum Civile,* even superficially, we notice the frequency and length of Lucan's apostrophes. This frequency is easily confirmed by a simple statistical analysis: apostrophe is used by Ovid, Statius, Silius, and Valerius Flaccus about twice as often as by Virgil, but Lucan uses it more than three times as often.[16] Moreover, the virulence of Lucan's invectives marks the narrator's involvement in the action.[17] In chapter 2, I analyze some of Lucan's apostrophes which are directed to characters considered negative by the narrator.[18] While I emphasize Lucan's ideological and stylistic distance from Virgil in the employment of this rhetorical device, I also underline the two authors' similar desire to control the reader's aesthetic reaction. Lucan's empathic description of Caesar's followers and the ironic comments offered in his direct addresses create a vivid and credible narration, but they also help the audience to evaluate the narrated events. Through the employment of these strategies the narrator wants to bar the readers from an uncritical identification with characters regarded as foolish and unable to understand what constitutes true virtue.

Indignation and emotional entanglement are particularly important as a means to promote the reader's active reaction to the narrated events. In a text dominated by the powerful presence of successful negative characters such as Caesar, the narrator's relationship with them is fundamental. Alessandro Schiesaro has perceptively underlined the risks that a forceful representation of vice can pose for the reader:

> At the level of "assent," which is the critical juncture in the development of forestalling of a passion, readers are left alone with their hermeneutic burden. They might have thoughtful teachers to guide them in the process, much as Plutarch recommends, but the author of the text, with his responsibilities and intentions, is inevitably out of the picture.[19]

Schiesaro's poignant observations on poetical reception can be applied to the *Bellum Civile* since Lucan's representation of Caesar and his minions occupies large sections and especially because the rhetorical luxuriance of narrative interventions reveals an author permanently preoccupied with the relationship between his words and the reader.

In the *Bellum Civile* characters and the narrator are voices in competition. Each character's voice expresses his or her own views, while the narrator's, like a counter-voice, frames the character's experience in a different light, presenting an alternative code of references for evaluation. The rhetoric of the narrative itself develops its effects through the relationship set up between the narrator, the emergent story, and his audience. This relationship produces irony. Irony is thus a byproduct of a narrative environment complicated by refractions and ambiguities since it is the outcome of a disparity between what is understood and what is known. What the character cannot see (or does not understand) is communicated by Lucan's narrator to him in apostrophe, which shapes the text as a dialogue. Didactic literature is often dialogic, and the presence of an interlocutor practically defines the genre:

> Alla funzione del 'tu' destinatario ogni testo didascalico assegna connotazioni diverse: e alle differenti caratterizzazioni dell'interlocutore corrispondono facies altrettanto diverse del progetto di insegnamento.[20]
>
> Every didactic text shapes his addressee, his "you" in a different way: different characterizations of the interlocutor correspond to the different kinds of didactic project.

For instance, in the archetypally didactic *Works and Days,* the primary addressee is Perses, the brother of the poet, represented as having cheated the poet out of a part of his estate. The poet (with the help of Zeus and the Muses) wants to teach him the path toward real justice, but Perses is often represented as completely unable to understand the full picture about justice; at times we wonder why the poet is even bothering. Jenny Strauss Clay convincingly explains the narrator's skepticism toward the more direct addressee as a well-conceived strategy: the entire lesson about justice and truth is reserved not for Perses but for the reader, who may be drawn to side with the poet, recognizing his superiority to the foolish Perses.[21]

This mechanism is also at work in the *De rerum natura,* where Lucretius generally presents himself as a dogmatic master and Memmius as his stubborn student. The master's lesson, we understand, is for all readers except Memmius:

> Lucretius allows his implied audience to eavesdrop on a therapy session conducted between himself as a teacher and Memmius as a pupil. This puts the wider audience in a privileged position: readers may perceive themselves as Lucretius' equals or partners in their self-conscious observations of the pedagogical process. Mitsis sees this larger strategy as manipulative or coercive in respect to the general reader, just as his image of Memmius does violence to the named addressee. However, in inviting the wider audience to identify with himself, Lucretius may also be implicitly identifying himself with the audience, thereby acknowledging that he too is a disciple.[22]

A similar narrative identification between narrator and external audience is fostered by Lucan's text, in which, as I hope to explain, the reader's reactions are the true object of the whole strategy of signification.

In addition, Lucan's reliance on apostrophe (as in general his use of a highly rhetorical language) is not a symptom of escapist evasion but rather an attempt to communicate more effectively the many sides of a complex reality.[23] The narrator's open comment becomes necessary to describing a reality in which words and symbols, fossilized and manipulated by the leaders, have lost their communicative efficacy. Lucan is aware that no member of a verbal community can ever find words in his language that are completely neutral and unbiased or exempt from the aspirations and evaluations of others.[24] Above all, he is aware that epic speech and in particular Roman moral vocabulary, has already been penetrated by the intentions of Caesar and his supporters. Lucan's aggressive tone—more typical of Roman satirical discourse than of Roman epic—betrays the moral orientation of the offered counsel[25]; and Lucan's narrator appears not as a nihilist, but as an individual deeply interested in ethics.[26] If, reproducing the perversion of the civil war and Caesar's manipulation of Roman ethical vocabulary, Lucan's language hosts oxymoronic expressions and terms that can have contradictory meanings, the Neronian author never affirms neutrality but, on the contrary, wants to denounce the rhetorical manipulation of language fostered by a perverted political environment.[27] And yet, since he is not at all confident that the true significance of narrated events can naturally emerge without an open comment or accusation, he uses apostrophe to balance out the "gap" between description and interpretation, between appearances and their meanings. In this attitude, Lucan discloses his engagement with history and concern for its victims.

Attacking the behavior of several "heroic" followers of Caesar, Lucan denounces their perversion of Roman *virtus* (which has shifted into senseless *furor*), their inability to think for themselves, and their mental enslavement to Caesar—in accepting the leader's transvaluation, eventually resulting in the establishment of the empire now presided over by Nero. At a narratological level, these interventions disrupt the reader's identification with what is being portrayed. Commenting too frequently on the action—there are at least 197 instances of apostrophe in the *Bellum Civile*—the narrator directs the reader's attention toward his own presence. In practice, by using apostrophe so often Lucan undercuts its possible effectiveness. Longinus stressed the importance of concealing figures of speech, to hide their effrontery in brilliant turn of phrases, to make them less obvious so as to avoid suspicion (*Sub.* 17.2). But Lucan does not conceal the effrontery, he does not seem willing to hide his presence as narrator and, in abusing the use of apostrophe he exposes it as an artifice which undercuts verisimilitude. However, his direct interventions are too frequent to be a rhetorical miscalculation. Lucan, to a degree, wants to *alienate* his readers from his text; he wishes to remind them that this is *just* a fiction, and that they should not be emotionally overwhelmed by the narrated events.

If, on the one hand, he strives to construct a poem which absorbs his audience through a vivid style and faithful representation of the characters' point of view, on the other hand, he also tries to hinder the audience's absolute identification with the fiction by allowing the narrator to speak extensively. The bifocal perspective from which Lucan portrays the narrated events forces the reader to become involved with the fiction but also to remain detached from it. In Lucan's aesthetic project, participation and alienation seem to be envisioned as fundamental phases through which the narrator accompanies the reader along the path of a correct reception of the work of art. Lucan crafts a poem in which distance and participation are as necessary as criticism and compassion toward the characters, in which the reader, with the aid of an eloquent narrator, questions everyone's actions and thus gains critical distance and ethical lucidity. In the twentieth century Bertolt Brecht tried to do something similar with his epic theater: he brought his audiences through a process of alienation (*Verfremdungseffekt*) in order to make the experience of the theater more profitably didactic. In the minds of both authors, poetry gives us imaginative opportunities to test, refine, and question ideas and values on which our understanding of the world rests; poetry teaches and delights, engaging our emotions as well as our capacity for reflection.

In chapter 3 I consider Lucan's use of apostrophe as a cognitively useful Stoic trope, as we have been reminded at least since Horace. Lucan's desire to encompass but also to guide his readers can be fully understood only if we place it within ancient rhetorical theory and in the context of philosophical (Platonic, Peripatetic, and Stoic) speculation on the risks and advantages of poetical discourse.[28] My examination of philosophical and rhetorical sources on poetry and poetics will be inclusive, not only because the distinction between philosophy and literary criticism cannot be unproblematically imported into ancient patterns of thought, but also because Lucan's biography suggests his exposure to different kinds of circles, scholars, and ideas.[29] Even if Lucan's allegiance to a poetics shaped by Peripatetic and Stoic preoccupations can be reconstructed only indirectly, it is rather useful to view the *Bellum Civile* in the context of Hellenistic and early Imperial ideas on aesthetics and rhetoric, rather than applying to it contemporary standards and expectations about the meaning and potential of the artistic endeavor.[30]

After clarifying what Greek and Roman rhetors and philosophers think about poetry, I will assess in what way some of these ideas are employed in the *Bellum Civile* and how an epic constructed to solicit strong emotional entanglement shows surprising allegiances to Stoic and Peripatetic aesthetics. Lucan's representation is, in part, built on and directly alludes to some of Aristotle's suggestions in the *Poetics*. At the same time his narrative anxiety to shield the reader from the negative examples portrayed in the fiction reminds us of Stoic didactic commitment to the reader's "ethical health." In addition, in this epic poem the presence of two important characters, one (Cato) portrayed as a Stoic sage and the other (Pompey) as a tragic victim, invites us to structure the discussion in terms of Lucan's Stoic and Peripatetic views on poetry.

The *Bellum Civile* is almost programmatically described by Lucan as a tragedy with Pompey as its tragic epicenter (*Bellum Civile* 7.210–213). Lucan accepts and, in a slightly modified version, re-presents Aristotle's definition of tragedy when he predicts that future readers of his poem, feeling "hope and fear" (*spesque metusque*, BC 7.211), will sympathize with Pompey. He manifests an almost "Virgilian sympathy" toward Pompey and explains that by facing the defeat of the better man, readers of all ages will at the same time suffer for Pompey and be filled with hope. The spectacle of courage and selflessness will endure for all ages as a powerful source of inspiration. Lucan's readers are called to react to the Republican defeat and, by wishing there had been a different outcome, to fight against their imperial present. This is Lucan's ultimate goal: the writing of a poem which will "allow the fearful to hope" (*liceat sperare timenti*, BC 2.15).

Lucan's apostrophes also convey the narrator's sympathy for Pompey's acceptance of defeat, his desire to protect the readers from the influence of negative characters, and his will to communicate an explicit "lesson" as informed by Stoic concerns about art. In fact, this kind of model of poetical reception—which both allows the use of emotions and makes room for a degree of mental dissociation between reader and fiction, permitting sympathy but not complete identification with the characters portrayed—had been developed by the Stoics. In this Stoic approach to art the reader is considered able to control his emotions even when under the charm of poetical mimesis supposed to use identifiable strategies to facilitate the reader's detachment from the object of contemplation (e.g., the text). In her article "Poetry and the Passions: Two Stoic Views," Martha Nussbaum has shown that in Stoic thinking we find two different approaches to poetry, each grounded in two different views of the nature of the soul. According to what she calls the "non-cognitive view," supported by Diogenes of Babylon and Posidonius, emotions are movements in the nonrational parts of a tripartite (essentially Platonic) soul; poetry educates through melody and harmony, by imposing order on nonrational impulses.[31] In the "cognitive view" (Chrysippus, Seneca, and Epictetus), on the other hand, emotions are evaluative judgments taking place in a one-part soul, and poetry educates by forming or changing these judgments. Poetry is dangerous because it delivers ambiguous or negative ethical messages through powerful images created in order to touch the audience's emotions and to be unreflectively accepted. Yet in this cognitive approach to poetry the Stoics consider poetic images as objects of assent; they offer them to the scrutiny of the mind.

This emphasis on the audience's ability to control its reactions is an innovative aspect of Stoic speculation on aesthetic reception. According to Plutarch, there are risks associated with poetry, but they can be overcome if the audience responds to the poetic enticement with the right kind of attitude (*De audiendis poetis* 15f–18b). Seneca knows very well that it is hard to resist the impressions triggered by the spell of poetic endeavor, but he is also aware that after the first unavoidable emotional reaction the alert reader should be able to decide about the ethical validity of the representation (*Eps.* 7 and 115). Moreover, in agreement with poets and philosophers like Panaetius, Lucretius, Cicero, Horace, and Persius, he recognizes the contiguity between the philosophical and literary endeavor. His desire to teach persuasively and effectively defuses his Stoic suspicions toward stylistic matters. Bred in this kind of philosophical eclecticism, Lucan shows a similar sensitivity toward the necessity to weld ethics and esthetics in a work of art.

Stoic texts recommend techniques useful to the formation of a critical stance and a detached spectatorship. Among these strategies we find the employment of frequent interventions and comments by the narrator. A desire to disrupt the identification process which prompts the reader to sympathize unreflectively with powerfully negative characters seems to be operating in Lucan's apostrophes as well as in his grotesque representation of characters utterly and foolishly devoted to their leaders. Through apostrophe, allegory, and irony Lucan wishes to alert his reader to the risks of believing in or passively endorsing all of his characters' doings. He develops an epic that features a vigilant narrator and promotes an awareness of the text as a mediated and mediating apparatus, a canvas where an object is never represented as a neutral entity. In his poem Lucan constructs powerful metaphors which, in accordance with Stoic *allegoresis*, must be interpreted by an audience in search of ethical guidance. In harmony with Stoic principles, he employs apostrophe as a powerful didactic tool and a formidable critical weapon to block identification between characters and audience. Since only the direct intervention of the narrator's voice can protect the reader from misunderstanding and successfully deliver the inspired message of political activism which Lucan wants to be heard, these passionate apostrophes must be considered a significant poetic choice.

Chapter 4 addresses Lucan's narrator and the character Cato. Here my concern is with the role of emotions in the *Bellum Civile*. Some scholars have tried to absolve Lucan's epic of philosophical preoccupations and have instead chosen to highlight what they see as the chaotic and pessimistic aesthetic temper of the poem. In order to substantiate this approach they have framed Lucan's characterization of Cato (especially in Book 9) as ironic and negative.[32] While some critics blame him for a stubbornness and rigidity allegedly connected to his Stoic allegiance, others condemn his ostensibly unwise and Unstoic "affair" with politics and emotions. These critics—often without giving serious consideration to the meaning of *apatheia* in Stoic discourse—view Cato's emotional entanglement with dramatic historical events as proof of the inefficacy of the Stoic creed or as a means to underline his philosophical failure.

In contrast with these recent critical tendencies, I believe that we cannot come to terms with Lucan's poem without dealing with its philosophical and didactic undertone. An exploration of the poem's philosophical mode can account for a passionate narrator who denies Virgil's civilizing providence and questions the rational Providence (*pronoia*) of the Stoics—all the while retaining a Stoic poetics.[33] Just as Lucan is unable to ignore the Virgilian model, so is he incapable of developing a defense of commitment outside Stoic discourse which, besides Virgilian epic, is the most important cultural framework employed and modified by the poet. If there is an attack against Stoicism in the *Bellum Civile*, this denunciation is not conducted as critics have suggested. I am aware that not everybody who reads this book will accept my argument that without irony and grimly parodic touches Lucan represents Cato as a Stoic hero who can teach the Romans political engagement and ethical health. But even those readers who see Lucan as a deeply ambivalent, sarcastic or despairing poet should appreciate this book for its attempt to seriously scrutinize the complex interrelation between poetry and philosophy. I hope that my discussion of Stoic attitudes toward fiction, poetry, and persuasion will illuminate the intellectual landscape inhabited by Lucan and his audience.

Lucan's allegiance to Stoicism is visible in several aspects of his work. To begin with, he shows dedication to a mimesis that openly and figuratively expresses cardinal truths about human existence such as the individual's moral responsibility and the absolute value of the good intentions.[34] The author's predilection for Pompey when he stoically accepts his doom, as well as for Cato, who by Nero's time had become a symbol of republicanism and Stoic commitment, demands a reconsideration of Lucan as a Stoic thinker, albeit of a particular brand of Stoicism. From a rhetorical point of view, there are important stylistic correspondences that tie the narrator's speeches to Cato's and allude to these characters' like-mindedness. Through textual analysis, I will show that Cato and the narrator share similar views and concerns. It should become progressively clear that a vivid representation that uses mythological allegory (*fabula*) as well as the spells of poetry (*ekplêxis*) is not inimical but necessary to philosophical depth and that the narrator of the *Bellum Civile* and its philosopher-hero Cato employ similar techniques (even emotional intensity) to engage their audiences and move them into right action.

Deeply concerned for the fate of the Romans, in the course of the *Bellum Civile*, Cato is associated with *metus* (*BC* 9.389; 2.291), *timor* (*BC* 2.240), *ira*

(*BC* 9.509–510), *furor* (*BC* 2.251–56), *gaudium* (*BC* 9.29), *dolor*, and *luctus* (*BC* 2.297–305; 2.378). Despite or *because of* the emotions which Cato harbors within his soul, he is praised by the narrator and is judged as able to guide and motivate those who seek advice, to produce effective apostrophes which, in turn, can stir powerful emotions in his listeners. Cato's feelings do not weaken his faculty to choose rationally what is best for those he loves. Lucan highlights the philosopher's concerns for Rome's political future without doubting the seriousness or the efficacy of his philosophical commitment and strategies. Whereas in chapter 2 I draw attention to the narrator's tendency to direct the reader's response to negative characters and in chapter 3 I explore the significance of Lucan's apostrophe to a relatively positive character (Pompey), in chapter 4, I explain how he uses apostrophe (and other techniques) to help the audience to evaluate the choices and personality of Cato as well as those of minor characters (e.g., Metellus, Brutus, the soldiers in Book 9) under the influence of Cato's rhetoric and behavior. By showing the philosopher's success in changing his interlocutors' opinions and conduct, the poet hopes that he too will be able to change the minds and resolutions of his fellow citizens.

Historically, the emotions have been studied mostly with respect to their negative influences rather than any positive role. Yet already Aristotle in his *Ethics* is fully aware of the importance of the sentiments or emotions; and even Posidonius, influential in Rome and head of the Stoic School in Rhodes during the first century BCE, seems to claim that if we are mature and rationally trained agents and if passions supervene upon beliefs, we ought to be passionate.[35] Paul Zanker has shown how an early statue of Chrysippus (c.280–207 BCE) depicts the philosopher with an intensity that seems to contrast with his professed doctrine of extirpation of the passions, suggesting that there was a role for the emotions in at least some kinds of intense pursuit, such as teaching.[36] And Panaetius (c.185–109 BCE), Scipio Aemilianus' associate and an influential figure of the Roman philosophical environment, argued, in a sort of compromise between Stoic and Aristotelian thought, that while it is important to be free from excessive passions, it is necessary to make the impulses obedient to reason. This evidence confirms the understanding that Panaetius was not advocating the eradication of the emotions but their moderation.[37] Among modern philosophers, Brad Inwood has recently emphasized that the sage lacks passions (extreme, irrational participation) because he lacks their constitutive false beliefs; yet—and this is very important for a correct evaluation of Cato's behavior in Lucan's Book 2—the sage retains some other elements of passion.[38] He can "rationally assent to just those impulses which would in the ordinary man be partial passions, doing so with an understanding of the hierarchical structure of permissible and instrumental goods."[39] Current studies on the psycho-emotional life of the Stoic sage underline that he has rational concerns on externals, reacts to them, and does not reject the information available to him through his emotional responses to reality.[40] The Stoic notion that external goods are indifferent cannot be used by the sage to maintain unresponsive behavior in the face of human suffering. Lucan's representation of Cato as a Stoic Sage does not uproot Stoicism; it undermines the notion of providence but also depicts the sage's *apatheia* as a complex phenomenon.[41] Cato's humanity certainly makes his archetypical idealism much more compelling.

By trying to join political militancy and philosophical idealism in one character, Lucan pursues a difficult path. Only a Cato who does not reject the passions but uses them constructively to fight against Caesar and mental lethargy can be appreciated and endorsed by a narrator so strongly involved with the political destiny of his city. Going beyond analysis of individual apostrophes, in the last part of the chapter, I reflect on the importance of Cato's emotions which I describe as consistent with the Stoic creed and central to a successful portrayal of Cato as a kind of anti-Aeneas. In fact, Lucan's humanization of Cato and his willingness to fight for a cause that, though just, is bound to fail make him worthy of admiration and similar to Virgil's *reginae* (Dido, Juno, Amata, Cleopatra, etc.). These vanishing yet unforgettable women who in the *Aeneid* refuse what has been willed by the gods (*Fatum*) and act in opposition to the way in which *pius* Aeneas acts become Lucan's models for a humane Cato.

In the *Bellum Civile* positive heroes are not blessed by victory. Lucan trumps the Virgilian idea of a material reward for the hero when he introduces a defeated philosopher-hero whose Stoic acceptance of the self-sufficiency of virtue is essential to counteract the power and psychological effects of defeat.[42] Living in a society in which, tragically, he sees ethical concerns defeated, Lucan abandons the orthodox Stoic notion of providence. He rejects the sage's *apatheia* as absolute indifference and defends political engagement by appealing to other notions also developed by the Stoics: for instance, the titanic fight of the sage against fate and the sheer importance of action.[43] While he may not believe that human society is a purposive system with a positive *telos* for action, he nevertheless believes in the moral necessity to fight tyranny. Cato is praised above all for his readiness to resist the nefarious powers sponsoring Caesar and for his awareness that defeat does not in itself prove the invalidity of a cause. Seneca had already emphasized the sufficiency of the sage who fights "unsuccessfully but equally stubbornly" (*tam infeliciter quam pertinaciter, Prov.* 3.14) against adverse circumstances. On this basis, against the premises originating with Roman epic, Lucan shows the insignificance of success and the moral superiority of the losing side. What matters in the end is not the triumph but the right pursuit (Cicero, *Fin.* 3.22 = SVF 3.18).[44]

With their apostrophes Cato and the narrator fight a conception of Roman history that Caesar's victory at Pharsalus seems to have sanctified: the legitimacy of the rule of the strongest.

Intruding into the text, the narrator (*BC* 9. 593–603) can rescue Cato from his material defeat by celebrating him as ideal commander of the Romans, perfect Stoic, and the only true Roman leader worthy of the title "father of the fatherland" (*ecce parens verus patriae*, *BC* 9.601). Only in the name of a philosophy that scorns human success, can the idea of historical triumph be minimized because Virtue, according to the narrator and the Stoics, must be considered in its "nakedness" (*nuda virtus*) separated from material success (*successu remoto*, *BC* 9.594). Too often in Roman history *fama* has been attached to unworthy events or insubstantial affairs. History, as Auden recognized, is carved "by the criminal in us." Goodness may be eternal but it is frequently silent and defeated; it is the task of Lucan's *vates* to celebrate it anyway.

Depicting Cato as the Stoic sage as well as an active political leader, Lucan also suggests that philosophical commitment must become active commitment. Cato's morality is not confined to his conscience but is at work in his fight against Caesar. If in Imperial Rome philosophers were imprisoned, exiled, and killed, they also gained authority and spiritual prestige by separating their wisdom and pursuits from the corruption of power. Lucan believes that the philosopher's scorn for power should not become indifference to his community. Cato's commitment to intervention in an imperfect political reality has been unjustly qualified as non-Stoic. It seems to me, however, that without undercutting the moral stature of the philosopher, his dedication turns him into a more sympathetic human being. His 'passion' (like the narrator's) is that not of the mad Caesar but of the good man outraged at a terrible outcome. Acting like Plato's philosopher in the myth of the cave, believing in altruism and personal responsibility, in the *Bellum Civile* the sage confronts the darkness of the world in order to teach his fellow citizens to fight for freedom.[45]

Throughout the discussion that follows I will try to focus my understanding of Lucan's rhetorical and philosophical program in his use of apostrophe: teaching, in this poem, takes place under the sign of apostrophe, which fills the gaps left opened by the gods' absence. When the gods (who favor Caesar) have abandoned the Republican cause, Cato must intervene and the narrator himself must communicate to his heroes the significance of their gesture in the face of death.[46] Even the historical Lucan, who in 65 CE was obliged by Nero to commit suicide for his participation in the Pisonian conspiracy, in the act of dying underlined the power of poetry. If we are to believe Tacitus, "feeling his hands and feet chilling and life receding little by little from his extremities, though his heart retained warmth and sentience, [Lucan] recalled a passage in his own poem (*recordatus carmen a se compositum*) in which he had described a wounded soldier dying a similar form of death; so he recited these very verses (*versus ipsos rettulit*), and those were the last words (*extrema vox*) he uttered" (*Ann.* 15.70). It does not matter which kind of government Lucan envisaged, an old fashioned Republicanism or a kind of enlightened monarchy. It is beside the point if at one point he was weak and tried to incriminate his mother to save his life (Tac. *Ann.* 15.57; cf. Suet. *Luc.* 25f.). Lucan's commitment to resist Nero is a "fact to be taken into account in any responsible judgment on his performance both in life and in art."[47] Writing his poem and becoming a tragic character in his own existence, he knew well how to create a sense of drama and how to inspire his audiences. Turning life into art and art into life, he chose a philosophical stance which allowed him to retrace and empower "the *not so fragile* limits of the speaking self."[48] He stood for commitment, fought his own battle of Pharsalus (*Pharsalia nostra, BC* 9.985), "followed the prescriptions of his own epic and plunged into the chance to create something new."[49] He demonstrated that poetry does effect a *transport* which takes us to another realm with different values and rules, a world that even the poet had not yet seen but about which he had only dreamt.

1

Lucan's Apostrophes as a Rejoinder to Virgil's Apostrophes in the *Aeneid*

> Talis pietas peritura querellas egerit.
>
> Love for the falling fatherland expresses such lamentations. (*BC* 2.63–64)
>
> Il lamento delle madri a Maratona
> [. . .] non fu udito da nessuno.
>
> The mothers' lament at Marathon [. . .] nobody heard.
> (Salvatore Quasimodo, *Maratona*)

Preliminary Observations on Virgil's Apostrophe

A vital legacy left by the Hellenistic poets to Roman epos and epyllion comprises poetic experimentalism, the mobility of the temporal levels, and the importance of the present as a funnel through which to reconsider and interpret all past events.[1] Rome also inherits from the Hellenistic world an interest in hexametric poetry devoted to the praise of monarchs, lofty themes, and historical exploration.

After Ennius and Naevius, history and national values had already become essential components of Roman epic, so that when in the *Aeneid*, Virgil decides to deal with the mythical past previous to the foundation (*ktisis*) of the Roman nation, he tries to bridge it to the present, to establish in which form that past influenced the present. The future (that is the poet's Augustan present) weighs on the action and conditions the "epic freedom" of the Virgilian hero; the knowledge and the burden of future history are the primary concern of the protagonist and increasingly shape all his decisions.[2]

Virgil's vision in the *Aeneid* is teleological. As Charles Segal explains:

Virgil's authorial persona not only takes in the whole course of the narrated events, but also comprehends the divinely destined course of history, from Rome's small beginnings to its domination of the world. Authorial prescience is, literally, divine prescience; it implies some measure of identification with Jupiter's grand sweep of knowledge and power over human affairs.[3]

The desire to talk about the present through a legend from the past is a major concern in Hellenistic epic. It is also prominent in Virgil's sparse but significant use of apostrophe. Yet, as I will show, the message communicated by the Augustan poet through this rhetorical device is not always consistent.

Let us glance at the beginning of the *Aeneid:*

> Arma virumque cano, Troiae qui primus ab oris
> Italiam fato profugus Laviniaque venit
> litora, multum ille et terris iactatus et alto
> vi superum, saevae memorem Iunonis ob iram,
> [. . .]
> Musa, mihi causas memora, quo numine laeso
> quidve dolens regina deum tot volvere casus
> insignem pietate virum, tot adire labores
> impulerit. Tantaene animis caelestibus irae?[4]

> I sing of warfare and a man who from the coast of Troy, in early days as a refugee, by destiny came to Italy and to the Lavinian shore, this man whipped cruelly on land as on the sea by the blows of the gods, by the grudging rage of cruel Juno
> [. . .]
> O Muse, tell me why, lamenting offenses to her authority, the queen of the gods compelled a man renowned for his virtue to undergo so many perils and enter on so many trials. Can such anger prey on the minds of the gods?
> (*Aen.* 1.1–4; 8–11)

The reader notices the similarities with the opening lines of the *Odyssey* and the recapitulative tone of the beginning of the *Iliad,* the arms and the battles. Importance is given to the first person "I sing," which signals the narrator's control and draws attention to his presence. Only at line 8 is a more direct tribute paid to tradition with the invocation to the muse; at the same time, the power of the narrator is highlighted with the apostrophe to the gods and the request for an explanation.[5] We have, at line 11, an example of what has been considered the hallmark of the *Aeneid*, the so-called "subjective style."[6] In this rightly famous verse, the narrator openly questions the anger of the gods and the origin of the events that he is about to sing.[7] Yet Virgil's intrusion in the narration does not always insinuate complaints and lack of understanding. In other instances, the narrator, through his remarks, seconds the story being narrated (or seems to) with his apostrophes, and so he propels and justifies the action in the plot.

The narrator's attitude toward his characters and narration has been established most systematically by Brook Otis.[8] Otis sees Virgil's voice expressed in two main ways:

1. through the use of apostrophe directed especially to characters destined to be overcome (sympathy).
2. through the characters' revelation of their own point of view (empathy).

First I would like to comment on the second device which had been noticed already in antiquity for giving to the narration a very memorable and distinctive flavor.[9] Apollonius of Rhodes in *Argonautica* 3 used Medea to focalize the story and to explore the intrinsically problematic choice that she was forced to face. Medea's psyche was portrayed with sophistication while the heroine was struggling to decide if she should help the Argonauts. The poet subordinated divine intervention to the psychological motivation of the heroine virtually to the point that the Olympians' designs and intervention could have been altogether eliminated from the action.[10] The novelty and significance associated with the figure of Medea are perceived and reused by Virgil on a larger scale.[11] The poet, in his epic, gives ample space to the point of view of characters other than the protagonist. For instance, he often directs his attention to the views and feelings of the losers and lets them openly complain against the gods. The most striking example of the freedom of speech granted to the losers is at *Aen.* 12.870–884. Here, in a fairly long speech, having understood that she cannot do anything more to save her brother Turnus, Juturna is allowed to criticize Jupiter for the cruelty of his decision but also for "the gift" of immortality which he once gave her:

> Quid nunc te tua, Turne, potest germana iuvare?
> [. . .] nec fallunt iussa superba
> magnanimi Iovis. Haec pro virginitate reponit?
> Quo vitam dedit aeternam? Cur mortis ademptast
> condicio? Possem tantos finire dolores
> nunc certe et misero fratri comes ire per umbras.

How now, Turnus, will your sister be able to help you? [. . .] I have not misunderstood the cruel commands of great-hearted Jupiter. In this way he pays me back after he has taken my virginity? Why did he give me an immortal life? Why did he take away death from me? Now I could put an end to these awful torments and be a companion of my poor brother among the ghosts." (*Aen.* 12.872; 877–81)

Juturna deems her immortality unbearable if her brother Turnus is taken away from her; she also condemns Jupiter for having taken from her virginity and her freedom to accept or reject the present. In the ancient world, women's capacity to complain in a way which preserved their honor was restricted and suicide was one of the few options open to them. Juturna's immortality obliges her to comply with what she would rather refuse, that is, to accept her brother's death and her own survival.

Gian Biagio Conte acutely frames "empathy" as a stylistic device operating in a wide system of signification within which Virgil grounds his work. Conte explains that traditionally a poet in a given society fills the epic code (the objective narrative structure, conventions, expectations defined by epic as a literary genre derived mainly from Homer) with the epic norm, that is, the cultural contents, the ideology which motivates his writing; yet, the poet knows how to conceal his point of view.[12] Apollonius of Rhodes is revolutionary in his choice to expose this feature of the epic genre and creating in the *Argonautica* a narrator who does not conceal his point of view.[13]

In the *Aeneid*, Virgil is being influenced by both Homer and Apollonius. Employing de Jong's useful narratological model, we could say that, like Homer, he does not allow the level of primary signification, identifiable with the narrator, to 'contaminate' the secondary level of signification, that of the characters, whose point of view is therefore faithfully portrayed by the primary narrator. The narrator's knowledge of the will of the gods and *fatum* does not compromise his objectivity and so allows minor characters to speak with their own voice.[14]

Virgil, probably under the influence of Apollonius' characterization of Medea, chose to reveal the biased perspective of the epic genre. According to Conte:

> Virgil introduces multiple points of view as a more powerful interpretative apparatus [. . .]. In the ideology of *epos*, History appears as a flat, static, monistic surface. This is the vision of a reality that has emerged into its final, definitive order [. . .]. But within the strata of History, covered over and pushed far into the background, lie the layers of suppressed crises and anguished, repressed memories, the price exacted by *imperium* and the

horrors of civil war. This wealth of lost events, which constitute in fact the linear movement of diachronic succession, is rearranged synchronically by Virgil as a simultaneous plurality of points of views. The absolute point of view of the norm is not obliterated; it is made relative [. . .] the upshot is not what a character is in the world but what the world is for the character and how he sees himself.[15]

The coexistence of Aeneas' point of view with that of his enemies springs from Virgil's will to grant them an autonomous *raison d être* which the historico-epic code had denied.[16]

According to Richard Heinze, something similar happens in apostrophe. Apostrophe is a manifestation of the narrator's "sympathy" (above, number 1) and can be viewed as responding to the same expressive need manifested in "empathy"; the poet is fully participating in the sufferings of the conquered and, emotionally, he is endorsing their points of view. Following Heinze, Block considers the role of apostrophe to be paradigmatic in the deaths of Euryalus, Nisus, and Lausus, whose misfortunes trigger the narrator's sympathy and sorrow. This understanding of the enemy, in her view, challenges the justifiability of the Latin war. Through apostrophe the narrator would express, at once, sorrow for the victims of Rome and his own doubts about the imperial project.[17] Block shares Heinze's and Otis' view according to which sympathy and the intrusive narrator threaten epic objectivity by foreshortening the necessary distance between the subject of the epic and its object.

Conte does not agree with this analysis which merges sympathy and empathy into the same narrative need. He maintains that sympathy and empathy are "genetically and functionally distinct and work in opposite directions."[18] While *empatheia* destroys epic objectivity through the multiplication of points of view and the consequent relativization of the epic norm's ideology, sympathy is Virgil's way to reorganize that fragmentation. Conte argues that apostrophe helps the reader to understand Virgil's agenda while writing the poem:

> . . . with the truth diffracted into individual, relative images, it is up to the poet to come forward as a 'monitor' able to assess the worth of each fragment by relating it to the objectivity of his own overview. That is the role played by the systematic intervention of the poet within the structure of the *Aeneid:* he creates an *objective consciousness* under which the various individual truths are subsumed.[19]

Conte assumes that, overall, the ideological biases of the epic norm in the

Aeneid are painfully displayed as reflecting only one particular point of view, but, at the same time, their norm is accepted. The Virgilian revelation of the agony of the leader and of the conquered can indeed be viewed as a type of apology that justifies power.[20] In this perspective, even sympathy becomes a blind closing of the eyes in front of war's bitter reality and the elegiac tone, an elegant way out, a surrogate for a more direct and outspoken protest.[21]

In the following pages I will examine the most extended apostrophes in the *Aeneid*, showing that while some of them definitely fit Conte's model, others do not. At crucial junctures in the *Aeneid* the narrator uses apostrophes to focalize our attention on his own voice. In those moments we are called to reflect on what seems most important to him. What the poet suggests often coincides with what Jupiter reveals to Venus in Book 1: Rome will hold forever *imperium*, an empire without end (*Aen.* 1.279), founded on the conquest of *furor impius* (*Aen.* 1.294–96). While the narrator as a public mourner and superior interpreter of the future appears in the invocations to Euryalus and Nisus, Pallas, and Turnus (*Aen.* 9.446–49; 10.507–9; 10.501–505), he figures as a disappointed interpreter of the gods' will and remains critical of his own inability to lament dutifully those who die in the appeal to Icarus (*Aen.* 6.30–33) and in the apostrophe to Jupiter at the beginning of Book 12. He also shares the sorrow and disorientation of the defeated in the apostrophe to Dido (4.401–405). While in the first charted group of apostrophes he focalizes the events with the foreknowledge of Jupiter, in the second cluster he assumes the confused point of view of *fatum*'s victims.

Providential Apostrophes:
A Narrator Near to the Conqueror

In the apostrophe to Euryalus and Nisus, the narrator's externalized reflections orient our reading and reconstitute the movement of the plot toward a more unified meaning. Advertising Rome's timeless glory, at *Aen.* 9.446–49, Euryalus and Nisus are praised for their behavior:

> Fortunati ambo! Si quid mea carmina possunt,
> nulla dies umquam memori vos eximet aevo,
> dum domus Aeneae Capitoli immobile saxum
> accolet, imperiumque pater Romanus habebit.
>
> You both are lucky! If my poetry has some power, no day ever will subtract you from the memory of time, as long as the house of Aeneas dwells on

the unshaken rock of the Capitoline and the Roman father maintains his
empire. (*Aen.* 9.446–49)

The narrator entrusts his certitude of Euryalus and Nisus' future immortality not so much to the power of the song as to the imperishable "*imperium*" of the Romans.[22] No matter how terrible and unfair *mors immatura* might seem, it is the price to be paid for the establishment of the new Roman nation. The adjective "*fortunati*" contradicts and corrects Nisus' judgment about his friend's and his own lot at 9.427–30 where, with the following words, he begged the Rutulian to spare Euryalus:

> me me! adsum qui feci, in me convertite ferrum,
> o Rutuli! mea fraus omnis; nihil iste nec ausus
> nec potuit (caelum hoc et conscia sidera testor),
> tantum infelicem nimium dilexit amicum.
>
> Me! Me! Here I am! I did it! Against me turn your swords, Rutulians. All the trickery was mine; he dared nothing, he could not—heaven is my witness, and the knowing stars—all he did was cherish too much a luckless friend. (*Aen.* 9.427–30)

Yet in the narrator's words, these friends are lucky despite their violent death. Gordon Williams thinks that they are lucky because "loving one another, they died together [. . .] Euryalus was lucky because he did not die alone and abandoned; Nisus was lucky because he did not outlive his lover, and his death on his lover's behalf was noble."[23] Williams argues that in the adjective "*fortunati*" we would have Virgil's recognition that what redeems and ennobles the warriors' final action is love as a private feeling, directed not toward the fatherland but toward each other. Yet if the main message of the apostrophe is that love as a private feeling is sufficient reason to bestow glory and praise, lines 448 and 449 contradict this quite non-epic impression. For, at 448–49, the narrator links the memory of the couple to the Roman future domain. Euryalus and Nisus will be remembered only as long as (*dum*) the city founded by Aeneas is standing. The narrator praises Nisus' action when, as Philip Hardie suggests, this "black hunter" has gained understanding of the importance of fighting as a true soldier in an army: "When Euryalus is captured Nisus continues to operate from cover, his spearthrows as unseen as any non-hoplite arrow, until the death of his beloved Euryalus forces him into the open to fight fair with his flashing sword."[24]

Conte's conclusions fittingly describe this apostrophe: the poet's intrusion works as a justification of the glory of Rome and an encouragement to be selfless soldiers. The deaths of many Italian soldiers (Camilla, Lausus, and all the young and brave warriors briefly invoked in Book 10) are mourned and justified in the same way. At *Aen.* 10.507–509 we have the narrator's invocation to the dead Pallas:

> O dolor atque decus magnum rediture parenti!
> haec te prima dies bello dedit, haec eadem aufert,
> cum tamen ingentis Rutulorum linquis acervos.
>
> O you who will come back as sorrow and great honor to your father! This first day brought you to war and took you away from it; nevertheless, you leave behind many heaps of Rutulians. (*Aen.* 10.507–509)

Pallas is the implicit addressee of the invocation (*rediture*). He has obtained his renown, fighting with pride and killing many enemies, and has behaved according to the expectations of his father as well as of Aeneas' and the epic code. Sorrow and public recognition (*dolor atque decus*) are interestingly juxtaposed, yet grief seems to be subordinated to the celebration of public virtues. Line 509 brings witness to Pallas' many victims (*ingentis acervos*). Williams, very perceptively, underscores this line's double entendre: "The glory lies in the slaughter; Pallas and his father could feel that, but the poet insulates himself in the ambiguous tone of *cum tamen*."[25] Williams could be right, the *cum tamen* might refer to the mounds of Rutulians slain by Pallas, but it could alternatively refer to *dies* (in the previous line), the little time available to this youth to gain his fame. If the latter is the case, we have not the revelation of a poet perplexed about the slaughter caused by war, but a poet who is amazed at the young warrior's ability to kill so many people in so little time. Confirmation of the second interpretation comes at line 507, where the narrator calls Pallas *rediture*, "the one who will come back." Deceptively the optimism conveyed by the verb helps the reader to forget that Pallas' resurrection is a trick: his return is granted only as a dead body memorialized in the praise of a poet.[26] The apostrophe is obviously focalized through the omniscient narrator of the *Aeneid* who can see the future and is able to understand that the deaths of Pallas, Euryalus, and Nisus can be meaningfully situated in the path that leads first to possession of Latium, and to *imperium* later.

As the examples above have shown, the narrator feels the urge to reveal himself especially when someone has been killed. In this matter his apostrophes resemble miniature lamentations or perhaps failed lamentation. If it is true that "lamentation is prototypical of epic as a genre that confers praise,"[27] it is also true that "lament is born from grief for the dead, and though praise is naturally combined with it, grief has the chief place."[28] While in Greek tragedy personal attachment expressed in lamentation threatens social order, in the Athenian public funeral orations, women's grief is inscribed in praise that minimizes the human cost of war.[29] In Virgil's apostrophe we find both impulses: on one side, there is a feminine desire to cry over the bodies of the war's victims which calls into question the glorification of death sponsored by a martial community; on the other side, we find the male urge to turn the lamentation into funeral oration with its public utility. Complaint, when present, is entrusted to minimally ironic signifiers[30] and it soon dissolves into the acceptance of the loss. Undercutting sorrow and desperation, the poet who apostrophizes the dead wants to turn even death into an *exemplum*, a display of glory and the spur to greatness, both useful devices to legitimize the needs of an expanding community. After all, as Elaine Fantham reminds us, in the city of Rome, men did not lament ritually; if we can believe Polybius' representation, they walked in the funeral procession, hierarchically arranged, wearing the death masks of their ancestors, and they listened to the *laudatio,* the eulogy publicly pronounced by the closest kin right before the lighting of the pyre.[31]

Thomas Greene has argued that the epic genre's primary concern "is not with heroic achievement in itself as with the affective cost of achievement"[33] and also that "[i]n European cultural history, the pivotal text that alters permanently the epic circle of projection and participation is the *Aeneid*."[33] Grief is dangerous and ambiguous; in Virgil's poem it is often associated with problematic characters (Juno, Dido, Amata, etc). Furthermore, with Virgil's apostrophe we have the impression that celebration and lament do not belong together anymore. The narrator seems greedy in his mourning of the dead; he does not say a word about Turnus' death.

Instead, Turnus' case is considered after he has slaughtered Pallas. This section is particularly interesting because it is immediately preceded by an address to the minds of men unaware of the future, in lucid opposition to the knowing narrator:

> Nescia mens hominum fati sortisque futurae
> et servare modum, rebus sublata secundis!
> Turno tempus erit, magno cum optaverit emptum
> intactum Pallanta et cum spolia ista diemque
> oderit. . . .

> O human minds unaware of the future and of how to find a balance in times of success! A time will come for Turnus when he will desire Pallas

alive ransomed at high price and when, with these spoils, he will hate this day. (*Aen.* 10.501–505)

Using the demonstrative *ista,* the narrator points to the *spolia* which Turnus is going to take. The demonstrative mimics a gesture, a dialogue between the narrator and the reader.³⁴ There is, here, an open message delivered not so much to Turnus but to the external audience, the readers of this work and future conquerors of the world. In the apostrophe, we are reminded of the importance of *clementia* (= *servare modum*). *Clementia* as *lenitas* or *moderatio* toward the defeated enemy had been employed by Caesar in 49 BCE at Corfinium, and Augustus in his *Res Gestae* (3.1–2) stressed that he acted in accordance with the principle.³⁵

Since the problem of preserving the right conduct toward the losers was one of the central issues in Roman politics between the age of Caesar and that of Augustus, it is perceived by Virgil as particularly prominent and deserving of an open meditation.³⁶ According to Alessandro Barchiesi, while in the implicit comments the narrator offers the reader the space of doubt and a locus in which the contradictions of the epic ideology are denounced, in his open comments, the narrator often endorses the epic genre with its ideological and literary corollaries.³⁷ For instance, although Virgil portrays the war between Trojans and *Latini,* at times, as a civil war, and although this image allows us to see the cracks inherent in the communicative structure of the *epos,* his ultimate message, his open comment, preserves the idea of a just war approved by the gods.³⁸

Dissenting Apostrophes:
A Narrator Near to the Defeated

In the apostrophe to Icarus (*Aen.* 6.30–33), the narrator's frustrations and the "dialectic of immobility" that Barchiesi has eloquently described are overtly manifested (in an explicit comment), and the narrator admits an inability to represent fully the reasons and unjust fate of those who are defeated.³⁹ In Book 6 Virgil seems to painfully acknowledge his silence as a betrayal of the losing side when he describes Daedalus. Several scholars have noted in the passage a marked identification between the author of the *Aeneid* and the artist Daedalus. Both artists create ambiguous works of art and, though with remorse, are not able to portray the victims of their enterprise.

Daedalus, successful in practically all his undertakings, not only fails as a father but also cannot immortalize his son through his art and "falls" in the attempt as Icarus had fallen from the sky:

> Tu quoque magnam
> partem opere in tanto, sineret dolor, Icare, haberes.
> Bis conatus erat casus effingere in auro,
> bis patriae cecidere manus. . . .
>
> Even you, Icarus, would have a great part in such an accomplishment if sorrow permitted it; twice he tried to carve your trials in gold, twice the father's hand failed. (*Aen.* 6.30–33)

No details are offered to explain the accident. Everything is condensed in the evocative *casus* (32) and *cecidere* (33) and in the sympathetic apostrophe to Icarus, absent from the life of his father and from his artistic endeavor. As Michael Putnam notices:

> both Daedalus within this initial segment of the narrative and the narrator expounding his tale seem in different senses careless [. . .] Daedalus thinks largely of his invention and the clever manipulation of it, not of its human consequences [. . .] neither at the start nor at the conclusion of the episode is the actual death of Icarus mentioned, a fact which invites the reader to fill in the text, to exercise his own imagination by re-creating and contemplating the most poignant incident in Daedalus' biography. In his role as a father Daedalus may have been lacking in understanding of his son. As an artist he is a double failure, first incapable of completely imitating nature, then unable to mime the disastrous results of this inadequacy.[40]

With Putnam, Fitzgerald, and Pöschl, I am convinced that at *Aen.* 6.14 "an artistic work is described in which the artist presents his own story"[41] and the accent is put on the inability of the artists (both Virgil and Daedalus) to portray reality fully. So strong is Virgil's identification with Daedalus that Virgil's narrator addresses Icarus directly, as if he were Daedalus, in explanation of his failure to carve his dead son into his relief. Through this failure Virgil does not trivialize grief but points to the difficulty of representing it adequately. As Putnam remarks, the episode is an extraordinary "study in artistic incompletion" and, I would add, serves as a symbol of the writing of the *Aeneid*. Daedalus stands for Virgil and Aeneas successfully accomplishing their journey and celebrating the greatness of Rome but also leaving behind, without much commentary, a train of victims who not only could not be spared but also cannot be adequately depicted and mourned.[42] It may be that this epic does not fulfill the reader's expectations of praise for Aeneas and that therefore it is a text that strives to deliver a positive message of accomplishment without fully managing the task. But it is certainly true that in its final segment there is no adequate and explicit lamentation for those who are vanquished.[43] The narrator behaves like Hercules when the latter is asked by Pallas for help against Turnus (*Aen.* 10.460–64). He listens to Pallas' prayers and asks for Jupiter's intervention; but ultimately he must agree with Jupiter that intervention is not possible. No one can change the fate of the dying youth, so Hercules must "suppress his groans" and "shed empty tears" (*corde premit gemitum lacrimasque effundit inanis, Aen.* 10.465).[44]

Another example of dissenting apostrophe occurs in Book 12. Juturna, skeptical about the gift of immortality given to her by Jupiter as a reward for her suffering, implicitly denounces the unfairness of (her) fate. In accordance with her dissatisfaction, Juturna not only does all she can to actively preserve Turnus from his fatal moment, she also bitterly laments his death.[45] Juturna-like, the narrator manifests his limitations and inability to understand what happens in the plot in the address to Jupiter at *Aen.* 12.500–504:

> Quis mihi nunc tot acerba deus, quis carmine caedes
> diversas obitumque ducum quos aequore toto
> inque vicem nunc Turnus agit, nunc Troïus heros,
> expediat? Tanton placuit concurrere motu,
> Iuppiter, aeterna gentis in pace futuras?
>
> What god will retell for me such a bitter story? Who in a song could describe that carnage and the death of the captains, how many of them over the entire plain Turnus hunted, or how many in turn the Trojan hero pursued? Was it your pleasure, Jupiter, that peoples afterward to live in lasting peace should rend each other in such a tumult? (*Aen.* 12.500–504)

The question to Jupiter recalls the remark about Juno and the anger of the gods at the beginning of the poem (*Aen.* 1.8–11). In both apostrophes, to Juno and to Jupiter, Virgil's narrator sounds confused.[46] But at *Aen.* 12.504, the narrator even more problematically questions Jupiter's agency: "Was the war which caused so many deaths really your will?" As in the apostrophe of Book 4 (see below), the narrator's omniscience here vanishes; what in other apostrophes is given as *the will of the gods* here becomes what is *perhaps* the will of the gods. It is a powerful maneuver that, as Wofford suggests, "raises the possibility that the epic, rather than representing divine teleology at work in human history, may instead tell an arbitrary story of human violence."[47]

The narrator withdraws his responsibility from the action which he describes as a cruel dance in which different captains in turn kill and are killed. He seems unwilling either to understand or endorse this story. Yet right afterward (at *Aen.* 12. 503) he recuperates his knowledge and affirms that the fight between the Trojans and Latini was despicable especially considering these people's future peace. The allusion to the *aeterna pax* would have not been lost on the Augustan reader. The narrator does not know who is the maker of *discordia,* but he capitalizes on this impasse by reminding the reader about the Augustan reestablishment of peace.

How can we explain (here and throughout) the double position of a narrator all-knowing and ignorant at the same time? Wofford concludes that Virgil in the *Aeneid* manages to balance both attitudes: he envelops the reader with rhetorical figures (like apostrophe) which "appear to affirm the ideological defense of Aeneas' epic mission" and are often connected to the omniscience of the narrator, while at the same time he describes the characters (the narrator included) as completely ignorant about the causes of the action.

The narrator's ignorance appears in the apostrophes of Book 4.408–12. Here he seems to forget about Aeneas' divinely ordained plans; he uses the sympathetic style to draw attention to Dido's feelings and to draw the reader close to the perspective of the defeated. At this moment he provides an indulgent and open comment on the behavior of the queen. The narrator invokes her name, tries to look at the situation through her eyes, and relieves her of responsibility by blaming *Amor* for the unavoidable events:

> migrantis cernas totaque ex urbe ruentis:
> ac velut ingentem formicae farris acervum
> cum populant hiemis memores tectoque reponunt,
> it nigrum campis agmen praedamque per herbas
> convectant calle angusto;
> [. . .]
> Quis tibi tum, Dido, cernenti talia sensus,
> quosve dabat gemitus, cum litora fervere late
> prospiceres arce ex summa, totumque videres
> misceri ante oculos tantis clamoribus aequor!
> Improbe Amor, quid non mortalia pectora cogis.

> And you could see them streaming as they rushed down from the whole city: even as ants, when they attack a giant stack of spelt to store it in their homes, remembering the winter, the black file swarms across the fields; they

haul the plunder through the grass on narrow tracks;
[. . .]
What were your feelings, Dido, then? What sighs did you utter at that sight when far and wide, from your high citadel, you saw the beaches boil and turmoil take the waters with such a vast uproar before your eyes? Voracious Love, to what do you not drive the hearts of men? (tr. Mandelbaum, modified) (*Aen.* 4.401–405; 408–12)

The narrator addresses the reader, Dido, and finally *improbus amor* as he strives to understand her feelings and desperation while staring at Aeneas' crew getting ready to leave. He allows Dido's perspective to be registered while at the same time he draws the reader's attention and sympathy to her. As Sarah Spence has written, "Book 4 grants voice to the cause of *furor* but, more than that, to the degree that it enlists sympathy for Dido, it engages us as audience on the side of difference and against the cause of empire, even if only temporarily."[48] The narration and preparation for the trip are interrupted as the narrator gives priority to his heroine's psyche. He does not employ his typical prophetic perspective but stares at the Trojans with the eyes of a regular reader or, rather, those of Dido. The Trojans are busy with their ships and to a spectator (*cernas*, 401) they might look like insignificant and weak ants rushing to store food for winter.[49] The sight of the spectator here merges with the glance of the queen who is described with the same verb as looking down (*cernenti*, 408) at the Trojans from the distant citadel: "Dido, the audience, and the emotional are each granted the superior position associated in the rest of the epic with power."[50] The verb *populat* is also invested with emotional significance. The ants (as well as the Trojans) consume everything around them; their alacrity appears to Dido as meaningless as it is devastating. In this line we have what Conte believes is missing from apostrophe in the *Aeneid*, a picture of "what the world is for the character."

The passage is striking because altogether the content of *Aen.* 4 betrays the narrator's negative judgment of Dido. At *Aen.* 4.69 she is called *furens,* and at 17 she is openly blamed for her conduct characterized as faulty: *Coniugium vocat: hoc praetexit nomine culpam* ("she calls it a marriage: with this name she disguises her guilt"). At 283, again and revealingly, in free indirect discourse, after the Trojan leader has been reproached by Jupiter and exhorted to set sail, the queen is categorized as *furentem* (*Heu quid agat! Quo nunc reginam ambire furentem / audeat adfatu?* 4.283–84).[51] If Virgil elsewhere prioritizes the destiny of Rome and justifies Aeneas' conduct,[52] he does not do so in the apostrophe to Dido, in which the trope is used to underline the queen's feelings and her perception of the events.

Conclusion: From Virgil to Lucan

Normally in the *Aeneid* the narrator is consistent in suppressing his own feelings and introducing the emotions of his characters without forcing his views upon the reader. *Empatheia* is the Virgilian strategy that allows this neutrality. Furthermore, Virgil for the most part does not allow the action to retreat into the background (especially when emotion is being expressed) and come to a standstill.[53] Yet there are important breaches in this objectivity and they typically occur in apostrophe, which can perform two rather different roles. In the apostrophes to Nisus and Euryalus, to Pallas, and to Lausus, Virgil's concern with the future is openly displayed. Even if, at times, his addresses contain a veiled irony, the Roman cause is nevertheless prioritized and narrative closure achieved. When communicating to the young victims of war, the narrator provides to his external audience directives for the appraisal of events that otherwise would be difficult to assess. In these apostrophes the polyphony created by the empathic rendering of each character's point of view is quickly corrected, and the *vates* establishes the priority of his interpretation and the justice of the fates willed by Jupiter.

Acknowledging a different perspective in the address to Icarus, Virgil admits that grief can hinder representation and celebration. In this apostrophe the "providential perspective" is momentarily forgotten and the narrator's point of view seems to coincide with that of the character addressed. Silence or the lack of representation (Icarus' absence) is all he can accomplish. Likewise lamentation is obliterated or rather constrained in this work. The poet does not indulge in his grief, nor does he question Jupiter's plan for too long. He behaves like Aeneas at *Aen.* 6.33–41, when the hero abandons the vain contemplation (*ista spectacula*, 37) of Icarus' grief and follows the Sibyl, the symbol of future knowledge. Like Aeneas, who in the confusion of the flight from Troy "did not look back" (*non . . . respexi, Aen.* 2.741) and left Creusa behind, the narrator forgets those who die; Virgil's success as a poet depends in part on his ability to forget the victims and rivalries of the Latin war, focusing instead on Rome's glorious future under Augustus.[54]

Finally, we find in Book 4 that apostrophe is a rhetorical strategy to preclude a unilateral endorsement of the plot. With this kind of rhetorical approach the plot is bent; it is forced to follow the inextricable paths of the human mind and the point of view of dissenting characters. In the address to Dido apostrophe is the mirror through which the writer and the reader can study and evaluate the events from Dido's point of view. In this section of the story apostrophe is used to provide further details that disrupt and complicate the narration and its intelligibility. In Book 4 we are allowed to see Aeneas' mission through the eyes of Dido and we are reminded of the "dark side" of *pietas*.

Roman epic at its inception with the *Bellum Poenicum* and the *Annales* is not introspective, does not question heroic values; rather it celebrates victories which are synonymous with happy endings. The topics chosen by Naevius and Ennius were morally unsophisticated and not tragic. As Sander Goldberg notices, the only episode endowed with real pathos in what survives of Ennius' *Annales* is Ilia's rape (34–50) and her persecution by Amulius. At any rate, even in this incident the gods remain on Ilia's side and her suffering is ultimately rewarded.[55] Roman legend (e.g., Livy's stories of Brutus 2.3–5 and Virginia 3.44–49) depicts suffering but does not question the course of action from which suffering springs forth. Sacrifice when embraced by Romans is always the morally right decision, the basis of the noble example. Brutus' consular office imposes upon him the duty of inflicting punishment on his own children; he executes the sentence without doubting the justice and necessity of the matter. Losers or enemy of the state can be treated in their misery with sympathy but not with tragic pathos.

In Roman epic the suffering-and-reward pattern becomes normative, but it is explored more deeply in Virgil's masterpiece. Although Virgil's subjective style problematizes "happy endings" by focusing on the enemy's suffering, it also seems to betray his unwillingness to consider fully the victims' experience. Andrew Laird has observed that in the *Aeneid*, much more than in the Homeric poems, speech is the privilege of the powerful.[56] In his book Laird establishes an interesting connection between ethnography and epic. Both discourses, he observes, despite their attempt to record facts impartially, reproduce the mores and preoccupations of their originating environment, that is, of imperial societies. Ethnographers are often aware of the difficulty in recovering, through the layers of the historical records, the identities of muted groups, minorities with unequal power to speak and be heard.[57] As I will try to demonstrate in the following chapters, Lucan's narrator takes on the task—unusual for a Roman epic—of giving voice to the defeated and of representing the world as they perceive it. Choosing as his subject the civil war, he depicts a universe in which there is no assurance of the triumph of the better cause.

In a poem that is about the losers, grief cannot get in the way of representation, nor can lamentation be contained. In fact, it occupies many of the narrator's apostrophes. In apostrophes that have the flavor of lamentations, Lucan admits that it is not possible to renounce certain things, that even the Stoics have not resolved with satisfaction the problem of external goods if political freedom is one of them. In their ethical theory the Stoics discussed wealth, health, or freedom as "preferred indifferents," objects that nature has set us to pursue (and therefore it is reasonable to pursue them) but that are not necessary to our flourishing and happiness. Yet by praising Cato's renunciation of his life for political freedom, even they admitted that the presence (or lack) of an external such as freedom matters greatly. The author complains indirectly when in his grotesque images he rejects the aesthetic of closure created by Virgil's reassuring and beautiful images. He abandons the idea that in the course of history virtue receives confirmation, legitimacy, and aesthetic appeal through victory and success. Some of his ironic descriptions or apostrophic tirades reveal the indescribable truth and ugliness of a world in which the good man is often brutally at a loss. In the poem, especially in its many apostrophes to different characters, the narrator offers a new lesson. He persuasively reveals that the epic dream of victory as the ever present companion of merit is a mystifying lie and that the philosophical *virtus* of the defeated Cato should be preferred to that of the triumphant Aeneas.

2

Addressing Negative Characters: The Didactic Nature of Apostrophe in the *Bellum Civile*

> Cum omnia quae excesserunt modum noceant, periculosissima felicitatis intemperantia est: movet cerebrum, in vanas mentes imagines evocat, multum inter falsum ac verum mediae caliginis fundit.
>
> While all excess are hurtful, the most dangerous is unlimited good fortune. It excites the brain, it evokes vain fancies in the mind, and clouds in deep fog the boundary between falsehood and truth. (Seneca, *Prov.* 4.10)
>
> It [my theater] by no means renounces emotion, least of all the sense of justice, the urge to freedom, and righteous anger; it is so far from renouncing these that it does not even assume their presence, but tries to arouse or reinforce them. The "attitude of criticism" which it tries to awaken in its audience cannot be passionate enough for it.
> (Bertold Brecht in a dialogue with the playwright Friedrich Wolf quoted in Willet 1964: 227)

The Narrator and Representation

The civil war and the advent of Caesar triggered a shift in Roman vocabulary.[1] The difficulty in interpreting a double-edged reality becomes the material on which Lucan's poem is founded. As both Thucydides and Sallust understood, the chasm between words and their meaning tends to become wider in time of internal strife and political instability. While Thucydides (3.82.4)[2] believed that during time of political turmoil words are affected by a change of customary meaning, in Sallust's work Cato speaks of a loss of true meaning. He insightfully observes:

> iam pridem equidem nos vera vocabula rerum amisimus: quia bona aliena largiri liberalitas, malarum rerum audacia fortitudo vocatur, eo res publica in extremo sita est.
>
> But in truth we have long since lost the true names for things. It is precisely because squandering the goods of others is called generosity, and recklessness in wrong doing is called courage, that the republic is reduced to extremes. (*C.* 52.11–12)

Cato perceives that "the present day is marked by *inter bonos et malos discrimen nullum* (*C.* 52.22): good men can no longer be distinguished from bad because, by implication, the loss of *vera vocabula rerum* has destroyed good and bad as conceptual categories."[3] Matthew Roller has clarified how during the Civil War we have a redefinition of Roman moral discourse and how this change is not founded on the creation of a new vocabulary and new terms but craftily hinges on Roman Republican symbols and traditional rhetoric.[4] The employment of words contrived by political ideology becomes evident in Lucan's text at *BC* 1.299–351 when Caesar attacks the Republic through his minion Laelius, who convinces his men to disregard the established ties (kinship and citizenship) binding them to the Pompeian faction. Laelius (and later on Caesar himself, *BC* 7.318–22) encourages the Caesarians to treat the Pompeians as *hostes*, external enemies, and explains that only those who participate in Caesar's mission form a community of moral obligations that must supplant consideration of previous civic commitments and even kinship.[5]

In Lucan's epic the flexibility of the word (under Caesar's attack) is explored and denounced. The author is fully aware that the republic and its values have been betrayed but are also displayed as an empty facade for the first time under the patronage of Caesar:

> Namque omnes voces, per quas iam tempore tanto
> mentimur dominis, haec primum repperit aetas.
>
> Oh, yes! all the voices by which for so long
> we have lied to our masters, that age was the first to fashion! (*BC* 5.385–86)

Dangerously, the advent of Caesar lends legitimacy to his "linguistic program," making those in charge as almighty as the gods:

> Bella pares superis facient civilia divos;
> fulminibus manes radiisque ornabit et astris
> inque deum templis iurabit Roma per umbras.
>
> Civil war will make deified men equal to deities;
> Rome will deck the dead with thunderbolts, haloes, and stars
> and in the very temple of the Gods swear by mere shades of men. (*BC* 7.457–59)

Lucan unmasks the dangers of political propaganda that divinized Roman emperors at their death and linguistically directs our attention to distinguishing real gods from fake ones. In the *Bellum Civile* the investigation of the gap or shift between words and their meaning is conducted through a rhetorical strategy that utilizes tropes such as irony, parody, paradox, accumulation of details, hyperbole, catachresis, and oxymoron as well as repeated questions to particular characters (apostrophe). Far from being accessory, these rhetorical figures try to turn the reader's mind aside from the basic literal meaning of a scene or its appearance and direct it toward its interpretation or possible interpretations. It is not simply *pathos* that Lucan is looking for[6]; rather, he wishes to focus his attention on situations for which either no words are available or only words that no longer convey a univocal meaning.

In Lucan's poem, the problem of "representation" emerges in connection with rhetorical and philosophical preoccupations about *phantasia*. *Phantasia* is viewed by the Stoics as the act of seeing connected to that of interpreting; according to Anthony Long, in Stoic thinking it has a centrality that it lacks in other schools of thought.[7] The Stoics defined dialectics as "the science of speaking well" and qualified "speaking well" as "speaking things that are true and fitting,"[8] yet they were profoundly aware that a representation can be false and misleading and indeed that it is not at all simple to apprehend the veracity of it.[9] Rist refers to Max Pohlenz's thesis (deriving from D.L. VII 54 = SVF 2.105, 1.631),[10] according to which Chrysippus wanted to think of the criterion of truth as present in the object of knowledge and not in the mind of the knower. Gerard Watson believes instead that the Stoics "were particularly insistent that all our statements were interpretations of reality, meanings imposed on reality rather than reality itself."[11] The available evidence suggests that dating back at least to Chrysippus there was debate in the school over the criterion of truth. Lucan, too, seems afraid that reality represented in its simplest form—i.e., in a plain, harmonious, and naturalistic style—does not supply enough meaning. He seems worried that his own descriptions fall short of the goal of unmistakably representing his own views on events, characters, and notions that have been already redescribed and reinvented by political and epic discourse.[12]

The Narrator's Ambiguous Intervention on Vulteius' *Virtus*

The notion of *virtus* and the meaning of *pietas* are explored by Lucan in the Vulteius episode.[13] When some of Antony's men are trying to escape the Pompeian troops led by M. Octavius and are trapped on a raft, Vulteius, the commander of the raft, convinces his men to commit suicide instead of falling into the hands of their enemies (*BC* 4.452–87). The episode has attracted the attention of several scholars, all of whom have recognized the perversity inherent in this collective suicide and in these soldiers' sense of duty. Frederick Ahl eloquently says of Vulteius:

> His *pietas*, his sense of duty, patriotism and proper conduct is, by his own admission, *militiae pietas* (4.499), dedication to military duty. This is the loyalty to individual generals (rather than to any ideal or to the state) that lay at the root of so many troubles in the late Republic. [. . .] Vulteius, like Scaeva, seems to think that love of death is the very essence of virtue, even though he never questions the moral worth of what he is dying for.[14]

Pietas, the defining virtue of Aeneas, his sense of duty toward his mission and his family, has been dangerously transformed into devotion to war itself. Virtue has become a generic desire to die and to fulfill the desires of one's leader. Yet Vulteius' invitation to his men is particularly convincing because it parasitically appeals to ideas and notions traditionally advertised as constitutive of the Roman nation:

> Quaecumque per aevum
> exhibuit monimenta fides servataque ferro
> militiae pietas, transisset nostra iuventus.
> Namque suis pro te gladiis incumbere, Caesar,
> esse parum scimus; sed non maiora supersunt
> obsessis, tanti quae pignora demus amoris.
> Abscidit nostrae multum fors invida laudi,
> quod non cum senibus capti natisque tenemur.

> Whatever records loyalty
> has preserved through the ages and those that Duty has kept

of the sword in active service—our young soldiers could have surpassed them!
Caesar, we know that to fall on our swords in your cause,
is not much; but, besieged as we are, greater deeds
elude us—deeds we would dedicate, pledges of deep devotion.
Hateful chance has cut away much of our praiseworthiness,
since we are not held captive with our old men and children. (*BC* 4.497–506)

Vulteius' desire to impress Caesar and his wish to die for him are couched in traditional epic vocabulary (*aevum, monimenta, fides, pietas, iuventus;* cf. esp. *Aen.* 9.446–49, the apostrophe to Euryalus and Nisus). Alluding to Aeneas' regret for not having been killed by the walls of Troy (*Aen.* 1.94–96),[15] Vulteius' disappointment over the absence of his relatives betrays his wish to have defended his city and relatives in a more traditional kind of defensive war. But it also betrays the character's perverted desire to bring sorrow to one's own relatives. In the *Aeneid* only a character like Turnus wishes that Pallas' father had been present at the death of the young boy (*soli mihi Pallas / debetur; cuperem ipse parens spectator adesset,* "to me alone Pallas is owed; I might only wish his father was here to watch." *Aen.* 10.442–43).[16]

Hopelessly trapped (*fuga nulla patet, BC* 4.485) Vulteius' men are "besieged" (*BC* 4.504) by fellow citizens intending to cut their throats (*stant undique nostris / intenti cives iugulis BC* 4.485),[17] they are summoned not to come to terms with the Pompeians (*BC* 4.507–510)[18] and like some of the Saguntines during the siege of their city, they commit suicide (*eodem plerique semet ipsi praecepitaverunt* [Livy 21.14.1]). Vulteius' behavior and invitation to his companions also resembles Aeneas' conduct during the last hours of Troy. Under the spur of *extrema cupido* (*Aen.* 2.348), the Trojan leader invites his companion to refrain from hopes of salvation (*Una salus victis nullam sperare salutem,* "Safety for the defeated is to hope for none" [*Aen.* 2.354]). The leaders' exhortation is successful, Vulteius' "ardor sustains all the spirits of the wavering youth" (*Sic cunctas sustulit ardor / mobilium mentes iuvenum, BC* 4.520–21) just as Aeneas' *furor* stimulates his young companions (*sic animis iuvenum furor additus, Aen.* 2.355). The similarity of Vulteius' words to those we found in Virgil's apostrophes to the young victims of the Italian war and the allusion to important events in the history of Rome deflect the audience's attention from the details of the situation. At this point the temptation might be to react sympathetically to Vulteius' speech and to his soldiers' suicide. The reader's pity depends on the hardship in which the soldiers find themselves and on Vulteius' appropriation of traditional epic language.

The idea that individual death is a spectacle to be contemplated and enjoyed is recurrent in the episode:[19]

> Conferta iacent cum corpora campo,
> in medium mors omnis abit, perit obruta virtus:
> nos in conspicua sociis hostique carina
> constituere dei. Praebebunt aequora testes,
> praebebunt terrae, summis dabit insula saxis,
> spectabunt geminae diverso litore partes.
> Nescio quod nostris magnum et memorabile fatis
> exemplum, Fortuna, paras.
>
> When mounds of dead bodies litter the field,
> every death is merged in the count, valor is drowned and vanishes.
> The gods have set us on a vessel in sight of friends
> and foes alike. The sea will supply us with witnesses;
> earth, too: mainland and craggy island will grant them;
> both sides will be watching us from opposite shores.
> I know not what mighty and memorable lesson you plan to
> draw from our death, Fortune. (*BC* 4.490–97)

Vulteius' desire to have men and gods as his witnesess can be framed in relation to Stoic athleticism and the Senecan idea of the *theatrum mundi* (*Prov.* 2.7–9; *Ep.* 43.4–5).[20] Stoic overtones permeate the entire episode, in which death freely chosen becomes the only way to counteract defeat. "Let the enemy learn that heroes have no masters," Vulteius exclaims at *BC* 4.505; and at *BC* 4.485–87: "everywhere fellow citizens are getting ready to cut our throats; choose death and chase all fears away" (*decernite letum, / et metus omnis abest*), "desire what is necessary" (*cupias quodcumque necesse est*). Vulteius' words to his men seem to echo Seneca's advice to Lucilius about how to minimize adversities in life at *Ep.* 107:

> optimum est pati, quod emendare non possis, et deum, quo auctore cuncta proveniunt, sine murmuratione comitari; malus miles est qui imperatorem gemens sequitur. Quare inpigri atque alacres excipiamus imperia nec deseramus hunc operis pulcherrimi cursum, cui quidquid patiemur, intextum est. [. . .]; paratos nos inveniat atque impigros fatum. Hic est magnus animus qui se ei tradidit; at contra ille pusillus et degener, qui obluctatur et de ordine mundi male existimat et emendare mavult deos quam se.

> That which you cannot reform, it is best to endure, and to attend uncomplainingly upon the god under whose guidance everything progresses; for it is a bad soldier who grumbles when following his commander. For this reason we should welcome our orders with energy and vigor, nor should we cease to follow the natural course of this most beautiful universe, into which all our future sufferings are woven. [. . .]; let Fate find us ready and alert. Here is your great soul—the man who has given himself over to Fate; on the other hand, that man is a weakling and a degenerate who struggles and maligns the order of the universe and would rather reform the gods than reform himself. (*Ep.* 107.9–12; tr. R. M. Gummere)[21]

Vulteius' men, making a virtue out of necessity and behaving indeed like the good soldier described by Seneca, embrace enthusiastically the suggestion of their commander. Vulteius himself is like the Stoic wise man who accepts all hardships as willed by the forces in supreme command of the Universe and imagines the gods as his witnesses. The vocabulary of moral freedom employed by the Stoics is interestingly and paradoxically borrowed by Vulteius, who does not die to preserve his freedom but to please Caesar and be admired.[22]

Virgilian and Stoic echoes characterize Vulteius' words again at *BC* 4.516–20:

> Proieci vitam, comites, totusque futurae
> mortis agor stimulis: furor est. Agnoscere solis
> permissum, quos iam tangit vicinia fati,
> victurosque dei celant, ut vivere durent,
> felix esse mori.
>
> I have discarded life, my friends; I am wholly aroused
> by the sting of immediate death: it is a frenzy. Only
> those whose onrushing fate is already upon them are granted
> the revelation; those who will go on living, the Gods
> keep them in the dark that they may endure to live on:
> death is a blessing! (*BC* 4.516–20)

According to Vulteius a special truth is revealed to those who are about to die: "only those touched by the imminence of fate can recognize how sweet it is to die."[23] Luca Canali's translation poignantly catches the strength of the adjective *felix* and its Stoic echoes. During the *laudatio funebris* for Pompey, Cato himself proclaims the happiness of the men quickly reached by death after defeat: "Happy are you [Pompey] whose death came close on defeat (*felix, cui summa dies fuit obvia victo* [*BC* 9.208]). Furthermore, at *BC* 4.520 the adjective *felix* seems to mimic programmatically the voice of the Virgilian narrator ambiguously calling "fortunate" the young victims of the Latin war (e.g., Nisus and Euryalus are called "fortunate" at *Aen.* 9.446). Virgil implies that even he who died a premature and violent death can be blessed if he realizes the fruitfulness of his sacrifice. On Virgil's use of *felix* in *Georgics* 2, Richard Thomas acutely observes that the adjective is employed to qualify trees that are propagated by arboriculture and through human intervention become productive (e.g., 2.81: *ramis felicibus*, "civilized branches," branches which bring fruit). Viticulture is like victory in war: sometimes fruit can only be brought into being by cuts and wounds.[24] We find the expression *insontes . . . proicere animas* (*Aen.* 6.435–36) sympathetically used by Virgil to characterize "the guiltless" in the underworld who, "renouncing life," committed suicide.[25]

Even if the concept of suicide as the ultimate free act is not present in the fragments from the Early and Middle Stoa collected by Von Armin, the exaltation of death as a supreme good is recurrent in early imperial philosophical discourse. John Rist observes that in early Stoic doctrine the word "freedom" does not appear in connection with suicide, and the act itself cannot be considered apart from the intentions triggering it.[26] Vulteius' behavior would not have been endorsed by Chrysippus.[27] Yet in the first century the suicide of figures like Cato, Thrasea Paetus, and Seneca made suicide philosophically acceptable: Seneca comes close to arguing that death freely chosen makes a person free.[28] Keeping in mind this Roman emphasis on suicide as a noble escape for those who are facing extreme circumstances (and the ennobling Stoic and Virgilian vocabulary on which the episode is constructed), it is very likely that Lucan's readers would have been brought dangerously close to sympathizing with Vulteius' decision to avoid the shame of defeat by preempting it with suicide. Vividly the poet puts in Vulteius' mouth words that persuasively describe his enterprise as a heroic undertaking. The narrator's point of view in the passages examined so far does not interfere with the description of the character's *aristeia*. Vulteius believes that his suicide and that of his soldiers will be a wonderful example of heroism (*memorabile . . . exemplum*, *BC* 4.496–97), and he does not wish his *virtus* to remain "buried" (*perit obruta virtus*, *BC* 4.491). To ensure that everybody watch the group suicide he waits for daylight to accomplish the deed (*orta dies*, *BC* 4.529). During the battle of Pharsalus the narrator reveals an opposite approach: not only does he wish that this event could be buried in darkness and silence (*BC* 7. 552–56), he also says that it is shameful to cry for individual deaths during the "funeral of the world":

Inpendisse pudet lacrimas in funere mundi
mortibus innumeris, ac singula fata sequentem
quaerere, letiferum per cuius viscera volnus
exierit, quis fusa solo vitalia calcet,
[. . . .]
   Mors nulla querella
digna sua est, nullosque hominum lugere vacamus.
Non istas habuit pugnae Pharsalia partes,
quas aliae clades:
[. . . .]
Maius ab hac acie quam quod sua saecula ferrent
volnus habent populi; plus est quam vita salusque
quod perit: in totum mundi prosternimur aevum.
Vincitur his gladiis omnis quae serviet aetas.
Proxima quid suboles aut quid meruere nepotes
in regnum nasci?

I am ashamed in this funeral of the world to waste
tears for countless deaths and tracing individual fates
to ask who suffered a death-dealing wound clean through his gut,
who stepped on his own intestines, spilled on the ground.
[. . . .]
   No one death
deserves its own lament, no one man do I have time to mourn.
Pharsalia played a different part in battle
from all other defeats.
[. . . .]
A blow too heavy for their own age to bear
was dealt to all nations by this battle; more than life and safety
was lost: throughout the world and for all time we are ruined.
Every age is conquered and will serve by these blades.
Why did these soldiers' offspring, why did their children's children
deserve to be born into tyranny? (*BC* 7.617–20; 630–33; 638–43)

The narrator makes clear that it is petty to mourn for individuals when there is at stake the freedom of all future generations. "No one death deserves its own lament" (630–31) when liberty is dying. Heroism is made vain by Caesar's victory. In the quoted lines Lucan's historical perspective is revealed: Pharsalus is the epicenter of ruin, the *birth* of freedom's death. *This* death is to be mourned.

Even if the narrator does not intervene directly to chastise Vulteius, Vulteius does not have the last word. Leigh has convincingly demonstrated how this episode implicitly attacks Roman culture, which used the *exemplum* in historiography and rhetorical discourse as a teaching technique.[29] A negative judgment of Vulteius' desire to die (and the superimposition of the narrator's point of view on that of the character) can be detected early on in the employment of the word *furor* by the centurion to describe his desire to serve Caesar (*BC* 4.517).[30] In texts dependent on Stoic sources the word *furor* characterizes the insanity of the enemies of the Roman state, and in the *Bellum Civile* it almost programmatically accompanies Caesar.[31] In epic, *furor* is normally attributed to negative characters or excessive acts.[32] During Troy's last hours, *furor* and *ira* upset Aeneas (*Aen.* 2.316–17) eager to find a glorious' death in combat (*pulchrumque mori succurrit in armis, Aen.* 2.317). But his desire is checked by Venus.[33] Appearing to him, she points out that his fury and anger made him forgetful of his family (*Nate, quis indomitas tantus dolor excitat iras? / Quid furis aut quonam nostri tibi cura recessit?*, "Son, why let such suffering goad you on to fury, where is your thoughtfulness for me, for us?" [*Aen.* 2.594–95]) and that Troy is doomed to destruction (*Aen.* 2.601–618).[34] *Furor impius,* personified at *Aen.* 1.295, will be rejected in the new Roman order prophesied by Jupiter to Venus (*Aen.* 1.257–96).

Even the images employed by Lucan to represent Vulteius' dying soldiers indirectly disclose the perversion of their act and the presence of the narrator's point of view. While the centurion invites his soldiers to survey their own death as an exciting and admirable spectacle, the simile at lines 573–79 encourages the reader to be distressed by it:[35]

> Concurrunt alii totumque in partibus unis
> bellorum fecere nefas. Sic semine Cadmi
> emicuit Dircaea cohors ceciditque suorum
> volneribus, dirum Thebanis fratribus omen;
> Phasidos et campis insomni dente creati,
> terrigenae missa magicis e cantibus ira
> cognato tantos inplerunt sanguine sulcos,
> ipsaque, inexpertis quod primum fecerat herbis,
> expavit Medea nefas.
>
> The others clashed: they, a single faction, enacted
> war's every horror. In this way the men who sprang from the seed
> of Cadmus, Dirce's cohort, were felled by wounds received
> from their own kinsmen, a hideous omen for Theban brothers;

in this way the Earthborn, bred on Phasis' plains from sleepless
dragon's fangs, when magic incantations fanned their rage
made Jason's furrows brim with kindred blood;
Medea herself paled at this, the first horror worked
by her untried herbs. (*BC* 4.548–56)

The two episodes recounted in the simile—one from the Theban cycle, the other from the Argonauts' saga—are both dealing with internecine fighting among kindred people and produce an effect of *mise en abîme* for the Vulteius passage. The fight between the Earthborn, focalized through Medea's horrified eyes, is called *nefas* (556) and recalls the mutual slaughter between Vulteius' men, also qualified as *nefas* (549). Leigh has emphasized that amused passivity in the face of death is a rather ambiguous stance since it is the attitude characterizing the gladiatorial audience conditioned to marvel during games where not much is at stake.[36] While Vulteius encourages his soldiers and his readers to believe that their actions and *virtus* will be amazing, the mythic episodes paradigmatically instruct the audience to react to it with consternation and disgust. A *glossa* in the *Supplementum Adnotationum super Lucanum* underscores that at lines 548–49 we find the point of view of the narrator and not that of Vulteius' soldiers: "it is said by the poet's persona, for the action would have not appeared to them as a horror" (*ex persona poetae dictum est* [aA]; *nam ipsis non videbatur nefas* [A]).[37]

The narrator's negative judgment of Vulteius, embedded in the simile, is not completely disclosed but redirected in his final comment:

> Nullam maiore locuta est
> ore ratem totum discurrens Fama per orbem.
> Non tamen ignavae post haec exempla virorum
> percipient gentes, quam sit non ardua virtus
> servitium fugisse manu, sed regna timentur
> ob ferrum et saevis libertas uritur armis,
> ignorantque datos, ne quisquam serviat, enses.

> Fame prattled
> of this vessel longer than of any other, scurrying over the globe.
> Yet despite the example these men taught, cowardly
> nations will not perceive that it is no arduous feat
> to escape slavery by one's own hand. They fear tyranny
> because of its sword, and liberty is destroyed by savage steel;

they forget that weapons were granted that none need live as a slave. (*BC* 4.573–79)

We are told that Vulteius' deed is immortalized by Fame as "greater than any other," but that future people "do not get it" (*non . . . percipient gentes*, 575–76), do not understand in what way even this episode can teach something. The narrator, in the brief postscript to the episode, tries to clarify the lesson: if Vulteius' men foolishly died to please their leaders, future generations should not be afraid to lose their lives in fighting for a much better cause: to struggle against their enslavement. The open reflection testifies to Lucan's concern to make his text intelligible *and* serviceable: the generalization and clarification will be useful for future readers of the *Bellum Civile*.[38] We saw how Virgil's address to some characters involved the future: in the name of future peace (that is, the poet's and his readers' Augustan present), Virgil tries to explain past suffering and to convince his audience about the necessity of accepting that suffering. Future readers are mentioned and made significant players also by Lucan, who employs personified *Fama* and the past in order to teach them a lesson about their present, namely the importance of rejecting their existing environment to fight against tyrants.

Several scholars have emphasized Lucan's extraordinary capacity to evoke a past which is "seen as still unfolding and not irrevocably lapsed, where some options are felt to be still available" in order to create the illusion of a history still open to change.[39] The use of present and future tense in the *Bellum Civile* fosters that illusion created to move the readers into a hypothetical, yet not impossible, realm of actions. This temporal flexibility spurs them to imagine parallel realities, the possible outcomes of actions they have not performed so far. If Pharsalus enslaved all future generations (*vincitur his gladiis omnis quae serviet aetas*, "these blades conquer all who will be slaves hereafter" [*BC* 7.641]), the appeal to futurity at *BC* 4.573–79 wants to compensate (and find a solution) for that enslavement in the plea that "coward nations" (*ignavae . . . gentes*) cease "being ignorant" (*ignorant*) and be told how they can rescue their freedom. When the desperation caused by tyranny is evoked, the hope of struggle is also brought in to play a part: *sed par quod semper habemus, / Libertas et Caesar erit* ("but the struggle which we always have with us will be between Freedom and Caesar," *BC* 7.695–96). As David Quint suggests:

> The confusion of tenses—present and future describing a past event—again spells out the message. Precisely at the moment of crushing republican defeat, the poem announces a sequel of ongoing resistance: this is the war we are still fighting, despite setbacks. Such assertions at the beginning and

ending of the narration of Pharsalia counterbalance the despairing declaration of finality that lies between them. The narrator's differing reactions—of jumping to pessimistic conclusions about history or holding out hope in the openness of the future—mirror the alternatives that faced Pompey of rushing to a single decisive battle or staying the course of a larger drawn-out strategy. Where Pompey, who knew better, chose badly and failed, the narrator stakes the project of his poem upon bravely keeping faith and waiting upon history.[40]

All things considered, we can say that in Book 4 through Vulteius' desire "to discard life" (*proieci vitam, BC* 4.516) Lucan conducts a subtle meditation on the legitimacy of political suicide, a typical Roman answer to defeat. The legitimacy of suicide is inserted in the wider exploration of the meaning of *virtus* and right behavior in defeat. If Seneca had praised suicide as the rational act of the *sapiens*,[41] Vulteius' suicide during the civil war becomes a supreme act of irrationality and spiritual enslavement.[42] Vulteius not only renounces his life, but above all he renounces an independent evaluation of the war. He has internalized the point of view of his commander and considers it a blessing to die for him. He has unreflectively appropriated Caesar's motivations as well as his cruelty, fury, and ambiguously parasitic language, which renders his behavior hard to assess without a direct intervention by the narrator. Even if the narrator's viewpoint emerges from contradictory signals given in the portrayal, Lucan's criticism of the character risks being buried in the tangled fibers of a text that is vividly reproducing competing points of view.

The Narrator's Emphatic Intervention on Scaeva's *Virtus*

If Vulteius' actions are criticized only indirectly, the narrator openly expresses his opinion on Scaeva's conduct, which closely resembles Vulteius'.[43] In Lucan's epic Caesar's centurion Scaeva makes his memorable entrance in Book 6 during Pompey's siege of Dyrrachium (48 BCE) when, according to Suetonius' historical record, his cohort "held up four of Pompey's legions for some hours, though almost all were struck by the mass of enemy arrows" (*quattuor Pompei legiones per aliquot horas sustinuit paene omnis confixa multitudine hostilium sagittarum*, Suetonius, *Jul.* 68.3). Facing defeat, Scaeva spurs his men to refrain from fleeing and offers his behavior—his desperate fight against the Pompeians—as an example of virtue. Scaeva's frantic desire to die during his *aristeia* is ultimately judged a perverted act by Lucan's narrator; yet the centurion's actions during most of the episode are problematically focalized through his own eyes and framed in the vocabulary of Roman traditional virtue. Scaeva's behavior recalls positive exemplary figures of the Roman historiographic and epic tradition: Horatius Cocles and Mucius Scaevola (Livy 2.10–12). His perverted *devotio* can also be read as an example of Stoic virtue.[44] The entire scene is further complicated by the references to Mezentius' *aristeia* and death (*Aen.* 10.870–905).

For Scaeva, *pietas* is devotion to his generals, not to his *pater* or his *patria*. This feeling has become his motivating force, triggering brutality and blind desire for massacres. In the name of *pietas* Scaeva accuses those who want to abandon the battlefield:

> Non ira saltem, iuvenes, pietate remota
> stabitis?
>
> Having forgotten loyalty, young men, won't you hold
> your ground at least from anger? (*BC* 6.155–56)

According to the centurion, the young soldiers are running away because they have abandoned *pietas*. Now *ira* should move them to do what *pietas* could not. He puts *pietas* on the same level as anger, assigning a positive value to an irrational instinct:

> Movit tantum vox illa furorem,
> quantum non primo succendunt classica cantu,
> mirantesque virum atque avidi spectare secuntur
> scituri iuvenes, numero deprensa locoque
> an plus quam mortem virtus daret.
>
> His voice excited such fury
> as never was kindled by bugle's first brassy blare.
> Admiring the hero and eager to watch him, they follow,
> young men bound to find out if courage—outnumbered, hard-pressed—
> has more than death to offer. (*BC* 6.165–69)

Scaeva is like a gladiator committed to die. His desire for death (*amor mortis, BC* 6.246) is stronger than the Pompeians' devotion to Pompey (*BC* 6.245–46). His voice kindles the army's desire for battle. His *virtus* is an inspiring spectacle. The emphasis on "watching," together with the mention of exotic animals to which Scaeva is compared (a panther, *BC* 6.183ff.; a Pannonian bear, *BC* 6.220ff.; and a Libyan elephant, *BC* 6.207ff.), evoke the games in the amphitheater. Like a titan that can only be crushed by a war machine (*BC* 6.196–200), he is "an indestructible wall defending Caesar" (*non fragilis pro Caesare murus, BC* 6.201).[45] If Mucius Scaevola mutilated himself in order to save the freedom of Rome (Livy 2.12), Scaeva is ready to partly blind himself (*BC* 4.214–19) rather than disappoint Caesar. Hit by a Gortynian arrow in the left eye, Scaeva, having extracted both arrow and eyeball, tramples on both (*intrepidus telumque suo cum lumine calcat, BC* 6.219). As already mentioned, this act reminds us of Scaevola's mutilation and of Cocles. Yet Scaeva's blinding of one eye at *BC* 6.214–19 also confers on the scene a negative symbolism: Scaeva has lost every insight into things; the civil war has made him blind. We recall *Aen.* 10.763ff., in which Virgil compares Mezentius to the blind Orion. At the beginning of the Republic Mucius Scaevola had offered a false swearing and a self-inflicted mutilation to help his city (Livy 2.12); similarly, Scaeva's wounds and deception, his false request of mercy at *BC* 6.230–235, reveal his commitment to Caesar, openly mentioned at *BC* 6.243.

Scaeva faces an entire army alone:

> Illum tota premit moles, illum omnia tela:
> [. . .]
> parque novum Fortuna videt concurrere, bellum
> atque virum.

> the entire mass of soldiers presses him, all weapons seek him
> [. . .]
> Fortune saw an odd pair fighting, an army pitted against a man. (*BC* 6.189; 191–92)

A few lines later, we are told again that "he goes to meet alone all the war's wounds (*tot vulnera belli / solus obit, BC* 6.204–5). Scaeva's strength and isolation allude not only to H. Cocles but to Mezentius (*Aen.* 10.689–802), described by Virgil as facing alone the enemy's ranks: *Concurrunt Tyrrhenae acies atque omnibus uni, / uni odiisque viro telisque frequentibus instat* ("all the Etruscan forces come together and with all hatred and all weapons attack that man alone," *Aen.* 10.691–92; *ille autem inpavidus partis cunctatur in omnis*, "yet he resists fearless against all sides," *Aen.* 10.717). Also like Scaeva, he is a kind of wall (*ille velut rupes, Aen.* 10.693), or a boar (*Aen.* 10.708–13) or lion (*Aen.* 10.723), or the blind Orion (*Aen.* 10.763).[46]

Finally, Scaeva's disregard for his life when an entire army is pitted against him conjures up the earlier scene in which Cato confesses to Brutus his desire to fight alone against all sides:

> Me geminae figant acies, me barbara telis
> Rheni turba petat, cunctis ego pervius hastis
> excipiam medius totius volnera belli.
>
> Let it be me the twin armies stab, me the Rhine's
> barbarous horde targets with darts; I will stand in the path
> of each spear and intercept the wounds of the whole war. (*BC* 2.309–311)

Both Cato and Scaeva are ready to sacrifice their lives for a cause, and their speeches fill their audiences with enthusiasm for the war.[47] But their behavior and wishes are only superficially identical. Lucan's linguistic choices and imagery interestingly link together Scaeva, Cato, and Mezentius: three characters who despite their differences share a sense of physical and spiritual self-sufficiency. What La Penna has observed about Mezentius can also be said about Scaeva or Cato: their *autarkeia*, their sense of invulnerability in the face of the external world, has no *comparanda* in epic or ancient tragedy but can be found in ethical models developed by Hellenistic philosophies. Not only Epicureanism but also a certain brand of Stoicism can rescue men from fearing death as well as the gods: "if it is *sapientia* to grant freedom and absolute *autarkeia*, this *autarkeia* once obtained cannot be reached, not even by Jove; so the *sapiens* is the antagonist of Jove in a sort of duel."[48]

Lucan's allusion to Mezentius in the Scaeva episode further confuses our evaluation of the Caesarian because Virgil is far from depicting Mezentius as a completely dark figure. In the *Aeneid*, the Lausus and Mezentius section presents the reader with an intriguing investigation of *pietas* concealed in the breast of a negative character. Virgil combines in the Etruscan king the figure of the loathed tyrant exiled from his *patria* with that of a tender *pater*. In war what renders father and son vulnerable is their mutual devotion: Lausus hurries to rescue his wounded father (*Aen.* 10.789; 796–810),[49] while Mezentius, famous for his atrocity and hatred for the gods, cannot bear his son's death.[50] Ultimately, Lausus' demise triggers in the *contemptor divum* a different evaluation of the world and, in the reader, a feeling of compassion toward Mezentius, whose anguish becomes a powerful equalizer:[51] As Harold C. Gotoff suggests:

> For this quintessential warrior the question of life and death had never been a consideration. His code was to enter battle neither giving nor asking any quarter, without regard for the prerogatives of gods or the opinion of men. From this independence came his magnificence. Only now does he realize

that he had a hostage to fortune and that his freedom from fear about his own mortality was illusory. All this is summed up in the phrase *morte tua vivens*—an uncompromising statement of interdependence [. . .] what has changed is his realization that he is vulnerable to emotional pain."⁵²

Unable to live without his son, Mezentius rushes to meet his doom, lifts his hand toward the sky, and talks to his horse. According to Georgia Nugent, the gesture symbolizes his newly acquired connection to human and divine society; it indirectly manifests his reestablished links with the community and makes him a sympathetic human being.⁵³ Nugent writes:

> The quintessential Roman virtue of *pietas* typically entails an appropriately reverential recognition of one's place in the "great chain of being," stretching from the divine father through the senatorial "fathers" of the Roman state to one's own father and on into the endless future of Rome through one's own son, with corresponding obligation, responsibilities, and privileges at each link in the chain. In the character of Mezentius, however, Virgil has boldly severed this chain [. . .]. Mezentius [. . .] identified with the stock epithet of *contemptor divum* (7.648, 8.7), explicitly claims that he has no concern for the gods (10.880), and at one point declares his own right hand his god (10.773); yet at the moment when he learns of Lausus' death he spreads his hands to heaven in a gesture recognizably that of Roman prayer, and the extraordinary power of his love for and sense of obligation to his son is not just ennobling but ultimately salvific.⁵⁴

Suffering in this episode can be considered as a profoundly civilizing force. The painful awareness of loss turns Mezentius into a human being who understands better than before the meaning of *pietas* exemplified by Aeneas' behavior toward his victim:

> At vero ut voltum vidit morientis et ora,
> ora modis Anchisiades pallentia miris,
> ingemuit graviter miserans dextramque tetendit
> et mentem patriae subiit pietatis imago.
> "Quid tibi nunc, miserande puer, pro laudibus istis,
> quid pius Aeneas tanta dabit indole dignum?"

> Beholding the lips and brow of the agonizing [boy], so astonishingly white in death, Anchises' son groaned aloud in pity and reached over him his right

> hand, as filial love, mirrored here, touched his heart. "Unhappy boy! What reward for such laudable acts, what now can I, pious Aeneas, grant you worthy of your generous nature?" (*Aen.*10.821–26)

Looking at the body of Lausus, Aeneas does not behave like a winner, but like a suppliant he extends his hands toward the corpse (*dextramque tetendit*) and lifts him up (*et terra sublevat ipsum*, 831).[55] Aeneas' mind is filled with images of fathers and sons. At once he imagines the death of his own Ascanius and Mezentius' distress at the sight of his dead son.[56] He even recalls the death of his beloved father, Anchises (notice the patronymic at line 822), since a *pietas* similar to that which has cost Lausus his life linked him to his father. Thus he groans aloud (*ingemuit fortiter*), and sends the youth's body intact to Mezentius. The awareness of his own familial ties humanizes Aeneas and gives to this scene a unique and unforgettable quality: for the first time in the genre an enemy's body and weapons are left unscathed in the name of *pietas*. In the *Iliad* the gods had to intervene to restore Hector's body, making it presentable to Priam's eyes and to the Trojan community; in the *Aeneid* it is Aeneas' humanity that performs the miracle. Aeneas' conception of *pietas* resembles Stoic *oikeiosis*, which is the process by which an individual comes to interconnect with other individuals. It is like a web that connects human beings in their basic similarity (e.g., Cic. *Fin.* 3.16–31). At the very end of his life, Mezentius finally recognizes it. Not only does he learn to accept death with the resignation of a hopeless man rather than with the enthusiasm of a reckless warrior; by asking Aeneas to preserve his body from the fury of his foes and to bury it with Lausus, he also starts to treat his archenemy as a fellow human being on whom he can rely. Mezentius' sorrow for his son will be remembered by Lucan when he describes Cato's paternal anguish for Rome.

The dense web of allusions enveloping Lucan's characterization of Caesar's follower provides the reader with a vivid description of the character involved in an *aristeia* realistically rendered through his own eyes.[57] The Roman audience might have pitied the centurion and admired his behavior, responding to it with the awe felt by Scaeva's internal audience. Aware of this danger, the narrator intervenes directly to comment on Scaeva's actions. The apostrophe to Caesar's centurion sets the record straight, breaks the spell that might have fascinated the reader, and with unmistakable strength unravels the message otherwise buried in the description. It illustrates the narrator's typical approach to negative characters on the Caesarian side.

As soon as the battle is over, Scaeva cannot stand up anymore. The fight itself has given strength to the centurion, and now that the military engagement is concluded he suffers from its cessation. The narrator observes with irony how Scaeva's soldiers, like delighted fans, take him on their shoulders and cheer him as some kind of idol in a parade. The description of their brazen tinkering with the body of the general suggests that now the narration is filtered through the eyes of a critical reporter who can look at the scene with a higher degree of detachment. Lucan's bitter tone helps his readers to dissociate themselves from Scaeva and proclaims the absurdity of losing one's life for Caesar:

> Subducto qui Marte ruis; nam sanguine fuso
> vires pugna dabat. Labentem turba suorum
> excipit atque umeris defectum imponere gaudet;
> ac velut inclusum perfosso in pectore numen
> et vivam magnae speciem Virtutis adorant.
> Telaque confixis certant evellere membris
> exornantque deos ac nudum pectore Martem
> armis, Scaeva, tuis: felix hoc nomine famae,
> si tibi durus Hiber aut si tibi terga dedisset
> Cantaber exiguis aut longis Teutonus armis.
> Non tu bellorum spoliis ornare Tonantis
> templa potes, non tu laetis ululare triumphis.
> Infelix, quanta dominum virtute parasti!

> And with the War god gone, down you crashed; although your blood;
> was shed, combat gave you strength. His men crowd round, catch him
> as he faints, rejoice to take his slumped weight on their shoulders;
> they worship the divinity as if sheltered within
> his punctured breast, the living image of great virtue.
> They compete, plucking the barbs out of your quilled limbs,
> decking the gods and bare-chested Mars with the spoils,
> with your weapons, Scaeva. Happy in your famous name
> had the sturdy Iberian fled you, or the wild Cantabrian
> with his diminutive shield, or the Teuton with his long one!
> You cannot adorn the thunderer's temples with spoils of war,
> cannot cheer in joyful Triumphs; unhappy man!
> With all your courage, you got yourself a master! (*BC* 6.250–62)

Gian Biagio Conte notices that the placement of the two verbs at the beginning and end of line 253 (*excipit . . . gaudet*) is a practice particularly employed by Virgil to slow down the action.[58] The *adagio* rhythmically signals the conclusion of the combat and introduces a comment on the act: in the final apostrophe Scaeva is revealed as "unhappy" because his virtue was foolishly used to promote Caesar and ultimately the advent of Caesarism. In Virgil's *Aeneid* the future is employed to convince the reader to accept the present (Augustus' rule); for instance at *Aen.* 6.377–81 the Sibyl appeases Palinurus' and the reader's heart by prophesying the eternal glory which will be granted to Palinurus' tomb (*aeternumque locus Palinuri nomen habebit, Aen.* 6.381); and in the apostrophe to Nisus and Euryalus (*Aen.* 9.446–49) Virgil's omniscient narrator accepts their death in the name of the future glory of the Roman nation. In marked opposition, in Lucan's apostrophe we find the prophetic look authoritatively employed by the narrator to reject the Neronian present.

As we will see, the forward perspective of Lucan's narrator is also implicitly in competition with that of his internal audience. Scaeva's soldiers adore Scaeva "as if there were a *numen* sheltered" within his breast and worship the "living image of great virtue." The *velut* as well as the *speciem* suggests that there is something strange happening in the section. Certainly this is not the godlike *animus* praised by the philosopher Seneca in several of his epistles and granting men equality with the gods (e.g., *Ep.* 31.11). The grotesque and slightly blasphemous nature of the scene is highlighted by the observation of what these soldiers do with their idol.[59] They treat the body of their hero as a toy, and they hurry to bring the weapons extracted from it before the "naked Mars." Conte explains *nudum pectore Martem* as a realistic detail: "in sculpture Mars was represented bare-chested [. . .] perhaps here we have a reflection of the Hellenizing taste of that time."[60] But the *Commenta Berniensia* say, *quasi sine huius armis Mars nudus esset et istis deberet ornari* ("as if without his weapons Mars would be naked and with those must be embellished").[61] In what way does this perverted harvest of arrows represent a suitable gift to Mars? Are those weapons a sign of Scaeva's courage or of his lack of understanding? In *Ep.* 31.10 Seneca explains with a completely different poignancy that a god is not made by what he wears but is naked in his absolute sufficiency, *praetexta non faciet: deus nudus est* ("a robe will not help: god is naked").

Yet in the end the external audience is not left with the hermeneutic burden of evaluating Scaeva's "appearance of virtue"—an ambiguity which seems totally lost to his troops. The narrator's apostrophe reveals how Scaeva's actions in the civil war represent a macabre *antiphrasis* to the Virgilian glorification of family devotion. The last lines of our apostrophic sequence (*BC* 6.256ff.) clarify what so far the narration has only indirectly communicated through allusions, irony, and ridicule. The ambiguity is finally resolved in the narrator's direct apostrophe to this (anti)hero, whose courage is evaluated as insanely misguided and harshly mocked. Scaeva's glory is openly called a self-deception. Parroting Virgil's sympathetic voice, Lucan's narrator suggests that Scaeva *might* have been *felix* fighting against the right kind of enemy; instead he selected the wrong cause, the wrong war, and the wrong adversary.[62] It is not important simply to wield a sword but also to wield it for the right reason and with the right intentions. Caesar's soldiers are paradoxically sacrificing their lives to become slaves. The word *virtus* attached to an improper target mutates into a negative agency for which no name is readily available. Taking the place of an acute *sententia*, the narrator's final exclamation remarks that Scaeva is sweating only to gain a master for Rome and himself. Instead of fighting for the party of freedom and the Republicans, by employing his heroism in the service of Caesar, Scaeva accelerates the path to Pharsalus, Munda, and Actium. He is part of the chain of events that resulted in the reign of the Julio-Claudian dynasty. If Scaeva and Curio's deaths can superficially be judged pitiful or glorious, Lucan's comments allow the reader to understand that they are in fact completely misguided.

Against Crastinus and Petreius

The narrator uses the Vulteius episode to urge future readers of the *Bellum Civile* to be ready to sacrifice their lives for the sake of freedom and the Scaeva episode to underline the foolishness of Caesar's followers. While he wishes everybody to be able to judge a course of action properly and independently, he knows that men are often persuaded by the wrong example and speech. For instance, at Pharsalus the soldiers do not respond to their first instinct—to avoid the conflict—and instead follow Crastinus into battle. Both sides, face to face with their parents and brothers, are stricken by *pietas* and realize the monstrosity of what they are about to do. Their attitude is emphatically and realistically portrayed with a wealth of psychological and physical details:

> Ut rapido cursu fati suprema morantem
> consumpsere locum, parva tellure dirempti,
> quo sua pila cadant aut qua sibi fata minentur
> inde manum, spectant. Vultus, quo noscere possent
> facturi quae monstra forent, videre parentum
> frontibus adversis fraternaque comminus arma,
> nec libuit mutare locum. Tamen omnia torpor
> pectora constrinxit, gelidusque in viscera sanguis

> percussa pietate coit, totaeque cohortes
> pila parata diu tensis tenuere lacertis.
>
> When their swift charge had eaten up the space delaying
> fate's finalities, the men, parted by a little strip of land,
> picked out where their javelins might fall, whose hand over there
> threatened them with death. The faces they saw forced them
> to acknowledge what atrocities they intended—fathers
> with hostile scowls, brothers' swords close enough to touch.
> But there was no urge to shift ground.
>   And yet numbness
> froze every chest; blood congealed in their guts,
> their piety received a blow; and for a long time
> whole cohorts, their muscles tensed, just held javelins ready. (*BC* 7.460–69)

Only when the Caesarian Crastinus hurls the first lance does the battle begin and the massacre unfold. In his account of the Civil War, Caesar presents Crastinus as a man of outstanding valor (*vir singulari virtute*, 3.91) while mocking Pompey's order not to attack:

> . . . sed quod nobis quidem nulla ratione factum a Pompeio videtur, propterea quod est quaedam animi incitatio atque alacritas naturaliter innata omnibus, quae studio pugnae incenditur. Hanc non reprimere, sed augere imperatores debent; neque frustra antiquitus institutum est, ut signa undique concinerent clamoremque universi tollerent; quibus rebus et hostes terreri et suos incitari existimaverunt.
>
> . . . but it appears to me that Pompey did this without any reason, for there is a certain eagerness of spirit and innate keenness in everyone which is inflamed by desire for battle. Generals should encourage this, not repress it; nor was it for nothing that the practice of giving the signal on both sides and everyone's raising a war cry began in antiquity; the custom was believed both to frighten the enemy and to excite one's own men. (Caes., *B.C.* 3. 92)

Caesar puts the battle of Pharsalus on the same level as other battles in the history of Rome and judges Pompey a fool for restraining the soldiers' "innate desire" for battle (*incitatio atque alacritas naturaliter innata omnibus, quae studio pugnae incenditur*). In contrast, Lucan's description of the soldiers' hesitation makes clear that in a civil struggle the natural instinct of the combatants is to avoid conflict.

Before action is resumed and the battle begins, we hear the outraged narrator intervening in an apostrophe to curse Crastinus' crime:

> Di tibi non mortem, quae cunctis poena paratur,
> sed sensum post fata tuae dent, Crastine, morti,
> cuius torta manu commisit lancea bellum
> primaque Thessaliam Romano sanguine tinxit.
> O praeceps rabies! Cum Caesar tela teneret,
> inventa est prior ulla manus?

> May the Gods give you, Crastinus, not death—a punishment
> prepared for all—but to your corpse sense(s) intact after death:
> for by your hand was hurled the lance that launched the war
> and that first stained Thessaly red with Roman blood.
> Headlong insanity! When Caesar withheld his weapons,
> what hand was found more ready? (*BC* 7.470–75)

I would like to pause a moment to understand the kind of punishment that the narrator wishes for Crastinus. *Sensus* in Latin is an ambiguous word that ranges in meaning from sensation, feeling, and attitude to judgment, perception, understanding, or sense. Generally the word is used in Lucan more with the idea of "awareness/consciousness/the ability to perceive and reason" than just with reference to perception.[63] It seems quite likely that in this passage the narrator wishes Crastinus to experience a full recognition of the horror of his action. A guilty conscience is considered by our narrator the most appropriate punishment for the deluded soldier. He should understand in death what he did not realize in life.

The better instinct yields to the worse again at Ilerda (*BC* 4.1–401). In an episode remarkably similar to the one described above, we find once more the presence of soldiers unwilling to engage in combat and a general, Petreius, who eloquently persuades them to return to their posts. A comparison between Crastinus and Petreius (*BC* 4.212–35) underlines the resemblance between the two men's actions and Lucan's negative evaluation of both.

Misinterpreting the fraternization between Caesarians and Pompeians as a surrender of his soldiers to the Caesarians (*seque et sua tradita venum / castra videt*, "he saw that he and his camp had been sold" [*BC* 4.206–7]), Petreius interrupts it (*iunctosque amplexibus en se / separat et multo disturbat sanguine pacem*, *BC* 4.209–10) and "leads his men back to their love of crime" (*scelerumque reduxit amorem*, *BC* 4.236).[64] Petreius' speech to his men, though formulated on the wrong premise of his army's treason, is powerful and persuasive:

Inmemor o patriae, signorum oblite tuorum,
non potes hoc causae, miles, praestare, senatus
adsertor victo redeas ut Caesare? Certe,
ut vincare, potes. Dum ferrum, incertaque fata,
quique fluat multo non derit volnere sanguis,
ibitis ad dominum damnataque signa feretis,
utque habeat famulos nullo discrimine Caesar,
exorandus erit? Ducibus quoque vita petita est!
Numquam nostra salus pretium mercesque nefandae
proditionis erit; non hoc civilia bella
ut vivamus, agunt. Trahimur sub nomine pacis.
Non chalybem gentes penitus fugiente metallo
eruerent, nulli vallarent oppida muri,
non sonipes in bella ferox, non iret in aequor
turrigeras classis pelago sparsura carinas,
si bene libertas umquam pro pace daretur.
Hostes nempe meos sceleri iurata nefando
sacramenta tenent; at vobis vilior hoc est
vestra fides, quod pro causa pugnantibus aequa
et veniam sperare licet. Pro dira pudoris
funera! Nunc totum fatorum ignarus in orbe,
Magne, paras acies mundique extrema tenentes
sollicitas reges, cum forsan foedere nostro
iam tibi sit promissa salus.

Oblivious of fatherland, forgetting your standards!
Soldiers, if you cannot offer *this* to the Senate's cause
—to march home as champions, Caesar's vanquishers—then surely
you can offer to be defeated. While you have your swords,
a fate unsettled, and blood to flow from many a wound,
will you run to a master, take up standards you once despised?
and you beg Caesar to think no less of you
than his other slaves! You also plead for your leaders' lives!
Never shall our safety be the price and wages
of unspeakable treason! Civil war is not fought
that we may live. We are dragged away in the name of peace.
Nations would not haul up iron from shafts that run deep
underground, no fortifications would barricade towns,
the valiant charger would not go to war, nor the fleet

to sea, ready to strew the ocean with turreted ships,
were it at all proper to trade liberty for peace!
Sworn oaths bind my foes to unspeakable crime
while you consider your vow less valid than theirs,
since men who fight on the side of justice are granted the right
to hope—even for pardon! Oh the hateful demise of honor!
Magnus! Ignorant of your fate, you are at this
moment raising levies all over the world, rallying
kings who rule far-flung lands—though perhaps by our 'treaty'
you are already promised your safety! (*BC* 4.212–35)

The speech is entirely given from Petreius' perspective. He sees himself as a liberator against Caesar. Echoing and attacking Augustus' propagandistic claims in *Res Gestae* 1.1 (*rem publicam dominatione factionis oppressam in libertatem vindicavi*, "I freed the republic oppressed by the rule of a faction"), Petreius depicts himself as an *adsertor libertatis* (212) and employs the language of archaic manumission ritual previously used by Augustus to describe his reestablishment of the Republic.[65] Petreius bares the ugly face of acceptance of Caesar's pardon and, very significantly, objects to that intolerable blackmail which, with the *pax augusta*, had become a reality: peace in place of freedom (*BC* 4.227). He cannot accept that those who fight for freedom and legality capitulate (*BC* 4.228–31), nor does he endorse the idea that Caesar is a king with the right to decide on matters of life and death (231).[66] The general's line of argumentation (esp. in *BC* 4.212–16) is consonant with that of Cato during the desert march: it is important to fight even without being victorious and losing one's life (*cum non maiora mereri quam vitam veniamque libet?*, "Why not to try to win greater gains than life and pardon?" [*BC* 9.275–76; cf. above *BC* 4.220–21]). Petreius employs apostrophe to make his speech more effective. He addresses Pompey as if he were present to remind his troop that while in remote parts of the world Magnus is trying to summon foreign kings to fight for him, his own people have already rejected battle, choosing for everybody a despicable compromise (*foedere*, 234) in order to preserve their lives (*salus*, 235).

Petreius is another character in the *Bellum Civile* who strategically employs Stoic accents and Virgilian language in an episode remarkably similar to *Aeneid* 4. The fraternization at Ilerda strongly reminds us of the amity between Trojans and Carthaginians, and Petreius' disapproval of it evokes Mercury's harsh reproach of Aeneas after the hero's elopement with Dido.[67] At *BC* 4.196–202, the association of the Pompeian and Caesarian armies is characterized by "joint banquets" (*concordes . . . mensas*, 197), "libations made at the light of fires" (*libamina . . .*

graminei luxere foci, 198–99), "linked beds" (*iunctoque cubili,* 199), and "the spinning out of sleepless nights with stories of war" (*extrahit insomnis bellorum fabula noctes,* 200). In similar terms, Virgil's description of Aeneas' intimacy with Dido includes a banquet (*Aen.* 1.695ff.), "libations by torchlights" (*Aen.* 1.723ff.), and "endless tales prolonging the night" (*Aen.* 1.747ff.). Echoing Mercury's words in reprehending Aeneas (*regni rerumque oblite tuarum,* "forgetful of your kingdom and of your concerns," *Aen.* 4.267), Petreius begins his reproach to the Pompeians:

> Immemor o patriae, signorum oblite tuorum,
> .... miles ...
>
> Oblivious of fatherland, forgetting your standards,
> ... soldiers ... (*BC* 4.212–13)

He does not approve of the fraternization that is, instead, cherished by the narrator and qualified as a rare moment of truthful realization (*periere latebrae / tot scelerum,* "all shadows concealing these crimes have vanished," *BC* 4.192–93), a beam of unexpected hope in the bleak universe of the civil war. In the apostrophe to *Concordia,* identified as "the Universe's sacred love which, enveloping everything in an eternal embrace, protects life and the world's harmony" (*aeterno complectens omnia nexu, / o rerum mixtique salus, Concordia, mundi / et sacer orbis amor, BC* 4.189–91), it is clear that only in reconciliation, by looking into each other eyes, do men of both factions realize the brutality of killing a kinsman:

> Arma rigant lacrimis, singultibus oscula rumpunt,
> et quamvis nullo maculatus sanguine miles
> quae potuit fecisse timet. Quid pectora pulsas?
> Quid, vaesane, gemis? Fletus quid fundis inanis
> nec te sponte tua sceleri parere fateris?
> Usque adeone times quem tu facis ipse timendum?
> Classica det bello, saevos tu neglege cantus;
> signa ferat, cessa: iam iam civilis Erinys
> concidet, et Caesar generum privatus amabit.
>
> They soak their weapons with tears, sobs interrupt their kisses,
> and, though not yet stained with a drop of blood, the soldier
> dreads the deeds he could have done.
> Why do you beat your breast?

> Why groan aloud, poor fool, and pour out useless tears?
> Why not confess that you choose to obey the command of crime?
> Do you so fear the man you yourself made fearsome?
> If his bugles signal battle, ignore their savage blare;
> if his standards advance, halt; in a flash civil fury will fade;
> a private citizen once more, Caesar will love his son-in-law. (*BC* 4.180–88)

At the moment of the emotional joining of the two armies the narrator comes forward. The apostrophe and sustained interrogations witness to his ability to construct dramatic immediacy and to "treat the action of the civil war as something coming and not yet past."[68] The apostrophe is fundamental because in it the *miles* summoned in line 181 emerges as a moral agent who can find the power to decide for himself what to do (*tua sponte*, 184) and is called upon to refuse Caesar's orders (*neglege . . . cessa*, 186–87).[69] Once again, the narrator considers the future and reminds the soldiers that in their decision, thanks to this reconciliation, the war might have come miraculously to an end. At the thought that "these men had a choice, crucial to future ages" (*magnum nunc saecula nostra / venturi discrimen habent*, *BC* 4.191–92) he cannot contain his enthusiasm. The narrator's praise of the *Concordia* of the soldiers underlines the narrator's concern with the future and with what philosophers called *oikeiôsis*. Troels Engberg-Pedersen has indicated that the concept of *oikeiôsis* is the kernel of Stoic moral theory. Using Cicero's *De finibus* 3.21 and 62–63, he shows that for the Stoics "to live according to nature" means above all to use rationality. Mature rationality is the force convincing people not only to take care of their material needs but especially to realize that all human beings are part of a community.[70] Men's understanding of familial and social ties (*concordia*) is for Lucan and the Stoics the only possible *salus*, the only available civilized resolution.[71]

Unfortunately, Petreius' order and the Pompeians' willingness to obey him destroy this chance of rationally oriented peaceful salvation. Within the Ilerda episode Lucan's judgment of Petreius and of his men is indirectly revealed by the emphasis on the terrible consequences of his speech and through the allusion to *Aen.* 4. As Sergio Casali argues, the implicit comparison—of Petreius to Mercury and of the troops to Aeneas—underscores an important ethical message:

> Petreius is wrong to stop the fraternization, and his soldiers are wrong as well when they obey the order. Many readers have felt that even Aeneas should have rebelled against Jupiter's and Mercury' orders; this is what Lucan explicitly recommends: to go against unjust commands. Instead, Aeneas gives up his desires leaving responsibility in the hands of fate. The

invitation to disobey, proposed by Lucan to the soldiers engaged in civil war, is directed to Aeneas himself. Obeying is not a virtue. We should not follow unjust orders. To obey orders is no justification: we should not give up our individual responsibility. The soldier who cries thinking of the atrocities which he is about to commit, which he will eventually perpetrate, cannot clear his conscience by invoking someone else's responsibility.[72]

To cry without trying to do something is foolish (*Quid, vaesane, gemis? Fletus quid fundis inanis, BC* 4.181); "to shed empty tears" is Aeneas' typical reaction when he faces the impositions of fate (*Aen.* 4.449). In chapter 1 I have discussed how Hercules' painful repression of grief and the hero's will to submit to Jupiter are communicated with the same expression (*lacrimasque effundit inanis, Aen.* 10.465–73). In the *Bellum Civile* Lucan does not accept Aeneas' behavior as paradigmatic; he proposes for his characters a different kind of attitude and a new kind of ethics. According to this alternative code, facts are to be evaluated without considering fate and divine will but simply by appealing to one's own conscience. The new ethics are embraced by Cato, who distrusts oracles and, for the well-being of the community, is titanically willing to go against fate.

Against Caesar's Tears (*Clementia* at *BC* 9.1045–1062)

The extraordinary liveliness (*enargeia*) of Lucan's poem is particularly evident in his representation of Caesar, who is compared to a lightning bolt and "is in a sense being revealed to be a lightning bolt."[73] Some critics have suggested that throughout the poem Caesar's figure is strongly magnetic and that even the narrator is captivated by the spell of his power and ultimate triumph.[74] Doubtless the general's victory march is formidable and his brilliant personality fully revealed in Lucan's simile of the thunderbolt (*BC* 1.143–57). Yet the narrator is deeply and constantly aware that, like thunder, no matter how spectacular its appearance in the sky, Caesar brings destruction. Lucan's hatred toward him is manifested openly through memorably ironic tirades (e.g., *BC* 1.31–45):

(At tu, quos scelerum superos, quas rite vocasti
Eumenidas, Caesar? Stygii quae numina regni
Infernumque nefas et mersos nocte furores
inpia tam saeve gesturus bella litasti?)

> And you—what High Gods of crime, what Furies have you
> duly invoked, Caesar? What powers of the Stygian realm,
> infernal evil, what night-steeped horrors have you
> hymned, you that will so savagely wage unholy war? (*BC* 7.168–71)

Even what tradition preserved as a positive trait of Caesar, his clemency, is revealed by the narrator as a ruse since the meaning of words (*clementia, virtus*) fundamental to the construction of Roman identity and to the political identity of the Augustan Age have been profoundly altered by Caesar.[75] As Debra Herskowitz forcefully explains:

> Caesar is not only the prime motivator of events and, often, the prime actor in them, he is also the prime shifter of significations, the man who, in [John] Henderson's words, "displaces the aboriginal centralities of Roman culture, rejigs '*the force of every Latin word.*'"[76]

Virgil never addresses Aeneas directly in the *Aeneid*, but he manages to communicate with him and with the future Roman conquerors through his addresses to the losers. In advising the winner to be merciful and to offer *clementia*, Virgil felt the need to establish directives for the conduct of the winners in victory, in the process becoming the prophet and counselor of the prevailing party.[77] Lucan, on the other hand, is concerned with the hazards that clemency imposes on the conquered. While *pietas*, Lucan suggests, has been reinterpreted by the winners as militaristic devotion to a commander, *clementia* has become a tool to break ideological resistance to the Caesars.[78] The man whose life is spared owes it to his enemy and with it must renounce any independence of mind and any future resistance. The complex relationship between clemency and power is lucidly summarized by Paul Plass:

> [G]ift giving and clemency alike are methods of exercising power, with clemency being a comparatively negative way of doing so by *not* taking something (life or property) rather than granting it. Since clemency created a strong impression of what had been lost, that is, freedom, it exemplifies the principle of loss aversion and was all the more resented for concealing the loss behind a show of goodwill. What one got had first been taken away and then given back on loan, with interest due in form of grateful compliance. The logic of clemency and gift exchange unfolds along much the same lines to generate the same antinomies. As veiled exercise of power, each reverses meanings and intentions and makes what is otherwise an

elementary relationship deeply problematic, so much, in fact, that the correct response may seem rejection, even when the offer is survival.[79]

In Caesar's letter to Oppius and Balbus (Cic. *Att.* 9.7c), when the dictator explains why he spared the rebels of Corfinium, the function of "clemency as a gift" is fully articulated:[80]

> Haec nova sit ratio vincendi, ut misericordia et liberalitate nos muniamus.

> Let this be a new means of conquering: that we fortify ourselves with our clemency and liberality.

In normal circumstances victory is gained and preserved through military force, but Caesar hopes that his clemency will achieve the same ends as violence. In the *Bellum Civile* any statement of a valid and unilateral way to react to Caesar's clemency is deferred; yet if no definitive answer is provided about how to make a dignified escape from defeat, irony effectively helps the narrator to denounce Caesar's political practices and his manipulation of Roman ethical vocabulary.

Through irony and parody the narrator unmasks the riddles of Caesar's *clementia* and underlines his manipulation of the concept. A play upon the shifting notions (*clementia, pietas*) advertised in Imperial ideology forms a subtext to Lucan's apostrophe at the end of Book 9, when Caesar, having arrived in Egypt, receives the ultimate gift, Pompey's head (*BC* 9.1045–1062).[81] The conqueror, having made sure that it is the right head he is examining, starts the good-father-in-law act:

> Non primo Caesar damnavit munera visu
> avertitque oculos; vultus, dum crederet, haesit,
> utque fidem vidit sceleris tutumque putavit
> iam bonus esse socer, lacrimas non sponte cadentes
> effudit gemitusque expressit pectore laeto,
> non aliter manifesta potens abscondere mentis
> gaudia quam lacrimis, meritumque inmane tyranni
> destruit et generi mavult lugere revolsum
> quam debere caput.

> Caesar at first neither condemned the gift nor turned his eyes
> from the sight: he stared hard at the visage until he was sure;
> when such scrutiny proved the crime, when at last he thought

it safe to play the good father-in-law, he squeezed out
tears in a forced flow and wrung groans from his gleeful heart—
not otherwise able, except with tears, to conceal
the obvious joy he felt. He belittled the tyrant's
vicious service, preferring to mourn the severed head
of his son-in-law than to be indebted for it. (*BC* 9.1035–43)

The description presents us with another kind of "empty tears," the fake tears of Caesar. Secretly rejoicing, he cries and deplores the evil deed; for, we are told, he does not want to owe anything to the Egyptian king in consequence of that *munus* (*BC* 9.1041–1043). Even mourning—a basic sign of human concern—has been manipulated by Caesar. His tears are a scheme: the master of *clementia* knows the way to effectively counteract its choking power. At *BC* 9.1045 the narrator breaks in with his corrosive commentary:

> O sors durissima fati!
> Huncine tu, Caesar, scelerato Marte petisti,
> qui tibi flendus erat? non mixti foedera tangunt
> te generis? nunc nata iubet maerere neposque?
> credis apud populos Pompei nomen amantes
> hoc castris prodesse tuis? Fortasse tyranni
> tangeris invidia, captique in viscera Magni
> hoc alii licuisse doles, quererisque perisse
> vindictam belli raptumque e iure superbi
> victoris generum. Quisque te flere coegit
> impetus, a vera longe pietate recessit.
> Scilicet hoc animo terras atque aequora lustras,
> necubi suppressus pereat gener. O bene rapta
> arbitrio mors ista tuo! quam magna remisit
> crimina Romano tristis fortuna pudori,
> quod te non passa est misereri, perfide, Magni
> viventis!

> Oh cruelest twist of Fate!
> Have you, Caesar, pursued this man with heinous war
> only to weep for him? Don't the ties of your united families
> touch you? Now your daughter and grandchild bid you grieve?
> Do you hope that among the nations who love Pompey's name
> this action will help your cause? You are, perhaps, stung with envy of

> Ptolemy,
> vexed that another should have a free hand
> with the life of the captured Magnus? You fret that war's
> revenge has been lost, your son-in-law snatched from under
> your proud victor's thumb? Whatever the impulse prompting
> your tears, it was far removed from true affection!
> Clearly you raced across land and sea for this one reason—
> fear lest your son-in-law perish somewhere in hiding.
> A good thing his death was snatched from your hands! What hideous crimes
> sardonic fortune has spared Roman decency
> in not suffering you, you fiend, to have mercy on the living
> Magnus! (*BC* 9.1046–62)

The narrator is denouncing Caesar's fake clemency and tears and is helping the reader to make sense of what is happening; for he finds it very strange that someone mourns over his worst enemy's death.[82] He observes that Caesar is not affected at all by his relationship with the dead man, nor worried about the sorrow he must have caused to his daughter and grandchildren. The general is crying because he thinks that the spectacle will make him well received by his troops (*castris prodesse tuis*, 1051). Or perhaps, the narrator adds, Caesar is suddenly attacked by envy for the Egyptian king; after all, only his hit man could lay hands on Pompey, exempting the *gener* from the "law of the proud victor" (*iure superbi / victoris*, 1054–55). Not exactly sure about the meaning of these tears, the narrator understands that they do not signify what tears usually stand for: they are not a sign of sadness or desperation or pure glee. Indeed, Caesar's pleasure could have been more complete if Pompey had never been killed. Yet if the narrator cannot securely identify the *impetus*, the kind of feeling that prompted those tears, he firmly believes that it was not *pietas*. While even the monstrous Mezentius in the *Aeneid* was capable of feeling *pietas* at least for his son, no feeling for his family makes Caesar vulnerable.

The apostrophic assault continues under the sign of irony: "Clearly you raced across land and sea for this one reason—fear lest your son-in-law perish somehow in hiding" (1057–58). The description cleverly juxtaposes *suppressus* and *pereat*. At first the verb *supprimo* (to suppress), paired with the verb *pereo* (to die), appears redundant. Instead, in it is invested the true significance of the action. What Caesar cannot stand is not Pompey's death but the silence that surrounds it. This is a death that he cannot claim, that he cannot use for any of his propagandistic goals, because he was unable to transform Pompey's defeat into a spectacle of his mercy.

Let us reflect on the power of the narrator's invocation to Caesar. Barbara Johnson has suggested that through apostrophe

> the absent, dead, or inanimate entity addressed is thereby made present, animate, and anthropomorphic. Apostrophe is a form of ventriloquism through which the speaker throws voice, life, and human form into the addressee, turning its silence into mute responsiveness.[83]

Johnson believes in the positive power of apostrophe, its intrinsic capacity to give a voice to something or someone that does not have one, at least not anymore.[84] Johnson assumes that the narrator in apostrophe frames events according to the character's perspective, but at *BC* 9.1045ff. something quite different is happening. Lucan does not give a voice to Caesar; he is interested in making him present without really allowing him to talk. Here apostrophe does not allow the characters to be reunited, and it does not entail an exchange otherwise impossible. Instead it creates a situation of imbalance: Caesar is made present only to be silenced. If history cannot be reversed, at least through apostrophe, the losers can abuse their abusers. Virgil had sympathetically apostrophized Nisus and Euryalus to encourage the reader to accept their death and to reconcile themselves with these victims of fate. Lucan addresses Caesar to reject his actions and to keep the reader alert to the spectacles put up by the leader to create consensus. Here apostrophe and irony are allied to create a form of invective; irony, as Aristotle thought, can become a species of *oligoria* or contempt.[85]

The intervening exclamation even more openly makes the point already suggested at *BC* 9.1058: justly (*bene*), this death at least has been snatched from Caesar's *arbitrium* so that he was denied a chance to take any decision regarding Pompey's life and could not exercise his fake *pietas* (*misereri*, 1061) on his son-in-law. The narrator's negative view of Caesar's mercy is also present in his apostrophe to Domitius Ahenobarbus after his rejection of Caesar's pardon in *BC* 7.599–604. While at Corfinium Domitius had accepted Caesar's pardon, at Pharsalus he rejects it. His death is described as free and happy, also as hopeful since he has not yet seen Pompey's defeat. Domitius accepts the Stoic idea that virtue is sufficient for *eudaimonia*. One's virtuous will and the ability to reason are the only things of intrinsic worth. Domitius is described as refusing *Caesaris venia* and the gift of life: "so often defeated by Caesar, he died a free man; he sank under a dozen wounds, jubilant, rejoicing because he thus escaped a second pardon" (*victus totiens a Caesare salva / libertate perit, tunc mille in vulnera laetus / labitur ac venia gaudet caruisse secunda, BC* 2.602–4). The narrator talks to the character in the second person and reveals how pleased he is about Domitius' decision to "flee the gift" of Caesar (*Caesaris effuge munus! BC* 2.524–25).[86]

At *BC* 9.1064ff. Caesar's *clementia* appears again, when he says, "I have lost the only reward of civil war, the chance to grant life to the defeated" (*Unica belli / praemia civilis, victis donare salutem / perdidimus, BC* 9.1066–68). Staring at Pompey's head, the general regrets his inability to spare Magnus and to become his friend:

> Laeta dies rapta est populis, concordia mundo
> nostra perit. Caruere deis mea vota secundis,
> ut te complexus positis felicibus armis
> adfectus a te veteres vitamque rogarem,
> Magne, tuam, dignaque satis mercede laborum
> contentus par esse tibi.

> A happy day is taken away from the nations, our accord
> is lost to this world. Magnus, my prayers lack the gods' favor:
> I asked to embrace you once my successful arms were laid down,
> to beg you, Magnus, to love me again and to go on
> living; for my labors' worthy reward
> I would have been happy to be your equal. (*BC* 9.1097–1102)

In marked contrast with what the narrator has previously affirmed (*BC* 9.1058: *o bene rapta arbitrio mors ista tuo* . . . , "yes, such death has been justly snatched from your power . . ."), the action is viewed through Caesar's eyes. According to the leader, a happy day (*laeta dies*) has been wrenched from the Roman people. His prayers have not been fulfilled because even if he could win the war, he was deprived of the possibility of saving Pompey and establishing *concordia* (1097) for all the world. With supreme rhetorical ability the Rubicon's trespasser invokes the *concordia* earlier invoked by the narrator (*BC* 4.190). Echoing the narrator's wish for friendship between son and father-in-law (*Caesar generum* . . . *amabit, BC* 4.188), Caesar presents himself as a maker of accord and amity. The language in the passage is worthy of comment because besides mentioning the Stoic notion of harmony, it mirrors Caesar's subtle manipulation of Roman traditional vocabulary. In Latin *complexus* implies the double notion of embracing and strangling. It is also a word with strong epic echoes: in epic the verb *complector* is often linked to the accusative *genua;* and the formula *complectere genua* (to embrace the knees), together with *tendere dextram* (to stretch the right hand), is topical when someone having been defeated is asking to have his life spared. In our passage, though, to the reader's surprise *complexus* is unexpectedly qualifying Caesar, the winner. Caesar is the one clasping Pompey (*te*, 1099) in an eccentric and paradoxical reversal of roles. The same kind of shift is at work in the syntactical link *rogare vitam* (1100), whose subject once again is Caesar: the victor would have asked Pompey, the defeated, "for life and affection." In his mention of *concordia* Caesar not only speaks the language of the Stoics; he also portrays himself as a novel *pius* Aeneas. As discussed above, the expression *dextramque tetendit* is rather originally used by Virgil at *Aen.* 10.823 to designate the winning Aeneas in the exceptional act of lifting his victim's corpse: real *pietas* (that of Aeneas) and fake *pietas* (that of Caesar) use the same gestures and language.[87]

In line 1102 Caesar persists in his manipulation of words: the leader's compensation (*mercede*) for all his labors lies in the feigned restoration of a *par*. While the use of *merces* hints realistically at the negotiation under way and at the contractual level of the exchange (Caesar earning the life and freedom of Pompey in the deal), *par*, a word particularly resonant in the lexical universe of Lucan's *Civil War* and semantically rich in meaning (equal/antagonist/pair), momentarily reconstructs the equality between the two.[88] The pair Pompey-Caesar would have been preserved but with their equality completely obliterated.[89] Caesar's *clementia*, while it preserves one's physical body, destroys identity, one's deeper beliefs, and the possibility to externalize them, to make them public. Like all sadistic practices it aims at humiliation rather than at pain because, as Elaine Scarry has demonstrated, it makes you say, desire, and think what you will later regret, what "unmakes" your world of truths and ideas.[90] Lucan's narrator seems rather aware of the importance of openly expressing one's ideas. Not only is he not duped by the appearance of Caesar's speech, in apostrophes he even voices his opposition to his manipulative habits and establishes himself as his own master of signification.

More concerning the complex relationship between silence and voice, appearance and interpretation, is revealed in the coda of this episode. At the very end of Book 9, after Caesar's speech and false tears on Pompey's head, we have Caesar's soldiers' reaction to the general's hypocrisy:

> Nec talia fatus
> invenit fletus comitem, nec turba querenti
> credidit: abscondunt gemitus et pectora laeta
> fronte tegunt, hilaresque nefas spectare cruentum,
> o bona libertas, cum Caesar lugeat, audent.

> He spoke thus,
> but found no companion to share his tears; the crowd put no

> credence in his grief, but concealed their mourning; they hid their
> hearts beneath a mask of joy, and, happy, they dared to gaze at bloody
> sacrilege—
> o sweet Liberty—while Caesar was mourning.[91] (*BC* 9.1104–1108)

The soldiers' response to Caesar's hypocrisy is hard to interpret. We are told that while the general cries, they do not believe in his lamentation and do not mourn with him. Hiding their sorrow and real feelings, they "dare" (*audent*, 1108) to show a happy face. What exactly is happening in these lines? It looks as if the troops regret Pompey's fate, they would like to cry but do not want to give Caesar the idea that they buy into his fake behavior and sympathize with his grief. They know that Caesar's tears are just a spectacle staged for "the nations who love Pompey's name" (*populos Pompei nomen amantes*, *BC* 9.1050) and "for the sake of the army" (*castris prodesse*, *BC* 9.1051). Their cheerful faces are in turn an "act," a gesture to spite the general, to signal their capability to think independently, to penetrate Caesar's lies. Of course the situation is highly ironical. The happy Caesar pretends to be sad for the sake of his cohorts; while the soldiers, who understand the real nature of that sorrow, disregarding the way they feel, put on a gleeful mask.

The narrator intervenes with his invocation *o bona libertas*, interestingly inserted between the soldiers—who, *hilares*, become the spectators of that bloody *nefas*—and weeping Caesar. On *bona libertas* Arnulfus Aurelianensis (late 12th cent.) in his *Glosule super Lucanum* writes: *que demonstrat illud quod habet in animo, quod non erant ausi facere milites Cesaris, uel yronice O BONA LIBERTAS quasi diceret: hec libertas non est libertas* ("which [the exclamation] demonstrates what he [the narrator] has in the soul, what the soldiers of Caesar did not dare to do or ironically 'o good freedom,' almost as if he were saying, this freedom is not freedom").[92] Similarly, the *Commenta Berniensia* suggest that *ironia quibus palam non licet flere, cum lugeat Caesar* ("irony, because to them it is not allowed to openly cry while Caesar cries"). These comments reveal that there might be a further reason why the soldiers do not cry: they might be afraid of Caesar's reaction at the sight of their devotion to Pompey. The soldiers' inability to cry recalls the assertion of a Roman mother at the outset of the civil war:

> "Nunc" ait "o miserae contundite pectora matres,
> nunc laniate comas neve hunc differte dolorem
> et summis servate malis; nunc flere potestas,
> dum pendet fortuna ducum; cum vincerit alter,

gaudendum est."

> "Now is the time," she says, "to pummel your breasts,
> mournful mothers, tear your hair out *now!* Do not delay this grief
> or save it for evils much worse! Now we can choose to weep,
> while the leaders' fortunes sway; but once one of them wins,
> we will have to rejoice." (*BC* 2.38–42)

What this anonymous mother feared is now happening. Caesar is winning, and it is not possible anymore for the soldiers to express their *flere potestas*. They cannot manifest their sorrow for the death of Pompey lest Caesar get upset about their emotions. The importance and inability of expressing sorrow are displayed by Lucan's narrator at *BC* 7.37–44, where he addresses Pompey and the pitiful Romans who were obliged to mourn in silence for his defeat:

> Te mixto flesset luctu iuvenisque senexque
> iniussusque puer; lacerasset crine soluto
> pectora femineum, ceu Bruti funere, volgus.
> Nunc quoque, tela licet paveant victoris iniqui,
> nuntiet ipse licet Caesar tua funera, flebunt,
> sed dum tura ferunt, dum laurea serta Tonanti.
> O miseri, quorum gemitus edere dolorem,
> qui te non pleno pariter planxere theatro.

> You they would have mourned: young and old, blending their grief,
> even children unprompted; throngs of women with their hair unbound
> would have clawed their breasts as they did for the death of Brutus.
> Now, though they fear the harsh victor's weapons,
> though Caesar himself proclaims your death, weep they will,
> even while they fetch incense and laurel wreaths for the Thunderer.
> Pitiful folk! They swallowed their grief, groan by groan,
> forbidden to weep as once they clapped, thronging your theater! (*BC* 7.37–44)

The "negative antithesis," the act of enumerating what was not there, reveals more effectively what should have been there; it highlights how Caesar's triumph has wrongly displaced public mourning for Pompey's death. Gordon Williams sees in the apostrophe a "characteristic shift of time scale" as the narrator "looks back from Nero's reign to pity the Romans who had to choke their grief."[93] And Andrew Walker observes that "like the negative antithesis, apostrophe functions as a *lure* in the text, constantly calling forth the past in all its visual plenitude only to collapse the vision by calling attention to the here and now of composition."[94] The narrator effectively reminds the reader of the importance of being able to freely express your opinion and your sorrow.

Arnulfus Aurelianensis says that that the exclamation *o bona libertas* (*BC* 9.1108, see above) is ironic. But in what sense? Is the narrator trivializing the soldiers' reaction? Is he suggesting that they should have mourned Pompey and used their grief to rebel against their leader? *BC* 9.1104–1108 is one of the few passages in which Caesar is shown without the support of his soldiers.[95] Faced with Pompey's severed head, they would like to mourn, to show that they miss Pompey; instead, they rejoice or at least pretend to do so. Only a minimal gesture is left to them to affirm dissent. *Libertas* has been reduced to an ineffective posture, a wordless rebellion of the spirit.

The quiescent laugh of the soldiers recalls some of Czeslaw Milosz' finest observations in *The Captive Mind*, where Milosz discusses the attitude of intellectuals obliged to live under Stalin's totalitarian regime:

> Officially, contradictions do not exist in the minds of the citizens in the people's democracies. Nobody dares to reveal them publicly. And yet the question of how to deal with them is posed in real life. More than others, the members of the intellectual elite are aware of this problem. They solve it by becoming actors [. . .] such acting is a highly developed craft that places a premium upon mental alertness.[96]

I am not suggesting a close parallel between Communist states and the Roman Empire. More modestly, I wish to stress a similarity in the state of mind of those who cannot sincerely express their thoughts. Milosz calls this mental rebellion "Ketman," a word that he finds described by Arthur de Gobineau as qualifying the attitude of dissidents in the Muslim East:

> Ketman fills the man who practices it with pride. Thanks to it, a believer raises himself to a permanent state of superiority over the man he deceives, be he a minister of state or a powerful king; to him who uses Ketman, the other is a miserable blind man whom one shuts off from the true path whose existence he does not suspect;[. . .] the feeling of superiority over those who are unworthy of attaining the truth constitutes one of the chief joys of people whose lives do not in general abound in pleasures.[97]

There are obvious similarities between Ketman and (Stoic) cultivation of spiritual freedom, especially a disquieting emphasis put on man as isolated from his environment, individually satisfied and separated from whatever happens outside his soul. Milosz concludes his reflections on Ketman with the following remarks:

> In short, Ketman means self-realization against something. He who practices Ketman suffers because of the obstacles he meets; but if these obstacles were suddenly to be removed, he would find himself in a void which might perhaps prove more painful. Internal revolt is something essential to spiritual health, and can create a particular form of happiness. What can be said openly is often much less interesting than the emotional magic of defending one's private sanctuary. For most people the necessity of living in constant tension and watchfulness is a torture, but many intellectuals accept this necessity with masochistic pleasure [. . .] Ketman brings comfort, fostering dreams of what might be, and even the enclosing fence affords the solace of reverie.[98]

Ketman can become a dangerously self-indulgent practice. Resistance that is not externalized into action resembles a toxic paradise of useless hindrance that ultimately sponsors alienation and lack of interest in one's social surroundings. This particular problem, the alleged sufficiency of the mind sponsored by a certain brand of Stoicism, is explored (and rejected) by Lucan especially through the account of Cato's participation to the war. Lucan's description of Cato as the only real mourner of the Republic (*BC* 2.297–305) and as actively involved against Caesar is a precise response to Caesar's manipulative tears and fake *misericordia* in *BC* 9.1044ff. but also to his soldiers' repression of sadness and action (*BC* 9.1104ff). Internal revolt and the defense of private independence are not enough for Lucan's sage.

Conclusions

Lucan is concerned with following the mutations of clemency and *pietas* and their acceptance by those who are loyal to Caesar. He is particularly preoccupied with the way in which the reader will react to the characters' reception of Caesarian "values." If Lucan's descriptions of the deaths of several Caesarians tend to reproduce the transvaluation of Roman ethical terms that are used without distinctions to qualify negative examples of heroism, the narrator's apostrophes counteract this tendency.[99]

While Valerius Maximus assumes that characters like Scaeva (3.2.23) or Caesar (3.2.19) can properly exhibit Rome's traditional values and patriotism, Lucan is profoundly skeptical about their heroism.[100] In Valerius' didactic project exemplary deeds are considered a source of instruction for those present at the event and those who will read about it.[101] In Valerius' compendium Scaeva appears in a chapter devoted to the exemplification of *virtus* as self-sacrifice for the cause of one's own country. Lucan has a different view, but he does not underestimate the appeal of characters portraying themselves as Roman heroes inspired by traditional *virtus*. He is aware of writing on a sensitive subject manipulated and filtered by a precise ideological bias. This bias portrays the history of Rome in terms of continuity since in the eyes of the creators and supporters of the new Imperial order all of those who contributed to the construction of the Caesarian state had to be not less worthy than the champions of Republican freedom.[102] If some Roman historiographers represent the Civil War with the language and images also employed to describe Rome's Republican past, Lucan's irony and narratorial comments signal a disruption without ambiguity.

The "*mise en scène* of spectatorship" enhanced by a narrator telling his audience how to judge "the spectacle" of his fiction and by the portrayal of the reactions of different internal audiences, invites the external audience's critical reflection.[103] Having created an effective mimesis in which the character's point of view is faithfully represented, the narrator interposes his comments and feelings, disrupting the audience's absolute identification with the fiction.[104] Lucan strives to create a compelling narrative that involves his reader with the presence of vividly represented characters and an involved narrator who, despite his strong emotional reaction, does not lose the ability to judge what he sees, is not duped by the pseudo-heroism of his characters, but eloquently reacts to it. Through this technique he effectively avoids a possible "misinterpretation" of the text and ensures the efficacy of his ultimately didactic and Republican epic project. Through the narrator's rhetorical maneuver, the illusion of the fiction is destroyed and its focalization adjusted. The perspective of the character in question is eclipsed while the hyperbolic details or a pointed question stimulate the reader to reevaluate the action from the angle of the intervening narratorial persona.

If stylistically—in tone, content, and ideological orientation—some of Lucan's addresses are very different from Virgil's, the two writers' tactics are not unrelated. In both there is a desire to guide the reader's response to the story being narrated. In the apostrophes analyzed above, as well as in the *Aeneid*'s apostrophe to Nisus and Euryalus, to Pallas, and to Lausus, the enacted lyric mood is only superficial because the intentions and ideas of the authors prevail over those of the characters.[105] The narrator discourages the reader from uncritically accepting what his characters are suggesting.

Lucan's narrative technique is strikingly similar to that used by Bertolt Brecht in his epic theater. Brecht, one of the most prominent figures in the twentieth-century theater, criticizes Aristotle's aesthetics, which in his view fosters empathy with the characters and leads the viewer to submit uncritically to the social message contained in the drama.[106] In light of Plato's generalized anxiety about the persuasiveness of (not exclusively theatrical) *mimesis,* what Brecht considers threatening about theater can certainly be extended to all forms of art. According to Brecht, the spectator's attraction to the spectacle is a dangerous phenomenon since emotional identification with the characters on the stage prevents the audience from considering critically the circumstances that directed the actors' actions and the power structures that bound the protagonists' very existences.

Brecht's epic theater is created with the intention of helping the spectator to distance himself from the characters and situations represented so that he can "weep when they laugh," maintaining a critical attitude toward the represented events. In Brecht's project the stage begins to tell a story, the narrator is no longer missing, and the background shapes an attitude toward the staged events. In order to foster a critical reaction, particular techniques are enacted. The staged action receives a commentary "by big screens recalling other simultaneous events elsewhere, by projecting documents which confirm . . . and contradict . . . what the characters sa[y], by concrete and intelligible figures to accompany abstract conversations, by figures and sentences to support mimed transactions whose sense [i]s unclear."[107] Since the production puts the subject matter and the incidents shown through a process of alienation (*Verfremdungseffekt*), the spectator is no longer allowed to submit to the fiction uncritically by means of simple empathy with the characters.[108] In his illuminating discussion of the *Bellum Civile* centurions, Leigh underlines the dangers of a text that transforms readers into passive spectators and also considers how Lucan's irony introduces a gap between narration and external audience.[109] The bifocal perspective from which Lucan observes the narrated story can be understood in terms of Brechtian alienation. Even Shadi Bartsch has considered "alienation" an essential element to understanding Lucan's poetry:

> Our alienation is supremely important for Lucan: it ensures that we will find it difficult to become emotionally embedded in his narrative, that we will feel a sense of detachment from the events [. . .] at the same time (and again, it is this double reaction that is the essence of the grotesque) we cannot help but react viscerally to the sheer violence done to the human

body. We are divided between distance and detachment, embeddedness and alienation. We are riven in the middle.[110]

This is exactly where I believe the narrator wants the audience to stand in relationship to his narrative. Lucan cannot avoid cogently describing the extreme acts which Caesar or Vulteius consider glorious and thus remains trapped in the ambiguity of a language affected by the drifting of signification triggered by the civil war and Caesarism. Nevertheless, he can ultimately reobtain control on his *poiesis* through direct intervention and disapproving irony.

Some of Brecht's reflections on empathy and the emotions can also be applied to Lucan's poem. He writes:

> We make no attempt to share the emotions of the characters we portray, but these emotions must none the less be fully and movingly represented, nor must they be treated with coldness but likewise with an emotion of some force.[111]

And again:

> A considerable sacrifice of the spectator's empathy does not mean sacrificing all right to influence him. The representation of human behavior from a social point of view is meant indeed to have a decisive influence on the spectator's own behavior [. . .]. A creation that more or less renounces empathy need not by any means be an "unfeeling" creation [. . . b]ut it has to adopt a critical approach to his emotions, just as it does to his ideas. Emotions, instincts, impulses are generally presented as being deeper, more eternal, less easily influenced by society than ideas, but this is no way true. The emotions are neither common to all humanity nor incapable of alteration; the instincts neither infallible nor independent of the reason; the impulses neither uncontrollable nor spontaneously engendered, and so on. A character's piecemeal development as he initiates more and more relationships with other characters, consolidating or expanding himself in continually new situations, produces a rich and sometimes complicated emotional curve in the spectator, a fusion of feeling and even a conflict between them.[112]

Brecht's theory explores the meaning of emotional identification with the characters without renouncing emotional involvement. Aristotle himself understood well that experiencing emotions requires judgment and cognition, since feeling pity for someone calls for the idea that the suffering experienced by the subject in question is (for the most part) undeserved (*Po.* 1453a).[113] He believes that there must be reasonableness in another's sorrow or joy. Immersion in another's world will help us to judge the other's feelings and reactions, for we must be sensitive to what circumstances the other is responding to and to the motives and intentions the person in question brings to those circumstances. Yet ultimately the immersion is "framed by a guiding interest in judgment. Propriety and reasonableness, rather than empathetic understanding for its own sake, prevail."[114] These observations can be related also to Lucan's epic, in which vicarious transportation of the reader is not everything. Lucan wants his readers to experience the hopes and fears of his characters through immersion in an empathic process but without becoming themselves so enmeshed in those emotional vicissitudes as to be unable to exercise their observational skills and critical stance. We could say of his epic what Theodor Adorno has said about Brecht: that his theater of alienation "cause[s] the viewer to think."[115] Such considerations on the emotions and reasoning alertness are compellingly resonant with Stoic theorization on the function of art. In the next chapter the audience response sought by Lucan through his apostrophic technique will be more carefully characterized as peculiarly Stoic.

3

Addressing Pompey: Lucan's Mimesis as Cognitively Useful Poetry and Apostrophe as a Stoic Trope

> spes o fidissima Teucrum . . .
>
> most trustworthy hope of the Trojans . . . (Virgil, *Aen.* 2.281)
>
> *Cum moriar sperare licet.*
>
> Although I die, it is possible to hope. (Lucan, *BC* 7.615)

BC 7.210–213: A Programmatic Statement

A fundamental statement of what Lucan wishes to do with his poem is presented at *BC* 7.210–13:

> cum bella legentur,
> spesque metus simul perituraque vota movebunt,
> attonitique omnes veluti venientia fata,
> non transmissa, legent, et adhuc tibi, Magne, favebunt.
>
> Whenever accounts of these wars are read,
> they will stir hope and fear alike, and useless prayers;
> astonished, all will feel that these are fates yet to unfold,
> not known facts, and oh Magnus, men will again warm to you! (*BC* 7.210–13)

Matthew Leigh persuasively links the ability to see something in one's mind and to capture it in words to the sphere of prophecy and rhetorical theory. He connects the aim and style of Lucan's narrator with the style employed by the augur Cornelius as he sits on the Euganean hills "seeing" (*perspexit, BC* 7.209) the signs of Pharsalus' battle in the sky and conveying the vision in prophetic utterance (*BC* 7.191–210). Cornelius' ability as a prophet and powerful narrator is attested to and qualified in even more detail by Aulus Gellius (*Noctes Atticae* 15.18.1–3: "Cornelius . . . with his mind in sudden turmoil said that far off he had caught sight of a most bitter battle being fought, and then proclaimed that he could see before him, just as if he himself were caught up in the battle, one side retreating, the other pressing . . ."); and Dio Cassius (41.61.4–5: "some birds not only announced the battle but in some sense performed it. For a certain Caius Cornelius accurately adduced all that had happened from them and recounted it to those present"). *BC* 7. 210–13 reveals that Lucan is committed to Cornelius' style and also to the vivid representation of Pompey's dramatic downfall for astonished readers (*attoniti*, 212) who, "seeing" the narration as history unfolding in front of their eyes (*veluti venientia fata, / non transmissa*, 212–213), will become so emotionally involved in the fiction to the point of formulating prayers (*spesque metusque peritura vota*, 211).[1] The narrator himself appears as an involved spectator of his fiction when he tries to influence history by praying (in vain) for different outcomes (*BC* 4.110–20; 4.189–92; 5.297–9).[2]

Rhetorically speaking, what allows the reader to be fictitiously present at the event is the narrator's effective employment of *phantasia* (mental picture) and *enargeia* (vividness). *Phantasia* came to occupy an increasingly prominent part in the artistic and aesthetic theories of the imperial period, even if it did not pose a substantial threat or a strikingly different alternative to the older hegemony of mimeticist thinking.[3] According to Longinus, the employment of *phantasia* and *enargeia* (*Subl.* 15.2) are conducive to shock (*ekplêxis*) in poetry and vividness in rhetoric, both qualities necessary to arouse the passions that are also mentioned by Quintilian in connection with *phantasia*:

> Quas phantasias Graeci vocant (nos sane visiones appellamus), per quas imagines rerum absentium ita repraesentantur animo ut eas cernere oculis ac praesentes habere videamur, has quisquis bene ceperit is erit in adfectibus potentissimus.

> Whoever masters those experiences which the Greeks call *phantasiai* (and we, of course, may call visions), through which images of things absent are so presented to the mind that we seem to see them with our eyes and to have them present, he will have immense power over the emotions.[4] (Quint. 6.2.29)

In short, as Leigh has underscored, the most important attribute of the family of concepts clustered around the term *enargeia* is its capacity to give the listeners or readers of a text a representation so vivid as to be visual as well as the illusion of being emotionally involved in the action.[5]

The effect of poems on the emotions or passions of the hearer is taken into consideration not only by rhetors but also by philosophers. The Stoics recognize that pleasure and fear are poetry's legitimate effects to the extent that they provide a means for the betterment of the auditor. According to Strabo, the famous geographer whose work shows a strong alignment with Stoic sources, pleasure is the most important feeling inspired by a poem, while fear serves to intensify the pleasure. The fear aroused by a poem is designated with the terms *ekplêxis* or *kataplêxis*.[6] The reader's emotional reaction seems a necessary and important consequence of his exposure to the text. "Hope and fear," the emotions mentioned by Lucan at *BC* 7.211 as effects of his narration, can be linked to two of the four main species of emotions categorized by the Stoics: namely, to "desire," defined as "the opinion that some future thing is a good of such a sort that we should reach out for it," and to "fear" "the opinion that some future thing is an evil of such a sort that we should avoid it" (SVF 3.391, 393, 394).[7] In the *Bellum Civile* these two particular emotional reactions that look forward to the future—and allow Lucan a chance to comment on his own time—are invested with special value since they are specifically mentioned.

The necessity of involving the audience emotionally is an aspect of drama emphasized by Aristotle in the *Poetics*.[8] In Lucan's account of the effect of epic on his readers the emotions stirred in the audience are not exactly those described by Aristotle for the viewers of tragedy: *Poetics* 1449b25–29 mentions *pity* and *fear* (*eleos* and *phobos*) not *hope* and *fear*.[9] Yet his narrator's wish to stir emotions and make his readers *attoniti* bears witness to the similarity between his model of epic reception and that conceived by Aristotle for staged drama. Employed by Lucan to qualify the reader's response to the narration, the expression *spesque metusque* is used in Latin from Cicero onward in connection to the emotional sphere, and the adjective *attonitus* "is marked by the glossaries as the Latin equivalent of the Greek *ekplektos*."[10] As a matter of fact, not only does Aristotle mention *ekplêxis* at *Poetics* 14.1454a4 and 16.1455a17, he also "attaches particular weight to metaphors that place things 'before the mind's eye' (*pro ommatôn*) and that therefore 'involve *enargeia*' as able to give the illusion of activity or actuality."[11] While the "fear" and "astonishment" of Lucan's viewers can be connected to Aristotelian *phobos* and *ekplêxis*, the emphasis on "hope" seems new. It comes, I believe, from Lucan's attentive reading of the *Aeneid*.

SPES

At *Aen.* 1.450–52, Aeneas is struck (*stupet, Aen.* 1. 495) while contemplating the images of the Trojan War depicted on the temple of Juno in Carthage. The images are witnesses to the Trojan defeat, yet they inspire hope:

> Hoc primum in luco nova res oblata timorem
> lenit, hic primum Aeneas sperare salutem
> ausus et adflictis melius confidere rebus.

> Here for the first time, in this grove, new things that met his eyes calmed Aeneas' fear; here for the first time he dared to hope for safety and even in affliction to trust his destiny more. (*Aen.* 1.450–52)

The only pleasure left to Aeneas, agitated by the insecurity of the future and by the hardship of his journey, "is envisaged by art. The sufferings of the Trojans, as Aeneas sees them in Carthage, have become fixed in art, literally: they are paintings. And it is here first, Virgil tells us, that Aeneas began to hope for a kind of salvation."[12] The images produce a strong emotional impression on Aeneas, who starts to regain confidence in men's ability to cry and to be touched by the limitations of life (*sunt lacrimae rerum et mentem mortalia tangunt, Aen.* 1.461). What Adam Parry has said of the *Aeneid*, I believe we can also say of the *Bellum Civile:* it is a poem about the *imperium* of art as much as it is a poem on the *imperium* of Rome.[13]

When Lucan tells us that the reading of his poem will provoke fear, empty prayers and hope, he exhibits the same trust as do Aeneas and Virgil. The sad account of the civil war will bring fear to viewers who will pray in vain for a different ending and consequently a different reality. Yet even in the desolate landscape of despair sketched by Lucan, hope is foreshadowed as a possible reaction to his work of art. In several *loci* the narrator complains because the gods have filled the universe with signs which, foretelling the future catastrophe, deny people even hope:

> Tum, ne qua futuri
> spes saltem trepidas mentes levet, addita fati
> peioris manifesta fides, superique minaces
> prodigiis terras implerunt, aethera, pontum.

> Then, that no hope of future—
> none—should alleviate fearful minds, unmistakable

proof of worse to come was added: the glowering gods
above filled land, air, and sea with omens. (*BC* 1.522–25)

Lucan seems to write his poem "to make the mind of men oblivious of future fate" (*sit caeca futuri / mens hominum fati*, *BC* 2.14–15) and "to allow the fearful to hope" (*liceat sperare timenti*, *BC* 2.15). At *Aen*. 2.281 the shade of the dead Hector is called by Aeneas "most trustworthy hope of the Trojans" (*spes o fidissima Teucrum*). At *BC* 2.242, Cato is "the only hope of virtue" (*virtutis iam sola fides*); and at *BC* 7.588 Caesar's slayer, Brutus, is apostrophized by the narrator himself as "glory of our nation, supreme hope of the senate" (*o decus imperii, spes o suprema senatus*, *BC* 7.588). It is the presence of men like Hector, Cato, and Brutus that inspires hope in the reader. In the desert, nature barred Cato's march (*iter mediis natura vetabat / Syrtibus*, *BC* 9.301–302), but his "daring virtue hoped to make her [nature] yield" (*hanc audax sperat sibi cedere virtus*, *BC* 9.302).

BC 7.210–13: Pompey as a Tragic Character

Apart from apostrophe Pompey often emerges as a fragile and guilty leader whose realistic portrayal is lucidly sketched by Cato (*BC* 9.204–208), who underscores that Pompey was the protector of a Republican façade, not of the Republic itself.[14] Yet at *BC* 7.213 (*et adhuc tibi, Magne, favebunt*, "men will again warm up to you, Magnus") Lucan's enthusiasm for Pompey drastically and intentionally contradicts the Republican's negative characterization "outside" the extended yet bracketed space circumscribed by the apostrophes themselves. Even when the narrator is finally ready to describe "the ultimate day" of Pharsalus (*summa dies, BC* 7.195), he does not forget Pompey. Indeed, he anticipates his death in order to describe the sorrow of the Romans and to join their sorrow in a sympathetic apostrophe to the leader (*te mixto flesset luctu iuvenisque senexque / iniussusque puer; lacerasset crine soluto / pectora femineum . . . vulgus*, "You [Pompey] they would have mourned—a wailing chorus of young and old, of children unprompted; throngs of women with hair unbound would have clawed their breasts," *BC* 7.37–40). In moments such as the one just described, the narrator's benevolent attitude toward Pompey—whose tale is qualified as one of tragic depth inspiring strong emotions (*spes metusque*) and amazement in his readers—is clearly revealed and the programmatic statement of *BC* 7.213 actualized.[15]

In Book 7 Lucan's benevolent attitude toward Pompey can be observed when he prefigures Pompey's imminent collapse describing a dream the general had on the eve of Pharsalus' battle. Lucan also encourages the audience to see Pompey as a tragic figure by contriving to represent him in his theater, being celebrated and applauded by the Roman crowds:

> At nox felicis Magno pars ultima vitae
> sollicitos vana decepit imagine somnos.
> Nam Pompeiani visus sibi sede theatri
> innumeram effigiem Romanae cernere plebis
> attollitque suum laetis ad sidera nomen
> vocibus et plausu cuneos certare sonantes;
> qualis erat populi facies clamorque faventis,
> olim, cum iuvenis primique aetate triumphi
> post domitas gentes quas torrens ambit Hiberus,
> et quaecumque fugax Sertorius impulit arma,
> vespere pacato pura venerabilis aeque
> quam currus ornante toga, plaudente senatu,
> sedit adhuc Romanus eques: seu fine bonorum
> anxia venturis ad tempora laeta refugit,
> sive per ambages solitas contraria visis
> vaticinata quies magni tulit omina planctus,
> seu vetito patrias ultra tibi cernere sedes
> sic Romam Fortuna dedit. Ne rumpite somnos,
> castrorum vigiles, nullas tuba verberet aures.

> But night—the end of happiness in the life of Magnus—
> beguiled his troubled sleep with an empty image:
> He dreamed that he had taken his seat in his Theater
> and was scanning the numberless faces of a Roman crowd. . . .
> By their joyful voices his own name was tossed starward,
> section vying with section, chanting and stamping;
> such was the aspect of the people, such their ovation
> long ago, when as a youth he enjoyed his first Triumph
> —for having defeated the tribes the Ebro's current encircles
> and every guerrilla force Sertorius flung against him—
> he had pacified the West and
> he was acclaimed in his pure white
> toga, as if it were conqueror's scarlet.
> Senators stood clapping when he,
> still a Knight, took his seat. Perhaps at the end of prosperity
> his mind, apprehensive about the future, fled back to glad days;

perhaps clairvoyant sleep, working its old ambiguities,
brought him, in guise of applause, omens of heavy grief-blows;
perhaps, this way, Fortune presented Rome to you, doomed
nevermore to see your ancestral home. Don't shatter his dreams,
watchmen of the camp: let no trumpet beat upon his ears! (*BC* 7.6–25)

With ingenuity in the dream the narrator can prolong Pompey's success while unraveling his future defeat. He is on Pompey's side and wishes him one more moment of happiness before his catastrophic end. In the *Bellum Civile,* Pompey is thus identified as a tragic protagonist whose unlikely downfall will draw the audience's sympathy. Lucan does not mention explicitly, but he does imply, a *reasonable,* cognitively grounded tragic pity (cf. *Po.* 1453b–b5). The reader will side with Pompey because of his unexpected defeat and because, though not perfect, he is a decent character facing at Pharsalus reversal of fortune (περιπέτεια, *Po.* 1452a20) and gaining a better understanding of the human condition (ἀναγνωρίσεις, *Po.* 1450a33–35 and 1452a30–35).[16] In discussing elements constitutive of tragedy's best plots, in chapter 13 of his *Poetics* (1452b35–53a3) Aristotle mentions the misfortune of a man who is not preeminent in virtue nor absolutely wretched. At 1453b10 he also emphasizes the fact that the poet must delight in creating a mimesis that brings commiseration and fear (ἀπὸ ἐλέου καὶ φόβου) through the plot (ἐν τοῖς πράγμασιν) and not through special effects (παρασκευάζοντες). Pompey is Lucan's morally "average" man whose rectitude *and* mistakes become relevant in the plot, compelling the audience to feel pity and fear. Lucan's mention of "hope and fear" can be considered an allusion to some of the most interesting ideas contained in the work of Aristotle, the first literary critic to have "theoretical appreciation of emotions in a cognitivist perspective,"[17] and the *Bellum Civile* can be regarded as a poem that elicits emotions without debilitating the spectator's intellectual faculties.

According to Berthe Marti, besides being represented according to Aristotle's recommendations Pompey is constructed by Lucan as a Stoic *proficiens* who will acquire knowledge, dignity, and humility only when abandoned by fortune.[18] Pompey's rectitude emerges at Dyrrachium (*BC* 6.1–132) and Pharsalus (*BC* 7).[19] During these battles Pompey makes obvious tactical mistakes because he does not want to take advantage of enemies who are his kinsmen. The narrator feels close to Pompey's desire to delay combat and understands Pompey's wish to spare lives before he democratically yields to the Senate's decision to wage war.[20] Plutarch informs us that during the Civil war Pompey had been harshly criticized for his passivity (Plutarch, *Pomp.* 67 and *Caes.* 41.1–5), but at *BC* 6.299–313 the narrator transforms this passivity into a redeeming quality. He avoids a direct accusation of the general, centering all the guilt in Caesar and fate.[21] While Caesar suggests in his own recounting of the war at *BC* 3.70 that Pompey recalled his troops for fear of an ambush, in a poignant apostrophe Lucan's narrator reveals that act as a sign of Pompey's *pietas:*

> Totus mitti civilibus armis
> usque vel in pacem potuit cruor: ipse furentes
> dux tenuit gladios. Felix ac libera legum,
> Roma, fores iurisque tui, vicisset in illo
> si tibi Sulla loco. Dolet heu semperque dolebit,
> quod scelerum, Caesar, prodest tibi summa tuorum,
> cum genero pugnasse pio. Pro tristia fata!
> Non Uticae Libye clades, Hispania Mundae
> flesset et infando pollutus sanguine Nilus
> nobilius Phario gestasset rege cadaver,
> nec Iuba Marmaricas nudus pressisset harenas
> Poenorumque umbras placasset sanguine fuso
> Scipio, nec sancto caruisset vita Catone.
> Ultimus esse dies potuit tibi, Roma, malorum,
> exire e mediis potuit Pharsalia fatis.

Civil warfare's worldwide bloodletting could have
spilled towards peace; but the leader himself
restrained his raging swordsmen. Happy and free in respect of laws
and rights, Rome, if only Sulla had won
this fight for you! But alas, it hurts and it will always hurt
since you, Caesar, have profited by the worst of your crimes—
fighting that man of scruples, your son-in-law. How grim is fate!
Libya's tears for Utica, Spain's for disastrous Munda
need not have fallen; the Nile, defiled with hideous bloodshed,
need not have borne a corpse nobler than Pharaoh's;
nor would Juba, naked, have weighted Marmaric sands.
Scipio would not have appeased Punic shades with his spilled
blood, nor would life have been shorn of sanctified Cato.
This could have been the last, Rome, the last day of evil!
Pharsalia could have made its exit from destiny's stage. (*BC* 6.299–313)

Apostrophizing Rome and then Caesar, the narrator underlines that his worst crime is to have fought against a decent man (*genero pio,* 305). He also reveals the absurdity of civil war and the insoluble ethical dilemma in which *pietas,* one of the founding virtues of Roman morality, is caught: Pharsalus could have been avoided and future freedom obtained only through viciousness; an ethical behavior produces bondage and the demise of the ethically best (*sancto caruisset vita Catone,* 311). The narrator's indignation stems from the awareness that morality, in this case, does not accomplish anything, that *pius* Pompey is destined to fail.[22] If Sulla instead of Pompey had fought this battle, final defeat could have been prevented (*BC* 6.302–303).

While the narrator's direct apostrophes to Caesar (e.g., *BC* 6.304) distance him from the leader, his apostrophes to Pompey underline Lucan's psychological closeness to this tragic character represented as a second unlucky Aeneas, for whom victory is not available and whose piety is not enough to succeed.[23] In Virgil's poem the suffering of the defeated *pius* Aeneas not only attracts sympathy, it also "mak[es] a moral claim"[24] that justifies the logic by which Aeneas later on was victorious over the Italians. In the *Bellum Civile* Pompey, *despite* his love (*amor*) for Rome and *because of* his reluctance to kill fellow citizens (*pietas*), does not rise from his ruin. Lucan pities him and is profoundly touched by his suffering.[25] In apostrophe, the narrator tries to console Pompey by invoking the Stoic idea of the self-sufficiency of virtue, which establishes the intrinsic moral superiority of the right intention and minimizes the worth of practical results. *BC* 7.703–708 makes manifest the narrator's sympathy toward Pompey as well as his endorsement of Stoic principles:

> Quidquid in ignotis solus regionibus exul,
> quidquid sub Phario positus patiere tyranno,
> crede deis, longo fatorum crede favori,
> vincere peius erat. Prohibe lamenta sonare,
> flere veta populos, lacrimas luctusque remitte.
> Tam mala Pompei quam prospera mundus adoret.
>
> Whatever you suffer in lands unknown, a lonely exile,
> whatever trials at hands of the Pharian tyrant,
> trust the Gods, trust the long-lasting favor of Fate:
> to win was worse! Allow no sound of lamentation,
> forbid the people to weep, forgo tears and grief!
> Let the world hail Pompey's woes as they hailed his prosperity! (*BC* 7.703–708)

There is in this passage a desire to see defeat as the last good thing to happen to Pompey in a benevolent turn of events, prompted not by Caesar's gods of victory but by those rational forces in the universe which (according to the Stoics) direct it toward its ethical perfection (Cicero, *Off.* 3.21–28). The gods are on the side of Pompey because, while allowing his demise, they do not allow him to become guilty. They preserve his virtue because they do not allow his name to be associated with the victory that destroyed the republic, paving the way to the empire and Nero. According to Ellen Zyroff, this apostrophe ends "with rebounding optimism that what happened to Pompey is all for the best."[26] The narrator uses his foreknowledge of Pompey's future defeat, much as Virgil had employed his knowledge of Rome's future victory, in order to convince the reader to accept Pompey's misfortune. His tribulation is, Stoically considered, a blessing because it does not compromise the leader's moral disposition but helps him to gain a deeper sense of the futility of triumphs and glory. In this passage the narrator lumps together *mala* and *prospera* (708), looking at Pompey's fate with the eyes of the Stoic sage who assesses facts not on the basis of political success or favorable outcome but exclusively on that of moral excellence ("to win was worse," 706).[27] Since according to the Stoics right judgment, i.e., wise and virtuous thinking (*phronesis*), is happiness (*eudaimonia*),[28] Pompey should be relieved simply by the awareness of his right conduct. From this perspective lamentations do not make sense since Pompey is being granted the best possible destiny.

The narrator does not encourage the reader to identify with Pompey always and indiscriminately. Pompey is described in an unfavorable light particularly in Book 2 and 8. For instance, at *BC* 8.335–45 the narrator is against Pompey and on the side of Lentulus, who is painfully aware of the selfishness of Pompey's plan; an idealist and a serious Republican, Lentulus believes that Pompey should not view the war as a private affair. He is outraged because Pompey is ready to bow to the Parthians in order to obtain help and victory against Rome itself. He is firmly convinced it would be better for Pompey to die than win in such a disgraceful way (*BC* 8. 395–96: *sed tua sors levior, quoniam mors ultima poena est, nec metuenda viris,* "yet your path is smoother, since death, the ultimate suffering, need not make men afraid"). Lentulus' speech is openly praised by the narrating voice at *BC* 8.454.[29] The narrator sympathizes with Pompey only when he stoically accepts his loss and suffers not for his downfall but for that of the Republic. Here his resignation becomes similar to "Cato's noble despair at the start of the war":[30]

> Non gemitus, non fletus erat, salvaque verendus
> maiestate dolor, qualem te, Magne, decebat
> Romanis praestare malis. Non impare voltu
> aspicis Emathiam: nec te videre suberbum

> prospera bellorum nec fractum adversa videbunt;
> quamque fuit laeto per tres infida triumphos,
> tam misero Fortuna minor.

> Not a groan, not a tear escaped you, your grief deserves respect
> and preserves intact your dignity, Magnus—it is just the grief
> Rome in her troubles requires. With no change in expression
> you gaze at Emathia: success in war has never
> seen you swagger, nor will adversity see you broken;
> fickle fortune falls as far short of you now, in this woe,
> as she did when you reveled in three triumphs. (*BC* 7.680–86)

Pompey did not rejoice in his triumphs, and now he does not weep in disgrace. He suffers with a dignified sorrow that shows his care for the destiny of his city and his mastery of *infida fortuna* (685–86). In this apostrophe, and also later when he will describe Pompey's death (*BC* 8.595–636), the narrator shares his sorrow, highlights the horrific cruelty of his enemies, and stimulates the reader to be sympathetic with him. In the moment of tragic reversal, Pompey's abandonment of kingly desires,[31] his altruistic looking to his people,[32] and his contained grief are underlined by the narrator and judged as worthy of the audience's pity (*BC* 7.681–82; *BC* 7.682).[33]

According to Shadi Bartsch, the incongruity which surrounds Pompey is "a deliberate tactic of the writing, thinking poet, who has set himself up as a character in the poem as well, a character of wild partisanship."[34] It is certainly true that a deliberate tactic is being employed by Lucan in the construction of the character of Pompey, but not one of illogical "wildness" since the narrator sides with him only when it is reasonable to do so: i.e., when Pompey finds himself trapped in his own *pietas* or is finally unconcerned with his personal glory. Emanuele Narducci qualifies the contradictions surrounding Lucan's Pompey as the result of two different narrative projects: one in which the author accepts what the historical sources recorded about the general of the senatorial cause (i.e., Pompey), another in which he composes an "apology and philosophical transfiguration of Pompey."[35] Lucan, Narducci speculates, might have drawn on reevaluations of Pompey elaborated by anti-Caesarian coteries tending to create a "myth" of Pompey and his family destined to the blessedness of the Elysian fields (*BC* 6.802–809).[36] In these circles Pompey's *gens* had to be programmatically opposed to the *gens Iulia* sponsored by the imperial group. Yet almost nothing in these elaborations suggests the use of an ennobling philosophical "*coloritura*," which instead is quite uniquely employed by Lucan to confer greatness on the figure of Pompey.[37]

Apart from Narducci's hypothesis, the recognition of Lucan's profound sympathy for a Stoic Pompey is evident. The narrator's predilection for Pompey should be understood as the predilection for a tragic character making mistakes under the pressure of difficult circumstances but ultimately committed to right action. The narrator in this epic is on the side of Pompey and wants the reader to bond emotionally with this character, especially when, in the most tragic hours of his life, perhaps better than the narrator himself he accepts defeat and behaves like Cato.[38] Lucan's verses are embedded within a dramatic context composed of vividly imagined particulars conveying a sense of immediacy that stimulates our participation and, in the case of Pompey, also attracts our sympathy. Lucan's depiction of Pompey as a *proficiens* caught in a tragic turn of events can ultimately be understood within the poem's Stoic temper, while the poet's will to involve the reader by stirring his emotions resonate with Aristotle's aesthetic formulations.

Yet, as will become clear in the next section, the fact that Lucan's aesthetic agenda is put in the mouth of his narrator and offered as an explicit "lesson" also moves the poem away from Aristotle's *Poetics* in the direction of Stoic poetics. Aristotle insisted on the need of concrete immediacy steering poetry away from didactic statements and perceived narrative intervention as incompatible with effective fiction (*Po.* 24.1460a5–11).[39] Instead, for Lucan a mimesis that reveals ethical standards of behavior in a vividly dramatic action only by "showing" is definitely not enough. He relies on his narrator to create a moving narration but also to warn his reader about problematic aspects of his narration. He often spells out the message contained in the action. His preoccupation with the effect of poetry on the audience seems to stem from Stoic discussion on the role and goal of poetry.

Philosophy, Poetry, and the Passions

So far, through textual analysis I have analyzed the way in which apostrophe is employed by Lucan, what aspects of it he borrows from Virgil, and what features of Virgilian style he prefers to dispense with. The study of apostrophe has shown us *how* Lucan's narrator makes didactic interventions that guide the reader toward rejection or acceptance of the examples proposed in the text. I will try to understand now why Lucan might make such didactic interventions. In the following pages of this chapter I will examine several theories on how poetry affects the passions in order to decide which theory Lucan may have preferred and endorsed. In particular, I will show that a Stoic model of poetical reception—one that makes room for a degree of mental dissociation between reader and fiction, allowing for the reader's sympathy but not for his complete identification with the characters portrayed—seems to have been adopted by Lucan. According to this model not only is the reader considered able to control his passions even when he is under the charm of poetical mimesis, but the poet is called upon to use specific techniques that facilitate the reader's detachment from the text.

There is general agreement among ancient commentators and different philosophers on the fact that, at least one of the ways in which poetry makes its impact on the soul is by altering the reader's emotional disposition. This alteration is produced through *ekplêxis*. In antiquity the notion of *ekplêxis* is quite complex, and in order to appreciate properly its wide field of application as well as its role in Lucan's text we must consider its theoretical elaboration more in depth. Ismene Lada describes *ekplêxis* as "the power to 'unhinge' men's minds, thrusting them under the domination of the affect." [40] She connects it to the captivation of the soul (*psychagogia*) mentioned by Polybius as the goal of tragedy (2.56) as well as by Plato in connection with the singing of the rhapsode, described as able to transport the listener imaginatively and emotionally into the fictive world of epic (*Ion* 535b). In another work (*Republic* 10.605c–d), Plato's Socrates specifies that the world of the representation, as we would put it, "infects" the listener's mind, altogether reinforcing his capacity to suffer not on account of a personal experience but vicariously, on account of "the lives of others" (606b1).[41] In Plato's judgment, comedy or tragedy can induce the members of an audience to suspend standards and beliefs to which they normally subscribe. As Stephen Halliwell suggests, "part of the 'yielding' or 'surrender' contained in the experience, part of what it means to 'follow' the emotional force of a dramatic portrayal, is precisely, according to Plato, to take on the underlying attitudes and values of the figures with and for whom one feels, and hence, to that extent, to imperil one's true self."[42]

But this is not the entire story about *ekplêxis*. Lada adds an important dimension to the meaning of this phenomenon by explaining that in the Platonic dialogues *ekplêxis* also portrays the soul's response to philosophical *logos*. For instance, in the *Symposium* Alcibiades compares Socrates to the mythical Marsyas and says that even "without instruments, by mere words," Socrates is able to emulate the aulos' insuperable enchanting power (*Symp.* 215c–d).[43] Thus Alcibiades attributes to Socrates' speeches the capacity to make the listeners *ekpeplêgmenoi* and possessed (*Symp.* 215d). He compares the enthrallment caused by Socrates' discourses with the image of the ecstatic entrancement caused by the Corybantic rites:

> When I listen to him my heart is leaping much more than the hearts of those possessed by Corybantic frenzy, and tears stream forth from my eyes at the sound of his speech. (*Symp.* 215e) [44]

Socrates' philosophical speeches are depicted by Plato as provoking in the mind of the listener the same effect provoked by the verses of a poet, and the event of "listening to the truth" is characterized as enchanting. Philosophy can provide audiences with an experience of deep revelation accompanied by intense emotional entanglement analogous to that bestowed by poetry.[45] This subterranean similarity between philosophy and poetry, perhaps only intuitively grasped by Plato, is fully acknowledged by the Stoics. As we will see, not only did the Greek Stoics praise the advantages of poetry; in the Roman world, too, poetry is accepted among the tools necessary to philosophers. In Lucan's *Bellum Civile* Cato's words, like those of Socrates, deeply affect his internal audiences.

In order to retain the benefits of poetry and to avoid its dangers, the Stoics elaborated well-articulated views about human psychology, developed theories about how poetry affects the human psyche, and formulated strategies to be enacted in order to minimize or stop the perils associated with poetic enchantment. All Stoics, no matter which psychological model of the passions they endorsed, admitted poetry because they focused on its potential educational value.[46] They were famous for their hostility to all emotions, which in their view had to be extirpated from human life; yet they wrote treatises dealing with the topic of poetry (which feeds the passions) and were fond of citing long poetical excerpts at crucial moments of their arguments.[47] Chrysippus, for example, used quotes from tragedy and epic as sources of inspiring insight.[48] We also find explicitly positive discussions on the role of poetry in education in Cleanthes, Posidonius, Seneca, Epictetus, Strabo, and Plutarch, some of whom seem to have seriously taken up Plato's challenge to reconcile poetry with philosophy.

Although we do not have any direct Stoic source about poetics, it is possible to reconstruct some basic ideas held by the Stoics about this topic. Stoic poetics maintains a boundary between the word and its meaning and is consequently divided between the study of a poem as a form of language (*lexis*) and as an expression of meaning (*logos*).[49] Concerning the criteria and goals of a poem as *lexis*, Phillip De Lacy has shown that the Stoics had different approaches to poetry.[50] Aristo, Zeno's pupil (fl. c. 250 BCE) in Philodemus' account, emphasized the importance of the arrangement (*synthesis*) of sounds and words primarily for their irrational effect and only secondarily for their "serious meaning" (*dianoia spoudaia*).[51] As in Cleanthes (c. 331–232 BCE; SVF 1.487), we find in Aristo an understanding of the importance of poetry as an effective aid to train the irrational side of the soul toward control.[52] Similar ideas can be ascribed to Posidonius (c.135–50 BCE), according to whom *lexis*, like music, affects the hearer thanks to harmonious sounds and pleasing composition irrespective of the content it expresses.[53] As irrational movements of the soul the pleasures of *lexis* should normally be avoided, but they are accepted and justified by Posidonius because of their educational benefits, since only an irrational inducement can educate the irrational part of the soul. Posidonius seems to have accepted Plato's tripartite model of the soul (*Republic* 435d, 504a–c and *Laws* 7), in which the passions are treated as irrational urges that must be trained and undermined by noncognitive strategies.[54] Poetry, in Posidonius' model, is valuable particularly in its noncognitive components.

Crates of Mallus, a Greek grammarian and Stoic philosopher of the second century BCE, leader of the literary school and head of the library of Pergamum, formulated the criterion of excellent poetry differently. In his view poetry is not good simply because it pleases the ear and it is written according to established criteria, but because of the "rational speculations that are naturally present in the poem" (Philodemus, *On Poems* 5.25.19–29).[55] This position, consonant with another important Stoic idea requiring that perception be always subjected and scrutinized by reason, is connected by Martha Nussbaum to what she defines as a "cognitive view of poetry," a perspective that demands from poetry a sort of *didaskalia*, not "irrational *psuchagôgia*."[56] According to Nussbaum, besides Posidonius, the Stoics who welcomed poetry the most were Chrysippus, Seneca, Strabo, and Epictetus; that is, those who appreciated it not as a pattern of pleasing sounds which tame the mind toward harmony and control but as a *logos*, ideas having a rational impact on the human psyche.

For instance, the geographer Strabo, active in Rome between the first century BCE and the early first century CE, has been shown to be influenced by Posidonius in his definition of *poiesis* as "significant poetic diction, containing an imitation of things divine and human" (Strabo 1.2.5 cf. D.L. 7.60). But rejecting Erathostenes' belief that all poetry aims at "enchantment" (*psuchagôgia*), he considers it a form of "instruction" (*didaskalia*).[57] Strabo concedes that poetry cannot always be read literally: fiction, he says, fulfills people's desire to learn by arousing emotion and is useful especially for women and children (1.2.8). In the Homeric poems there is an element of fictional discourse (*mythos*) mixed with things said "in a historical and instructive manner" (*historikôs kai didaskalikôs*, 1.1.10). Yet he sees the core of Homeric poetry (and geography) as truthful and didactic.

The Stoics who elaborated a cognitive view of poetry consider passions as assents (evaluative judgments) to appearances (*phantasiai* in Greek, *species* or *visiones* in Latin).[58] According to them passions are modifications of the rational part of the soul: not animal reactions or urges but judgments about how to view the world.[59] Typically, these judgments wrongly persuade the subject to ascribe too high a value to items that, according to Stoic doctrine, are neither important nor under the agent's control. At any rate, in the model under consideration these wrong evaluations can be rationally modified. Chrysippus does not endorse Plato's tripartite structure of the soul, but his conception of the passions can be ultimately derived from Plato's *Republic,* in which *thumos* (the passionate part of the soul) is said to be responsive to belief and an "ally of the reasoning part." (441a).[60] The Stoic theory of passions posits a distinction between instinctive reaction and rational assent. When confronted with appearances, including those generated by poetry or painting (Sen. *Ira* 2.2.5–6), a human being, even the wise man, will receive an involuntary "impulse" (*ictus*) that will make him react involuntarily. But the impulse *is not* a passion (*pathos/adfectus*): the latter arises only when the receiver of such an impulse gives to it rational assent (Sen., *Ira* 2.3.1). In connection with Alexandrian poetics and chapter 15 of the treatise *On the Sublime,* Claude Imbert has explained that a *phantasia* is a vision communicated by language. While language makes the vision explicit, the vision in turn brings language into existence.[61] *Phantasia* is the frame through which the poet views, depicts, and apprehends the world. What the poet conveys is not the way the world is but a model (*phantasia*) of the world. To this model we can give or not give our approval. Thus, the Stoics treated images produced by poetic endeavor as objects of assent "so that the distinction of image (representation/*phantasia*) and judgment tended to dissolve."[62] For them representations are not always veridical, but they always present something to the "commanding part" of the soul (*hegemonikon*), which in Stoicism constitutes the mind.[63]

In several passages Seneca hints that it is not easy and in fact practically impossible to resist impulses and impressions produced through poetry (e.g., *Eps.* 7 and 115). Yet he also insists that after the first involuntary reaction for which we cannot be considered morally guilty, it is up to us to embrace (or reject) the representation.[64] Anthony Long calls attention to a similar emphasis on assent in Epictetus:

> [t]he faculty of assent [. . .] constitutes a person's moral identity, and, as such, it is a character formed by experience, a disposition to make or decline to make specific commitments and choices. The content of these is given in representations. It is representation that provides selves with the viewpoint which they can select as appropriate to who they are, or reject as inappropriate. The Stoic self of Epictetus is constituted not by assent *simpliciter* but by the way assent uses representations.[65]

Plato considered poetry dangerous because it often contains false opinions (*doxai*) persuasively put in the mouth of admirable characters and passively accepted by the audience (*R.* 377b7).⁶⁶ Widening the discussion, Nussbaum notes that the passion-arousing power of tragic and epic poetry is connected in Stoic writing not only to the identification between character and spectator but also to the idea that the character is suffering something truly terrible and is powerless to prevent the damage. All three beliefs are wrong and pernicious from a Stoic point of view. Yet the Stoics find ways to defuse these mistaken ideas contained in the fiction, indicating strategies that will empower the audience by making the spectacle a positive and rewarding didactic experience. A Stoic spectator, armed with the right mental attitude, will not indiscriminately give assent to the characters' actions, but she will be able to criticize them. A proper mental disposition allows the audience to approach critically any kind of representation.⁶⁷

The emphasis on the hearer's ability to control his reaction is an important innovation in Stoic speculation on aesthetic reception. Before the Hellenistic period the hearer was conceptualized as a more or less passive recipient, but in the Stoic system he is no longer envisioned as defenseless against external impressions. Lada underscores the novelty of the phenomenon by observing that the Stoics developed a form of "reader response theory" that charged the hearer with some responsibility with respect to the fiction.⁶⁸ The Stoics invite the readers to realize that the values offered on stage can be wrong and that poets can lie. In fact, what we have in the fiction "is not the way the world is, but only someone's appearance (*phantasia, phainomenon*), therefore we have to ask ourselves, as we do about any impression that comes before us, whether we are going to assent to it or not."⁶⁹ In *De audiendis poetis* Plutarch, approaching the subject of the role of poetry in the education of the young man, seems influenced by Stoic ideas when he states that because it combines pleasure with ethical values, poetry should be employed as a propaedeutic to philosophy (15f–16a). According to Plutarch, the dangers of poetry can be overcome if the young man is aware of poetry as a *pseudos,* that is, when the audience does not regard what is successfully depicted in mimetic works as either "true" or "excellent" (*kalon,* 18b). He reminds us that we praise mimesis "for achieving likeness, whether the object be bad or good" (18a). Yet he strives to posit a disjunction between technical considerations of artistic merit and appreciation of ethical truths present in the work. The proper exercise of ethical judgment remains for him an integral part of the poetic experience; consequently, he offers an extensive analysis of how ethical criticism should be applied to a work of fiction.⁷⁰

Among the techniques useful to the formation of a critical stance and a detached spectatorship, Stoic texts recommend providing a running commentary on the action. This commentary will offer to the reader "a criticism that approximates to the criticism philosophy itself would offer."⁷¹ Plutarch says that in making use of a medical analogy Chrysippus also proposed to employ the technique of generalization. If a poetic statement seems significant, the audience should "not allow it to be linked to one matter only, but move it over to all similar cases, and accustom the young people to see the common link and to make intelligent transfers of what is pertinent, through many examples getting practice and training in sharpness of discernment."[72]

In his *Discourses,* the addresses of the philosopher Epictetus to Medea offer another technique fostering critical spectatorship.[73] Epictetus is brusque with his imagined interlocutor. He does allow his fictional reader to admire Medea for her courage (2.17.18) and to be sympathetic with her, but using direct address he also criticizes her ideas and behavior. Epictetus' approach to this character is particularly important because it reveals that an author can take an active role in his text and provoke readers to be, in their turn, active recipients of the fiction. Indeed, a Stoic spectator should regard fictional characters as a good doctor regards his patients: he should be strongly involved with them without being infected with their maladies.[74] Sometimes even harsh humor and satire are powerful weapons to bar the reader from extreme involvement with the characters of the text.[75]

Some of these ideas about the dangers and advantages of poetic reception can be found *in nuce* in Plato's *Republic.* According to Halliwell, at *Republic* 10.605c10–11 Plato alludes to the possibility that artistic representation might foster ethical understanding, which does not entail the complete psychological immersion present when an actor impersonates somebody. This pattern of poetical reception makes room "for a subconscious degree of mental dissociation between the hearer and the poetic character, positing 'sympathy' or 'fellow feeling' (*sumpaschein,* 605d4) where it is more appropriate to speak of 'identification' in the case of Book 3's argument."[76] In other words, in Halliwell's interpretation the better model of reception envisages sympathy that is not identification *tout court,* but an aesthetic emotion felt in response to an artistic spectacle that does not impinge directly on the spectator's own life.[77] Even if Plato does not explore the issue systematically, we can deduce from the various passages in which he discusses it that he conjectured:

> a series of psychological positions that can be occupied in the experience of poetry—a series of grades of imaginative absorption in the mimetic world that extends from the adoption of a quasi-participant point of view to the holding of an attitude of critical detachment. At one hand of this range we can accordingly locate the intense assimilation, the self-likening identification, of *Republic* 3, which takes place when a performer's (or we must remember, a poet's) mind plays out the role of a character, whether

in first person verbal recitation or physical enactment. This experience, which partially recalls the *Ion*'s description of the performing rhapsode as "outside himself," involves something close to a wholly "participant" point of view, and one understanding of the term, a strong degree of "empathy": a point of view, in other words, from which the mind experiencing the poetic representation is so immersed in the mind of the character as to have no room for emotional or critical dissociation. But . . . this is not a class of experience which Plato ever ascribes to audiences of poetry in the strict sense, only to reciters or actors [. . .]. For audiences as such, *Republic* 10, no doubt drawing on the scrutiny of the behavior of mass audiences in the Athenian theater, posits a psychically deep engagement with the characters, and a "surrender" to the emotions they evoke, but one that takes the form of "sympathy" rather than "identification" and leaves some degree of (sub)conscious dissociation from the characters ("these are other people's sufferings," 606b1). Audiences of tragedy, at any rate, are thus conceived of as engaged observers or "witnesses," but not "quasiparticipants."[78]

A similar kind of audience and mimesis are envisioned by Lucan, who wishes to involve his readers but not to the point of full absorption and elimination of their critical ability. Commentary, generalization, satirical tone, and apostrophe are techniques devised by the Stoics to bar the reader from extreme involvement with the fiction and to make the aesthetic experience didactically useful. Lucan uses them all and especially apostrophe. He vividly depicts Pompey's downfall; but by intervening in the fiction he spurs us to side with him only when he becomes aware of the futility of success. Much less sympathetically, he apostrophizes Caesar's followers when they act without truly considering the foolishness of what they are doing.[79] Through the narrator's ironic comments and generalizations Lucan hopes to help his readers to see the mistakes of his characters as well as the common links between the represented situation and theirs, the past and the present.

The Roman Environment: Seneca on Style, Literature, and Philosophy

So far I have given priority to Greek speculation about poetry. Now it is time to consider texts produced in the Roman environment. The kinship between philosophy and rhetoric is emphasized in Cicero, for whom the two cannot be dissociated. In his *Orator* he says that he wants to find not simply an eloquent man but "eloquence itself" and that the latter can only be found and seen with the "eyes of the mind" (101). Style is not simply the ability to add elegance to an already formed thought because philosophical and mental clarity are necessary to elaborate a persuasive and well-structured thought (*Orat.* 14. 113–115; *De orat.* 3.142) . In 77 BCE, after his Greek training in rhetoric and philosophy, Cicero returned to Rome more convinced than ever that those two fields of endeavor were inseparable.[80] In one of his most influential works, the *De officiis*, Cicero demonstrates that "it is the bearing of philosophy on human conduct which matters most."[81]

Seneca's ideas about philosophy and literature constitute another important moment in the reception history of Stoic doctrine in the Roman world and are a source to keep in mind when approaching Lucan's stylistic practices. Seneca recognizes the dangers of poetry but is not at all ready to renounce its advantages.[82] He considers emotional engagement a fundamental moment of the process of persuasion toward right understanding and action. The employment of poetry and rhetoric aims to involve the senses as well as the mind of the reader. This understanding seems to be shared by Lucan, whose poetry strives to produce in his readers an echo stimulating minds and senses toward proper behavior.

Seneca's main complaints against the poets are that they are typically indifferent to ethical truth and that they construct false stories about the underworld, the gods, or the importance of wealth. By constructing powerful but false stories, they affect the soul of the listener through the formation of a judgment. For instance, the poet's representation of a sad fate awaiting individuals after death triggers fear of death: "there are no ills to be suffered after death [. . .]. All these things are the fancies of the poets, who stirred us with groundless terrors" (*Ira* 2.35.4; *Cons. Marc.*19.4). Moreover, their depiction of Jupiter's lust feeds human errors by convincing people that it is acceptable to act as Jupiter acted (*dare morbo exemplo divinitatis excusatam, Brev. vit.* 16.5).[83] Sometimes in his philosophical work Seneca highlights the dangers of poetical elaboration (e.g., *Ep.* 7. 115; *Ep.* 90.20; *Ep.* 100.2), and he admits that it is hard to resist the impression made by the representation and associated with the pleasure of poetry (*per voluptatem facilius vitia subrepunt*, "vices creep more easily through pleasure," *Ep.* 7.2). A negative spectacle will not affect the wise man, but it is likely to harm the morally weaker, those who are "progressing" toward virtue (*proficientes*). At any rate, at *De ira* 2.2–3 the philosopher justifies poetry (*spectacula et lectiones rerum vetustarum*, 2.2.3) with his theory of assent. He says that passion (*adfectus*) does not consist in being moved by the impressions (*species*) presented to the mind but in surrendering to these promptings (2.3.1).[84] Seneca's entire philosophical enterprise bears witness to his deep awareness of the importance of poetic diction for those who are concerned with true persuasion.

I have already mentioned that the Stoics study a poem for its speech (*lexis/synthesis*) as well as for its meaning (*dianoia/logos*) and that some Stoic thinkers (Aristo and Crates) believed the arrangement of words to be a matter of relevance to the irrational captivation of the soul.[85] It would seem logical to assume that Stoics like Seneca, who gave importance to poetry above all as a "container" of rational ideas, should not pay much attention to the question of style. Yet this does not seem the case.

In general, the Old Stoa is remembered as equating speaking well with speaking the truth (*Ep.* 90.20; 49.12) and with following nature. Aristotle's pupil Theophrastos distinguished between a style created for the delight of the general public and another suited for the philosopher devoted to dispelling mistakes and showing the truth.[86] Zeno and Chrysippus only approved of the latter and in their most stern theorizations seem to be almost distrustful about any concession toward ornamentation (SVF 1.23.14; SVF 2.96.19).[87] The Old Stoics concentrated on "nature" as the will and capacity of the single good man to tune into the *logos* and believed that there is only one way to describe logically and coherently the truth sought after. For the Stoics speaking well was not a result of technical instruction but the natural consequence of a correct disposition of the mind. Minimizing the individual's contribution to the formulation of the truth, they stressed the fact that if the truth is always the same, then the language expressing it must also be always identical to itself. There are traces of the Stoic indifference toward stylistic elaboration in Cicero's criticism of them as *duriores et oratione et moribus* ("full of asperities in their style and manners," *Fin.* 4.78). Cicero condemns their style as entirely ineffectual, that is, unable to produce a change in the soul of the hearers and as such unfit for *admonitio* since *etiam qui adsentiuntur nihil commutantur animo et idem abeunt qui venerant* ("even those who approve are not changed inside and, having come, they go away untouched," *Fin.* 4.7).[88]

In the Roman environment the Stoics' skepticism toward stylistic care seems to have been bypassed. We do not know of the philosophical writings by Cato the younger, who was judged by Cicero (at *Brutus* 118) to be the *Stoicus perfectissimus* and is featured prominently in Lucan's *Bellum Civile*. Yet, when he is presented as a character in the third Book of *De finibus*, his speeches embrace the classic principle of *decorum*.[89] In *Paradoxa Stoicorum* 3, once again, "oratorical flourishes" (*oratoria ornamenta*) are considered a supplement to Cato's way of speaking.[90] According to Cicero, even Panaetius deviated from the rigid stylistic principles of the older tradition and "censured alike the harshness of the Stoic doctrines and the crabbedness of its logic; in doctrine he was mellower and in style more lucid" (*Fin.* 4.79). Following Aristotle (*Rh.* 3.1404), he admitted that if we can theoretically separate an objectively better style designed for philosophical argumentation from another devoted to creating a psychagogic effect on the audience, in practice the speaker must use the latter to convince a public untrained in logic. Panaetius, according to Aldo Setaioli, welcomed the psychagogic element in the *sermo* since he understood that the plain expression will not easily persuade people to embrace the right kind of life: it will not be effective for *hortari, persuadere, consolari*, and giving *praecepta*.[91] Panaetius was very much aware that he is talking to people not yet committed to wisdom (*prokoptontes*), and he adapted his language for their benefit. For their sake he used powerful images and strove to obtain the *enarges* (fr. 109 Van Straaten).[92] In different ways Horace and Persius have been shown to be extremely sensitive to stylistic matters and the necessity to persuade.

A similar opening toward rhetorical elaboration can be detected in the writing of Seneca, who agrees with the stylistic ideas of the Old Stoa only at a theoretical level. For instance, in *Ep.* 49.12 he says, quoting Euripides, that the truth uses a simple language that should not be made complex (*nam ut ait ille tragicus "veritatis simplex oratio est," ideoque illam implicari non oportet*, "For as the tragic poet says 'The language of truth is simple'; therefore, it should not be made complicated," *Ep.* 49.12).[93] In *Ep.* 90.20 he is scandalized because good men can easily be driven away from the truth by the "sweetness" of words (*quam facile etiam magnos viros dulcedo orationis abducat a vero*, "how easily the sweetness of a speech drags even good men away from the truth," *Ep.* 90.20). He also reminds his addressee Lucilius, who criticized the unadorned philosophical writings of a certain Fabianus, that he is dealing with a philosopher (*oblitus de philosopho agi compositionem eius accusas, Ep.* 100.1), whose words "are chosen, not hunted down or, in the manner of the present day, arranged contrary to nature and inverted" (*Ep.* 100.2). According to Kirk Freudenburg, Seneca defends Fabianus in the name of Stoic theories, postulating the existence of a natural arrangement of words: "Like the Atticists and neo-Chrysippeans of the previous century, Seneca admits that Fabianus's 'natural flow' of words will not always smoothly caress the ear" since he writes for the minds, not for ears (*animis . . . non auribus, Ep.* 100.2).[94] Despite this talk about simple style and natural flow, Seneca is far from accepting those Stoic prescriptions that establish a univocal relationship between truth and its expression.[95]

Following Aristotle (*Rh.* 3.1404) and Panaetius, in *Epistulae* 38, 100, and 75 Seneca theoretically recognizes the stylistic differences between *sermo*, the simple conversation most suited to philosophy, and *disputatio*, a discourse rhetorically elaborated for the persuasion of the general public. Nevertheless, he explains that both modes must be employed in order to "bend" (*flectere*) the soul. Though committed to marks of logically good reasoning such as consistency, clarity, and breadth of scope, he realizes that it is necessary to search for techniques that are more engaging than those routinely used by philosophers.[96] In persuasion it is crucial to appeal through rhetorical means to the imagination and inner world of the hearer.[97] Seneca permits rhetorical tools in the philosopher's arsenal because he considers the necessity of convincing the senses as well as the mind. In his philosophical work he gives great importance to the idea of emotionally moving the audience (*movere*), since he is convinced that a discourse cannot be appealing only to the intellect (*probare*) but must capture all the senses of the listener.

In order to persuade his audience successfully, Seneca is careful to employ effective language; rejecting Ciceronian syntax, he fully embraces the fashionable *sententia* as the building block of his philosophical dialogues.[98] He has an almost historicist approach to writing (*adice nunc, quod oratio certam regulam non habet; consuetudo illam civitatis, quae numquam in eodem diu stetit, versat,* "add that rigid stylistic laws do not exist: they follow fashion that is continuously changing," *Ep.* 114.13) because he believes that to choose current writing practices is a necessary step to create effective communication.[99] Even a philosopher can "introduce verses among his wholesome precepts, that he may thus make those verses sink more effectively into the mind of the non-wise" (*cum salutaribus praeceptis versus inseruntur, efficacius eadem illa demissuri in animum imperitorum? Ep.* 108.9–10).

What is particularly interesting in Seneca's approach to literature and stylistic practices is his detection of the proximity between poetry and philosophy.[100] At *Ep.* 8.8 he observes that many poets say things that could be said or should be said by philosophers (*quam multi poetae dicunt, quae philosophis aut dicta sunt aut dicenda*); in *Ep.* 33.2 he remarks that poetic works have many ideas shared by Stoic doctrines *(eiusmodi vocibus referta sunt carmina, refertae historiae)*. At *Ep.* 59.5–7, tropes (metaphors and similes) are considered useful for poets as well as philosophers when they are exploited to give clarity and strength to the context. In this letter Seneca seems to discuss metaphors (that is a species of poetical utterance) from the point of view of the audience, as a device for "presentization" used by all who try to cope with the weakness of the human mind:[101]

> Illi ([= antiqui], qui simpliciter et demonstrandae rei causa eloquebantur, parabolis referti sunt, quas existimo necessarias, non ex eadem causa qua poetis, sed ut inbecillitatis nostrae adminicula sint, ut et dicentem et audientem in rem praesentem adducant.
>
> They [the ancient prose writers], talking with simplicity to make themselves understood, introduced metaphors which I believe necessary not for the

same reasons of the poets but as aids to our weakness, in order to expose the hearer and the speaker to reality. (*Ep.* 59.6)

For instance, Seneca tells Lucilius that he was captured by one of the similes of Sextius (*movit me imago ab ille posita*). The Greek philosopher compares the sage to an army marching in a square formation (*Ep.* 59.7, *quadrato agmine exercitum*), "fortified against all inroads" (*ad omnem incursum munitum*, *Ep.* 59.8) and ready to face the enemy. Thus, because of its strength and because of the mind's weakness, poetry should be woven into ethical statements since "when meter is added and when regular prosody has compressed an excellent idea (*egregium sensum*), then the same thought (*eadem illa sententia*) comes as it were hurtling with a fuller fling" (*Ep.* 108.10).[102]

Besides Seneca, in his *Ars Poetica* Horace explains that it is not enough for a poem to satisfy the canons of art; it must also make an impression on the mind of the hearers. The delight (*dulce*) and ethical instruction (*pulchrum*) provided by poetical *psychagôgia* is underlined by Horace:[103]

> Non satis est pulchra esse poemata; dulcia sunto
> et quocumque volent animum auditoris agunto.
>
> It is not enough for poems to be ethically relevant; they must delight
> and drag the soul of the listener where they will. (*A.P.* 99–100)

Some hearers want to be delighted but others demand instruction; thus the poet must combine instruction with delight (*A.P.* 343–44). Furthermore, Horace seems to link poetry and philosophy when he requires from the poets the knowledge of *sapientia*:

> Scribendi recte sapere est et principium et fons:
> rem tibi Socraticae poterunt ostendere chartae,
> verbaque provisam rem non invita sequentur.
>
> The beginning and source of good writing is wisdom: the Socratic pages will
> be able to indicate to you your matter, and once you have determined your
> subject the words will follow without difficulty. (*A.P.* 309–311)

According to J. Tate, not only does *sapere* mean moral wisdom but the term *Socraticae chartae*, in connection with *A.P.* 309 and 311ff., also refers preeminently to

Stoic philosophy: "Stoicism claimed to be, and was called, Socratic . . . Heraclitus (*Quaes. Hom.* 79) clearly means Stoicism by *Sôkratikê sophia* . . . [and] Persius (5.37) speaks of the 'Socratic bosom' of his Stoic teacher Cornutus."[104] Even in ancient times wisdom was the distinguishing mark of the poet (*A.P.* 391–407). The myth of Orpheus as charmer of tigers and that of Amphion, who could move rocks and stones, allegorically hint at the fact that the primitive poets were lawgivers and founders of cities. Homer was a better teacher than Chrysippus (*Ep.* 88.5ff.), and in the person of Odysseus he set before us an example of the efficacy of virtue and wisdom.[105] The prioritization of content over form seems also to derive from Stoic doctrines.[106]

What poetry fosters according to Seneca is not an irrational *enthusiasmos* but a return to reason, an impulse to reanalyze the context under the guidance of rationality.[107] According to Mazzoli, in *Ep.*108.7 Seneca fuses the language of inspiration with that of frenzy, which in turn can be connected to Cleanthes (SVF 1.486), Plato's *Ion* (535b7–c3), and *Phaedrus* (534b4–6):

> A certain number are stirred by high-sounding phrases, and adapt themselves to the emotions of the speaker with lively change of face and mind—just like the emasculated Phrygian priests [*Phrygii . . . semiviri*], who are wont to be roused by the sound of the flute and go mad [*furentes*] to order. But the true hearer is ravished and stirred by the beauty of the subject matter, not by the jingle of empty words [*rapit illos instigatque rerum pulchritudo, non verborum inanium sonitus*]. (*Ep.* 108.7; tr. R. M. Gummere)[108]

In Seneca's statement the language of irrationality is certainly present. But in this passage the emphasis on a superior knowledge to be found in *the beauty of the poetic content* should be put in context with what Nussbaum has called a cognitive approach to poetry.[109] In Seneca's view, powerfully poetical discourse does not produce irrationality in the soul; it reawakens "the seed of virtue" and reestablishes the boundaries of sanity:

> Facile est auditorem concitare ad cupidinem recti; omnibus enim natura fundamenta dedit semenque virtutum. Omnes ad omnia ista nati sumus; cum inritator accessit, tunc illa animi bona veluti sopita[110] excitatur. Non vides quemadmodum theatra consonant, quotiens aliqua dicta sunt, quae publice adgnoscimus et consensu vera esse testamur?
>
> It is easy to incite a listener so that he will crave the love of the good; for nature gave to everybody the foundations and the seed of virtue. We are all

born for virtuous actions. If an educator comes by, he awakens this good disposition that is asleep. Can't you see how much our theaters resound (with applause) whenever words are pronounced which we publicly acknowledge and which with our consensus we declare true? (*Ep.* 108.8)

Praeterea ipsa, quae praecipiuntur, per se multum habent ponderis, utique si aut carmini intexta sunt aut prosa oratione in sententiam coartata, sicut illa Catoniana: "emas non quod opus est, sed quae necesse est"; . . . qualia sunt illa aut reddita oraculo aut similia. . . . Advocatum ista non quaerunt; adfectus ipsos tangunt et natura vim suam exercente proficiunt. Omnium honestarum rerum semina animi gerunt, quae admonitione excitantur non aliter quam scintilla flatu levi adiuta ignem suum explicat. Erigitur virtus cum tacta est et inpulsa. Praeterea quaedam sunt quidem in animo, sed parum prompta, quae incipiunt in expedito esse, cum dicta sunt. Quaedam diversis locis iacent sparsa, quae contrahere inexercitata mens non potest. . . . Ingenii vis praeceptis alitur et crescit novasque persuasiones adicit innatis et depravata corrigit.

Furthermore precepts which are given have a lot of weight in themselves, especially if they are woven into the fabric of poetry or condensed into well-constructed maxims like those by Cato: "Buy not what is useful but what is indispensable" . . . equally useful are oracles given by the gods or similar statement. . . . These statements do not need someone who will provide a proof: they go straight to our emotion and are useful because in them is manifested the force of nature. The soul contains the seeds of all virtues which, by an exhortation, are stirred to growth, as a spark that is fanned by a gentle breeze develops its natural fire; likewise virtue develops under the impulse of incitement. Furthermore, there are in the mind notions that are not clear, and which become evident when they are expressed by words; other [notions] lie scattered here and there and it is not easy for an untrained mind to arrange them in order. . . . Precepts nourish the strength of the mind, add to innate ideas new points of view and correct those which are distorted.[111] (*Ep.* 94.27–28; 28–29; 30)

In practice Seneca seems to suggest that an effective style "going straight to our emotions" produces the same effects of philosophical exhortation, reawakens the spark of virtue, inspires proper behavior, and can dispel mistaken judgments.[112] Arid and "naked" expressions are not at all demanded by philosophy, which does not reject an "ingenious" style (*non mehercules ieiuna esse et arida volo quae de rebus tam magnis dicentur—neque enim philosophia ingenio renuntiat, Ep.* 75.3).

Stylistic tools, Seneca writes, must be used like medicine, which ultimately fosters health: *non delectant verba nostra sed prosint . . . alia artes ad ingenium totae pertinent, hic animi negotium agitur* ("our words should aim not to please, but to help . . . the other arts are wholly concerned with cleverness, but our business here is the soul," *Ep.* 75.5–6).[113] The delight that good eloquence produces is never for itself but subordinated to the awakening of good behavior in the audience. The good listener "will not become excited for the jingle of the empty word but will be stirred by the beauty of the content" (*rapit illos instigatque rerum pulchritudo, non verborum inanium sonitus, Ep.* 108.7). Literary and rhetorical strategies are a methodological premise to solid and persuasive speech. There is no escaping from persuasion, and so none from rhetoric. In Lucretius' and Seneca's works we find impressive models of philosophical-literary investigation in which poetic diction engages the reader's full attention in a way that an abstract and scientific prose could not.

A. D. Leeman believes that Stoic theory on style did not have an overly strong impact on Seneca's views on poetry. But he adds that Seneca probably felt that his style, resting on directness and compression and stretching the truth to "impress the reader in the most effective way," did not contradict the teachings of the Stoics.[114] Aldo Setaioli characterizes Seneca's style as dependent on Panaetius' elaboration. Gian Carlo Mazzoli connects his positions to the Stoic theory of the "impulses (ἀφορμαί) from nature toward virtue" (SVF 1.566) probably already present in Cleanthes and developed in Posidonius. He suggests that in keeping with the tradition of the Stoa, Seneca, far from a conception of *l'art pour l'art*, "welds ethics and poetics as rings of a unique and unbreakable chain" and emphasizes the pedagogical function of the artistic endeavor.[115] At this point it should be clear that whether we believe that Seneca was influenced more by Panaetius than by Posidonius or vice versa, we should understand that he considers emotional engagement a fundamental moment of the process of persuasion toward right understanding and action. He values the aesthetic experience because it involves the senses as well as the mind. A similar conviction is embraced by Lucan, whose poetry strives to produce in his readers an echo stimulating minds and senses toward proper behavior.

POETRY AND CRITICAL READERSHIP IN THE *Bellum Civile*

Despite their claim that the wise man is the only true poet (SVF 3.654 and 655), our Stoic sources (with the exception of Seneca) do not show philosophers actively engaged in the creation of "philosophical" poetry. They reveal instead philosophers limiting themselves to commenting on Euripides or to interpreting Homer. Seneca alone openly defends poetry and dramatic plots for their ability to engage the reader with philosophical themes as well as for their capacity to encourage moral self-scrutiny. For Nussbaum he is the only Stoic who seems to have reflected in a serious way on the relationship between poetry and spectatorship, creating in some of his tragedies a practical example of Stoic "reformed" poetry.[116]

For instance, in the play *Medea* the philosopher not only portrayed Medea's emotional conflict as a Stoic struggle of judgments; he also crafted her as a main character "repellent to the audience." Moreover, through the chorus' criticism of Medea he highlighted for the audience a correct model of critical reception.[117] Not everybody agrees with this interpretation of Seneca's drama nor on the degree of didactic success achieved in his poetic inventions.[118] Schiesaro, as I mentioned earlier (see Introduction), by highlighting the gap between representation and reception in Seneca's plays, expresses reservations concerning the didactic success of his tragedies since he is of the opinion that the chorus' flat criticism of Medea does nothing to isolate the reader from the heroine's ensnaring passion or to persuade the audience that she is wrong in hating Jason and in killing her children.[119]

Lucan's poetry can be considered another attempt of Stoic fiction to promote through rhetorical means the right kind of relationship between representation and audience. Although Lucan is not a philosopher and in the *Bellum Civile* even expresses his impatience with some Stoic philosophical premises (e.g., *pronoia*), he believes in poetry as an instrument for effective teaching and exhortation.[120] The narrator's desire to stimulate awareness of the fiction seems influenced by Stoic recommendations on how to approach art. With his *Bellum Civile* he succeeds in crafting a poetry that is not an obstacle to critical thinking. Lucan employs rhetorical devices that shield the reader from negative examples and draw him toward positive ones. Reawakening the reader's hope, Lucan's poetry rekindles his desire to struggle against moral and political lethargy. His "philosophical" poetry is not an isolated example. During the first century CE we see an interesting fusion of the horizons between philosophy and artistic creation: philosophical prose becomes artistic (Seneca) while poetry becomes philosophic (Persius). Already in the *Aeneid*, according to Heinze, Virgil employed epic divine machinery allegorically to represent his belief in a Stoic *theologia physica*, with Jupiter as the symbol of an omnipotent and imperturbable Providence.[121] Even though the *Aeneid* cannot easily be forced into a Stoic paradigm, in it Virgil carefully couches his plot and discourse on the origin of the Roman state in a divine plan according to which *kosmos* and *imperium* are welded together. He strategically connects the winning side (Aeneas/Augustus) with the Olympians, order, and civilization.[122] Earlier we saw how Virgil's narrator is attracted to (and sometimes ambiguously fosters) the idea of historical progress guaranteed by Jupiter. We also saw how forcefully Lucan's narrator defuses Virgil's scheme, showing that Caesar's victory at Pharsalus proves Jupiter's complete indifference to human affairs.

The exploration of the identification mechanism through which the reader tends to sympathize with the character was analyzed by Plutarch in *De audiendis poetis*. In this text there is a defense of poetry associated with an "upright standard of reason" (15d); Plutarch considered poetical works harmless and indeed beneficial if received by a critical audience.[123] In chapter 2 I showed how Lucan promotes a similar program with his employment of apostrophe and irony to make didactic interventions in his text so as to create critically aware readers. With Seneca and some philosophers of the Middle Stoa, Lucan is aware of the power of poetical discourse for persuasion, and he exploits it in full. But he is also careful to avoid the dangers connected with the poetical spell (*ekplêxis*). Through the narrator's exegesis he powerfully leads his audience to assent to certain images (e.g., Pompey's acceptance of his trial, Cato's commitment to fight) and to reject others (e.g., Scaeva's death, Caesar's *pietas*). The narrator's irony prevents his reader from sympathizing with ambiguous characters. His generalizations (e.g., comments on the suicide of Vulteius' men) clarify what the readers should learn from the fiction: the similarities between the past and the present and how individual mental alertness can make a difference.

The emotional engagement of the audience is recognized by philosophers and orators as necessary for persuasion. Likewise, Lucan wants to produce a profound effect on the reader's psyche. According to Seneca, the right type of mimesis will be conducive to a kind of moderate shock. Readers as well as spectators will identify and sympathize with the characters but will not become completely absorbed with their passions:

> This [= mental shock, *ictus animi*] crops up even among the spectacles of the theatrical stage and readings recording the events of history [*spectacula et lectiones rerum vetustarum*]. . . . Sometimes singing and an excited rhythm and the well-known martial blare of the trumpets arouse us; even a horrible picture and the sorry sight of the most just punishments move our minds; this is why we laugh with those who laugh, why a crowd of mourners saddens us [*inde est quod adridemus ridentibus et contristat nos turba maerentium*], why we grow excited [*effervescimus*] at the struggles of others [*ad aliena certamina*]. Such sensations, however, are no more forms of anger than it is sadness that furrows our brow at the sight of a fake sea-battle,

no more than it is fear that runs through the minds of readers as Hannibal besieges the city walls after Cannae [*timor qui Hannibale post Cannas moenia circumsidente lectorum percurrit animos*]; all these, rather, are the emotions of minds reluctant to be moved; they are not passions but the very initial stages prior to passion [*nec adfectus but principia proludentia adventibus*].
(*Ira* 2.2.3; 4–6)¹²⁴

The dynamics of poetic reception in which involvement and distance must be attentively calibrated is well illustrated by Seneca in this passage; involvement and distance also play an important role in Lucan's aesthetics of reception. The reference to "readings recording the events of history" and to the fear "that runs through the minds of readers" parallels the fear (*metus*) that Lucan predicts in his audience at *BC* 7.205–213. Yet according to Seneca, this *metus* is not a real passion and does not preclude a rational approach to the spectacle. Fostering emotional arousal but also reluctance to be moved through several devices (apostrophe, irony, generalization, harsh humor, allegory), Lucan promotes a fiction that will fuel the reader's critical ability and his awareness of the fiction *qua* fiction. In fact, through his style Lucan creates a mimesis that can be easily identified as such. Since the frequent direct addresses call our attention to the narrator's mediating presence, they are defined by a lack of naturalism. They break the spell of the fiction and move the narration beyond *enargeia* (the stimulation of inward vision and the arousal of concomitant feelings aiming at evoking the scene of portrayed action as if it were real).[125] By pointing out his presence in the poetic texture, the narrator programmatically destroys the *enargeia* that he has striven to construct in his poetic environment; by so doing he encourages detachment.[126] If realism in a text is definable as verisimilitude achieved by narrative techniques that induce the greatest awareness of the text's content and least of its form, the *Bellum Civile*, with its voluminous amount of narratorial interventions, is certainly not always a very realistic text.

Lucan destroys the illusion of the spectacle formally, through his narrator and especially in his narrator's use of apostrophe whose content—often informed by values and ideas in competition with those of the fictional characters—betrays an external frame of reference. Apostrophe in the *Bellum Civile* can be defined as the artist's attempt to craft in his work a sort of second consciousness. In this effort Lucan abandons Aristotle's prescriptions, according to which the poet should "talk as little as possible" (*Po.* 1460a5) and, in line with Stoic recommendations, adopts a more didactic role for himself and his poetic enterprise. Recently there has been a tendency to read Lucan's rhetorical strategies, especially his irony, as directed against Stoicism.[127] For instance, Shadi Bartsch has suggested that the narrator who creates the dreadful images of the "subject under siege" and the "*grammatica* of deconstruction" is impatient with Cato's philosophical steadfastness. She suggests that it "is only the effort of our will to understand that keeps us shifting back and forth between ways of understanding, making sense of the contradictions, paradoxes, and collapses of opposites by supplying exegetical supplements to explain what the narrator really means."[128] The oscillation in meaning of cardinal words and notions is certainly a key feature of Lucan's work: paradox in the *Bellum Civile* entails the charging of morally positive terms (such as "piety" and "clemency") with negative meaning (like "crime" and "punishment") or the merging of normally separated words. Yet, as I explained in the previous chapter, this confusion of linguistic boundaries is not a sign of disengagement; it is not an attempt to flatten all ethically charged terms but to draw attention to them. Lucan's style tries our hermeneutical capacities and, as the Stoics recommend, sharpens our exegetical aptitude. His desire to show the self's political potential and creativity compels him to acknowledge the strength of the linguistic system in the shaping of consciousness without acknowledging that system's autonomy or priority.

Above all, Lucan's reader is not alone in facing the poem's linguistic puzzle since he can count on the frequent "exegetical supplements" offered by the narrator. In his apostrophes Lucan's narrator primarily manifests a resistance to disengaged spectatorship:

> when a sea battle is like a *naumachia* or a soldier like a gladiator, the reader as a spectator is transported to one of the institutions on which the power and hegemony of the emperor rest. Yet there is a choice. *If complicity with the coming of Caesarism is associated with the dispassionate gaze of the spectator,* the mentality which Lucan represents as most appropriate to the Republican is that of *constant emotional intervention against history.*[129]

The link between the civil war and gladiatorial contests is drawn in Lucan's narrative by the foolish Curio at *BC* 4.703–710:

> variam semper dant otia mentem.
> Eripe consilium pugna: cum dira voluptas
> ense subit presso, galeae texere pudorem,
> quis conferre duces meminit? Quis pendere causas?
> Qua stetit, inde favet; veluti fatalis harenae
> muneribus non ira vetus concurrere cogit
> productos, odere pares.[130]

>   Idleness always encourages doubt:
>   root out reflection with battle! Once sadistic pleasure
>   swells at the sword's heft, once visors disguise the blush of shame,
>   who thinks to judge his leaders or weigh the worth of causes?
>   Men back the side they're on, just as in games at the deadly arena
>   no long-standing anger makes gladiators clash;
>   they hate their rivals, whoever steps into the ring. (*BC* 4.704–710)

The passage faithfully represents the point of view of the Caesarian Curio, who is rushing his men to fight against the Pompeians. Curio is against *otia* (703) and *consilium* (704); he does not want to give his soldiers time to reflect and think about what they are about to do. He underscores the similarities between the war and the arena. He believes that both are games. As if they were fighting in the circus, according to Curio, soldiers in the civil war should not consider the cause of battle and the reasons of the leaders but should blindly fight against who is in front of them (*pares*).[131] In this speech it is clear that Curio wants to erase crucial differences, make everything the same. He doubts men's ability to reason and has completely internalized Caesar's perverted logic according to which violence and victory are legitimizing tools in war.[132] Lucan is subject to this environment and to the power of Imperial rhetoric, but he does not passively record it. Instead, he incites his characters to follow their own mind not that of their generals. With his apostrophes he fights against those who try to neutralize men's critical awareness, to erase distinctions and discourage moral reflection.

Lucan's Uses of *Fabula:* Allegorical Poetry

Besides encouraging his readers to exercise their critical abilities, Lucan is fond of highlighting the gap between poetry and straightforward facts. He distances himself from Homer's and Virgil's *fabulae* and considers the Trojan War a famous legend (*vetus . . . fabula*, *BC* 6.48–49; *BC* 3.212–213). He rejects the *Götterapparat* and does not allow the gods to interact with human beings. He is considered by some ancient critics an historian rather than a poet; yet as D.C. Feeney has said, "his outrageous procedures and spectacular poetics place him in a totally different dimension from even the most colourful historian." Lucan is a master at blurring the boundaries between history and poetry; he effectively uses allegorical discourse, which sits at the intersection between the two.[133]

Retelling the myth of the garden of the Hesperides, the narrator accuses as "envious the man who impairs the credit of past ages by calling on the poets to tell the truth" (*invidus, annoso qui famam derogat aevo, / qui vates ad vera vocat, BC* 9.359–60). He knows well that, "as the gods have wished," the "causes" of the working of the universe "remain hidden" to him (*at mihi semper / tu, quaecumque moves tam crebros causa meatus, / ut superi voluere, late, BC* 1.417–19). He cannot represent the gods in action because he is uncertain about their motives and plans. The *vera* offered to a reader by a *vatis* are not *causae;* they go beyond the literal surface and can become *fabulae*, surpassing the truth discernible in historical data. They reveal a more subtle message. Recounting Pompey's demise effected by a Roman sword, Lucan calls it "a tale that will never lack reproach of gods on high" (*numquam superum caritura pudore / fabula, BC* 8.605–606). In this instance, the term *fabula* is not employed to frame Pompey's story as a worthless or untruthful fiction; on the contrary, it calls attention to its allegorical meaning and message. Arguing that "the dissociation of truth from fact, of ideals from history, is a grand illusion capable of changing facts," Frederick Ahl connects Lucan's *fabulae* with an ideal reality, which an alert reader can find in poetical discourse and from which he will derive not factual information but a powerful source of inspiration.[134]

Even this idea might have been borrowed from philosophical discourse. Beginning in the sixth century BCE with philosophical interpretations of Homer, interpretative allegorists claimed to discover the truthful message hidden beneath the surface of a text.[135] Chrysippus, as advocate of allegorical interpretation, was himself an interpreter of *fabulae*. He understood well that there are higher truths to be discovered beyond what seems patently false and that we must set ourselves to discover the *hyponoiai* "intention[s] that lie below the surface."[136] He did not hesitate to interpret paintings and poems allegorically (SVF 2.1071). Though the relation of words to meanings is, in Stoic terms, natural rather than conventional, there is no one-to-one correlation between words and meanings; for things can have different names and, as Gellius reports, Chrysippus thought that all words are ambiguous, particularly in poems.[137] Allegory is defined by the Stoics as a trope in which the poet says something and means something different (cf. Quint. 8. 6. 44).[138] For instance, the allegorist Heraclitus (1st cent. CE) interprets the labors of Heracles as a symbolic representation of the wise man's fight against the passions.[139] The Stoics affirmed that the interpreter must not simply pay attention to the propositional level of the sentence; he also should construct analogical meaning out of it.[140] Above all Cornutus, like Zeno (SVF 1.274, 275) and Strabo (1.1.10), emphasized that Homer said some things *kata aletheian* and others *kata doxan*. He believed that "the myths of the poets contain an element of philosophic truth which they inherited from an earlier age," from men "able to understand the nature of the universe and given to philosophizing concerning it in symbols and enigmas."[141] Only rational beings can express themselves and their actions self-consciously and reflectively in thought and language.[142] Epictetus reminds his reader that the power of constructing or synthesizing a sign is not a passive capacity:

> Our intellect is so structured that we are not simply passive receivers of impressions from sensible objects, but select and abstract from them and add to them and construct things out of them, and indeed make transitions from some of them to others which have some sort of connection with them. (*Diss.* 1. 6.10)[143]

Various kinds of relationships link words to their meanings. As De Lacy points out, a Stoic reader must be sensitive to the way in which a poet constructs these relationships:

> The Stoic critic must know the various kinds of relations that may exist between a word and its meaning, and he must be able to determine what the relation is in any particular occurrence of a word in a poem. He must not expect the poet always to use words in their proper senses, or to present the thought in technical terms, but he must be able to resolve the poet's allegories, and show how the words are appropriate to the meaning.[144]

Thus for the Stoics the correct use of impressions is a profoundly hermeneutic activity since "God"—Epictetus explains—"introduced man as a student of himself and his works, and not merely as a student, but also as an interpreter of these things (*Discourses* 1.6.12–20 = LS 63E)."[145] The Stoics do not ask a poet for a narrative that is true but admit a narrative that can be false. As Jon Whitman states, "Chrysippus attributes human impropriety to a lapse in the dynamic continuum of the personality, and more importantly for our purposes, he is beginning to relate such impropriety to the oblique turn of language . . . the Stoics thus expose that pervasive duality in language which will later inspire systematic allegory."[146] Poetry can lie; it is up to the individual reader/interpreter to decipher and decide how these lies fit in the poetic message.[147]

At *BC* 9.411ff. it seems to me that not only does Lucan's narrator himself suggest that we read Cato's Libyan march allegorically by alluding to "the first true personification allegory in the West, the 'Choice of Heracles' of the fifth-century BCE sophist Prodicus."[148] He also openly warns us *not* to read literally Cato's accidents in the desert:

> Cur Libycus tantis exundet pestibus aer
> fertilis in mortes, aut quid secreta nocenti
> miscuerit natura solo, non cura laborque
> noster scire valet, nisi quod vulgata per orbem
> fabula pro vera decepit saecula causa.
>
> Why the Libyan climate abounds in such plagues, breeding
> so much death, or what secretive Nature has mixed
> in with the poisonous soil, our care and labor is not
> strong enough to learn—except that a myth, popular worldwide,
> has deceived the ages replacing the true cause. (*BC* 9.619–23)

Here the narrating persona emphatically calls our attention to the fact that he does not have the will or the power to know the truth (*non cura laborque / noster scire valet*, 621–22) and that "the explanation related in the text is actually *not true*."[149] He points out that what he reports is only a famous legend (*fabula*, 623), without scientific value (*pro vera causa*, 623). He is not able to know the truth about Libya, but he does recount extensively a false story about it, a long aetiology in which he tries to account for why there are so many snakes in Libya.

In Glenn Most's opinion, the lines above contain a criticism of Cornutus' allegorical approach to poetry: myth would not reveal the truth about nature when correctly interpreted but would conceal it by confusing mankind.[150] Expressing a certain impatience with the sort of allegorical explanations promulgated by Cornutus in his *Epidrome*, already Seneca discarded the project of allegorizing Homer as fundamentally useless (e.g., *Ben.* 1.3–4; *Ep.* 88.5; *Phaedra* 195–203).[151] Lucan, however, does not seem to attack allegorically deceptive interpretations by squarely opposing them to "truth." Instead, he warns his audience about the fictional nature of the *fabula* he is about to relate in order to help the readers raise their critical antennae.[152] His poem is not a historical account and does not need to always relate what actually happened (Aristotle, *Po.* 1451b). A poet can strive for a different kind of truth, for a "more philosophical" (*philosophoteron*, *Po.* 1451b5) kind of signification. This in part explains why he is not afraid to include in his epic gods in which he does not believe. He invokes them and mocks their inactivity to underline their indifference and deny theodicy.[153]

Martha Malamud acknowledges that in Book 9 there is evidence for interpreting Cato's fight against the Libyan hardships as an allegory of the harsh path toward virtue. Yet she is skeptical about the possibility of constructing too neat a picture of correspondences between Cato and Hercules or the desert snakes and the passions.[154] At any rate, in her discussion she does link poetry to philosophy when she suggests that even the Stoic sage Cato drinks from the spring of poetry. While on the one hand she dissociates the narrator who repeats a *fabula* and is unable to find out "true causes" from Cato, "the *true* father of the fatherland" (*parens verus patriae, BC* 9.601), on the other she connects Cato to poetry by interpreting the singular, snake-infested spring (*fons unus,* 9.607, 616) encountered by Cato at *BC* 9.606–618 as symbolic of the *fons* of poetry. The episode of Cato's drinking from the *fons* is immediately followed by the story of Medusa's severed head from whose blood the Libyan snakes were generated. Lucan casts Medusa as a symbol of the horrors of civil war as well as of poetic inspiration by echoing Ovid.[155] Ovid had written of "Pegasus and his brother born from their mother's blood" (*Pegason et fratrem matris de sanguine natos, Met.* 4.786) and had called Hippocrene, the spring created by the winged horse and symbolizing poetical inspiration, "*Medusaeo fonte*" (*Met.* 4.312):

> Lucan's careful reworking of Ovid's Medusa story reveals that the spring from which Cato drinks is identical to the Pierian spring, the source of Lucretius' inspiration as well as the site of confrontation between Ovid's battling sets of Muses. This is the tainted source of Lucan's inspiration as well.[156]

Malamud is thus identifying Cato's drinking from the *fons* with Lucan's poetic endeavor. By clustering together the spring, the snakes, and Cato, Lucan manifests his awareness that when philosophers (or poets inspired by philosophical ideals) drink from the spring of poetry, they too must confront the unfathomable threats associated with it: old threats envisioned by Plato or Chrysippus weary of poetry's enchantment and ambiguity, as well as new ones dependent on the Roman political environment. Despite these threats, Cato drinks and exhorts his companions to drink:

> Vana specie conterrite leti
> ne dubita miles, tutos exhaurire liquores,
> noxia serpentum est admixto sanguine pestis.
>
> Frightened by death's empty appearance,
> do not hesitate, soldiers, to drink safely that water.
> The snakes' poison is lethal only if blended with blood. (*BC* 9.612–614)

Cato explains that the snake poison in this case does not represent a threat, and he proves the truthfulness of his interpretation by surviving the drinking of the suspect fluid (*dubiumque venenum / hausit, BC* 9.615–616).

Conclusion

Overall Lucan's employment of techniques such as apostrophe and allegorical discourse shows his reliance on Stoic discourse about art. With Plato, Seneca, and Cicero, Lucan shares the understanding of the affinity between the literary and the philosophical endeavor. Enlightened by Stoic speculation he believes that each of us can be a reader capable of containing the emotional tide triggered by the aesthetic engagement and of profiting from literature. Our exposure to art can be transformed into an ethically useful and life-changing experience. An analysis of Cato's behavior and a deeper acquaintance with this character will confirm the character's allegiance to effective rhetorical discourse and his ultimate resemblance to the narrator.

4
ADDRESSING THE EMOTIONS: LUCAN'S NARRATOR AND THE CHARACTER CATO IN THE *Bellum Civile*

> Prosperae res et in plebem ac vilia ingenia deveniunt; at calamitates terroresque mortalium sub iugum mittere proprium magni viri est.
>
> Success comes to the common man, and even to average minds; but to triumph over the calamities and terrors of mortal life is the part of a great man only. (Seneca, *Prov.* 3.4.1)
>
> Hoc enim est, quod mihi philosophia promittit, ut parem deo faciat.
>
> For that is exactly what philosophy promises to me, that I shall be made equal to god. (Seneca, *Ep.* 48.11)

CRITICISM OF CATO

Some scholars have tried to absolve Lucan's epic of philosophical preoccupations and have viewed the aesthetic temper of this seemingly chaotic and pessimistic poem as opposed to the harmonious universe conceived by the Stoics. How do these critics accommodate Cato's presence in the poem? W. R. Johnson portrays Cato as a caricature of Stoic virtue. Stubborn and unaffected by the destiny of his soldiers, the Stoic saint does not stir the sympathy of the reader, who instead finds himself attracted to wicked characters like Caesar or the witch Erichtho. According to Johnson, during the desert march Cato is so busy persuading his troops of the importance of fighting for freedom that he does not care about anything else. "Cato's fanaticism," Johnson argues "is no less ruinous of freedom [. . .] than is Caesar's countervailing fanaticism."[1] Johnson reaches his negative verdict against Cato mainly in considering his behavior during the desert march.

Berthe Marti and W. Hemmen formulate similar conclusions by looking at Cato's behavior in Book 2.[2] Even if they consider the Stoic Cato the hero of the poem and the symbol of freedom and justice, they judge him to be a cold and passionless individual unable to be affected by external circumstances: "[r]ather than a magnetic leader of men," Marti writes, "he remains a lifeless abstraction" who "feels no pity, no tenderness, no imaginative sympathy (*Const.* 15.3)."[3]

Matthew Leigh formulates an equally pessimistic characterization of Cato. He uses the episode of the crossing of the desert (esp. *BC* 9.734–846) to depict Cato as too rigidly attached to the Stoic creed.[4] In Leigh's reading, Cato is the gladiator who "challenges fortune at every hour" (*omni fortunam provocat hora, BC* 9.883) and does not care about the fate of his soldiers. To them he brings "strength in death" (*in letum vires, BC* 9.886) while he is unable or, worse, unwilling to preserve their bodies from destruction. In Leigh's opinion, Cato does not really liberate men from the passions and from their suffering, for they still suffer but "are ashamed to die groaning with Cato looking on" (*puduitque gementem / illo* [sc. *Cato*] *teste mori, BC* 9. 886–87). Ultimately, the Republican leader seems to be satisfied with the show of his soldiers' sad and unusual deaths (*tristia fata suorum / insolitasque, BC* 9.735–36). He is happy with a *mise en scène* of Stoic virtue. Like the gods in Seneca's *Prov.* 2.7–17 when they gladly admire the spectacle of Cato's unbroken stance, in the desert Cato has become the insensitive viewer of a bloody production.[5]

Shadi Bartsch also discusses Cato's march in the desert as well as his dialogue with Brutus in Book 2.[6] She acknowledges that Book 9 is a challenge to those critics who, wanting to frame the Stoic saint as unmistakably triumphant over pain, avoid explaining the grotesque aspects of the episode.[7] She points out that in the desert tragic elements, violent details, and amusing touches coexist uneasily. She believes that the desert snakes (like the civil war) stand for "a principle of boundary violation" while Cato symbolizes "the principle of boundary maintenance."[8] Bartsch's interpretation is powerful and reasonable given Cato's traditional portrayal as protector of the law.[9] Her reading charges the desert battle with symbolic power: the desert becomes the metaphorical arena of the formidable competition between chaos and order, matter and spirit, enslavement and freedom. Considering Book 9 as the place in which a confused and violent physical reality challenges philosophy and rationality, Bartsch tries to establish the winner in this paradigmatic conflict. And yet in answering the question she wavers. Certainly mind and rationality triumph when Cato induces his suffering men to suppress their lamentations; yet the "vile body" is victorious in the episode of Aulus consumed by thirst and unable to refrain from drinking his own blood (*BC* 9.747–48).[10] Although in the *Bellum Civile* "the criteria for making political decisions have become irrevocably tarnished, just like the vocabulary in which they are couched"; and although the snakes impressively represent those confused human situations with which Stoicism is unable to cope effectively, she is not ready to assign a full victory to the snakes.

Bartsch employs a different argument when she discusses Book 2. Here Cato's actions would not be completely consistent with the Stoic creed.[11] In fact, Cato's condemnation of the man who can remain "free of fear" (*expers metus*, *BC* 2.289–90) during Rome's collapse does not square with the traditional portrayal of the Stoic sage who preserves himself free from fear in every situation (e.g., Horace's *impavidus vir* of *Odes* 3.3.8).[12] Surprisingly, in Lucan's text Cato asks the gods to preserve him from the madness of remaining indifferent: *procul hunc arcete furorem, / o superi, motura Dahas ut clade Getasque / securo me Roma cadat*, "O gods, keep far from me this madness that I should be indifferent while Rome falls and this tragedy affects even the Goths and the Dahae" (*BC* 2.295–98). Commenting on these lines from the point of view of Stoic orthodoxy, Elaine Fantham draws a conclusion similar to Bartsch's: she notes that "Cato's obedience to his grief is contrary to Stoic teaching, which rejects such emotion."[13]

Besides the oddness of Cato's prayers to the gods (*BC* 2.295–98), Bartsch argues, Lucan's Stoic saint has lost the conviction to fight for a restorable "party of liberty."[14] At *BC* 9.204–206 he proclaims that true freedom died at the time of Sulla and Marius but irrationally acts against his awareness. Embracing *fides ficta libertatis* ("a fake faith in freedom"), he decides to intervene in the war. He "practices ideology—not with Brutus' mistaken heat (*calorem*, *BC* 2.324), but in cold blood."[15] The tag "in cold blood," emblematically included in the book's title, evokes the sage's *apatheia*. Cato's decision to intervene in the war would be calculated, illogical, and not in harmony with Stoic formulations; yet it is admirable. Bartsch praises Cato precisely because he stood for what had no concrete possibility of coming true; he is an idealist who believed that freedom lives wherever someone is willing to fight for it.[16] Although "[Cato] could not have known or expected it to be possible," Bartsch explains, he was ultimately able to make a difference since "he taught Pompey's army to fight for *libertas* rather than for a master. By participating, by acting, despite his despair, Cato made the idealistic fight between liberty and tyranny possible."[17]

The two images of Cato traced by Bartsch are not completely overlapping.[18] While in Book 9 he is described as a man whose philosophical creed is ultimately unable to handle successfully a concrete life situation, in Book 2 he is praised for his illogical and ultimately successful philosophical commitment. Cato is criticized for doing too little in Book 9 and too much in Book 2. Philosophical idealism is considered a stricture as well as a powerful motivating political force.[19] This evaluation of Cato is in a way similar to that formulated by Plutarch. The

Greek historian analyzed Cato's political shortsightedness more realistically than the majority of previous Roman writers; at the same time he concentrated on Cato's intentions and emphasized the philosopher's spiritual greatness. The Cato of Plutarch's biography is not a flawless Stoic saint and not at all a perfect political leader. Nevertheless, he is a man of outstanding virtue and morally triumphant in political defeat.[20]

Cato, the Narrator, and Poetry

In the mimetic structure of the *Bellum Civile* there are several signs of the association of Lucan's narrator and Cato with poetical endeavor. They both manifest reservations toward oracles. Stylistically they may adopt oracular vividness, but they superimpose their voices upon those of seers. Ultimately they criticize oracular utterance. While in Book 5 the narrator corrects the Pythia and complains about the gods' unwillingness to talk about Pharsalus, in Book 9 the voice of Cato silences the oracle of Ammon and prophesies in his place. Narrator and philosopher are similarly inspired by the awareness of men's mortality. Above all, *enargeia* and *ekplêxis* bestow upon Cato and the narrator's speech the effectiveness necessary to persuade and move their audiences to action. Our fight to attain moral salvation or freedom depends on our "drinking" the words of the sage (Seneca, *Ep.* 59.9), who in turn has drunk from the *fons* of poetry (*BC* 9.607, 616).

At *BC* 5.70–236 Appius, afraid to face the risks of war, goes to Delphi to consult the Pythia and to try to learn about his future. The prophecy itself (*effugis ingentes tanti discriminis expers / bellorum, Romane, minas solusque quietem / . . . tenebis,* "you escape the war's cataclysmic menace; you have no part in this mighty struggle, Roman; you alone will find peace," *BC* 5.194–96) is short and ambiguous; it seems to predict Appius' peaceful survival (*quietem*) and instead predicts his death.[21] The narrator criticizes Appius' preoccupation with himself when the freedom of all Romans is at stake and mocks his foolish concern with his survival. Apostrophizing Appius, he interprets the ambiguous oracle for him:

> Nec te vicinia leti
> territat ambiguis frustratum sortibus, Appi;
> iure sed incerto mundi subsidere regnum
> Chalcidos Euboicae vana spe rapte paras.
> Heu demens! Nullum belli sentire fragorem,
> tot mundi caruisse malis, praestare deorum
> excepta quis Morte potest? Secreta tenebis

litoris Euboici memorando condite busto.

      But the nearness of death holds no
terrors for you, Appius, beguiled by the riddling oracle!
With the world unsettled by an uncertain law,
you, carried away by vain hope, sought refuge in Euboean Chalcis.
You idiot! Not to notice the clangor of war,
to avoid the whole world's misfortune—which of the gods
except Death has power to grant you this? Yes! You will dwell in seclusion
on Euboea' coast, hidden away in a memorable tomb. (*BC* 5.224–31)

Yet even more harshly he mocks the gods for their decision to let Pharsalus happen and for their reticence to talk about it:

Custodes tripodes fatorum arcanaque mundi
tuque potens veri Paean nullumque futuri
a superis celate diem, suprema ruentis
imperii caesosque duces et funera regum
et tot in Hesperio conlapsas sanguine gentes
cur aperire times? An nondum numina tantum
decrevere nefas et adhuc dubitantibus astris
Pompei damnare caput tot fata tenentur?
Vindicis an gladii facinus poenasque furorum
regnaque ad ultores iterum redeuntia Brutos
ut peragat fortuna taces?

Tripod, custodian of destiny, Mysteries of the Universe!
And you, Paean, prince of Truth, from whom the gods
above have concealed not one day of the future—why do you
fear to disclose the final throes of the empire's collapse,
slaughtered leaders and the deaths of kings, all nations drowned
in Hesperia's blood? Have the gods not yet resolved
upon a crime so dire? Does the stars' reluctance
to have Pompey beheaded withhold many destinies?
Or are you silent to ensure that fortune may carry out
the deed of the avenging sword and the punishment for ambition,
tyranny met once more by a vengeful Brutus? (*BC* 5.198–208)

The repeated questions disclose the indignation of the narrator and his doubts about the gods' ability to direct the world with justice. His rhetoric accuses their unwillingness to reveal Pharsalus' bloodshed and defines Brutus' killing of Caesar as an honorable act. Like a coward, Apollo—ironically called "prince of truth"—is afraid (*times*) to disclose Pharsalus. He participates in the righteous punishment of a criminal by simply staring at a human *ultor*, silently (*tacere*) witnessing an accidental happening (*fortuna*). Perhaps, the narrator speculates, the gods have not decided yet "to condemn Pompey" (*damnare caput*). His fate and that of the universe hang on the gods' hesitation to "decree a crime (*nefas*) so dire." The narrator cannot explain how a *nefas* can fit into a providentially ordered, just universe directed by the gods. He can renounce these gods if they choose *nefas* (*mentimur regnare Iovem, BC* 7.447), but he cannot renounce justice.[22] He is committed to righteousness even if he doubts the gods' commitment to it.

A similar pattern—the superimposition of a human character's voice upon that of an oracle—is used in Book 9. Here Cato, urged by his soldiers (*comitesque Catonem / orant, exploret . . . numina, BC* 9.546–48) and by Labienus (*BC* 9.550–63) to interrogate the oracle of Ammon, rejects the proposal but with oracular wisdom and divine inspiration talks to his men:

> Ille, deo plenus tacita quem mente gerebat,
> effudit dignas adytis e pectore voces:
> "quid quaeri, Labiene, iubes? An liber in armis
> occubuisse velim potius quam regna videre?
> An, sit vita brevis nil, si longane, differat, aetas?
> An noceat vis ulla bono? Fortunaque perdat
> opposita virtute minas, laudandaque velle
> sit satis, et numquam successu crescat honestum?
> Scimus, et hoc nobis non altius inseret Hammon.
> Haeremus cuncti superis, temploque tacente
> nil facimus non sponte dei; nec vocibus ullis
> numen eget, dixitque semel nascentibus auctor,
> quidquid scire licet. Sterilesne elegit arenas,
> ut caneret paucis, mersitque hoc pulvere verum,
> estque dei sedes, nisi terra et Pontus et aer
> et caelum et virtus. Superos quid quaerimus ultra?
> Iuppiter est, quodcumque vides, quodcumque moveris.
> Sortilegis egeant dubii semperque futuris
> casibus ancipites; me non oracula certum,
> se mors certa facit. Pavido fortique cadendum est:

hoc satis est dixisse Iovem."

> Cato, filled with the god that he silently kept in his mind,
> poured out a heartfelt response as good as an oracle's:
> "What do you bid me ask, Labienus? Whether I would rather
> fall in battle a free man or see a monarchy?
> Whether all that counts in life is whether it be short or long?
> Can violence do the good man harm? Does Fortune waste
> her threats when virtue lines up againt her? Is it enough to wish
> what's praiseworthy? Is honor increased by success?
> We know this, and Ammon will not implant it more deeply.
> We all cleave to the gods; even if this shrine falls silent,
> we do nothing without god's will; nor does the deity
> need any word—at our birth the Creator told us
> all we are given to know. Did he bury his truth in this dust,
> choose barren sands, choose to foretell to only a few?
> Does god have a home, if not earth and sea and air
> and virtue? Why do we look for gods beyond these?
> All that you see and feel is Jupiter;
> leave it to doubters to hanker after fortune tellers
> constantly worrying how the future will eventuate.
> Oracles don't make me sure: sure death does.
> Brave and timid alike must fall:
> this Jove has said; it suffices. (*BC* 9.564–84)

Cato "ends with a declaration of his own status as a *sapiens,* a status which Lucan's authorial voice has acknowledged in advance by introducing Cato's speech with *ille deo plenus* (9.564): Cato, his rational faculty developed to the utmost, is full of godliness in the Stoic sense."[23] *Scire,* the knowledge that matters, comes to the sage from within. Cato's behavior and his relationship with the truth seem to put him in opposition to Caesar.

In Book 10 Caesar asks Acoreus, the counselor of the young Ptolemy XIII and the symbol of philosophical wisdom, about the Nile's origin.[24] In this episode, Lucan characterizes the desire to know "the truth" as an ambition of powerful kings. Caesar's "love of truth" (*amor veri, BC* 10.189) and "sure hope of seeing the location of Nile's spring" (*Niliacos spes . . . certa videndi / fontes, BC* 10.191–92) are defined as a *cupido* (*BC* 10.268) typical of tyrants (*Phariis Persisque . . . Macetumque tyrannis, BC* 10.269). *Sacer* Acoreus (*BC* 10.193) only superficially satisfies Caesar's thirst. He reveals a will to legitimately disclose the gods' secrets to the Roman (*fas mihi magnorum, Caesar, secreta parentum / prodere, BC* 10.194–95), but in practice he only recounts many "vain stories" (*vana, BC* 10.219) and "mistakes of the ancients" (*vana vetustas, BC* 10.239; *BC* 10.219–10; 240ff.; 247ff.). Ultimately, Acoreus' long and dubious speech turns him into the spokesman of "lying fable" (*fabula mendax, BC* 10.282). Nature, in his view, "wants people's awe not their knowledge" (*maluit ortus / mirari quam nosse tuos, BC* 10.297–98).[25]

It seems clear that in Book 10 we are presented with a tyrant who, counting on his personal prestige, demands the mysteries of the universe from a philosopher-figure: "If your ancestors initiated the Cecropian Plato to your mysteries," Caesar asks Acoreus, "which guest ever there was more worthy (*dignior*) and capable (*capacior*) than I to be initiated into the mysteries of the world?" (*BC* 10.181–84). In rather traditional fashion, Caesar conceives of the gods as granting favors (e.g., long life, *BC* 10.176–77) and practical information (e.g., the geographical location of the Nile's springs) to their protégé. By contrast, in the section about Ammon's oracle we have instead Cato as a sage who looks for wisdom inside himself and who believes that the gods have given all an access to truth. In the Stoic fashion Cato identifies the gods with nature and virtue (*dei sedes, nisi terra . . . / et caelum et virtus, BC* 9.578–79).[26] According to him, violence has no power over the good man, fortune's threats are in vain when virtue is set against them, and success is not at all the measure of virtue (*BC* 9.566–71). What is worth *knowing* is already in us, and Ammon cannot "implant" it any deeper. Cato's pursuit of *virtus* doesn't depend on the gods' approving response.[27] His ideas are presented as "oracular pronouncements," important lessons that cannot be buried in the sand because they are directly opposed to Caesar's belief in success as proof of the gods' favor. At *BC* 1.226–27, while crossing the Rubicon, Caesar equates *fortuna* and *fatum*: *Te fortuna sequor; procul hinc iam foedera sunto. / Credidimus fatis, utendum est iudice bello* (fortune, I follow you! Let us put pacts aside; / I put myself in the hands of fate, my judge now is the war").[28] Cato keeps the two concepts distinctly apart (*BC* 9.592–98).

On Cato's pronouncements R. Sklenár has written, "our *scire* does not automatically follow from the divinity's *dixit*; rather, the acquisition of *scire* is precisely the task to which we must devote our lives."[29] The *sapiens* devotes his life to the acquisition of knowledge and uses this knowledge to help others. When Seneca urgently asks himself, "Why is it that folly holds us with such an insistent grasp?" the answer is the following:

> Primo quia non fortiter illam repellimus nec toto ad salutem impetu nitimur, deinde quia illa, quae a sapientibus viris reperta sunt, non satis credi-

mus nec apertis pectoribus haurimus leviterque tam magnae rei insistimus.

First of all, it is because we do not reject it strongly, because we do not struggle toward salvation with all our energies; furthermore, because we do not put sufficient trust in the discoveries of wise men and do not drink in their words with open hearts; too lightly do we approach this great problem. (*Ep.* 59.9)

While Lucan's Caesar relies on the fates (*credimus fatis,* 1.227), Seneca suggests that we rely on the sage (*sapientibus viris . . . credidimus . . . haurimus*), that our struggle to obtain moral salvation is dependent on our "drinking" of the sage's words.

Besides qualifying Cato's utterances, in an apostrophe the adjective *sacer* is employed in the *Bellum Civile* to qualify the task of the poet:

> O sacer et magnus vatum labor! omnia fato
> eripis et populis donas mortalibus aevum.
> Invidia sacrae, Caesar, ne tangere famae;
> nam, si quid Latiis fas est promittere Musis,
> quantum Zmyrnaei durabunt vatis honores,
> venturi me teque legent; Pharsalia nostra
> vivet, et a nullo tenebris damnabimur aevo.

> O sacred and mighty labor of poets, you snatch
> everything from fate and grant immortality to mortals!
> Caesar, be not stung with envy of ever-lasting fame.
> For if Latin Muses can promise anything,
> so long as the honors of Homer, poet of Smyrna, shall last
> posterity will read me and thee; our Pharsalia,
> will live and no generation will banish us to the shadow! (*BC* 9.980–86)

The word *fatum* at 980 should be interpreted not simply as "the erosion of time" or "death" but as "history" shaped by the victors. The poet's effort is sacred because it has the gigantic task of reinterpreting Roman history. The poet's mission is sacred because it can present something different, a sort of counterfactual history, a *fabula* (something that cannot be checked against facts), a moral tale able to snatch events from the evaluations imposed on them by the winners. For the sake of future generations (*venturi,* 985), the *vates* Lucan must rehearse Caesar's triumph, but he gives the story *his own* ideological bent (*me* precedes *te*, 984). Virgil's message in the apostrophe to Nisus and Euryalus (*Aen.* 9.446–49)[30] is reversed by Lucan in his apostrophe to the *vatum labor*. For Lucan fame is not linked to the imperishable *imperium* of the Romans (*Aen.* 9.449) but to its poets (*Latiis . . . Musis, BC* 9.983). The name of Achilles (not accidentally suppressed in the text) lives because of Homer's *honores,* and that of Caesar will live because of Lucan's *Pharsalia.* As Dolores O'Higgins has noted, sooner or later "emperors and commoners join the helpless dead, who may act or speak only at the command of a *vates.*"[31]

There is one more important and crucial connection between the narrator and Cato. Their words are described as producing in the audience an identical effect:

> Dixit et omnes
> haud aliter medio revocavit ab aequore puppes
> quam, simul effetas linquunt examina ceras
> atque oblita favi non miscent nexibus alas,
> sed sibi quaeque volat nec iam degustat amarum
> desidiosa thymum, Phrygii sonus increpat aeris,
> attonitae posuere fugam studiumque laboris
> floriferi repetunt et sparsi mellis amorem:
> gaudet in Hyblaeo securus gramine pastor
> divitias servasse casae. Sic voce Catonis
> inculcata viris iusti patientia Martis.
>
> So he spoke and his words summoned
> all ships back from water—the way, once their eggs
> hatch, files of bees abandon their waxen nurseries and,
> heedless of the comb, cease to cluster in swarms, wing on wing;
> each flies off on her own and, indolent, no longer sucks
> pungent thyme. But let clashing Phrygian brass rebuke them—
> stunned, the bees dawdle no more but resume with zeal
> their bloom-born labor, their love of far-flung honey.
> The shepherd in meadows on Monte Ibleo, eased of cares,
> rejoices: he has assured the wealth of his cottage.
> Thus Cato with his voice drummed into his men courage to face a just war.
> (*BC* 9.283–93)

After Pharsalus, the troops loyal to Pompey mutiny at the prospect of war prolonged under Cato's leadership (*BC* 9.217–54). With a powerful speech (*BC* 9.254–83) Cato persuades the soldiers to remain with him and to do what in the mind of the Stoic sage is the only right thing to do, to fight for their own freedom. The soldiers who are persuaded by Cato's argument and rhetoric to go back to battle are compared to bees summoned back to work by Phrygian brass. They are also indirectly described with the adjective "stunned" (*attonitae, BC* 9. 289), referring to the bees, the same adjective previously used by the narrator to portray the effect of his epic on future readers (*attoniti, BC* 7.213). The soldiers' shock commits them to fight for a just cause at the side of Cato. The troops' reaction to Cato's speech (*BC* 9.283–93) and that of Lucan's reader to the poem (*BC* 7.210–213) point us toward a model of poetical reception in which a rational response and an emotional reaction are not diametrically opposed. We understand from the context of Cato's speech that the bewilderment of the audience does not produce irrationality but brings the listeners to right conduct. Cato's soldiers are persuaded by the philosopher to fight for freedom as Lucan's contemporary readers should be persuaded by his poem to recover their independence.[32]

In the passage quoted above, the "Phrygian brass" must be read in connection with other texts concerned with the effect of poetical and philosophical *logos*. It alludes to Seneca's "Phrygian priests roused by the sound of the flute" and "stirred by the beauty of a concept" (both in *Ep.* 108.7). It brings back to our memory Alciabiades' enchantment at the sound of Socrates' voice (*Symp.* 215b–d) and Cleanthes' metaphor of the trumpet mentioned by Seneca at *Ep.*108.10: "as our breath produces a louder sound when it passes through the long and narrow opening of the trumpet and escapes by a hole which widens at the end, even so the fettering rules of poetry clarify our meaning."

In Lucan, *enargeia* and *ekplêxis* bestow upon the sage and narrator's speech the effectiveness necessary to persuade and move their audiences into action.[33]

The Power of Allegorical Discourse and Apostrophe: Praising the Philosopher-Hero at the Crossroads

It is unquestionably true that in the *Bellum Civile* similarities exist between Caesar's and Cato's behavior and that this parallelism is, to a degree, programmatically woven into the text. I have emphasized how the perverted logic of the civil war can easily manipulate traditional Roman language and even Stoic rhetoric, uprooting both from what they normally signified. Yet the intentions behind the rhetoric and behavior of characters are never ignored by Lucan's narrator. Being aware of the opacity of appearances, through his apostrophes, direct interventions, and textual allusions, he helps the reader to appraise his characters' intentions.

A powerful acknowledgment of Cato's spiritual superiority and of his similarity to the narrator marks the beginning of Book 9. Here the Stoic leader, apostrophizing the soldiers, describes the difficult journey around the Syrtes and across the Libyan desert as an allegory of the arduous path toward virtue:

> Atque ingressus steriles sic fatur harenas:
> "O quibus una salus placuit mea signa secutis
> indomita cervice mori, componite mentes
> ad magnum virtutis opus summosque labores.
> Vadimus in campos steriles exustaque mundi,
> qua nimius Titan et rarae in fontibus undae,
> siccaque letiferis squalent serpentibus arva.
> Durum iter ad leges, patriaeque ruentis amore
> per mediam Libyen veniant atque invia temptent,
> si quibus in nullo positum est evadere voto,
> si quibus ire sat est. Neque enim mihi fallere quemquam
> est animus tectoque metu perducere volgus.
> Hi mihi sint comites, quos ipsa pericula ducent,
> qui me teste pati vel quae tristissima pulchrum
> Romanumque putant. At qui sponsore salutis
> miles eget capiturque animae dulcedine, vadat
> ad dominum meliore via."

> About to cross the barren sands, [Cato] addressed them [his soldiers] thus:
> "Men who have resolved that your one salvation was to join
> my camp and die with neck unyoked, steady your minds
> to meet a mighty task of valor and grave ordeals.
> We are marching to barren plains, the parched zone,
> where the sun is too close and water in the springs is scarce,
> where scorched fields are crawling with deadly poisonous snakes.
> Hard the road to law and our failing nation's love!
> Through central Libya let them come, let them try the wasteland—
> any for whom to desire escape is pointless
> and to march is enough; now I don't mean to deceive,
> to cover up fear and lead the crowd on.
> The men I would have as my comrades are those actually
> enticed by danger, men who consider it glorious—
> and Roman—to suffer even the most grueling ordeals
> with me as witness.

But, the soldier who craves assurance
of safety, the man entranced by life's sweetness—he can
find his master by an easier path. (*BC* 9.378–94)

Cato impels his soldiers to face a paradigmatic choice. In his speech labors and sufferings, leading to virtue (*virtutis opus summosque labores,* 381), are juxtaposed with a sweeter and safer path (*animae dulcedine . . . meliore via,* 393–94), a road only apparently better which, at the end, leads to servitude (*ad dominum,* 394). He asks his men to welcome the difficult climb toward virtue and law (*durum iter ad leges,* 385), the path that will reveal their "love for a falling fatherland" (*patriaeque ruentis amore,* 385). Later in the book even the narrator will characterize the episode as a *fabula* (*BC* 9.623), inviting the reader to view Cato's march in the desert as metaphor. In fact, the "two roads" available to the leader and his troops allude to the myth of Hercules at the crossroads, the tale narrated by Prodicus of Ceos and reported by Xenophon in *Memorabilia* 2.1.21–34 (= 84B Diels-Kranz). The story, which featured Hercules wavering between virtue (*arete*) leading to law (*nomos*) and *voluptas* (*Kakia*) leading to vice, was fairly well known in antiquity, especially among the Cynics and the Stoics.[34] The allusion to the tale of Hercules at the crossroads qualifies the philosopher Cato—despite his historical defeat followed by the suicide in Utica—as the *Bellum Civile*'s Hercules *invictus*.[35] In Xenophon's text (*Mem.* 2.1.24) *Kakia* promises to keep her followers from warfare. In the *Bellum Civile* Cato, like Hercules, having chosen *Virtus,* is not interested in the physical *salus* (*BC* 9. 395) guaranteed by *Voluptas;* instead, he selects participation to the war and the salvation "of dying with [his] neck unyoked" (*BC* 9.380). At the command of virtue, Cato undertakes the desert journey (*hac ire Catonem / dura iubet virtus, BC* 9.444–45).

Throughout the Libyan excursus, the Hercules myth is even more pervasive. Alluding to the garden of the Hesperides (*BC* 9.355–67) and setting forth the Libyan march as a journey beyond the boundaries of the known world to a land from which there is no return (*BC* 9.859–62), Lucan views Cato as a new Hercules.[36] In the description the presence of the river Lethon with its springs in the underworld (*BC* 9.355–356), as well as the expression *inredux via* ("road without a return," *BC* 9.408) denoting the Libyan route, remind us that Cato finds himself in a sort of allegorical Hades.[37] The fight against the snakes (*BC* 9.644–48) evokes Hercules' battle against the Hydra and the serpents protecting the golden apples of the Hesperides.[38] Cato's march in the desert grants the soldiers a chance to inhabit a unique mythic space; far from being an aimless expedition, it is the *only* trial that brings the soldiers toward their renewed commitment to Republican *virtus* (*sola potest Libye turba praestare malorum, / ut deceat fugisse viros*, "Libya alone, with all its plagues, can prove that men who fled can still be men," *BC* 9.405–406). It establishes the Stoic sage as Rome's new *numen tutelare (patriam tutore carentem / excepit,* "[Cato] embraced the fatherland which was lacking a protector," *BC* 9.24–25). He surpasses the greatest heroes of myth and Roman history.[39]

During the Libyan sojourn, in the address to his soldiers (*BC* 9.378–94) Cato's image is consonant with that traced by Lucan at *BC* 2.295–98. Lucan does not typify the Stoic leader as a cold and abstractly detached philosopher but as a sincere and concerned human being. Lucan makes the Stoic sage confess that he "does not want to deceive anybody." He "will not cover up fear while leading the crowd on" (*neque enim mihi fallere quemquam / est animus tectoque metu perducere volgus, BC* 9.388–89). He knows that his troop is facing a great danger and feels a certain anxiety about the outcome. Cato's attitude is rather different from that of Aeneas at *Aen.* 1.208–209:

> Talia voce refert curisque ingentibus aeger
> spem voltu simulat, premit altum corde dolorem.

> [Aeneas] preoccupied by profound concerns said these things; he displayed
> false hope on his face while burying deep affliction in his heart.

Aeneas talks to his companions about their future optimistically but deceptively (*Aen.* 1.198–207). In marked opposition, Cato does not hide his feelings and communicates sincerely the dangers of the journey. Having been worried about the spiritual safety of the entire human race (*BC* 2.312–316), in this episode he is preoccupied with the hardship his comrades will have to face in the desert, even though he realizes that the dangers will test their newly acquired loyalty to the Republic (*BC* 9.405–406).

Since Jupiter and victory are on the side of Caesar, the only comfort that Cato can offer to his suffering companions are his physical presence (*me teste pati,* "suffer with me as a witness," *BC* 9.391) and his willingness to be the first to face every danger (*primus harenas / ingrediar,* "first I will approach the desert," *BC* 9.394–95). Far from disproving his words or alienating the soldiers, Cato's actions motivate them to be brave. In his presence they can endure great toils and even death:

> Omnibus unus adest fatis; quocumque vocatus
> advolat atque ingens meritum maiusque salute
> contulit, in letum vires; puduitque gementem

illo teste mori. Quod ius habuisset in ipsum
ulla lues? Casus alieno in pectore vincit
spectatorque docet magnos nil posse dolores.

He [Cato] alone is present at every deathbed; summoned,
he speeds to confer a tremendous gift, one greater than life—
the strength to face death. Dying men are ashamed to groan
with such a witness. What power did any plague
have against him? He conquers crises in other men's hearts;
watching, he teaches that even severe pain lacks power. (*BC* 9.884–89)

Since Jupiter has already forgotten Pompey and is concentrating on Caesar's victory, Cato is the only one who can appreciate and be a witness to the suffering of the defeated. Matthew Leigh has suggested that *illo teste* does not imply philosophical *autarkeia* in the behavior of the soldiers but incriminates "Cato, the spectator, the man involved with the surfaces of things," happy with a mere spectacle of virtue. He is right to note the emphasis on "witnessing," but his explanation is perhaps a bit harsh.[40] He does not consider that Cato "is called" (*vocatus*, 884) by the soldiers to be present in the hour of their death and that the courage his witnessing inspires is called "a great boon, more important than life itself" (*ingens meritum maiusque salute*, 885). The presence of Cato reminds his men that pain is ultimately powerless over the spirit; the *iunctura "spectatorque docet"* (889) underscores not so much Cato's passivity but his power to teach a lesson even by being a mere spectator.[41]

There is a further point to consider. Some of Seneca's reflections on "looking" should be used to contextualize Lucan's description. In some of his letters Seneca makes clear that we must live as if we were under the public eye (*Quid autem prodest recondere se et, oculos auresque vitare?* "What profits it, however, to hide ourselves away, and to avoid the eyes and ears of men?" *Ep.* 43.4–5). In this letter, he urges Lucilius to live as if he could be heard and watched by him (*sic vive tamqum quid facias auditurus sim, immo tamquam visurus*, "Live just as if I could hear what you are doing, or better, as if I could see what you do," *Ep.* 32.1) and "to choose worthy companions" who will be able to teach him how to die (*ad meliores transi: cum Catonibus vive, cum Lelio, cum Tuberone . . . cum Socrate . . . te docebit mori*, "Change therefore to better associations: live with the Catos, with Laelius, with Tubero . . . with Socrates . . . he will teach you to die," *Ep.* 104.22). In the *Bellum Civile* Cato is the advisor who, according to Seneca's *Ep.* 94.72–74, everybody should choose in order to pay attention to what really matters (*itaque si in medio urbium fremitu conlocati sumus, stet ad latus monitor et*

... *suscipiat . . . animum ab externis ad sua reversum,* "therefore if we are placed in the middle of a tumult of cities, let an advisor stand at our side and . . . let him admire the spirit that, removed from externals, is concentrated on itself"). Discussing some of the letters mentioned above, Matthew Roller notes how in Seneca's prose, human conscience—the highest possible form of moral authority that lives within us as a fragment of the divine mind regulating the universe—is often described with images and metaphors drawn from traditional mechanisms of external, community-oriented moral evaluation.[42] Similar considerations can be applied to Lucan's description of Cato's soldiers dying under his eye. In this passage Cato has become the "personification" of their newly acquired Stoic and Republican conscience.

The Narrator's Apostrophe to Roma

While Caesar is the incarnation of foolishness and of all the vices of the enemies of Rome, Cato, his ideological antagonist, epitomizes Stoic wisdom and the perfect Roman political leader who is committed to public service to the point of renouncing everything in order to assure the success of the state.[43] Attachments (e.g., to wealth, personal success, safety) rather than public concern do not have any relevance in the mind of a leader emphatically portrayed in an exemplary mode as the true father of the dying Republic (*BC* 2.297–305, 2.389–91) as well as the ideal Roman general who never lies to his troops, marches side by side with his soldiers, and does not request special privileges.[44] Among the many major and minor leaders of the *Bellum Civile,* Cato is the only one urging his men to fight not for his personal success but for a worthwhile cause (*BC* 9.379–408). As long as the soldiers have made that cause their own, Cato's personal death does not matter. In his behavior he clarifies what Caesar wants to forget, that "drawn swords belong not to the general but to the soldiers" (*BC* 5.252–54). By making himself a *miles,* Cato becomes the true *dux* of the army.[45] At *BC* 9.587–97, his paradigmatic military and Stoic qualities are dramatically juxtaposed and praised. The narrator's admiration for Cato and his acknowledgment of the importance of the desert march become fully revealed in an apostrophe to Rome (*BC* 9.586–604) which seems ultimately directed toward Lucan's contemporary readers. Having previously mocked the Roman custom of conferring divine status upon all dead emperors (*BC* 1.33–66; 6.805–9), the narrator now declares Cato to be the only human being worthy of being immortalized as a divinity:[46]

Ipse manu sua pila gerit, praecedit anheli

militis ora pedes, monstrat tolerare vapores,
non iubet, et nulla vehitur cervice supinus
carpentoque sedens; somni parcissimus ipse est;
ultimus haustor aquae, quam, tandem fonte reperto
indiga cogatur laticis certare iuventus,
stat, dum lixa bibat. Si veris magna paratur
fama bonis et si successu nuda remoto
inspicitur virtus, quidquid laudamus in ullo
maiorum, fortuna fuit. Quis Marte secundo,
quis tantum meruit populorum sanguine nomen?
Hunc ego per Syrtes Libyaeque extrema triumphum
ducere maluerim, quam ter Capitolia curru
scandere Pompei, quam frangere colla Iugurthae.
Ecce parens verus patriae, dignissimus aris,
Roma, tuis, per quem numquam iurare pudebit,
et quem, si steteris umquam cervice soluta,
nunc, olim, factura deum es.

Packing his own javelin, Cato on foot forged ahead
of his panting soldiers, showing them
not commanding how to bear hardship. No one shouldered his weight
while he lolled at ease in a sedan-chair. First awake, last asleep,
he was the last to drink at a spring when water was found,
and his parched troops fought to slake their thirst;
he stood back till even the camp cook had drunk. If great renown
is awarded for true merits, and if one examines virtue
naked, with success stripped off, all that we praise in our forebears
was luck. Which of them, when it comes to battles won
or the blood of nations spilled, has earned a name so great?
This is the triumph—crossing Sidra and the remotest parts of Libya—
that I would want to lead, more than riding three times
up the Capitoline in Pompey's car, more than breaking
Jugurtha's neck. Behold! The true father of his country,
the man most deserving of altars from you, Rome; the man
by whose name you need never be ashamed to swear on oath:
if ever you stand with neck unyoked
—now, someday—you will make this man a god. (*BC* 9.587–604)

Significantly in the *laudatio*, the narrator talks in the first person (*hunc ego* . . .

*triumphum / conducere maluerim, BC.*9. 597–98) and casts the Libyan march as *the* triumph which he himself would have wanted to achieve, an accomplishment more important than all of Pompey's celebrated victories. At *BC* 9.603–604, echoing Cato's previous words to his soldiers (*indomita cervice mori, BC* 9.380), the narrator asserts that Libya marks a crucial event for those who believe in the importance of preserving their spiritual emancipation (*cervice soluta,* "standing with a neck unyoked," 603), those who, like the soldiers and the narrator, have accepted Cato's lesson to die free.

The importance of the narrator's open evaluation of the Libyan march in the passage quoted above has not been stressed enough. As we saw, scholarly attention has been drawn toward the grotesque details of the episode and the snake-induced *insolitae mortes* (*BC* 9.734), which do not seem to square with a celebratory intent. Lucan might have given Cato's soldiers a splendid victory over the snakes; instead, he depicts their defeat and their bodies horribly torn apart. If the narrator wished to glorify intentions and spiritual strength, why do we find this emphasis on the body? I believe that Lucan's "uglification" of death can be understood first of all as a response to its "aestheticization" by Virgil. In the *Aeneid* the narrator, facing human loss and defending the epic ideal, makes his apostrophized victims beautiful and adopts a melancholy register. As Thomas Greene has observed, "[t]he perpetual elegiac note of the *Aeneid* never turns to tragic because tragedy involves the confrontation of loss and purgation that follows acceptance. Virgil wants always to exalt the loss even as he winces at it."[47] In contrast, Lucan rejects the lyric mode and adopts an ironic attitude. The grotesque details employed in the description are not meant to criticize the soldiers' attempt but to underscore the tragic futility of their sufferings. The snakes, Lucan explains, "fight for Caesar" (*pro Caesare pugnant / dipsades, BC* 9.850–51), and Caesar will be ultimately victorious. The carnage of the Republican army in the desert reminds the readers of all its historical defeats: at Actium, Pharsalus, Thapsus, and Munda. It expresses Lucan's bitter disappointment at the downfall of the Republican forces, his bitter awareness of the tragic destiny of freedom.

Despite, or perhaps because of, this disappointment in order to communicate to his audience more than mere disappointment, Lucan uses his own narrative voice to celebrate Cato. Having already suggested that Cato loves the state with the devotion and sorrow of a father (*BC* 2.297–305; 2.388), he now considers him the only man worthy of the title *pater patriae* (*ecce parens verus patriae, BC* 9.604).[48] In a truly philosophical vein the narrator also proclaims that virtue should be valued per se, "naked, with success stripped off" (*successu nuda remoto, BC* 9.597). It does not matter if Cato does not accomplish anything practical while fighting in a secluded corner of the universe against an army of snakes. The victories of the ancestors are the result of luck and perhaps something even more ambiguous than that. Lines 596–97 attack the massacres and wars on which the Roman empire is built: "Who with the favor of Mars, through the sanction of victory and the blood of nations, deserved such a name?" Who in the history of Rome deserves praise if his success is built on human blood and his virtue mingled with slaughter? *Fortuna* in Hellenistic historiography had been understood sometimes as blind chance but often, especially in Polybius and Plutarch, is conceived as a mysterious force active in the historical process and promoting the creation of Roman *imperium* (e.g., *Rom.* 8.9, *De Fort. Rom.* 320a–321b).[49] Even Livy explains in his histories that the creation of the Roman establishment was fostered by *fortuna* and *virtus*.[50] In the passage above (*BC* 9.587–604) Lucan instead interprets *fortuna* as political success he wants to dissociate from virtue. Victory in epic writing as well as in historiography is considered a legitimizing phenomenon; but Lucan loathes this idea and elects Cato as his hero specifically because, being a Stoic, he does not care about success and practical results.

According to Mary Beagon, the dichotomy between *virtus* and *fortuna* is replayed by Pliny in the description of M. Sergius at *Natural History* 7.106 with the observation that some individuals conquered men but Sergius vanquished fortune.[51] In Pliny, as in Lucan, fortune is thus constructed as an enemy to be conquered by a superior personal effort. While the impossibility of judging a moral contest by criteria of worldly success goes back to Aristotle (*E.N.* 1099a–1101a), it is most forcefully exhibited in Lucan's description of Cato and in Seneca's portrayal of the virtuous man. In both authors the sage is represented as arming himself against fortune and, not content to remain on the defensive, offering himself to her blows (*BC* 9.569–71; *Ep.* 98.4; *Prov.* 4.12).[52] As we will see, the sage's will to resist and antagonize fortune marks Lucan's Cato as the titanic "counter-figure" of *pius* Aeneas. In Julio-Claudian literature the emphasis on moral triumph is symptomatic of a sociocultural milieu in which the opportunities traditionally offered by political and military careers were reduced and withdrawal from public life sometimes became the only possible active resistance to a tyrannizing emperor.[53] Beagon's observations are correct; yet in the *Bellum Civile* Lucan does not simply show Cato's spiritual resistance but also his active, though ultimately vain, efforts to fight Caesar.

Defending Emotions

In the narrator's apostrophe to Rome, Cato is depicted in an exemplary mode and is immortalized as a true god. In other sections of the poem Lucan connects his sublimity to his humanity: Cato is like a god who has human emotions and cares about men. We clearly see his implication in the troubled world of civil war and his distance from the tranquil abode of the gods at *BC* 2.284ff:

> Sic fatur, at illi
> arcano sacras reddit Cato pectore voces:
> "Summum, Brute, nefas civilia bella fatemur;
> sed quo fata trahunt, virtus secura sequetur.
> Crimen erit superis et me fecisse nocentem.
> Sidera quis mundumque velit spectare cadentem
> expers ipse metus? Quis, cum ruat arduus aether,
> terra labet mixto coeuntis pondere mundi,
> compressas tenuisse manus? Gentesne furorem
> Hesperium ignotae Romanaque bella sequentur
> diducti fretis alio sub sidere reges,
> otia solus agam? Procul hunc arcete furorem,
> o superi, motura Dahas ut clade Getasque
> securo me Roma cadat."
>
> Thus [Brutus] spoke, and unto him
> from his inmost breast Cato then spoke these sacred words:
> "The greatest evil, Brutus is civil war, I grant;
> but where the fates beckon, confident virtue will follow.
> The crime of the gods will be that they made me guilty, too.
> Who would want to watch the stars and cosmos fall,
> feeling no dread himself? Who, while the fiery firmament tumbles
> and earth trembles under the jumbled weight of the crashing cosmos
> would want to sit, hands folded? Will unknown lands
> and kings cut off by the waves beneath some alien sky
> play a part in Hesperian frenzy and the Roman wars?
> Shall I alone live at ease? Ward off this frenzy,
> o gods, that Rome, whose doom will shake Goths and Dahae,
> should fall, leaving me unaffected!" (*BC* 2.284–97)

The passage is riddled with paradoxes. With divine wisdom (*sacras . . . voces*, 284) Cato explains that his virtue will have to be tried by the evil convulsion of the civil war; he does not want to be like those inert gods who can watch the world's destruction without lifting a finger.[54] Out of a sense of duty for his country and insofar as its participation can positively affect Pompey (*me milite vincat / ne sibi se vicisse putet,* "let him [Pompey] win with me a soldier in his ranks lest he thinks he won for himself," *BC* 2.322–23), Cato chooses to fight; fighting for Cato is a "preferred indifferent." We should not think that the choice of these "indifferents"—whether preferred or not preferred—is a trivial matter since it is exactly through their selection and rejection that, according to the Stoics, every person exercises his moral faculties.[55] The sage's self-sufficiency does not lead him to neglect or abandon the people for whom he feels natural affection. Sometimes, Epictetus says, it may become necessary for a Stoic to run a risk for a friend and even to die for him (*Disc.* 2.7.3).[56] A man's life is an external which is strictly speaking an "indifferent," but the use a sage makes of his life does matter since that pertains to the morality of his character. Cato believes that he is required to fight for freedom (and eventually sacrifice his life for it) in order to preserve his virtuous character. Even in the midst of chaos his virtue is *secura* while he himself is not *expers metus* (292). Lines 284 and 292 must be put in context with *BC* 2.240–41, where the narrator explains that "Cato fears for everybody but has no concern about himself" (*cunctisque timentem / securumque sui*). As Fantham perceptively observes, "Cato is *securus sui* because *virtus* is *secura* (287), but he cannot be free of care while Rome is at risk; hence he rejects such impassivity in 297. Brutus sets up the ideal of serenity as a prerequisite of wisdom; Cato counters with the claim of *virtus,* which he interprets as the social virtue of justice (and less prominently self-control and courage) rather than contemplative *sapientia.*"[57] Cato reacts to the sad *spectacula* of the destruction of the world (*mundumque . . . spectare cadentem,* 289) with *metus* (cf. *BC* 1.134) and believes that to react with indifference is a frenzy (*furorem,* 297) comparable to the frenzy of civil war (*furorem,* 291).

In the course of the *Bellum Civile,* Cato is associated with *metus* at *BC* 9.389 and 2.291. He is also linked with *timor* at *BC* 2.240, with *ira* at *BC* 9.509–510, with *furor* at *BC* 2.251–56, with *dolor* and *luctus* at *BC* 2.297–305 and 2.378, and with *gaudium* at *BC* 9.291.[58] In all these cases the emotions of the Stoic saint are characterized by Lucan as praiseworthy. Even the intense feelings felt by those who follow Cato's leadership seem approved by the narrator.

Traces of Cato's humanity and exemplarity are visible at *BC* 9.509–510. In this section of the desert march the general is offered a helmet filled with water and is described as *iratus*. Aware of having stimulated the army's envy (*dux . . . / invidiosus erat,* "the commander . . . was the object of envy," *BC* 9.504–505), he harshly addresses the soldier who gave him the water (*BC* 9.505–509) and rejects the gift:

>Sic concitus ira
>excussit galeam, suffecitque omnibus unda.

> So, shaken with anger,
> he dashed the helmet aside and the water was enough for everybody. (*BC* 9.509–510)

During the Libyan march the leader's *duritia* does not grow into sadism and his *ira* separates him from the impassive Stoic sage.[59] The leader is concerned with the physical and psychological welfare of the soldiers. By example and not only by empty words he wants to teach that he is different from Caesar and values equality above everything else. As we saw, like a *bonus imperator* he walks on foot, sleeps little, attends the wounded, and does not accept privileges.[60] The *sententia* of line 510 (*suffecitque omnibus unda*) reveals that the spilled water quenched everybody's thirst and that the spiritual fulfillment provided to the soldiers by Cato's words and gesture has triumphed over their bodily needs.[61] Ultimately the decision to refuse the water is manifested as the correct choice: it reveals that anger has not clouded Cato's rational ability to choose what is best for himself and for everybody. We could say with Seneca that "this prompting of the mind which is submissive to reason" cannot be called anger; "anger is that which overleaps reason and sweeps it away" (*hanc iram non voco, motum animi rationi parentem; illa est ira, quae rationem transsilit, quae secum rapit, Ira* 2.3.4).[62]

Cato's anger is noteworthy because in the *Bellum Civile ira* and the adjective *iratus* are typically associated with Caesar. Debra Hershkowitz has suggested that in Lucan's poem *virtus* survives by shifting its signification away from positive qualities and toward negative attributes associated with the semantic sphere of *furor*.[63] Yet in the passage above, and in several other moments of the epic, the semantic trajectory of words like *ira* or *furor* seems to follow a direction opposite to that proposed by Hershkowitz. When they are attributed to Cato and those who try to imitate him, they tend to assume a positive slant. For instance, in Book 3 the noun *ira* is employed in the account of Metellus' attempt to protect the Treasury against Caesar's greediness:

> Tamen exit in iram
> viribus an posint obsistere iura, per unum
> libertas experta virum.
>
> And yet in one instance freedom burst into anger,
> testing whether right could resist might
> by one man's means. (*BC* 3.112–114)

In Lucan's ambiguous linguistic universe, the same word is not always univocally tied to the same concept. In the lines above Metellus' love for freedom "grows (*exit*) into indignation (*in iram*)" (112), but we do not have the impression that the development is a degeneration since it is produced in the defense of law (*iura*, 113). Metellus' brave behavior and speech upset Caesar, who in turn "burns with great anger" (*magnam . . . in iram / . . . accensus, BC* 3. 133–34). A few lines later, Caesar is again described as "overcome by fiercer anger" (*acrior ira subit, BC* 3.142). By qualifying each man's reaction with the same term Lucan juxtaposes a "good" anger and a "bad" anger. While the first is rooted in the devotion to freedom, the latter is fostered by pride and especially by an unmistakable sense of superiority.[64] During this episode Caesar mocks Metellus—*te vindice tuta relicta est / libertas?* ("with *you* as guardian freedom should be safe?" *BC* 3.137–38)—when the soldier, in a sort of *imitiatio Catonis*, acts as the protector of freedom and legality. With biting irony the proud general reminds him that "not yet has time so jumbled sublime with low that if Metellus' voice could save the Laws, they'd not rather have Caesar annul them!" (*non usque adeo permiscuit imis / longus summa dies, ut non, si voce Metelli / servantur leges, malint a Caesare tolli, BC* 3.138–40).

At the end of this episode Metellus is removed from the building by Cotta, whose speech defends passivity and assumes a vaguely Stoic cadence:[65]

> "Libertas" inquit "populi, quem regna coercent,
> libertate perit; cuius servaveris umbram,
> si, quidquid iubeare, velis."

> He said, "People whom tyranny coerces lose Liberty
> by taking liberties: you will at least preserve her shadow
> if you do what you are ordered to willingly." (*BC* 3.145–47)

Cotta's words echo Cato's in Books 9 and 2. Yet while the former wishes to preserve a simulacrum of freedom *by conforming* his will to the will of those who are in charge, the latter follows "the ghost of freedom" (*fides ficta libertatis, BC* 9.204–205) and its "vain shade" (*inanem umbram, BC* 2.303) by doing exactly the opposite: *by fighting* the unjust will of the leaders.[66] Cotta's reaction is important because once again it allows us to note the poem's linguistic ambiguity and how the acceptance of the Stoic creed can produce diversified reactions: compliance with the status quo in the case of Cotta and the will to resist it in the case of Cato.

Another positive conceptualization of *ira* is discernible in the description of Pompey's death. At *BC* 8.663, Lucan explains that those who were able to see

Pompey's head after it was cut from his body noticed an expression of "anger" toward the gods in his face:

> At Magni cum terga sonent et pectora ferro,
> permansisse decus sacrae venerabile formae
> iratamque deis faciem, nil ultima mortis
> ex habitu vultuque miri mutasse fatentur,
> qui lacerum videre caput.
>
> But, while Magnus' shoulders and breastbone crunched against steel,
> the venerable beauty of the sacred visage remained,
> his face still angered at the gods, and in death's extremity
> nothing in the hero's bearing or countenance was altered—so say
> those who saw his severed head. (*BC* 8.663–67)

Despite the presence of *ira*, Pompey's beauty remains unchanged (*permansisse decus*, 664; *nil . . . mutasse*, 666). Emanuele Narducci observes that some modern editors find the *lectio* "*dis iratam*" rather strange in the context of Pompey's unaltered beauty. In ancient times as well as in modern an emotion as strong as anger is believed to produce physical alterations. However, he defends *iratam* as perfectly consonant with the characterization of Pompey developed by Lucan in the *Bellum Civile*.[67] After Pharsalus the leader of the senatorial cause has several reasons to be upset with the gods, who maliciously want to bring him down. During the battle of *BC* 7.85 "the pilot of the state" is depicted as "groaning seeing the gods' deception and aware of the fates' opposition to his plan" (*ingemuit rector sensitque deorum / esse dolos et fata suae contraria menti*, *BC* 7.85). At *BC* 7.113 he also realizes that Pharsalus is the gods' fulfillment of Caesar's "unjust prayers" (*vincis apud superos votis me, Caesar, iniquis*). In the *Aeneid* a similar attitude seems to characterize Turnus, Aeneas' defeated opponent, who is described as dying with a "resentful lament" (*vitaque cum gemitu fugit indignata sub umbras*, "with a groan his life fled indignant down to the shades," *Aen.* 12.952). Servius explains *indignata* as Turnus' reaction to the fact that his prayers have not been heard.[68] Approaching death, Turnus seems very aware of the gods' ill will against him (*vos o mihi, manes, / este boni, quoniam superis aversa voluntas*, "You, shades, be kind to me since the gods above manifest their adverse will," *Aen.* 12.646–47). At the moment of his death in the *Iliad*, even Hector perceives the bitter truth of the gods' unjustified hostility against him and says to himself, "Alas! the gods have lured me on to my destruction" (*Iliad* 22.297).[69] In the *Bellum Civile*, Pompey's defeat is seen as despicable not only by Pompey himself. It is perceived as a "cruel crime of the gods" (*crimen . . . deum crudele*, *BC* 8.55; *nefas*, *BC* 8.638) by his wife; moreover, the narrator describes Pompey's end as "a tale that will never lack reproach of gods on high" (*numquam superum caritura pudore / fabula*, *BC* 8.605–606) and the stones that cover Pompey's tomb as "replete with the gods' crime" (*crimine plena deum*, *BC* 8.800).[70]

Pompey's justifiable resentment toward the gods, however, is made to coexist with his commitment to die a serene Stoic death. A few moments before being fatally wounded, the general "wraps his face and . . . head in his cloak; he shuts his eyes and holds his breath lest he should let loose any words and ruin his eternal fame with weeping" (*involvit voltus atque . . . caput; tum lumina pressit / continuitque animam, ne quas effundere voces / vellet et aeternam fletu corrumpere famam*, *BC* 8. 615–617). He is satisfied with the result (*seque probat moriens*, "he approves of his dying self," *BC* 8.621). *Watching* himself being watched, he has successfully rehearsed a Stoic death in the "theater of the world" (*theatrum mundi*) and obtained the right composure in a difficult moment.[71] Eventually, he consoles himself with the Stoic idea that no power can take his past happiness away from him:

> Spargant lacerentque licebit,
> sum tamen, o superi, felix, nullique potestas
> hoc auferre deo.
>
> Though they rend and scatter me,
> I am, o gods, still happy; no power above
> can take that away.[72] (*BC* 8.629–31)

This conceit is formulated with pride and almost as a challenge to the gods. With resentment and spiteful satisfaction Pompey seems to say, "My happiness remains and not even you up there can deprive me of it."[73] The gods, who in the epic cosmos as well as in Stoic thought are considered the guarantors of the world's providential order, are perceived by Pompey (and as we will see to a degree even by Cato) as forces strongly opposed to the moral fulfillment of the universe and of the individual.

The dying Pompey is thus poised between rebellion and acceptance of his fate, between voiced complaint and silence. His *venerabile decus* (664) and *felicitas* (630) are juxtaposed with his *ira* (665). He strives to preserve a dignified look and does not want to "corrupt his eternal fame with weeping" (*aeternam fletu corrumpere famam*, *BC* 8.617). Yet he shows a sort of unrelenting anger, and he is dressed like a mourner. In Martha Malamud's words:

as he veils his head and closes his own eyes, he acts as mourner at his own funeral [. . .] his mourning garb imitates the costume of Cato, who is described similarly at the beginning of the epic (*BC* 2.371–378). Cato's untended hair and beard and mournful face mark him here as unique, the *only* person equipped (through disinterest) to mourn for the human race. Pompey, belated character that he is, enacts the role of Cato, right down to the costume, when he tries to die as a Stoic sage.[74]

While with his composed face Pompey displays the acceptance of his destiny, with his rightly angry brow and attire he mourns the unfairness of his doom and evokes Cato, a figure characterized by Malamud as Rome's ultimate mourner, whom I will also characterize as the *Bellum Civile*'s ultimate rebel, willing to go against Caesar as well as the gods' "prevailing cause" (*victrix causa deis placuit, BC* 1.128).

Strong emotions animate Brutus and Cato's conversation in Book 2. Here we have a fourth example of *ira* employed to qualify a correct reaction when the word is used to describe Brutus' newly acquired desire to fight in the civil war:

> Sic fatur, et acres
> irarum movit stimulos iuvenisque calorem
> excitat in nimios belli civilis amores.
>
> So speaking, he [Cato] plied
> indignation's stinging lash, and the young man's fervor
> he roused all too successfully to love for civil war. (*BC* 2.323–25)

In this episode Brutus is at first unwilling to embrace the war; after hearing Cato's reasons he changes his mind and sides with him. As we saw, the Stoic leader apostrophized the youth and revealed to him that because he considered passivity a *furor* (*otia solus agam? Procul hunc arcete furorem, / o superi, BC* 2.295–96), he chose involvement. Eventually, in the passage quoted above, Cato's concerns rouse Brutus too. A similar pattern was employed by Lucan in Book 9. With a powerful apostrophe Cato incites his soldiers "to steady their souls" (*componite mentes,* 380) and "to meet a mighty task of valor and grave sufferings" (*ad magnum virtutis opus summosque labores,* 381); "as a result he inflames their trembling spirits with courage and love for toils" (*sic ille paventes / incendit virtute animos et amore laborum, BC* 9.406–407). In Lucan's work the power and originality of Cato's representation resides in his decision to fight in the war and in the strong but righteous emotions which it inspires. Cato's apostrophes make people burn (*excitat calorem, incendit*) with love for virtue and labor.⁷⁵ Heat and fire envelop Cato's adamantine virtue and illuminate the lives of those who follow him.

Brutus is aroused by the excitement for a war previously deprecated (*feralibus armis, BC* 2.260; *scelerata in proelia, BC* 2.251) but eventually legitimized by Cato's presence. What drives the young man into it, his *amor,* has nothing in common with the "private purposes" (*suae... causae, BC* 2.249) motivating those already involved in it:

> Quemque suae rapiunt scelerata in proelia causae:
> hos polluta domus legesque in pace timendae,
> hos ferro fugienda fames mundique ruinae
> permiscenda fides. Nullum furor egit in arma:
> castra petunt magna victi mercede; tibi uni
> per se bella placent?

> Private reasons sweep each man into heinous battle:
> some think of a sullied name and laws fearful in peacetime;
> some need steel to escape starvation and the world's downfall
> to break their sworn promises: not one is driven to arms by mere *furor;*
> they join a camp, swayed by hefty bribe; do you alone
> choose war for itself? (*BC* 2.251–56)

In these words we see Brutus' conviction that everybody (except Cato) joined battle for selfish reasons. Persuaded by Cato's speech, he changes his mind and realizes that it is possible to join the conflict for a pure and selfless enthusiasm. The passage significantly problematizes the meaning of the word *furor,* which, as I have already observed, though generally used with a negative connotation (*BC* 2.296) and in connection with Caesar, in this particular instance (*BC* 2.252) qualifies a righteous emotion. Discussing *BC* 2.249–323, Fantham perceptively notes that by Stoic standards greed, lust, and fear—the emotions mentioned by Brutus at lines 2.249ff. as characterizing those who have agreed to fight for private calculations—are forms of *furor* (e.g., Cic. *Tusc.* 3.10). But at line 252 *furor* seems a different kind of feeling and the one motivating Cato, the only man who "chooses the war for itself." Cato's *furor* (internalized by Brutus at *BC* 2.323–25) is "the madness of the man who fights for an ideal."⁷⁶ It is a praiseworthy indignation that though different from pernicious *furor* cannot be properly designated by any separate word.

Brutus' longing to fight for the Republic alludes to Aeneas' yearning for glory after Anchises' account of the future exploits of Rome in the Elysian Fields:

> Quae postquam Anchises natum per singula duxit
> incenditque animum famae venientis amore.

> After Anchises led his son through each successive stage, he made his spirit burn with love for the coming glory. (*Aen.* 6.888–89)

The burning desire of Aeneas is kindled by the words of Anchises. Aeneas' enthusiasm is not thwarted at all by his father's mention of the sad fate of Augustus' nephew Marcellus who, dying at a young age, did not have a chance to pursue greatness. Right after the famous "parade of heroes" Marcellus is mourned by Anchises, who composes an exquisite *laudatio funebris* for the boy (*Aen.* 6.872–86).[77] He agonizes over him as if he were his own dead son:

> heu miserande puer . . .
> . . . Manibus date lilia plenis,
> purpureos spargam flores animamque nepotis
> his saltem accumulem donis et fungar inani
> munere.

> O boy, worthy of my sorrow. . . . Bring me lilies, all of you, with full hands; let me scatter the bright purple flowers for my grandson's shade to heap, at least, these gifts and pay the vain tribute. (*Aen.* 6. 882, 883–86)

The parade of unborn heroes commemorates the dead by celebrating the continued vitality of the *gens* through various generations.[78] But in the *epicedion Marcelli* that concludes the parade, "intangible gloom hovering about Marcellus' head, Anchises' tears (867), and the programmatic word *luctus* (868)" are intensely present.[79] E. Skard suggests that the parade describes the procession of the ancestors at Marcellus' funeral. Even if his interpretation is not correct, his focus on death is legitimate.[80] In these melancholy lines Marcellus becomes the symbol of all the young Romans cut down in the flower of life to build the Roman empire; and Anchises, ritually lamenting the youth's death, stands for all the bereaved Roman fathers and mothers.[81]

Crying over the fate of Marcellus, Anchises *perhaps* blames the gods, envious of such great imperial progeny and of the accomplishments of Rome (*nimium vobis Romana propago / visa potens, superi, propria haec si dona fuissent*, "Too potent in your eyes, o gods, had seemed the Roman stock, were such gifts made to last," *Aen.* 6.870–71). He thinks about Marcellus as a kind of offering to divert the envy of the gods.[82] However, in Virgil's lines the complaint is indirect and craftily defused by the beauty of the description. Paternal sorrow and the idea that a human being is being sacrificed to avert the envy of the gods are instead amplified in Lucan's description of Cato (*BC* 2.297–305), who cries over the body of the dead Republic and compares himself to a bereaved father crying over his son's corpse. In the episode the images of mourner and mourned overlap: as Cato laments Rome's loss of freedom, he also considers himself the new *piaculum* (*BC* 2.304) demanded by the gods who are openly mocked for their cruelty:

> Ceu morte parentem
> natorum orbatum longum producere funus
> ad tumulos iubet ipse dolor, iuvat ignibus atris
> inseruisse manus constructoque aggere busti
> ipsum atras tenuisse faces, non ante revellar,
> exanimem quam te complectar, Roma; tuumque
> nomen, Libertas, et inanem prosequar umbram.
> Sic eat: inmites Romana piacula divi
> plena ferant, nullo fraudemus sanguine bellum.
>
> Anguish
> orders a parent, bereaved by the death of sons, to lead
> the long cortège to the tomb; it soothes him to thrust his hands
> into the bleak fires and, once the pyre-mound is raised,
> to hold the bleak torch himself: likewise, I will not be hauled back before
> I embrace you, lifeless Rome! I will walk to your grave,
> liberty, mourn your name, your insubstantial shade.
> Let the heartless divinities have Roman atonements in full;
> let us not cheat the war of its blood!" (*BC* 2.297–305)

If splendid images of future glory and iridescent flowers glorified Marcellus' death, there is nothing that makes bearable the death of the Republic in the *Bellum Civile*. Lucan (via Cato) constructs a bleak image that makes us deeply feel the anguish of death and the cruelty of the gods. Cato's condemnation of the gods echoes the narrator's resentment and highlights the poem's inconsistent metaphysical structure.

Retelling the dramatic events of the war, the narrator swings back and forth between the idea that the world is governed by deterministic laws and the opposite notion according to which the world is abandoned to pure chance (*BC* 2.1–15). Narducci points out how incoherently (at *BC* 2.1–15) Lucan juxtaposes a dialectic structured around the belief in a providential divinity to an argument constructed to reject the idea of providence.[83] Neither of these conflicting conceptions is rejected, but they are uneasily brought to coexist side by side. From their oxymoronic symbiosis the idea, more poetic than philosophical, of a "cruel providence" is born and is visible even in Cato's attitude toward the gods.[84] In Book 9 he seems to support the traditional Stoic notion of the omnipresence of god (*haeremus cuncti superis . . . / nil facimus non sponte dei . . . / Iuppiter est quodcumque vides, quodcumque moveris*, "We all cleave to the gods . . . we do nothing without god's will . . . all that you see and all your feelings, that is Jupiter," *BC* 9.573–74, 580), but is he really doing so? In his commentary Haskins equates *vides* with the external world and *moveris* with the soul, the inner world of each individual.[85] What happens when the sage's inner world is not pleased by the external world? Should he silently live in conformity with what he sees, or should he try to actively modify the environment around him according to his views and feelings about it? Anthony Long reminds us that in Stoic doctrine nature manifests itself "in the rational organization of the cosmos" as well as "in the normative voice of the individual's impulse and reason," although it can be challenging to do justice to the Stoic intuition that "our natures are parts of the whole" (D.L. 7.87).[86] The question of the relationship between internal nature and external nature in the Early Stoa is complex and has been carefully analyzed by Long. While in most cases he wants to make internal and external nature (the two criteria for acting) perfectly equal and ultimately pulling in the same direction, in one of his articles on the topic he seems to grant priority to internal nature, observing that Chyrsippus "entitles us to gloss the proposition about divine world government by reference to the 'community of reason.'" Here Long seems to grant that reason is an *internal* founding criterion and that even someone "who did not accept Stoic theology" might be willing to accept and respect the inferences about human nature dictated by the Stoic system.[87]

In his mourning at *BC* 2.297–305, Cato is defiantly at odds with the gods. He calls them cruel and, as we saw, is unwilling to accept impassively what they decree.[88] The sage's dissatisfaction echoes other parts of the text in which Jupiter is strongly condemned by the narrator for his indifference to human matters and for allowing Caesar's success and survival:

> Sunt nobis nulla profecto
> numina: cum caeco rapiantur saecula casu,
> mentimur regnare Iovem. Spectabit ab alto
> aethere Thessalicas, teneat cum fulmina, caedes?
> Scilicet ipse petet Pholoen, petet ignibus Oeten
> inmeritaque nemus Rhodopes pinusque Mimantis,

> Cassius hoc potius feriet caput! Astra Thyestae
> Intulit et subitis damnavit noctibus Argos:
> tot similes fratrum gladios patrumque gerenti
> Thessaliae dabit ille diem? Mortalia nulli
> Sunt curata deo.[89]

> For us, truly, there are no
> divinities: since blind chance drags the ages onward,
> we lie when we say Jove rules. Will he gaze from high
> heaven at Thessalian slaughter, holding still his thunderbolts?
> Will he hurl his fires at Pholoë, hurl them at Oeta,
> blameless Rhodope's groves, the pine-woods of Mimas,
> leaving Cassius to strike at Caesar's head? Upon Thyestes
> he brought the stars down and flung abrupt nightfall at Argos;
> will he grant the light of day at Thessaly bristling with brothers' and fathers'
> blades, so many and so alike? Mortal affairs have never
> been god's care. (*BC* 7.445–55)

When the narrator calls into question Jupiter's handling of mortal affairs, the notion of an orthodox and benign Stoic providence is challenged. If they can watch Pharsalus without intervening, it means that they do not care about human affairs. Already in Seneca's writing the idea of providence is marginalized while the individual's reaction to a hostile environment becomes a central focus. It does not matter if circumstances are ultimately part of a rational or divine project; what matters is the way in which men face these accidents (*Ep.*16.4–5; 107.2). Narducci detects an unresolved tension between Seneca's sage's "acceptance" of hardships and the "contempt" (*contemptus*) felt by the sage when facing them (*effugere ista non potes, contemnere potes*, "you cannot avoid these hardships, you can despise them," *Ep.* 107.3; *contemnite paupertatem . . . contemnite dolorem . . . contemnite fortunam; nullum illi telum quo feriret animum dedi*, "scorn poverty . . . scorn pain . . . scorn fortune; I have given her no weapon with which she may strike your soul," *Prov.* 6.6). Fortune, acting as a minister of the gods, is described by Seneca as the antagonist of Cato the Younger, who accepts his test but also challenges and defeats it with his death at Utica (*Prov.* 2.9).[90] In a hostile environment the sage becomes the *aemulator deorum*. He reaches and overcomes them: "in this you may outstrip god; he is exempt from enduring evil, you are superior to it" (*hoc est quo deum antecedatis; ille extra patientiam malorum est, vos supra patientiam, Prov.* 6.6).

The pessimism that only intermittently seizes Seneca is ostentatiously displayed by Lucan, who is tragically aware in his *Bellum Civile* that a man's path toward virtue does not depend on his ability to submit to the fates but rests precisely on the opposite: on his will to resist them. Yet, even within this dark picture, even in this fearful landscape in which the prayers of the readers are fated to die (*spesque metusque peritura vota, BC* 7.211), "hope" has a place and Lucan features a Brutus willing to ignore the cruelty of the universe to follow Cato, that "last surviving hope of virtue chased away and banned from all lands hereafter" (*omnibus expulsae terris olimque fugatae / virtutis iam sola fides, BC* 2.241–42).

The soldiers of Book 9 are also eager to fight a just war. Twice the narrative structure duplicates the pattern of Book 2. Mimicking Brutus's unwillingness to participate in the war (*BC* 2.251–84) as well as his change of mind (*BC* 2.323–25), the soldiers are at first reluctant to fight (*castrorum bellique piget*, "they are tired of the camp and of war," *BC* 9.218ff.); but later they are convinced by Cato to rejoin the combat (*BC* 9. 255–83). Even at *BC* 9.406–407, after Cato's powerful apostrophe (*BC* 9.378–406), the soldiers face the desert march with enthusiasm (see above).[91] Very persuasively Cato suggests that Pompey's death offers them a chance to fight not for a king but for themselves (*quod non in regna laboras, / quod tibi, non ducibus, vivis morerisque*, "you are now toiling not to produce a kingdom, you live and die not for your leaders but for yourselves," *BC* 9. 258–59). Since freedom is now at hand, they should not deny their lives and swords to the fatherland (*nunc patria iugulos ensesque negatas, / cum prope libertas? BC* 9.264–65).[92] Stirred by Cato's speech, the soldiers become keen to reenter the conflict; they are like bees driven back to their toils by the sound of Phrygian cymbals:

> Dixit et omnes
> haud aliter medio revocavit ab aequore puppes,
> quam, simul effetas linquunt examina ceras
> atque oblita favi non miscent nexibus alas,
> sed sibi quaeque volat nec iam degustat amarum
> desidiosa thymum, Phrygii sonus increpat aeris,
> attonitae posuere fugam studiumque laboris
> floriferi repetunt et sparsi mellis amorem;
> gaudet in Hyblaeo securus gramine pastor
> divitias servasse casae. Sic voce Catonis
> inculcata viris iusti patientia Martis.
>
> His words summoned
> all ships back from water—the way, once their eggs

hatch, files of bees abandon their waxen nurseries and,
heedless of the comb, cease to cluster in swarms, wing on wing;
each flies off on her own and, indolent, no longer sucks
pungent thyme. But let clashing Phrygian brass rebuke them:
thunderstruck, the bees dawdle no more but resume with zeal
their bloom-born labor, their love of far-flung honey.
The shepherd in meadows on Monte Ibleo, eased of cares,
rejoices: he has assured the wealth of his cottage.
    Thus with his voice
Cato drummed into his men courage to face a just war. (*BC* 9.283–93)

The army embraces civil war, which under the leadership of Cato and in the name of freedom has become just (*iusti . . . Martis*, 293). The language employed is apt for describing bees as well as soldiers: *examina* can designate swarms of bees as well as the ranks of soldiers, and the expression "*miscent alas*" (286) evokes the act of joining battle (e.g., *Romanae miscent acies*, *BC* 1.682; *miscenturque manus*, *BC* 3.569, etc.).[93] The soldiers' newly acquired desire to fight is described as a productive enterprise through the analogy with the bees, "lovers of far-flung honey" (*BC* 9.289–90).

The passage is significantly constructed to recall by contrast *Aeneid* 1.430–37 and *Georgics* 4.1–315. At *Aen.* 1.430–37 the Carthaginians' effort to build a new city is compared to the fervid toil of the bees:

> Qualis apes aestate nova per florea rura
> exercet sub sole labor, cum gentis adultos,
> educunt fetus, aut liquentia mella
> stipant et dulci distendunt nectare cellas,
> aut onera accipiunt venientum, aut agmine facto
> ignavum fucos pecus a praesepibus arcent;
> fervet opus redolentque thymo fragrantia mella,
> "O fortunati, quorum iam moenia surgunt!"

So in early summer labor impels the bees above fields of flowers amid sunbeams, as they lead abroad their nation's youthful brood or as they store the flowing honey, filling cells with sweet nectar, while they take their loads from the newcomers or, lined for war, chase the drones, lazy swarm, away from the hive; labor thrives, and fragrant honey smells of wild thyme. "How fortunate are these men whose city walls already are rising!" (*Aen.* 1.430–37)

Even more poignantly at *Georgics* 4.64, Virgil singles out "Cybele's cymbals" (*matris . . . cymbala*) as useful to persuade a swarm of bees to settle, and at *G.* 4.103–105 he explains that the beekeeper must strive to contain the bees' *instabilis animos*, which induce them to swarm away, neglecting their work:

> At cum incerta volant caeloque examina ludunt
> contemnuntque favos et frigida tecta relinquunt,
> instabilis animos ludo prohibebis inani.

> But when swarms fly without direction, play in the sky, disdain their honeycombs and leave their chilly homes, you will constrain their unstable spirits from empty play. (*G.* 4.103–105)

Besides showing how to maximize the bees' efforts Virgil illustrates their nature and develops an elaborate comparison between bees and a human society.[94] In the *Georgics* the bees are not the symbol of a golden or primitive age since they are subject to strife (*G.* 1.466–514) and to the love of possession (*amor habendi*, 4.177). Strife and greed, together with exertion, constitute typical traits of advanced civilizations. The bee society, unable to control its external environment, is also susceptible to fear (4.37).[95] Having mentioned some of the bees' defects, Virgil emphasizes some of their positive features, above all their profound communality and love of toil.[96] At *G.* 4.153ff., he describes the bees as sharing offspring (*natos*) and a city (*consortia tecta urbis*). He explains that they "regulate their life with mighty laws" (*magnisque agitant sub legibus aeuum*, 154), can work themselves to death (*animam sub fasces dedere*, 204), are absolutely devoted to their leader (*ille operum custos, illum admirantur*, 215), and can gloriously sacrifice their life in battle (*pulchramque petunt per vulnera mortem*, 218). Thus the bees exhibit the patriotism of the old Roman people, but their virtues and loyalty are not in the service of a Republican society. Virgil's bees, like Egyptians or Lydians, fight for a king (*G.* 4.210–218); they do not fight for themselves or for their country.[97]

Lucan's bees are informed by the models of *Aeneid* 1 and *Georgics* 4, but they are also different from them. Before listening to Cato's inspiring words, Lucan's bees are antiphrastically shown as lacking all the features Virgil attributed to those occupied with building a nation. While Virgil's bees take care of the reproductive cycle (*educunt fetus*, *Aen.* 1.432), store honey (*liquentia mella stipant*, *Aen.* 1.432–33), and productively interact with each other (*onera . . . praesepibus arcent*, *Aen.* 1.433–34), Lucan's are forgetful of their brood (*effetas ceras*, *BC* 9.285), fly with selfish motivations (*sibi quaequae volat*, *BC* 9.287), and do not interact (*non miscent nexibus alas*, *BC* 9.286).[98] This behavior, however, is displayed by Lucan's bees/soldiers only in the first part of the image (*BC* 9.283–88). After listening to the sound of Cato's voice, they are renewed and transformed, ready to care for their society. They display the virtue of Virgil's bees in the *Aeneid*, but are not inspired (like the bees of *Georgics* 4) by the love of a monarch (*BC* 9.289–93). Lucan's bees reject monarchy; they now fight for the liberty of their households.

The image of the soldiers' call back into battle (*BC* 9.283–92) unravels with a chiastic rhythm that diverts the reader's attention from Cato to the soldiers and from the bees to the *pastor* (290) who bangs the cymbals. At this point (*BC* 9. 292–93) the narrator clarifies the comparison by identifying Cato's voice (*sic voces Catonis*, 292) with the *Phrygii aeris sonus* (288) of the "shepherd on Monte Ibleo" who "is happy" (*gaudet*, *BC* 9.291) and confident (*securus*, *BC* 9.291) because through the work of the bees and the production of honey he can guarantee the household welfare.[99] Cato is like Seneca's "shepherd [*pastor*] who takes pleasure [*capit voluptatem*] in the increase of his flock" (*Ep.* 34.1). If in the *Georgics* honey is linked to peaceful pursuits, in the *Bellum Civile* it is linked to the persuasion of waging a just war. The contentedness of Lucan's *pastor* is similar to that of Seneca, who rejoices (*exulto*, *Ep.* 34.1) in having spurred Lucilius to grow up: *exhortatus sum, addidi stimulos nec lente ire passus sum, sed subinde incitavi* ("I exhorted you, I applied the goad and did not permit you to march lazily, but roused you continually," *Ep.* 34.2). The contentedness of Lucan's *pastor* also reminds us of Virgil's *pastor* Aristaeus (*G.* 4.317), who is able with the *bugonia* "to put aside cares" (*deponere curas, G.* 4.531) and to obtain new bees (*G.*4.554–58), as well as the satisfaction of Virgil's Corycian *senex*, who can thrive in a hard and unyielding environment by taking care of his bees (*G.* 4.127–29) and is perfectly satisfied with what he has (*G.* 4.132–33).[100] In the *Georgics* the Corycian old man "understands nature's limitations, stays within them and thereby achieves individual success."[101] In *BC* 9.283–93 Cato, "the shepherd" of his soldiers, also tries to put his knowledge and rhetoric at the service of a rather imperfect society.

Commenting on the character of Cato in the *Bellum Civile*, Hershkowitz suggests that he is caught up in the infectious and devastating passion that he stirs up in his adressees.[102] Yet in reading Lucan's descriptions of those who fall under the spell of Cato's words, and especially by considering the image connected to the soldiers' renewed love for labor, we do not get the impression that the enthusiasm promoted by Cato is being qualified as a negative but rather as a necessary and constructive feeling. Like the bees positively influenced by the sound of cymbals, those who listen to Cato are transformed and become newly committed to the cause of liberty and the pursuit of honey. They regain concern for their families and city. Once persuaded, they embrace a positive passion that ultimately fosters unity and prosperity.[103]

Cato's Mourning: Dissenting with a Female Voice

Some of my observations in this chapter have already emphasized that Lucan's description of Cato, besides highlighting his courage and attachment to virtue, portrays him as a hero intensely affected by the conditions of his fellow Romans. In Book 2 Cato's words to Brutus underline his commitment to the community and allude to the Stoic concept of *oikeiôsis* (affinity).[104] The Stoics held that the basis for all human society is the love that parents show their children. Cicero says, "it is held by the Stoics to be important to understand that nature creates in parents an affection for their children; and parental affection is the source to which we trace the origin of the association of the human race in communities" (*Fin.* 3.19.62).[105] And elsewhere: "nature, by the power of rationality, connects one human being with another for the purpose of associating in conversation and way of life and engenders above all a special love for one's offspring. It instills an impulse for men to meet together [. . .] and to be zealous in providing life's wherewithal not only for themselves but also for their wives and children and others whom they hold dear and ought to protect" (*Off.* 1.12).[106] Extending this notion, Seneca suggests:

> Omne hoc, quod vides, quo divina atque humana conclusa sunt, unum est; membra sumus corporis magni. Natura nos cognatos edidit, cum ex isdem et in eadem gigneret. Haec nobis amorem indidit mutuum et sociabiles fecit.
>
> All that you behold, that which comprises both god and man, is one: we are the parts of one great body. Nature produced us related to one another since she created us from the same source and to the same end. She engendered in us mutual affection and made us sociable. (*Ep.* 95.52, tr. R. M. Gummere)

The sage, possessing *oikeiôsis*, has knowledge of what is "properly his own"; in other words, he recognizes the various layers constituting his identity—his civic devotion, his sentience, his rationality—which coexist inside him in perfect harmony, none of them being suppressed or out of balance.[107] This knowledge would allow a Stoic sage like Lucan's Cato to see his bond to Rome in very personal terms. He laments the loss of Rome's liberty, vividly comparing himself to a devoted father who mourns over the bodies of his children (*BC* 2.297–305). The intensity of the image, as well as its poetic and conceptual ramifications, give to lamentation and fatherhood an almost programmatic importance.

At the beginning of the famous encomium to Cato (*BC* 2.380–391), Lucan's narrator points out that, like an exemplary Stoic *and* a good citizen, Cato distances himself from parochial interests and is free from excessively negative emotions. The idea that Cato is not touched by negative desires is spelled out at *BC* 2.390–91:

> Nullosque Catonis in actus
> subrepsit partemque tulit sibi nata voluptas.

> Into none of Cato's deeds did
> self-indulgence worm its way, in none did it play a role. (*BC* 2.390–91)

Being free from excessive concerns and loathing, he can fully perceive the tragedy of Rome's enslavement and is "the only one free to mourn" for the human race:

> uni quippe vacat studiis odiisque carenti
> humanum lugere genus.

> Only he was really free, lacking both zeal and hatred,
> to cry for the human race. (*BC* 2.377–78)

In his commentary C.E. Haskins glosses *studiis odiisque carenti* as "*imperturbato, showing the Stoic apatheia.*"[108] Yet it seems that this *apatheia* does not prevent Cato from crying. Not only is his involvement in the civil war regarded as blameless; in this *laudatio* (*BC* 2.380–91), which highlights Cato's traditional Stoic traits, even his tears (*lugere,* at line 378) are considered a sign of his superior conduct (line 377).[109] Epictetus says that "the power to love (*philein*) belongs to the wise one alone" (*Diss.* 2.22.3); Lucan adds that even the power to mourn belongs only to the sage.

Among our sources Lucan is not alone in juxtaposing the image of the stern and uncompromising Stoic sage to that of a more humane and friendly man. While he is depicted by Valerius Maximus and sometimes by Seneca as imperturbable and "almost divine," in Plutarch Cato is humanized.[110] Plutarch's portrayal of his death includes details that at first might be considered ill-designed to celebrate the greatness of a Stoic hero. In chapter 7 he shows Cato as capable of great anger against those who hurt him and in chapter 11 as filled with grief for the death of his half-brother. During his last hours Cato is said to become angry in the course of a conversation and to lose his temper with a slave who tried to hide his sword (*Life of Cato Minor,* 67 and 68.3). Vincenzo Tandoi points out that Plutarch's characterization of Cato's last acts does not emphasize his possession of Stoic *apatheia,* and Robert Goar believes that besides celebrating Cato's suicide as a moral victory, Plutarch shows us "Cato the man rather than the Stoic saint."[111]

In Lucan's Book 2 Cato's humanization is visible in the emphasis on his *luctus* and fatherly attachment to the Republic. These themes are highlighted in Cato's remarriage to Marcia (*BC* 2.326–50), whose mourning attire (*BC* 2.336–37)—logistically motivated by her previous attendance at her ex-husband's funeral—mirrors Cato's *luctus* for the death of *libertas* and prefigures his imminent death.[112] As Marcia welcomes Cato in her embrace, the shadow of her funereal robe eclipses the shining purple of Cato's senatorial toga (*obsita funerea celatur pupurea lana, BC* 2.367). The eclipse of color and brightness at *BC* 2.367 contrasts with the profusion of dazzling white and purple flowers employed by Virgil in Anchises' mourning scene at *Aen.* 6.882–83 (*purpureos spargam flores*). The Cato-Marcia remarriage is also constructed as an antithesis of the parting of Aeneas and Creusa in *Aeneid* 2:

> Whereas Aeneas must continue to live to preserve the remnants of Troy, Cato must die to preserve the notion of liberty. Thus Cato's death is not something essentially negative. For an ideal does not require physical transmission from generation to generation, as the Trojan blood of Aeneas does. It demands, rather, an individual capable of bringing the ideal into tangible, living dimensions. This is the role Cato fulfills as father of the city. But, in ideological terms, the father of the city is also the husband of the city, in the sense that his example is the regenerative force that inspires others to follow in his footsteps.[113]

Before the beginning of the civil war Roman women mourn for their children's death and connect their ability to lament to freedom: *nunc . . . contundite pectora, matres, / nunc laniate comas . . . / . . . nunc flere potestas, / dum pendet fortuna ducum; cum vicerit alter, / gaudendum est* ("now . . . strike your breasts, mothers, tear your hair out . . . now that you can while the leaders' fortune sway; but once one of them wins, you will have to rejoice," *BC* 2.38–42). At *BC* 2.297ff. Cato becomes the ultimate free mourner of Rome:

> Ceu morte parentem
> natorum orbatum longum producere funus
> ad tumulos iubet ipse dolor, iuvat ignibus atris
> inseruisse manus constructoque aggere busti

> ipsum atras tenuisse faces: non ante revellar,
> exanimem quam te complectar, Roma; tuumque
> nomen, Libertas, et inanem persequar umbram. [114]
> Sic eat: inmites Romana piacula divi
> plena ferant, nullo fraudemus sanguine bellum.

>   Anguish orders a parent
> bereaved by the death of sons to prolong the cortège
> to the tomb; it soothes him to thrust his hands
> into the bleak fires and, once the pyre-mound is raised, to hold
> the bleak torch himself; likewise, I will not be hauled back before
> I embrace you, lifeless Rome! I will pursue you,
> Liberty, mourn your name, your insubstantial shade.
> Let the heartless divinities have Roman atonements in full;
> let us not cheat the war of its blood! (*BC* 2.297–305)

I have already pointed out that the description alludes to Anchises' mourning for Marcellus (*Aen.* 6.870ff.) and, more generically, brings to mind the Roman ritual in which the male next of kin lights the funeral pyre and pronounces a speech to commemorate the deceased. The ceremony is well documented and described by Polybius, who underscores the political significance of mourning in Rome:

> But the most important consequence of the ceremony is that it inspires young men to endure the extremes of suffering for the common good in the hope of winning the glory that waits upon the brave. And what I have just said is attested by the facts. Many Romans have volunteered to engage in single combat so as to decide a whole battle, and not a few have chosen certain death, some in war to save the lives of their countrymen, others in times of peace to ensure the safety of the Republic. (*Universal History* 6.54; tr. Scott-Kilvert)

Even if the *funus* described by Lucan is of a private nature, Cato's lamentation is meant as a *laudatio funebris,* which should inspire his internal audience and external readers to care about their city.[115] The political and ethical overtones of *BC* 2.297–305 are evident through the allusion at *BC* 2.300 (*inseruisse manus*) to the Republican Mucius Scaevola, described by Livy in the act of placing his right hand in the fire and letting it burn without manifesting the slightest trace of weakness: " 'Behold me,' he said, 'so that you may learn how little the body counts for those who have glory in view' and placed his right hand on the fire lit for a sacrifice" ("*En tibi,*" inquit, "*ut sentias quam vile corpus sit iis qui magnam gloriam vident,*" *dextramque accenso ad sacrificium foculo inicit,*" Liv. 2.12). Emphasizing Scaevola's indifference to pain—*cum torret quam velut alienato animo ab sensu* ("when he continued to broil it as if bereft of all senses of feelings," ibid.)—Livy shows the hero's love for the fatherland to be greater than his concern for his personal physical well-being. Similarly, Lucan shows Cato's political commitment to be greater than his concern for physical salvation when he embraces the painful and dangerous fate of the tottering Republic.[116]

Cato's mourning is thus conceptualized by Lucan to communicate the sage's humanity and political commitment but, as we will see, also to indicate his resistance to fate. Cato as a mourner resembles some of the women who in the *Aeneid* lament their destiny, and these echoes enhance what Narducci has called Cato's "titanic identity." The rise of the funeral pyre at *BC* 2.300–1—*constructoque aggere busti / ipsum atras tenuisse faces*—conjures up the image of Dido's erected pyre (*Aen.* 4.504–505: *pyra . . . / erecta ingenti taedis,* "a big pyre having been constructed with torches"). More specifically, the presence of the two verbs *iubet* and *iuvat* at *BC* 2.298 (*ad tumulos iubet ipse dolor, iuvat ignibus atris*) alludes to the moment in the *Aeneid* when Dido is eager to erase from her mind the memory and love of Aeneas: "it is pleasing to destroy all the memories of the unfaithful and the priestess so directs" (*abolere nefandi / cuncta viri monumenta iuvat monstratque sacerdos, Aen.* 4.497–98). Considering Aeneas an *impius* consort for the betrayal of his newly acquired vows, Dido seeks peace and forgetfulness, destroying the memory of her beloved (*monumenta, Aen.* 4.498). In his mourning, Cato, the "father and husband of the city" (*urbi pater . . . urbique maritus, BC* 2.388), wants to keep alive the memory of his beloved freedom and the idea of a society of fathers and sons bonded by mutual ties of love and duty. Alison Keith has shown how often in Virgil's poem the *reginae* (Dido, Juno, Amata, Cleopatra, etc.) who instigate conflict collude with the Furies (the Greek Erinyes) to resist Jupiter's will. For instance, at *Aen.* 7.307–329 Juno summons Allecto to try to thwart Jupiter's resolutions. Later in Book 7 the war, Juno's terrible handiwork, is quite symbolically announced by her helper Allecto, who sounds the signal for battle on the curved horn (*cornuque recurvo, Aen.* 7.513) while Trojans and Latins assemble to fight (*Aen.* 7.519–22).[117]

At *Aen.* 4.384–86 Dido threatens to persecute Aeneas as a Fury after her death:

> sequar atris ignibus absens
> et, cum frigida mors anima seduxerit artus,

omnibus umbra locis adero.

> Though absent, with black torches I shall follow you; and when cold death has divided my limbs from my soul, everywhere I shall be present as a shade. (*Aen.* 4.384–86)

The lines quoted above are evoked in the *Bellum Civile* when Cato mourns for Rome, presenting himself like a father who holds "black torches" (*atras faces*, *BC* 2.301) by the tomb of his dead son and pursuing the "empty shade" of freedom (*inanem persequar umbram*, *BC* 2.303). At *Aen.* 4.384–86 Dido is visualized as a Fury, and at *Aen.* 4.607–610 she invokes the avenging Dirae (*Dirae ultrices*) to enforce her curse on Aeneas. But elsewhere in the book she is also represented as a surrogate for the sacrifice to Stygian Jupiter that she pretends to be carrying on (*Aen.* 4.638).[118] Similarly, at *BC* 2.295-307 Cato is characterized as an avenger *and* a victim. Philip Hardie considers the complex representation of Dido in *Aen.* 4 one of the points of reference for Lucan's extensive sacrificial imagery in the *Bellum Civile*.[119] Even Frederick Ahl reflects on the sacrificial nature of the blood spilled in Lucan's poem and reminds us that the gladiatorial games (*munera*) originated as ritual offerings for the dead.[120]

Like Dido, Cato is both victim and avenger. Resembling Juturna (*Aen.* 12.871–81), he unreservedly condemns the gods for their deplorable strategies (*BC* 2.304–305). As compelling as Allecto's war trumpet, his voice has the power of a Phrygian bronze spurring man into battle (*Phrygii sonus increpat aeris*, *BC* 9.289). The "Phrygian bronze" evokes the image of Cleopatra represented on the shield of Aeneas in the vain attempt to resist Caesar Augustus.[121] In Virgil's ekphrasis the queen is shown summoning her troops while followed by the snakes ominously foreshadowing her defeat and suicide:

> Regina in mediis patrio vocat agmina sistro,
> necdum etiam geminos a tergo respicit anguis.[122]

> The queen in their midst cheers her ranks with native timbres nor sees yet the twin snakes threatening from the rear. (*Aen.* 8.696–97)

Phrygian cymbals and snakes are prominent in Lucan's characterization of Cato's Libyan march. Cato's voice awakens his troops to battle and reminds readers of Cleopatra's war sistrum.[123] The snakes that according to Lucan vanquished Cato's army, according to some ancient sources also brought about Cleopatra's demise.[124] After Antony's death and Actium's defeat, Cleopatra preferred suicide to the degradation Octavian had in mind for her. She did not want to be paraded as a slave in the Egyptian cities over which she had ruled, so the queen of Egypt preferred suicide to humiliation. Either by means of an asp, symbol of the Egyptian monarchy and a bold assertion of her royal power, or by means of some other poison (Plu., *Ant.* 85–86), she affirmed her independence. Cato too will prefer death to submission to Caesar and his suicide, according to several scholars, was the intended end of the *Bellum Civile*.[125]

Besides Virgil's *Aeneid*, another text that might have fired Lucan's imagination in the description of Cato's army attacked by the snakes in the desert is the *Carmen de Bello Actiaco*. In this fragmentary early imperial epic poem, featuring Octavian's campaign against Antony and Cleopatra, the anonymous author describes with a great wealth of detail the varieties of death conceived by the Egyptian queen:

> [dele]ctumqu[e loc]um quo noxia turba co[i]ret
> praeberetque suae spectacula tri[s]tia mortis.
> Qualis ad instantis acies cum tela parantur,
> signa, tubae classesque simul terrestribus armis,
> est facies ea uisa loci, cum saeua coirent
> instrumenta necis u[a]rio congesta paratu.
> Und[i]que sic illuc campo deforme co[a]ctum
> omne uagabatur leti genus, omne timoris
> [. . .]
> Aut pendente [su]is ceruicibus aspide mollem
> labitur in somnum trahitur libidine mortis.
> Percutit [ad]flatu brevis hunc sine morsibus anguis
> uolnere seu t[e]nui pars inlita parua ueneni
> ocius interem[i]t, laqueis pars cogitur artis
> in[t]ersaeptam animam pressis effundere uenis,
> i[m]mersisque f[r]eto clauserunt guttura fauces.
> [h]as inter strages solio descendit et iter.[126]

> . . . the chosen place for the crowd of criminals to gather in and offer the sad spectacles of their own death. As when against impending forces weapons are readied along with standards, military trumpets, and fleets at the same time as land troops, such did the aspect of the place seem when the savage tools of death, brought together with varied preparation, assembled. Thus gathered there on the field from all sides, every disgusting mode of death wandered, every kind of fear [. . .] or, with the asp hanging from his neck, he drifts into soft sleep and is drawn on by desire for death. A small snake

kills another by its exhalation, without biting, or a small portion smeared on a slight wound kills more swiftly; some are compelled by tight nooses to expand their blocked breath from compressed passageways, the throats of those immersed in water closed their air passages. In the midst of this carnage the queen descended from her throne among . . . (col. v.36–43 and col. vi.45–52, Courtney).

During the desert march "the sad deaths of [Cato's] men" are provoked by "tiny wounds" of snakebite (*tot tristia fata suorum / insolitasque videns parvo cum volnere mortes, BC* 9.735–36). The snakes may symbolize extreme impulses that Cato has defeated, but in their deadly accomplishments they are also considered creatures of Caesar as they "fight for Caesar and carry through the civil war" (*pro Caesare pugnant / dipsades et peragunt civilia bella cerastae, BC* 9.850–51).[127] They might be ineffective against Cato's virtue: *quod ius habuisset in ipsum [Catonem] / ulla lues?* ("What power did any plague have against *him*?" *BC* 9.887–88). But they do decimate the Republican army, neutralizing its attempt to resist autocracy. Cato's army, fighting on the sands of Libya against a bestial and lethal enemy, symbolically becomes the first victim of the Caesars' arenas.[128]

At *BC* 2.297–305 and 304–318 Lucan's depiction of Cato recalls another female character of the *Aeneid*. Cato's speech alludes to that of Euryalus' bereft mother in *Aeneid* 9. Seeing her son's truncated head, the old woman suddenly becomes aware of his tragic death and starts to complain about her tragic destiny:

> "Hunc ego te, Euryale, aspicio? Tune ille senectae
> sera meae requies potuisti linquere solam,
> crudelis? Nec te, sub tanta pericula missum,
> adfari extremum miserae data copia matri?
> Heu, terra ignota canibus data praeda Latinis
> alitibusque iaces, nec te, tua funera mater
> produxi pressive oculos aut volnera lavi,
> veste tegens, tibi quam noctes festina diesque
> urguebam et tela curas solabar anilis.
> Quo sequar? Aut quae nunc artus avolsaque membra
> et funus lacerum tellus habet? Hoc mihi de te,
> nate, refers? hoc sum terraque marique secuta?
> Figite me, si qua est pietas, in me omnia tela
> conicite, o Rutuli, me primam absumite ferro;
> aut tu, magne pater divom, miserere tuoque

> invisum hoc detrude caput sub Tartara telo,
> quando aliter nequeo crudelem abrumpere vitam."
> Hoc fletu concussi animi, maestusque per omnis
> it gemitus: torpent infractae ad proelia vires.

> "Must I see you like this, Euryalus? You, the only comfort of my age, how could you leave me alone, cruel boy? Was not your poor mother given a chance to bid you, sent into so great a danger, a last farewell? Ah, now in a strange land, carrion for Latin dogs and birds, you lie; and I, your mother, never took your body out for burial nor closed your eyes, nor washed your wounds, nor dressed you in the robe I had been weaving for you night and day, in haste, before the loom, easing an old woman's pain. But where shall I go now? Where is the earth that holds your dismembered trunk and your mangled body? This is all of yourself that you bring back to me, my son? On sea and land I followed this? Put your spear into me, if you can be moved by *pietas,* Rutulians, let fly all your javelins at me, and with your arms kill me first; or else take pity, father of the great gods, with your bolt dispatch this hateful soul to the abyss. For I cannot otherwise break off my cruel life." All hearts were shaken by her cries, and groans of mourning came from all, their strength for battle broken and benumbed. (*Aen.* 9.481–99) [129]

Cato's resemblance to a grieving mother reveals his humanity. In the *Aeneid* as in the *Bellum Civile* we have instances where there is no burial ceremony but characters who, by imagining one, mourn for their beloved. In both texts the dirges communicate a concern for those who die. Poetically they restore a sense of justice and regret for human lives while forcing the reader to reflect on the implications of *pietas*.

Invoking *pietas,* Euryalus' mother wishes to die like a Titan hit by Jupiter's bolt (*detrude . . . caput telo*) or becoming the target of enemy spears (*in me omnia tela conicite*). In her speech the juxtaposition of gods and foes has a titanic quality since it puts them on the same level and reveals their hostility, their analogous unwillingness to pay attention to a wretched creature's desire. The act of granting death to those who invoke it is, in the eyes of the woman, a gesture of mercy which the gods and the Rutulians both deny. The "great *father* of the gods" is not touched by this *mother*'s suffering. Her desire to die after her son's death as well as her demand of a human foe to inflict the blow invite comparison with Mezentius' behavior after the death of his son Lausus.[130] In both characters the loss of a beloved inspires boldness and desire to die that is echoed by Lucan in his portrayal of the sage. In fact, the old woman's last wish is repeated and surpassed by

Cato's generous prayer to become the target of all factions, to receive the wounds of the entire war in order to redeem Rome's mistakes. Cato is ready "to sacrifice his life for the fatherland" (*patriaeque impendere vitam, BC* 2.382) and "believes himself born not for himself but for the entire human race" (*nec sibi, sed toti genitum se credere mundo, BC* 2.383). He is not concerned with his pain and suffering but with the destiny of the city. He hopes (*O utinam . . . liceret, BC* 2.306) that after his *devotio* his truncated head might not be (like that of Euryalus) a sight for tears and desperation (*Aen.* 9.498–99) but rather serve for Rome's expiation and the restoration of peace:

> Sic eat: inmites Romana piacula divi
> plena ferant, nullo fraudemus sanguine bellum.
> O utinam caelique deis Erebique liceret
> hoc caput in cunctas damnatum exponere poenas!
> [. . .]
> Me geminae figant acies, me barbara telis
> Rheni turba petat, cunctis ego pervius hastis
> excipiam medius totius vulnera belli.
> Hic redimat sanguis populos, hac caede luatur
> Quidquid Romani meruerunt pendere mores.
> [. . .]
> . . . Me solum invadite ferro,
> me frustra leges et inania iura tuentem.
> Hic dabit, hic pacem iugulus finemque malorum
> gentibus Hesperiis.[131]

> So be it: let the heartless divinities have Roman
> atonements in full, let us not cheat the war of its blood!
> Oh that my head, consigned to the gods of Heaven and Hell,
> might be granted the right to make all expiations!
> [. . .]
> Let it be *me* the twin armies stab, *me* the Rhine's
> barbarous horde targets with darts; I want to stand in the path
> of each spear and intercept the wounds of the whole war.
> Let my blood redeem the nations, my death cancel
> Any debt incurred by Roman immortality.
> [. . .]
> Strike me with your steel—me
> alone—as I keep futile watch over laws and empty rights.

> My throat will bring peace and end of woes
> to Hesperia's people. (*BC* 2.304–307, 309–313, 315–318)

While the gods demand atonement, Cato wishes to keep the Romans pure and to restore peace by offering his head as a gift to those heartless divinities. The lack of hope detectable in the imperfect subjunctive of line 306 (*utinam . . . liceret*) is minimized by the more assertive jussive subjunctives (*figant/petat/redimat*, 309–12) and eventually defused by the self-reliance of the future *dabit* (317). Cato as a parent is superior to the divine creators of humankind not only because he cares about his children but also because, unlike them, he can give his life for their salvation.

In Cato's mourning Lucan's multiple allusions (to Mucius Scaevola, Scaeva, Dido, the Furies, Euryalus' mother, etc.) contribute to the character's complexity. In the *Bellum Civile* Cato is concerned about his people and rebels against the gods for their indifference. In this portrayal dissenting Virgilian voices are woven around the Republican hero to create the impression of a Stoic sage at last unwilling to conform to *fatum* and the imperialistic epic code. Cato resembles those Virgilian characters at odds with the gods' plan for the loss of a beloved one. In his disagreement and lack of success he acts like the women who resist the will of Jupiter by more or less openly manifesting their discontent. As Georgia Nugent has written:

> Whereas Aeneas, Anchises, Evander, and Latinus yield unquestioningly to the exigencies of fate, female figures such as Dido, Camilla, Amata, Juturna, and others suggest the possibility of choice and independent volition. By refusing what has been spoken (*fatum*) by the gods, scripted by their society, or chosen for them by others, the strong women of the *Aeneid* assume a tremendous narrative burden for the poem: acting as counterpoint to *pius*, passive Aeneas, they serve as signposts to the road not taken. It may seem surprising that this exploration of independent judgment should be allotted to the women of the *Aeneid*. It is less surprising, however, when we note the regularity with which the memorable female characters of the *Aeneid* die—or wish to die. While representing alternatives to the "dominant voice" of the *Aeneid*, women also indicate and play out in the text the failure of these alternatives.[132]

Since Lucan wants to differentiate Cato's *virtus* from Aeneas' willingness to obey the demands of the gods regardless of any principle of justice or personal evaluation, he never explicitly characterizes Cato as *pius*. At the very beginning of the poem, his famous formulation "the conquering cause pleased the gods, but the conquered pleased Cato" (*victrix causa deis placuit sed victa Catoni, BC* 1.128) puts Cato on the same level as the gods, but also calls attention to the fact that his project is diametrically opposed to theirs. Seneca's dictum, "let men be pleased with whatever pleases god" (*placet homini quidquid deo placuit, Ep.* 64.20), seems purposefully reelaborated by Lucan's Cato, who rejects Jupiter's plan and tries to comply with the divine mandates of his conscience.[133] As we saw, distancing himself from the gods, he declines to strike an attitude of divine indifference toward the imminent war. If the sage's tranquility ("*tranquilla . . . otia,*" *BC* 2.281–82) is like the gods' *ataraxia*, Cato rejects it. In Cato's reply to Brutus—"confident *virtus* follows the fate's lead / the crime of the gods will be that they made me guilty, too" (*sed quo fata trahunt, virtus secura sequetur. / Crimen erit superis et me fecisse nocentem, BC* 2.287–88)—virtue and fate are deceptively placed on the same path. While on the one hand the answer evokes Cleanthes' well-known line, *ducunt volentem fata, nolentem trahunt* ("the fates lead the willing man and drag the unwilling" Sen. *Ep.* 107.11), the substitution of *trahunt* for *ducunt* "suggests unwillingness on Cato's part to follow the path prescribed by destiny."[134] The gesture marks him as ideologically opposed to Aeneas and also brings him closer to the women of the *Aeneid* who are at odds with *Fatum*, in particular with the women who pursue alternative destinies through suicide or active resistance. The *Aeneid*'s hero endures hardships without condemning Jupiter (e.g., *Aen.* 5.709). Cato instead takes on the adversities but criticizes what the god has planned for the Romans. With his conduct and his willingness to be defeated, he provides an antiphrastic comment to the Fate-abiding behavior of the victorious Aeneas. While Jupiter and Aeneas dream about greatness and a future empire, Cato, enlightened by his own conscience and following a deeper religious impetus, fights for freedom. Lucan replaces the silent grieving of Hercules (*Aen.* 10.465) and of Virgil's narrator (e.g., *Aen.* 6.30–33; 6.870–71) with Cato's and the narrator's mournful commitment to fight.

Whereas Stoicism provided some Romans with the philosophical justification to passively accept the political reality of the empire, in Lucan's poem it feeds rebellion. Cato successfully illustrates a new kind of Stoic sage. With his indignation and tears he does not use the name of god to accept what he judges unfair but, rebelling against a divinity who does not have at heart the common good, fights its darlings and rejects its oracles (*BC* 9.585–86). He appoints himself as the lamb for the salvation of the Romans; he hopes that his sacrificial throat (*iugulum, BC* 2.317) may be cut to bring peace to the world. In the desert he acts like the truly synecdochic hero by facing dangers before everybody else.[135] Not fearing for his personal destiny, Cato glorifies the Republic by exposing himself to death and rejecting the imperial logic that gave importance to the material body of one particular individual, the emperor, over all others. Virgil's melancholy over the death of Marcellus foreshadowed the problem of dynastic continuity faced by the Principate during the first century CE.[136] As a true republican Cato can put his individual fate at stake and hope for an eternal Republic.

According to Narducci, Lucan's *Bellum Civile* reveals a profound crisis of the Stoic system, an implosion caused internally by its logical premises and externally accelerated by historical circumstances. The crisis would be fully manifested in Lucan's rejection of Stoic *apatheia* in the characterization of Cato. In the light of recent philosophical studies on the meaning of Stoic *apatheia*, I am more inclined to claim that Lucan's sage is not too far removed from that portrayed by Stoic philosophers who do not require the Stoic sage to be coldly detached, prescribing instead that while the sage should not "appropriate his passions at face value," he should neither be "alienated from them."[137] The sage is not the cold and indifferent creature described by Stoic adversaries but a compassionate human being able to rationally control his feelings. In this chapter I have tried to emphasize those feelings and features that show the Stoic sage in the *Bellum Civile* as an emblematic paradigm for justice and attachment to virtue while still a sympathetic creature. Moderate detachment is essential to true fellow feelings since without it "we shall be driven to squabble over indifferents in competition with those we imagine we love, and shall find one wishing the other dead. We shall not truly love them (*philein*). True love for others, on this view, requires a certain detachment from things other than our own character and *proairesis*."[138] The common man, not understanding who and what he is, can be mistaken about what is truly valuable for his nature. But the sage possessing perfect self-understanding of "what is properly his own (*oikeiôsis*)" can be a "more actively devoted citizen and father than the common man."[139]

Close textual analysis of the *Bellum Civile* shows that Cato does not reject the emotions but only the passions, the irrational and excessive movements of the soul. His state is characterized by *eupatheia*, rational joy and other good emotions like benevolence, respect, affection, cheerfulness and mirth. Cato is not depicted as being insensitive to pleasure and pain. He feels them but can overcome them, recognizing that pain is not to be feared and that pleasure is not a true good. He also places a high value on his country and on relationships. Textual analysis also shows that Cato and the narrator have several traits in common. They employ vivid representation that uses mythological allegory (*fabula*) as well as the spells of poetry (*ekplêxis*) which is not considered contrary but conducive to philosophical depth. The narrator of the *Bellum Civile* and its philosopher-hero Cato employ similar techniques and try to stir strong emotions in order to engage their audiences and move them toward a better behavior. Not only does Lucan use apostrophe (and other techniques) to help the audience to evaluate the choices and personality of Cato and other minor characters under the influence of Cato's rhetoric and behavior, his portrayal of Cato as "detached" and "concerned" when approaching the spectacle of the world can be interpreted as the most perfect example of critical spectatorship.

Conclusion: Powerful Voices

> The two wept bitterly—Priam, as he lay at Achilles' feet, weeping for Hector, and Achilles, now for his father and now for Patroclos, till the house was filled with their lamentations. (Homer, *Iliad* 24. 509–513)

> When Cato had thus spoken . . . the majority, in view of his fearlessness, nobility, and generosity, almost forget (*eklathomenoi*) their present troubles (*tôn parontôn*) . . . they begged him to use their lives, property and arms as he himself judged best; for it was better to die persuaded [*peithomenous*] by him than to save their lives by betraying such virtue [*aretên*]. (Plutarch, *Cato minor* 60)

In her book *Roman Honor*, Carlin Barton has given a remarkable psychophysical account of the way in which the Romans experienced life. She has written, "*Virtus* and the *honores* won in the crucible of the contest were shining and volatile; the refining fire of the ordeal produced a heightened sense of vividness, a brilliant, gleaming, resplendent existence."[1] This fiery existence was consequently rapidly consumed; "everything human is fragile (*fragiles*) and fleeting (*caduca*)," Cicero reminds us in his *De amicitia* (27.102). "Being was ephemeral, but nonbeing was absolute. Valor was glass and fire, but humiliation was stone and ice."[2] And humiliation began "when men came to believe that the charisma of victory no longer resided in the collective entity of the *res publica* but rather in the figure of an individual leader; communal authority and republican government were doomed and monarchy was the only reality."[3] Suddenly life was no longer a fair game; the rules and outcome of every contest were arbitrarily decided by the emperor. "Who is so crazy to desire advancement through his own and his country's dishonor, in a state where the chief privilege of its highest office is that of being the first to pay compliments to Pallas in the Senate?" Pliny the Younger demands (*Epistulae* 8.6.3). Yet many had to promote themselves in order to preserve their lives or those of the people they loved. It was hope of survival that the clemency of Julius Caesar granted the Romans, "the hope of life, which crushes even great spirits" (Tac., *Historia* 5.26.1).

"With the loss of the good contest and the rules that framed it, cold, callous, brazen shamelessness became a cure for shame."[4] Hardship makes you hard; prolonged suffering triggers insensitivity. In the *Tusculanae Disputationes* Cicero speaks of the endurance of those who have suffered and can now bear their lot more easily because they have hardened themselves against fortune (3.38.67). According to Barton, Stoic *apatheia* (and its popularity) can be explained in this context: the loss of a good fight. She quotes Seneca: "Surround yourself with philosophy, an impregnable wall (*inexpugnabilis murus*); though fortune assault it with her many engines, she cannot breach it. The spirit that abandons external things stands on unassailable ground; it vindicates itself in its fortress; every weapon hurled against it falls short" (*Ep.* 82.5).[5] For Seneca the wise man resembles a stone: "Cato does not respond to insult; he does not blush; he does not defend himself; he does not play the game; it is beneath him."[6] The logic that sustains the wise man can be interpreted as a refusal to play. For Barton withdrawal (*otium*) developed into a value in Roman culture when "it became impossible to maintain one's being by contest and when the isolation of withdrawal was less painful than the humiliation that came with the active negotiation of one's honor."[7] "The abstract thinker could have a reality without others, a being without others."[8]

Lucan, however, does not construct a wise man who refuses the game. Inspired by those Romans—love poets, gladiators, Stoics, satirists, epicists—who never stopped wanting to be warriors, he creates his Stoic sage as the perfect *miles*. Not only does Lucan's Cato fight against Caesar's tyrannical desires, mental lethargy, and the indifference of the gods; in the fight he uses the fire of his emotions and the ice of his philosophical commitment. True love for others requires a certain detachment from things. Cato's philosophical creed empowers him with such a weapon so that his love for the Republic can stay focused on what is important. Recent philosophical studies have demonstrated that intensity is compatible with freedom from excessive emotions because what the wise man pursues so energetically is seen for what it is. In the character of Cato, Lucan develops a poetic symbol of this almost impossible intertwining of reason and heart; Cato fuses fire and ice, victory and defeat, emotions and rationality. After Pharsalus' massacre Pompey's ships "carry mourning cries, grief-blows and hardship able to stir the tears even of hard Cato" (*puppes luctus planctusque ferebant / et mala vel duri lacrimas motura Catonis, BC* 9.49–50). Not only is Cato moved by tears, being "the only one free from hatred and zeal" (*uni quippe . . . studiis odiisque carenti, BC* 2.377); in turn he "can cry for the human race (*vacat . . . / humanum lugere genus, BC* 2.377–78). He is the only true mourner of the republic because he can preserve himself free from excessive emotions without becoming indifferent. He is the "true father of the fatherland" (*ecce parens verus patriae, BC* 9.604) and, like a bereaved parent who is moved by sorrow (*ceu morte parentem / natorum orbatum . . . dolor, BC* 2.297–99), he embraces the lifeless body of the dying republic (*exanimem . . . te complectar, BC* 2.302). In his mourning he criticizes the cruel gods (*inmites Romana . . . divi, BC* 2.304), quick to require atonement (*BC* 2.297–305).

Cato is not afraid to lose his life confronting the anger of Caesar or of Olympus. He is similar to Ajax, who in the tempest "fights alone, undefeated by difficulties" (*solus invictus malis / luctatur Aiax,* Sen. *Ag.* 532–33). Challenging the bolts of Jupiter, "he stands out from the deep like a sheer rock" (*ardua ut cautes, salo . . . extat, Ag.* 539–49) and "shines amid the blind sea" (*caeco mari / conlucet Aiax, Ag.* 542–43).⁹ In this light Cato shines. He is depicted by Lucan as a titan who dares to challenge *fatum*. In his disagreement with fate, lack of success, and suicide he resembles those women in the *Aeneid* who resist the will of Jupiter by manifesting their discontent. Like Juturna (*Aen.* 12.871–81) he unreservedly condemns the gods for their deplorable strategies (*BC* 2.304–305). As compelling as Allecto's war trumpet (*Aen.* 7.513), his voice has the power of a Phrygian bronze spurring man into battle (*Phrygii sonus increpat aeris, BC* 9.289). Like Dido he is a victim and an avenger; like Cleopatra on the shield of Aeneas (*Aen.* 8.696–97) he is accompanied by snakes.

Yet entering Cato's space, "the serpent and the flame" lose their scorching power and are tamed.¹⁰ In the *Bellum Civile* the snakes, a suitable symbol of the threats posed by desire to the will and morality, have shed their power as well as their deceptive beauty. They evoke Seneca's snakes (in his *Medea*) but have become ugly. Lethal for many, they can do nothing against Cato ("What power did any monster have against *him?" BC* 9.887–88).¹¹ If the wise man as legitimate avenger of real guilt has the determination of a fury, Cato has the determination without having its inhuman cruelty. The rocky strength of the Stoic sage lashed by history's blows shows "no trace of savagery":

> quemadmodum quedam non possunt igne consumi sed flamma circomfusa rigorem suum habitumque conservant, quemadmodum proiecti quidam in altum scopuli mare frangunt nec ipsi ulla saevitiae vestigia tot verberati saeculis ostentant; ita sapientis animus solidus est et id roboris collegit, ut tam tutus sit ab iniuria quam illa quae rettuli.

> as certain substances cannot be consumed by fire but, though encompassed by flame, retain their hardness and shape; as some cliffs, projecting into the deep, break the force of the sea and, though lashed for countless ages, show no traces of this savagery, just so the spirit of the wise man is solid and has gathered so much strength as to be no less safe from injury than those things which I have mentioned. (*Const.* 3.5)

The Stoic saint responds to the commotion of the Civil War but preserves his balance and his compassion. He considers *otium* a *furor* (*BC* 2.295–96); and his lack of indifference gives power to his words, warms those who listen to him (*sic fatur*. . . *excitat calorem,* BC 2.323–24), and "inflames [*incendit*] fearful spirits [*paventes*] with virtue and love of toil" (*BC* 9.402–403). His apostrophes make his internal audiences hopeful (*BC* 2.242) and "amazed" (*attoniti, BC* 9.289).

Through *enargeia* (vividness) and *phantasia* (verbal image making) even Lucan's narrator wants to make his readers *attoniti*. With his elaborate style he strives to create a narration so compelling that it will stir them to formulate vain prayers:

> cum bella legentur,
> spesque metusque simul perituraque vota movebunt,
> attonitique omnes veluti venientia fata,
> non transmissa, legent, et edhuc tibi, Magne, favebunt.

> whenever accounts of these wars are read,
> they will stir hope and fear alike and useless prayers,
> all readers will feel shocked that these are fates yet to unfold
> not known facts, and O Magnus, men will again warm to you! (*BC* 7.210–13)

Lucan's style creates "a mode of intersubjectivity" through which "it becomes impossible to distinguish between the author and the audience. The second person singular, 'you,' denotes both individuals, so that 'you' both produces and views the description."[12] The sublime produced by Lucan enables the audience to identify with the facts narrated, as Longinus recommends in his treatise. It "lift[s] up the soul of an audience so that it believes itself to have produced what it has heard (*hôs autê gennêsasa hoper êkousen*), and thus the sublime effectively transfers the recipient into the position of author (cf. 7.2)."[13] At the same time, again in agreement with Longinus, Lucan "demands that his audience be discriminating and discerning."[14] Longinus "invites his named addressee, Postumius Terentianus, to give his judgment (*sunepikrineis*) on his project (1.2)"; Lucan demands the same from his reader.[15] The emotional intersubjectivity created between narrator and audience parallels their common necessity to judge what is produced in the artistic endeavor. In order to foster a detached spectatorship and an enlightening mimesis, Lucan uses allegory, commentary, generalization, ironic tone, ugly descriptions, and apostrophes to characters. Several of these techniques were recommended by the Stoics to bar the reader from extreme involvement with the fiction and to make the aesthetic experience didactically useful. Lucan's poetry, with its involved *and* critical narrator, can be considered an attempt to forge a

Stoic fiction capable of promoting through rhetorical means the right kind of relationship between representation and audience. The narrator's mention of "hope and fear" can also be connected to Aristotle's *Poetics*, "the first full-scale theoretical appreciation of emotions in a cognitivist perspective."[16] The *Bellum Civile* is a poem that elicits emotions without debilitating the spectator's intellectual faculties. As the narrator predicts, we will be drawn (*favebunt*, *BC* 7.213) toward Pompey (Lucan's tragic hero), but we will also be able to see his mistakes.

Something more must be said about Lucan's snakes, according to some critics Cato's most formidable enemies. I would like to focus my attention on the mode of their defeat at the hands of the Psylli. Lucan's taming of the snakes may have been inspired by the central episode of Seneca's *Medea*, Medea's incantation of the snakes. At lines 670ff., Medea is described by the nurse summoning the serpents of heaven and earth:

> Vocat quascumque ferventis creat
> harena Libyae quasqua perpetua nive
> Taurus coercet frigore Arctoo rigens,
> et omne monstrum. Tracta magicis cantibus
> squamifera latebris turba desertis adest.
> Hic saeva serpens . . .
> carmine audito stupet
> [. . .]
> Mortifera carpit gramina ac serpentium
> saniem exprimit . . .
> Addit venenis verba non illis minus
> metuenda. Sonuit ecce vesano gradu
> canitque. Mundus vocibus primis tremit.

> She summons all plagues generated from the sand of burning Libya—whatever Taurus, paralyzed by Arctic cold, keeps hidden in perpetual snow—and all kinds of monster. Attracted by her magic chants, the scaly horde rushes from its deserted den.
> Here, a cruel serpent . . . hearing the song is stunned
> [. . .]
> She harvests deadly grasses and squeezes the snakes' venom . . . to her poisons she adds words not less able to stir fear than they. Listen, there is the noise of her crazed footsteps, and the sound of her tune. The world trembles as she begins to sing. (*Med.* 681–86, 688, 731–32, 737–39)

In Lucan's Libyan episode, after the snakes and the elements have massacred the majority of Cato's army, the survivors are saved by the Psylli, a tribe immune to snake poison and committed to alleviate the snakebites suffered by the Roman army through magical formulas. According to Plutarch, Cato, making ready to traverse the desert, brought along the people called Psylli because they were able to heal the bites of serpents and to charm them (*Cato Minor* 56). The magical cures given by the Psylli to the wounded soldiers are described by Lucan in terms similar to those employed by Seneca to describe Medea's incantation (*Med.* 681ff.). Yet Lucan's description is much longer and includes details which suggest the power of poetry:

> Nec solum gens illa sua contenta salute
> excubat hospitibus, contraque nocentia monstra
> Psyllus adest populis. Qui tunc Romana secutus
> signa, simul iussit statui tentoria ductor,
> primum, quas valli spatium comprendit, harenas
> expurgat cantu verbisque fugantibus angues.
> [. . .]
>   At si quis peste diurna
> fata trahit, tunc sunt magicae miracula gentis
> Psyllorumque ingens et rapti pugna veneni.
> Nam primum tacta dasignat membra saliva,
> quae cohibet virus retinetque in volnere pestem;
> plurima tunc volvit spumanti carmina lingua
> murmure continuo, nec dat suspiria cursus
> volneris, aut minimum patiuntur fata tacere.
> Saepe quidem pestis nigris inserta medullis
> excantata fugit; sed, si quod tardius audit
> virus et elicitum iussumque exire repugnat,
> tum super incumbens pallentia volnera lambit
> ore venena trahens et siccat dentibus artus,
> extractamque potens gelido de corpore mortem
> expuit.

Nor does their own safety wholly preoccupy this tribe;
they look out for strangers, too; in his fight against fatal pests,
the Psyllan befriends humanity. Now he escorts Roman
standards: whenever Cato ordered the tents pitched,
straightway the Psyllan cleanses the sands enclosed by the rampart's

> length, driving adders away with spells and incantations.
> [. . .]
> But, if a snake by day
> represents a mortal threat, then miracles of the magical tribe
> take place, the great battle of the Psyllan pitted against the venom
> absorbed:
> first, with his saliva he marks off the limb afflicted,
> confining the poison and limiting damage to just the wound;
> then, many and many a charm he spins, mouth foaming,
> whispering without pause, for the speed of the wound allows for
> no breath, nor can the fates tolerate a moment's silence.
> Often the toxin squirted into the blackening marrow
> flees by incantations alone; but should the poison listen reluctantly,
> should it resist despite coaxing and commands to leave,
> then, leaning over the pallid wounds, the Psyllan sucks them
> and, squeezing the poison out through his lips and teeth, drains the limbs;
> using his powers to extract death from icy flesh,
> he spits it out. (*BC* 9.909–14, 922–36)

The Psylli have Medea's enchanting power, but they use it for opposite goals. They are a people concerned with the well being of their neighbors; their magic is directed toward saving other peoples' lives. They could enjoy a safe and happy existence conducted in isolation and indifference. Instead, they look out for strangers and make the desert safe for the Romans. With "songs and words" they drive the terrible reptiles away from the soldiers' path (*expurgat cantu verbisque fugantibus angues,* 914) and the poison away from their bodies (922–35). When someone is bitten by the snakes, the battle between the Psyllan and the poison begins. It is portrayed as a formidable struggle (*ingens . . . pugna,* 924) between silence and words. The Psylli "spin multiple songs in a continuous whispering" (*plurima tunc volvit . . . carmina, / murmure continuo,* 927–28) because "the course of the wound does not allow one to catch his breath" (*nec dat suspiria / cursus volneris,* 928–29). The metaliterary significance of the passage is emphasized by Lucan's frequent punning on the words *verba, cantus,* and *fata* (etymology: *fari,* to speak, to predict or to sing). Fate "cannot tolerate any silence" (*minimum patiuntur fata tacere,* 929). At one level the line is describing the destiny of the troop: if the Psylli stop their incantations, the soldiers will die. Poignantly, though, these incantations also symbolize the power of poetry.[17] As long as poetry releases its spells, there is a hope of keeping in check the lies repeated or silently hidden in celebrative epics, a hope to counterbalance the triumphal version of history created by the winners. This image can be linked to the figure of the apostrophizing narrator, who can counteract the poisonous perversity of imperial lies only through poetry. The malady, the snake's poison or laudatory propaganda, "insinuated in the marrow" (*inserta medullis*, 931), flees (*fugit*, 931) only when it is "sung out" (*excantata*, 931) and extirpated with the force of the incantatory song. The point is repeated with graphic vigor in the personification of the *virus* that "is slow to hear" (*tardius audit*, 931) and must be "extracted by mouth" (*ore venena trahens*, 934). According to Katherine Eldred, "the poet's interest lies in having his snakes recreate their own etymologies in the deaths they inflict" so that, for instance, an *haemorrhois* (*aimorreô* = to lose blood) turns his victim Tullus "into a stream of blood" (*BC* 9.806–14).[18] If the snakes "are speech-acts" and demonstrate "the danger inherent in speech,"[19] Cato, possessing the right kind of mind, shows himself to be immune to the tricks of linguistic manipulation; and the Psylli become the symbol of the benefits inherent in speech.

The vivid representation of the strength of poetry is the ultimate message given in Book 9. The "snakes fight for Caesar," and their poison decimates the soldiers; but they can be neutralized by poetry. We could say of Lucan's representation of poetry what Giancarlo Mazzoli has said about Seneca's poetry:

> *Carmen* is the formula of the magician and of the lawgiver, the oracle of the prophet, the verse of the poet, the prescription of the physician: it is the word that acts and constructs.[20]

In the *Bellum Civile* the narrator as well as Cato knows that words can act. Not only do they help readers to become critically aware; they also inspire them to search for the truth and to positively influence their environment. Cato and the narrator must ignore (past or future) defeat because they cherish the competition that may give freedom a chance. They both must persuade their audiences about the intrinsic value of this struggle.

In Plato's *Republic* Socrates condemns poetry because under the influence of tragic performances even the best people, instead of reaching awareness of the fragility of pleasures available through the body, sympathize with the suffering character. Even the best men desire to pity and express sorrow over the character's loss, "hunger[ing] for the satisfaction of weeping and wailing" (*R.* 606a4–5). Grief is fostered by poetry and, according to Socrates, impedes deliberation (604b9–c3). Yet at the end of the *Republic* he seems to readmit fiction in recounting the myth of Er. Ramona Naddaff argues that "poetic myth, despite and perhaps even because of its limitations, satisfies the philosopher's need to keep his desire for absolute philosophical knowledge alive and urgent, even if ultimately impossible and illusory. Poetry increases and encourages philosophy's desire to desire; it 'strengthens and fosters' the desire to know and to represent that which is."[21] Lucan's poetical tale unveils the fragility of language, but it also empowers it. Lucan's poetry unravels human weakness while also making the most of it. It produces fear but also hope (*spesque metusque, BC* 7.210–13).

In the *Prometheus Bound* we are told that before giving men the gift of fire, Prometheus prevented them from foreseeing the moment of death by implanting in them hope (*Pr.* 248–50). Thus hope marks the human condition and occupies a unique place in the human world suspended between the ignorance of the beasts and the omniscience of the gods.[22] Given the harsh reality of the *Works and Days*, in a world heading toward involution and annihilation Hesiod "can hope" (*eolpa*, 273) that the practice of justice will defuse such decay.[23] He hopes that the Muses with their imitative power to make things present, visible, and audible will help mankind in the construction of harmony. If kings cannot be ethically or socially transformed, the poet will be able to transform other polarities with the honey of his *logos*.[24] Even in the desolated landscape of despair sketched by Lucan in the *Bellum Civile*, hope is foreshadowed as a possible reaction. If the gods have left everywhere signs of future collapse depriving men of hope (*BC* 1.522–25), the poet writes "to allow the fearful to hope" (*liceat sperare timenti, BC* 2.15).

While the Republic is crumbling and even the gods seem to have abandoned their posts, while moral standards can be reconfigured by a new victor, one gets the impression reading this poem that it is crucial to stand for what is right even if it is destined to be overcome. Lucan's resistance to political and spiritual enslavement becomes ideologically important: *phantasia* makes visible what even the artist himself has not yet seen. Lucan's construction of "his own civil war" (*Pharsalia nostra, BC* 9.985) is significant because its ethical message contradicts that of the *status quo*. If this poem realistically includes the enemy's vocabulary with its competing and devastating ethical discourse, the narrator is never in doubt about which discourse is morally superior.

Appendix:
Stoic Inhumanity? A Philosophical Appraisal of Practical Pursuits and the Passions

> And what is compassion but a fellow-feeling for another's misery, which prompts us to help him if we can? And this emotion is obedient to reason, when compassion is shown without violating right, as when the poor are relieved, or the penitent forgiven. Cicero, who knew how to use language, did not hesitate to call this a virtue, which the Stoics are not ashamed to reckon among the vices, although, as the book of the eminent Stoic, Epictetus, quoting the opinions of Zeno and Chrysippus, the founders of the school, has taught us, they admit that passions of this kind invade the soul of the wise man, whom they would have to be free from all vice. Whence it follows that these very passions are not judged by them to be vices, since they assail the wise man without forcing him to act against reason and virtue; and that, therefore, the opinion of the Peripatetics or Platonists and of the Stoics is one and the same. (Augustine, *The City of God*, 9.5)

I have indicated that a lack of care and indifference to the environment are accusations launched by several critics against Lucan's Cato during his Libyan march. Historically, more than once Stoic agents have been described as callous because "[they] do not care enough about things that ordinary people care about, so that their detachment from ordinary human concerns makes them repellent rather than admirable."[1] Recently, the topic of Stoic inhumanity has been addressed by Martha Nussbaum, who asserts that the doctrine of indifferents requires an inhuman attitude from the side of the Stoics, who deny intrinsic worth to external things.[2] In Terence Irwin's words, "Nussbaum seems to assume that if we regard something as indifferent, even a preferred indifferent, then we cannot suppose that it warrants us in facing danger or taking risks to secure it."[3]

It is true that since preferred indifferents do not constitute or promote happiness, they are not considered goods by the Stoics. Yet Irwin rectifies that proposition by explaining that the same relationship that regulates "ends" (*telê/fines*) and "objectives" (*prokeimena/proposita*) in Aristotelian thought regulates the relationship between preferred indifferents and the good in Stoic philosophy.[4] In Irwin's view the claim that nothing except virtue is worthwhile for the Stoics does not imply that nothing except virtue is unworthy since rational concerns for ends are natural and do not exclude rational concern for objectives. The point seems clearly stated in Seneca's *De brevitate vitae* 22.4:

> Indeed, which of our sages—I mean, of our school, for whom the good is virtue—will deny that these things we call indifferents also have some value in themselves [*aliquid in se pretii*] and that some are preferable to others?[5]

In another passage (*Ep.* 92.11 = LS 641), Seneca explains that one should seek indifferents "in good judgment" and in accordance with nature:

> "Won't you seek them?" of course I'll seek them. Not because they are good, but because they are in accordance with nature, and because they will be taken by me with good judgment. "Then what will be good in them?" Only this, that they are chosen well. (Sen. *Ep.* 92)[6]

Thus the Stoic account of happiness allows and requires legitimate concern for other things besides the good, and this is why the Stoics describe happiness as doing everything possible to obtain preferred indifferents (Galen, *De placitis Hippocratis et Platonis* 5.6.10 = LS 64I) or as doing everything that lies in us to obtain the preferred indifferents (Plut. *De communibus notitiis adversus Stoicos* 1071a = LS 64c).[7]

The Stoics' "attempt to do everything possible in order to obtain the preferred indifferents" implies "within the limits imposed by virtue." Even in Aristotle's account virtuous people do what is most reasonable in the light of the information they have at the time of the choice; once they have done the best they could, "they are without regrets" (*E.N.* 9.4.1166a29). As long as they never fail to do what should have done, even in failure, they are always successful, just like the Stoic sage. Under these circumstances—if the sage fails to obtain the preferred indifferent—he can express disappointment for the failure. Without becoming desperate or unresponsive, he can regret the failure since he recognizes that the acquisition of the preferred good would have been the preferable course of action for himself and others. The sage's regrets are not even in conflict with his belief in providence.[8] He understands that what seems an unfortunate event happens for a universal reason. Yet this belief in the ultimate causes does not keep him from regretting an unfortunate circumstance nor from helping those involved in it. Determinism and deterministic inabilities do not put the agent at the mercy of external circumstances and do not free him from deciding and acting on the basis of his priorities and feelings.[9]

Finally, the idea according to which external goods are indifferent but not unimportant is also consistent with Stoic acceptance of suicide.[10] The Stoics are aware that external conditions can deteriorate to the point where suicide can become justifiable:

> A sage will make his own reasonable departure from life, for the sake of his country or his friends, or if he falls into excessively severe pain or suffers mutilation or contracts an incurable disease. (D.L. 7.130)

In short, the notion that external goods are indifferent is not sufficient ground to maintain unresponsive behavior in the face of human suffering. Tad Brennan insightfully describes the Sage's difficult yet unavoidable "navigation in a sea of indifferents" in the following terms:

> The key thought to keep in mind is that the Stoic theory of indifferents entails the view that the Sage must navigate through a world of indifferent affairs, and select among objects and actions that are per se indifferent; yet it makes all the difference in the world which objects and actions the Sage selects. The Sage must never have the false belief that any of the things around him are good; yet he must be endlessly, exquisitely sensitive to the respective values of the things around him. And he must act from that sensitivity; his virtue actually consists in his knowledge of indifferents and his expert handling of them.[11]

The above statement should be kept in mind when we deal with the conundrum faced by Cato, who (urged by Brutus) ponders choosing or rejecting war. According to Stoic thinking, even evil actions and their consequences can be understood to fit intelligibly into a context determined by divine nature. The Stoic sage is thus justified to believe that the will of the gods with its intrinsic justice permeates all matters. Yet he might have doubts about how exactly theodicy is at work in the world, about how the will of the supreme mind becomes manifest in human events. Considering Cato's specific situation, could it be possible that the will of an ultimately benevolent divinity manifests itself in the sage's attempt to defend freedom? Or is Cato irrationally resisting Caesar's superior might and illogically getting involved in the wrong cause (e.g., a war fought by the majority for personal advancement)?[12] If war is judged by Cato as an evil, why should he get involved in it? The problem of how the individual comports himself within this schema is complex. Should the sage allow himself to be moved and "propelled" by the rhythm of the Universe (in Cato's case, passively tolerating the evil of Caesarism), or should he seek ways to actively insinuate himself and his conduct in that rhythm (rejecting Caesarism)? At *Prov.* 5.5 Seneca remembers the valiant Demetrius saying, "Immortal gods, I have this one complaint to make against you: that you did not earlier make known your will to me." In this statement there is the idea that we struggle against the will of the gods because we do not understand that it is the will of the gods.

Not only do recent critics justify the sage's practical involvement in the world; they also reevaluate the sage's propensity to feel. Inwood explains that the sage lacks passions (extreme, irrational participation) because he lacks their constitutive false beliefs; yet the sage retains some other elements of passion.[13] For instance, reacting momentarily to a certain appearance without giving assent to it, he "goes pale" when facing a danger (Aulus Gellius, *Noctes Atticae* 19.1.17 = Epictetus fr. 9) and can jump when hearing a loud noise without really believing that there is a threat (Seneca, *Ira* 2.3.1). Affective reactions (like turning red or shivering) are not passions since they are often beyond the voluntary control of the agent. Passions can develop only with an assent that in the case of the sage is not present. Posidonius, suffering from gout, can groan (Cic. *Tusc.* 2.61); a sage, being a human being, may turn red in front of a crowd or tremble or feel distress before pronouncing a speech (*Ep.* 11.1–3).[14] In sum, wisdom does not obliterate the sage's humanity and feelings:

> I do not remove the sage from among human beings, nor do I exclude feelings of distress [*dolores*] from him as from some rock that is incapable of any awareness [*rupe nullum sensum admittente*] [. . .]. The sage will tremble and be distressed and grow pale; for these are all modes of awareness belonging to the body [*corporis sensus*]. (Sen. *Ep.* 71.27, 29)[15]

The sage can retain the sorts of appearances that in other people could signify being under the sway of a passion but without being under the full sway of passions.[16] He can "rationally assent to just those impulses which would in the ordinary men be partial passions, doing so with an understanding of the hierarchical structure of permissible and instrumental goods."[17]

Thus, as Inwood explains, affective responses occur even in the soul of a perfected human being:

> [W]e turn pale or tremble at a sudden shock; the most we can do is to reject this involuntary response and to refuse to give our assent to the proposition

that something frightening occurred. We can stop ourselves from having an impulse to avoidance or to contraction of the soul. But still, the involuntary response has occurred and it is at the very least peculiar to deny that it is a case of fear. For it is very similar to fear in its effects on us and is caused by the same stimulus. Yet the Stoics are committed to denying that it is fear, or even a cause for fear, not least because they concealed that even a sage would have these affective reactions.[18]

This acknowledgment of involuntary psychic reactions could seriously compromise the Stoics' monistic approach to psychology, but they defuse the potential risks of this admission by denying that "preliminary passions" are passions at all. In other words, according to them there is not a direct link between, for instance, passion on the one hand and tears or groaning on the other. If I groan it does not automatically mean that I am prey to passion since I can eliminate passions by eliminating assent, but I cannot eliminate the appearances triggering my suggestion. Then it is possible to conclude, as Augustine did in *De civitate Dei* 9.4 (see the epigraph to this appendix), that if the sage can be moved by suggestive appearances, he has emotions. The Stoics might call them "quasi-emotions" or "pre-emotions" due to their lack of assent, but ordinary people would call them emotions. Before Augustine, even Plutarch (*Virt. Mor.* 449ab) suspected that such reactions were simply emotions, but that the Stoic commitment to a monistic psychology forced them to qualify them as a different phenomenon.[19]

Suggestive appearances are cognitively important since they do provide all human beings with useful information about the world in which they live. For instance, the appearance that it is bad to be impoverished is not completely misleading since poverty, according to the Stoics, is a nonpreferred indifferent and since it causes hardship, which in normal circumstances should be avoided. Even the sage can profitably use the information contained in suggestive appearances. In Irwin's words, the Stoics "have every reason to agree with the claim that passions reveal important aspects of value to us, and they retain this cognitive function of the passions in the sage, insofar as they retain the appearances that make us vividly aware of preferred and non-preferred indifferents."[20] Seneca points out that freedom from passions does not leave the sage unconcerned about the losses that provoke passions in other people, and he reminds us that the perfected man values affective ties with other human beings: "the sage is self-sufficient, not in the sense that he wants to be without a friend, but in the sense that he can do without him" (*Ep.* 9.2–5). If he loses a friend, he will have the appearance of some important loss without assenting to the idea that something truly terrible has happened since, after all, the loss does not compromise his moral perfection.

Sages can feel sympathy because they understand the pain. They also recognize that they are liable to suffer significant nonpreferred indifferents and have vivid and insistent appearances of other people's sufferings, which gives them a good reason for doing something to relieve them.[21] According to this view, the sage is not simply engaged in the improvement of the self; he also "honors (*sebesthai*) his parents, is actively devoted to the welfare of his children (*philostorgian*), and—as his situation permits—takes active part in politics (D.L. 7.117–118, 120–21; Cic. *Fin.* 3.62–68 [LS 57F])."[22] Epictetus might have understood exactly this point when he linked higher integrity to sociability and invited his students to do "what is appropriate," that is "not to be unmoved (*apathes*)" but to dutifully maintain "natural and acquired relationships" with sons, brothers, fathers, and citizens (*Diss.* 3.2.2–4).[23]

In the end the Stoic sage has rational concerns about externals, reacts to them, and does not reject the information available to him through his emotional responses to reality. If we follow Irwin's reasoning and consider the matter from an Aristotelian point of view, it is not really plausible to accuse the Stoics of being inhuman because of their belief in a sage who does not let appearances interfere with his deeper commitment to virtue. Even Aristotle believed that the virtuous person has been trained to comprehend that the loss of external goods does not threaten the most important aspects of one's happiness (*E.N.* 1101a-5).[24] For the philosopher human emotions are natural and beneficial as long as reason imposes on them a certain boundary. We all can be angry, Aristotle says, but the hard part is "to be angry with the right person, to the right extent, at the right time, for the right moment, and in the right manner" (*E.N.* 1106a26). In this context the expression "moderate anger" might be misleading since, if the situation calls for it, Aristotle would suggest, extreme anger might be the individual's correct response. When he advises us to form passions always in harmony with reason (*E.N.* 1102b15 and 1102b25), he is really telling us nothing different from what the Stoics suggest when they require us to get rid of passions and to replace them with good affective states (*eupatheia*). Virtuous people's reactions and their consequences for the doctrine of good affective states are described by the Stoics in their doctrine of preferred indifferents.[25]

Among modern philosophers Irwin is not alone in tracing a more humane portrait of the Stoic sage.[26] Recently Richard Sorabji, pursuing a line of inquiry similar to Irwin's, has reconsidered the role of indifferents in Stoic doctrine. Sorabji reminds us that the Stoic Diogenes of Babylon and his successor Antipater (c.152 to 129 BCE), in redefining the early Stoic approach to the goal of life, thought that it is our duty to do everything in our power to secure the naturally preferred objectives such as health, prosperity, the family, and mankind.[27] Diogenes' attitude of indifference does not exclude the most energetic pursuit of what is preferred. The idea of indifference and reservation is not used by him to advocate lack of interest or uninvolvement in practical matters; rather it is employed to protect the subject from disappointment in case of failure. Marble representations of the Stoics, according to Paul Zanker, support the idea of their strong involvement in certain activities.[28] Early Stoic thinkers were portrayed as intensely absorbed in their thinking and in their teaching. "Intensity," Sorabji explains, "is entirely compatible with freedom from emotions, just so long as the indifferent things, so energetically pursued, are seen for what they are."[29]

At this point it should be clear that, with regard to indifferents and the emotions, the Stoics should not be considered so far removed from other schools of thought as modern and ancient commentators sometimes argue.[30] Among the early Stoics, Chrysippus (c. 280–207 BCE) believed in the importance of "good affections" (*eupatheia*); later Stoics as well as different schools of thought were ready to accept a psychological model which gave to the movements of the non-rational parts of the soul even a greater role.[31] For instance, if we are to believe Cicero's testimony, Panaetius (c.185–109 BCE), the most important representative of the Middle Stoa and a shaping personality of the Roman philosophical environment, perceived that it is important to be free from all perturbations of the mind (Cic. *Off.* 1.67; 1.69); yet at the same time he thought that it is necessary to make the impulses obedient to reason (Cic. *Off.* 1.67).[32] The latter statement suggests that Panaetius was not advocating the eradication of the emotions but their moderation.[33] Panaetius, returning to Plato and Aristotle as ultimate sources of Stoic doctrine, discussed the morally imperfect human being without rejecting the Stoic ideal of the wise man.[34] Posidonius (born in c.135 BCE) believed that an "enquiry about good and evil and about ends and virtues starts from the correct enquiry about emotions" (Galen, *De plac.* 5.469 = Posidonius, fr. 30 EK). He accepted *pathos* as "excessive impulse" but disagreed with Chrysippus about the causes of emotions as errors in judgment (Galen, *De plac.* 5.429–30 = frag. 152 and 157 EK). He believed that reason cannot be subject to excess and endorsed Plato's theory according to which reason is the highest faculty controlling the irrational parts of the soul (*R.* 4.434e–444e). Like Posidonius, the Academic philosopher Antiochus of Ascalon (130–68 BCE) "insisted that the wise person will not experience emotion. His position was unusual, however, in that he regarded this Stoic doctrine as fully compatible with early Academic and Peripatetic views. Indeed, he claimed that those supposedly conflicting positions were in fact the same position, distinguished only by trivial differences in terminology."[35] Sounding very much like a Stoic, the Epicurean Philodemus, who had among his students Horace and Virgil, wrote of a "commendable anger which arises from insight into the nature of things and from avoiding false opinion."[36]

Middle Stoicism, represented by Posidonius and Paenetius, brought about a pooling of philosophical orientations among which were Platonism and Aristotelianism. This syncretism had a great impact on Antiochus, a philosopher extremely influential in the history of late Republican Rome. In constructing his Academic skepticism Cicero accepted several Stoic positions. His work confirms a typical trait in the Roman attitude toward philosophy: its basic incapability or unwillingness to keep different philosophical traditions rigidly distinct.[37] It is also significant that the first-century BCE compendium of Stoic, Peripatetic, and Platonic philosophy, put together by the Stoic philosopher Arius Didymus, adviser of Augustus, reflects the idea that a good philosophical education involves training in different philosophical traditions.[38] Lucan's depiction of a Stoic sage moderately affected by passions seems particularly plausible in the context of Roman philosophical eclecticism.

Notes

Introduction

1. Pugliatti 1985: 203.
2. The three most frequent objects of apostrophe in the *Bellum Civile* are Caesar, Pompey, and Rome; sometimes mythological characters are addressed (e.g., the Cyclops at 6.388ff.), often the gods (1.37), sometimes places (Corcyra, 2.623) or abstract ideas (e.g., *Concordia mundi* at 3.190, *labor vatum* at 9.980). I do not think that the difference in object addressed drastically changes the nature of the apostrophe; what instead needs to be considered is Lucan's attitude toward his addressee, his desire to expose this addressee as a positive or negative example.
3. Corbett 1971: 460. See also, Horace, *A.P.* 99ff.; Cic. *De or.* 189ff.; Quint. 4.1.63, etc.
4. About "aesthetic positionality," see Fitzgerald 1995: 1–16.
5. Bartsch 1997; Leigh 1997.
6. Block 1982; Conte 1974a.
7. E.g., Pöschl 1950; Otis 1963; Heinze 1965; Johnson 1976; Rosati 1979; Block 1982; Conte 1986; Hardie 1989; Fowler 1997b; Wofford 1992; Quint 1993; Greene 1999. Good overview on the topic in Fowler 1997a.
8. Bal 1985:100–101. On focalization: De Jong 1987; De Jong 2001; Fowler 1990 and 1997a.
9. Basic contributions about narratology and focalization are in Bal 1985; Genette 1980; Pugliatti 1985; a good bibliography on the topic is in Conte 1986:154 n10 and Fowler 1990 pointing out the difficulty of 'surgically' separating coexisting points of view. About the *Aeneid*, see La Penna 1967 and Perutelli 1979.
10. O'Hara 1997: 254; on Virgilian ambiguity, see O'Hara 1997: 249–51 with bibliography.
11. Block 1982:16. On apostrophe in Homer, Nietzsch 1860; Parry 1972; Yamagata 1989: 91–103; Grillo 1988: 9–67. On the relationship between singer and audience in an oral performance, see Plato, *Ion* 535c–d and Havelock 1963: 167.
12. Heinze 1993; Otis 1964; Block 1982. Virgil's narrator intervenes more often than the Homeric narrator; if we accept Zyroff's calculations, in the *Aeneid* we find 69 apostrophes which come directly from the narrator, while in the *Iliad* and in the *Odyssey* there are, respectively, only 38 and 16; see Zyroff 1971: 500–501.
13. Conte 1986; Wofford 1992.
14. The first consideration belongs to Quint 1993: 9, the second to Feeney 1991: 137.
15. In his *Argonautica*, Apollonius manages to create a narrator and characters who move in opposite directions, creating a gap that enhances irony and the fictional level of

the narration; Fusillo poignantly observes that while in Homer the ideological domain of the narrator was absolute and tyrannical, but never open and explicit, in Apollonius it is possible to clearly perceive the narrator's dominating traits, his intellectualism, humanistic rationalism, pessimism, anti-heroic stance, etc. On Apollonius' innovations, see esp. DeForest 1994: 37–46; Fusillo 1985; Paduano 1972; more specifically on the narrator in the Greek and Roman epic tradition, see my article "The Narrator's Voice: A Narratological Reappraisal of Apostrophe in Virgil's *Aeneid*," in D'Alessandro Behr 2005.

16. Reporting Hampel's calculations: Barratt 1979 commenting on lines 527–31; Gagliardi 1975: xi: "Il dato più rilevante offerto dalla lettura del libro è la frequente intromissione del poeta . . ." ("The most relevant fact offered by the reading of the book is the frequent intromission of the poet . . ."). The practice of direct address is so diffuse in the *Bellum Civile* that some translators, completely missing its importance and significance, prefer to substitute the more normal third person in place of the second person. E.g., Duff's translation in Duff 1928 and his comment at viii. On apostrophe in epic and scholarly work on the subject as well as charts on the frequency of apostrophe in the most important Greek and Roman epic works, see Zyroff 1971: 4–8 and 500–36; for apostrophe in Lucan, Basore 1904.

17. Especially Seitz 1965: 204ff., and Narducci 1979: 117.

18. I have analyzed only a few significant ones, but they are omnipresent in the text: e.g., *BC* 8.550–60 to Ptolemy; *BC* 8.674–78 to Septimius; *BC* 8.781–85 to Cordus afraid of burying Pompey; *BC* 8.823–34 to Egypt; *BC* 8.835–50 to Rome. Even the many addresses to the gods or to Fortune are close to invectives: e.g., *BC* 1.510 to the gods generous to give supreme command to men but greedy in allowing them to maintain it; *BC* 5.198–208 to Apollo and his followers; *BC* 8.542–47 against the Egyptians who decided to murder Pompey; *BC* 8.600–604 and 8.795ff. to Fortuna. Sometimes the pessimism of the apostrophes and the portrayal of the gods emerging from them are hard to integrate in the Stoic texture of the work—they cannot square with an orthodox belief in the Providence—but their tone and content certainly emphasize Lucan's concern with political freedom and ethical awareness.

19. Schiesaro 1997: 109–110.

20. Schiesaro 1994: 129.

21. Clay in Schiesaro, Mitsis, and Clay, eds., 1994: 29 and 32–33: "The deeper truth—that the practice of justice may not always be rewarded and that even hard work may come to naught—are reserved not for Perses, but for Hesiod's ideal listener, ὁ πανάριστος, 'the man who can think for himself and sees how things will turn out in the end.'"

22. Konstan 1994: 14 summarizing Mitsis' points.

23. Cf. Conte 1974a: 82: "L' anima vera di quest' arte [Lucan's], l' impulso che la sorregge e la motiva internamente, è da ricercarsi nel suo tentativo di rovesciare per mezzo dell' artificiosità le fondamentali forme retoriche. Lo sforzo è tutto concentrato al sovvertimento interno di quelle forme, che operi un netto passaggio dalla retorica ad una pararetorica grazie ad un più profondo slancio comunicativo[. . .]. Nella nuova arte che rigetta i principi della classicità augustea, l'idea riesce ad esprimersi solo distorcendo la forma concreta, l' apparenza immediata" ("The true aim of Lucan's art, the impulse which supports it and motivates it internally, must be sought in its attempt to turn upside down fundamental rhetorical forms though artificial means. There is here a concentrated struggle to subvert within all main rhe-

torical forms, a clear switch from rhetoric to pararethoric because of a more profound desire to communicate [. . .]. In this new art which rejects the principles of Augustan classicism, an idea can be expressed only distorting its specific form, its immediate appearance"). On the "rhetoricized mentality," see Rudich 1997: 1–13.

24. The idea that words are not a neutral entity but have been shaped by the intentions of their previous users is developed in Bakhtin 1981.

25. As a general introduction on satirical techniques, see Brilli 1973; Wehrle 1992; Citroni 1980: 311–43. Particularly insightful on the relationship between satirist and the object of satire is Seidel 1979 suggesting that it is not difference but erosion or annihilation of difference between the poles of satire (the satirist and the satirized) that requires acts of ritual boundary-policing; in other words, satirists try to exorcize that erosion of differences using a kind of ritual invective.

26. Agreeing with Narducci 2002 rather than with scholars like Johnson 1987; Masters 1992; or Sklenár 2003, I am reluctant to accept Lucan as a fully blown skeptic or deconstructionist. I argue that deconstruction in the *Bellum Civile* is always employed in a search for meaning.

27. Roller 2001; Hershkowitz 1998; Bartsch 1997.

28. Schiesaro 1997: 109–110; his ideas are further developed in Schiesaro 2003: 234ff.

29. Halliwell 2002: 263–77; for the Roman cultural and philosophical environment of the first century CE, see Morford 2002: 162–239. L. Annaeus Cornutus, one of Lucan's teachers and a protégé of the Annaei, shows interests in several fields of study besides philosophy. Only his *Epidrome*, or *Summary of the Traditions of Greek Theology* survives together with few fragments of his commentary on Virgil. Aulus Gellius tells us that Cornutus was interested in epic (Aulus Gellius, *N.A.* 9.10.5 and 2.6.1). On Cornutus as a philosopher and on Stoic *allegoresis*, see Most 1989: 2014–59 (with extensive bibliography); Nock 1931: 995–1005; Lapidge 1989: 1379–1429. On Cornutus' grammatical studies, Zetzel 1981: 38–41; Geymonat 1984, 1: 897–98; Timpanaro 1986: 71–75. On Lucan's education, besides the classical Due 1970: 201–224, see more recently Morford 2002: 189–208 and Lapidge 1989.

30. Stoicism also shapes the *Bellum Civile*'s ethics, yet it is necessary to remark that the general Stoic tone adopted by Lucan does not oblige him to consistency to Stoic doctrines. If assessing the philosophical 'orthodoxy' of a philosopher can be a rather difficult task, assessing that of a poet would be also rather useless. Important methodological remarks on 'philosophical orthodoxy' are in Inwood 1993: 150–53.

31. Nussbaum 1993.

32. Leigh 1997; Bartsch 1997; Hershkowitz 1998.

33. My evaluation of Lucan's Cato is a development in line with an older critical tendency sketched by Ahl 1976 and Marti 1945b.

34. Zeller 1980, ch.7b3, 10b–c, 12c. The connections between Lucan's *Bellum Civile* and the didactic genres (especially Virgil's *Georgics* and Lucretius' *De Rerum Natura*) have been elucidated by Paratore 1943: 40–69.

35. Evidence for Posidonius' views is presented by Galen in his polemical work *Precepts of Hippocrates and Plato*, for *loci* and problems, see Appendix D in Graver 2002 as well as Cooper 1998: 71–111.

36. Sorabji 2000: 186; Zanker 1995.

37. Panaetius' views on the subject can be found mainly in Aulus Gellius 12.5 (fr. 3 Van Straaten) and Cicero, *De finibus* 4.23; cf. Graver 2002: xxxiv who also mentions our inability to understand with what argument Panaetius could reconcile Stoic ideas with those of the Old Academy; at xxxiii, she concludes: "the point of importance is that the human capacity to feel strongly toward what we see as good or bad for ourselves remains a natural capacity, in Stoicism as in other ancient systems. It is not in having feelings that we go astray, but in our judgments of value." See also Alesse 1994.

38. Inwood 1985.

39. Rorty 1998: 251.

40. See the appendix to this volume.

41. Narducci 2002: 398.

42. Cf. Von Albrecht 1999: 239. According to Stoic postulates, "nothing can ever prevent us from constantly willing to do what is right, even though the resultant action may fail to produce the effects intended; these effects are external to ourselves and do not or should not affect that permanent disposition of the soul in which our blessedness, security and freedom are to be found" (Brunt 1973: 11). In Lucan's poem, however, there is an unresolved tension between the narrator's knowledge of the self-sufficiency of virtue—which theoretically needs nothing in order to realize itself—and his disappointment at the material failure of virtue. On the Stoic background of the *Bellum Civile*, see Due 1970; Gagliardi 1968; George 1986: 362–89; George 1988: 331–41; Lapidge 1979; Le Bonniec 1970; Malcovati 1940: 56ff.; Schotes 1969; Syndikus 1958: 82–84; Viansino 1974.

43. For the sage's titanism, see *BC* 9.569–71; Seneca *Ep.* 98.4; *Prov.* 4.12; La Penna 1979 citing some of the Greek sources; for the sheer importance of action, see *BC* 9.593–97.

44. Even the Stoics do not seem to have resolved with satisfaction the problem of external goods if political freedom is one of them. In their ethical theory they discussed wealth, health, or freedom as "preferred indifferents," objects which nature has set us to pursue (and therefore is reasonable to pursue), but which are not necessary to our flourishing and happiness. Yet by praising Cato's renunciation of his life for political freedom, they admitted that the presence (or lack) of an external such as freedom matters greatly.

45. About the philosopher re-entering the cave, Gill 1996: 301–307; Irwin 1977. For the belief that altruism constitutes the deepest kind of self-realization, and that anyone can come to understand this truth, see Engberg-Pedersen 1984: 327–29 and Gill 1998b: 303–28.

46. Pucci 2002: 34 underscores a similar function for the narrator's response to the death of Hector (*Iliad* 22.270ff.): "For at this point Hector realizes that he has been abandoned by his gods, when he faces 'evil death' in an absolute theological void, at this point the poet himself comes to his assistance and communicates to him an awareness of the immortality of his glorious gesture. Though sometimes it is a divinity that grants glory to the hero, here divinity has abandoned him; accordingly, the poet intervenes not to provide Hector with glory itself but with the awareness that his gesture will acquire immortal glory through the song of the poets."

47. Rudich 1997: 185.

48. I am modifying the words of Kristeva 1982: 18 who writes: "the aesthetic task—a descent into the foundations of symbolic construct—amounts to retracing the fragile limits of the speaking being."
49. Bartsch 1997: 148.

Chapter One

1. On this topic see D'Alessandro Behr 2005. Of course the fragmentary state of Naevius' *Bellum Poenicum* and Ennius' *Annales* does not always allow critics to follow the exact development and history of the genre. Nevertheless, the available evidence suggests that Ennius was absorbed in experimental practices. About it, see Briggs 1981; Bulloch 1985; Cartledge and Gruen 1997; Reggiani 1979 and Grilli 1965, esp. 9–90. On the legitimacy of the category of epyllion, see Jackson 1913. *Contra* Allen 1940: 1ff. Recently, Merriam 2001.
2. Barchiesi and Conte 1989: 136; same idea in Knauer 1999: 110–111 and Goldberg 1995: 83–110.
3. Segal 1999: 44. On the importance of the present in Callimachus see Bing 1988; on the relationship between past and present in Apollonius, Fusillo 1985.
4. For the text of the *Aeneid* I have used the edition by Paratore 1990. Here and elsewhere in the book, translations of the *Aeneid* are mine unless indicated.
5. Beye 1993: 230.
6. Heinze 1993: 361–70 was the first to analyze Virgil in terms of portrayal of psychological attitudes manifested in speeches and to create the term "*subjectivität*"; on Heinze's seminal work, see Perutelli 1972 and 1973 and more recently Hardie 1999a.
7. Cf. Segal 1999: 45: "The questioning voice is unexpected, untraditional. There is no precedent in Homer. Homer's gods, of course, have frequent head-on collisions, but Homer's omniscient bardic voice never questions the world order in this way. The closest parallels are the hard demands of justice and meaning by the choruses of Greek tragedy." Yet the prominence of the narrating "I" is perceivable in Hellenistic literature, especially in Apollonius and Challimachus. See DeForest 1994; Beye 1999; Briggs 1981; Faedo 1970; Fusillo 1985; Hunter 2001.
8. Otis 1964. Otis' observations were inspired by Heinze 1993 (orig. published in German 1965). According to Heinze, Virgil's style, in the *Aeneid*, would encourage emotional identification with points of view other than those of the narrator. Otis' ideas have become widely accepted, e.g. Quinn 1968.
9. Rosati 1979: 539–62.
10. Paduano 1972:103–4, commenting on *Arg.* 3.818.
11. About Apollonius as a mediator between the *Aeneid* and tragic models, see Hardie 1997: 323.
12. Conte 1986: 97–100 and 141–54.
13. Apollonius (like Callimachus) did whatever he could to push the person of the narrator into the frame of the narrative itself. About this phenomenon and in general on Apollonius' innovations, see Bing 1988; De Forest 1994; Paduano 1985: 33–46; Paduano 1986:5–60.

14. Discrepancies in the story (e.g., death of Palinurus told by the narrator, *Aen.* 5.835–71; death of Palinurus told by Palinurus himself, *Aen.* 6.346–62; removal of golden bough retold by Sybil, *Aen.* 6.136–48, and by narrator, *Aen.* 6.196–211) confirm this point; at *Aen.* 5. 867–71, the action is focalized through Aeneas who thinks that Palinurus is dead and the narrator does not intervene to let us know what really happened.

15. Conte 1986: 154 with extensive bibliography. The notion of "point of view," is still useful when applied to the text with the right definition. Conte's definition of "point of view" is: "the semantic position that every character—every active subject—occupies in the text, the structure taken by things as they appear in the text."

16. In his discussion Conte does not consider enough Homer's characterization of Patroclus.

17. Block 1982: 22. About 'vatic empathy' see also Grandsen 1984:112–14.

18. Conte 1986: 169.

19. Conte 1986: 171–72; emphasis in the original.

20. Martindale 1993: 35ff. and esp. 42.

21. Wofford 1992:169–76. She explains convincingly that the idyllic tone is a well-planned "ideological strategy by which apparent solutions to irresolvable claims can be presented convincingly by the poetry" (Wofford 1992: 450 n26).

22. *Dum* with the future marks the transition.

23. Williams 1983: 206.

24. Hardie 1997: 321.

25. Williams 1983: 92.

26. The principal function of the *rediture* is to shift the attention of the reader towards what will make the fall of Pallas acceptable. Often the corpses of soldiers, through idyllic tone and their insertion in the natural world, are transformed by Virgil into objects of aesthetic contemplation (e.g. *Aen.* 1.422–36, 6.703–9, 7.30–36, 8.31–67, 11.67–71). See Wofford 1992: 169ff.; Guy-Bray 2002: 72 commenting on Euryalus' corpse compared to a flower cut by the plough: "The loss of a single flower is hardly tragic, especially if the flower and Euryalus are what military analysts call acceptable losses. Presenting Euryalus's death and the others like it as both inevitable and necessary is part of an attempt to present ideology (here, the belief in the establishment and maintenance of the Roman empire as an absolute good) as natural." The phenomenon is analyzed by Johnson 1976: 59ff. who notes how the beauty of many descriptions of death distracts our attention from the suffering of the victims. For Johnson, however, Virgil's pathos and lyrical emphasis are ultimately disturbing, not appeasing.

27. Murnaghan 1999: 204.

28. Ibid. (quoting Bowra).

29. Loraux 1986: 42–50.

30. See my comments above on *dum* and *fortunati*.

31. Fantham 1999: 225. About the importance of lamentation in the history of Greek Epic, Nagy 1979; Alexiou 1974; Holst-Warhaft 1992; Loraux 2002. Foley 2001 explores how during the Peloponnesian war tragedy presented a form of public lamentation that may have obliquely compensated an audience deprived of the full pleasures of expressing grief. Women historically played the role of mourners not only physically lamenting the dead but also expressing views about death and glory that might have been at odds with

mainstream public ideology. In tragedy such dissention is conveniently put into female mouths and, at the end of the century, it is also limited. For the transformation of funeral and elegy into a form of political propaganda in the *Aeneid*, see Guy-Bray 2002: 79: on Aeneas' gesture to honor Lausus' body with Dido's robes he says "Aeneas is clearly a man who can use anything: the destruction of his native city, love tokens from a woman who killed herself because of him. Ultimately the most important thing both Aeneas and Virgil use—the former for military reasons, the latter to advance the plot and to create the moments of pathos in which he excelled—is the recurring trope of the beautiful man who dies young."

32. Greene 1999: 192.
33. Ibid.: 197.
34. Barchiesi 1984: 47 where he also notes that this kind of demonstrative occurs in the *Aeneid* only in direct speech between characters.
35. The theme of the conquered that asks for *venia* is recurrent in Augustan official propaganda, *Res Gestae* 3.1: *victorque omnibus veniam petentibus civibus peperci;* Vell. 2.86.2: *Victoria fuit clementissima.* On Caesar's *clementia*, see Weinstock 1971: 233–43; Alföldi 1985: 173ff. On Augustus' *clementia* after Actium, see Syme 1939: 314; Southern 1998: 100–114; and Galinsky 1996: 84–85; 371–74.
36. Barchiesi 1984: 49–52.
37. Barchiesi 1984: 39ff. analyzes some forms of implicit comment: overlapping of different epic models, "*relais* intertestuali," "montaggio degli eventi" (construction of the events) and, as I have pointed out, the empathic rendering of the characters (Barchiesi 1984: 48ff.).
38. Ibid.: 86. The idea of Civil war in Latium was first developed by Pöschl 1977: 39ff.
39. According to Barchiesi 1984: 88 the implicit contradictions that pervade the text foster an ambiguity that "becomes the mirror of an insoluble ideological conflict: not the passive recording of a triumphant ideology rather the representation of a blocked dialectic, a dialectic of immobility."
40. Putnam 1995: 76.
41. The "artistic work" at *Aen.* 6.14ff. is Daedalus' craft on the doors of Cumae's temple; about it, see Paschalis 1986: 33–43; Fitzgerald 1984: 53 and Pöschl 1975: 119–23. In my reading "the artistic work" is also Virgil's *Aeneid.*
42. Sympathetic readings of Daedalus are in Otis 1964: 284–85 and Segal 1965b: 642–45; a more ironic view of how the suppression of details also obliterates guilt is in Fitzgerald 1984: 51–66, in Putnam 1995b: 73–99 and in Leach 1988: 356–59. No matter how we read the passage, in it "the narrator has arbitrarily taken over for the artist in order to make emptiness an index of emotional content" (Leach 1999: 119). Wofford 1992: 199 suggests that we find in apostrophe "a fundamental congruence between the sacrificial basis of Virgil's poetic power [the narrator fictionally setting himself in a position which resembles that of the victims] and the politics of the foundation and conquest that the poem narrates."
43. The abrupt end of the *Aeneid* has been the object of critical discussion since the Renaissance. For instance, the humanist Maffeo Vegio (1407–1458) indirectly admits the moral ambiguity of Virgil's ending by adding to it a thirteenth book (known as the

supplementum) which picks up where Virgil left off. Besides adding Aeneas' marriage with Lavinia, the foundation of a city and Aeneas' apotheosis, Vegio includes the funeral for Turnus. For Vegio's work, see Cox Brinton 2002; for an overview of the discussion on Virgil's ending see Kallendorf 1999; Putnam 1999: 210–30; and Horsfall 1995a.

44. Since it obliterates guilt, the suppression of lamentation can also be interpreted in the opposite direction. Since Hercules in this passage is a divine actor with Jupiter in Olympus, we are reminded that his legendary labors and afflictions were in the end rewarded with immortality. As a symbol of rewarded suffering Hercules accepts Pallas' suffering because he has embraced Jupiter's vision of the future (*fatum*): life is short and it is the task of virtue to prolong memory on earth (*Aen.* 10.467–68). Confident on account of his own reward, he optimistically knows that somehow, sooner or later, good things issue even from pain and labor.

45. Barchiesi 1984: 16–30 and Barchiesi 1999: 326–29, where both episodes are discussed.

46. He strikes us as similar to Apollonius' narrator preoccupied in Book 4 with his retelling of Medea's tragic cases. Cf. A.R. 4.1–5: "Now you yourself, goddess Muse, daughter of Zeus, tell me of the labor and wiles of the Colchian maiden for, inward with speechless fright my mind wavers as I ponder whether I should call it the lovesick grief of blind passion or a panic flight, through which she left the Colchian people."

47. Wofford 1992: 202.

48. See Spence 1999: 83 and 95 (quoted).

49. The simile was already employed by Apollonius of Rhodes at A.R. 4.1452–56.

50. Spence 1999: 93. Fowler 1990: 42–63 suggests how sometimes in the *Aeneid* it is hard to understand whose point of view is being described and endorsed.

51. On the negative characterization of women in the *Aeneid*, see Keith 2000: 65–101.

52. Suzuki 1989:103–122.

53. Heinze 1993: 234. This is what happens, for example, with Catullus' Ariadne (poem 64) or the lament of Carme in the *Ciris*.

54. Gale 2003: 338 and 341. Furthermore, she observes that "the speech of Anchises that fires Aeneas with love of the future is also the speech in which artistic endeavor is rejected in favor of Rome's true destiny of conquest and government" (p. 341).

55. Goldberg 1995: 147.

56. Laird 1999: 197.

57. Ibid.: 13 with appropriate bibliography on ethnographical studies.

Chapter Two

1. Well characterized in Henderson 1987: 141–42: "Caesar will be the signifier which projects into the totality of the discourse of the Empire the assurance that all discourse will orbit around the imperial signifier, that meaningfulness will radiate from *Caesar* at its center, that *Caesar* will serve for the World as the master-sign dispensing legitimacy, propriety, identity, the right to exist, to 'own' a name, the World-of-the-Father to Roman culture, that is to human culture. . . ."

2. "The ordinary acceptations of words in their relation to things was changed as men thought fit. Reckless audacity came to be regarded as courageous loyalty to party, prudent hesitation as a specious cowardice, moderation as a cloak for unmanly weakness, and to be clever in everything was to do naught in anything." Th. 3.82.4 (trans. C.F. Smith 1953–59). For the relevance of the Thucydidean passage to the language of paradox employed by Lucan, see Martindale 1976: 48.

3. Sklenár 1998: 215; on political and language *stasis* see also O'Gorman 2000, esp. 14–22; Roller 2001: 45; Lebek 1976: 233; Barton 1993: 157 and n65.

4. Roller 2001: 18–126.

5. Ibid.: 59–62 and 39–40. Laelius' assertions bear a striking resemblance to the imperial "oath of loyalty" administered at the beginning of an emperor's reign. Whether the rhetoric of these oaths emerged from the Civil War is not clear; yet Roller presents it as consistent with and already at work in the alienating language of the Caesarians. Caesar's antagonist, Pompey, is less interested in the redefinition of Roman vocabulary because he represents the senatorial side and can more legitimately and logically claim that drastic measures must be taken against those who are threatening the constitution. Roller shows that in historical reality Pompey, more than Caesar, was actively involved, through his propaganda, in the manipulation of Roman communal vocabulary. On civil war and victory in the Republic and at the beginning of the empire, see Gagé 1933; Weinstock 1957: 224–26; and Fears 1981: 736–826.

6. Cf. Seitz 1965: 204–32.

7. Long 1996a: 264–85. See also my chapter 3.

8. Long 1996b: 86 quoting Alexander of Aphrodisias. Cf. "Only the wise man is a dialectician" (SVF 2:124).

9. Rist 1969: 136 "All potential knowledge is presented to the mind after the sense organs have performed their particular acts of sensation. This presentation *(phantasia)* is defined by the Stoics as an experience that arises in the soul, and is explained further by Zeno as an impression." Rist provides us with Cicero's *Acad. Post.* 1.40–2 (SVF 1.55, 60, 61) and *Acad. Pr.* 2.145, in which we have Zeno's exposition of the process of acquiring knowledge, but also with some rebuttals by Zeno's antagonists (e.g., Zeno used to say that "recognition is assent to a recognizable presentation, that is, that it is achieved both by the wise and the foolish, and that is the criterion of truth. Arcesilaus objected that, if this assent can occur in both the wise and the foolish, in the wise being knowledge and in the foolish opinion, then 'knowledge' and 'opinion' must be two different names of one single thing [Sext. Emp. *M.* 7.152–53]." (Rist 1969: 140 and esp.138ff.) See more recently on Stoic epistemology and with updated bibliography on the question of the Academics' skepticism on Stoic criteria of truth, Hankinson 2003, esp. 72–77. Despite all their problems, Hankinson is right to point out that the Stoics were committed to truth and believed that we can make ourselves into better cognizers.

10. Pohlenz 1938: 173–210. The thesis and evidence for it are discussed also in Annas 1980: 84–104 and Kidd 1989: 137–50.

11. Watson 1966: 70.

12. Conte 1974: 85: "la meta dell' opera anticlassica di Lucano è l' analisi della realtà, cioè non un immagine della realtà ma una serie, quasi un cumulo di contributi diversi per quell' immagine. Sembra che sottesa a quest' arte ci sia sempre la paura che la realtà rap-

presentata nelle sue forme semplici sia poco significativa" ("The goal of Lucan's anticlassical work is the analysis of reality or better not one image of reality but a series of images, practically a mound of different propositions for that image. There seems to be implicit in this approach the fear that reality simply represented is not significant enough." Important observations about the "fundamentally dichotomic nature" of an autocratic Augustan regime that continues to present a Republican façade are in Rudich 1993: 247ff. and 1997: 1–16, esp. 6: "As for *virtus*, the concept had been gradually disintegrating [. . .] the original meaning of *virtus* had been an irrevocable commitment to the service of the community, *civitas*, and now this presented irreconcilable choices for those concerned. The state and the law had now become incarnated in the person of the emperor, who thus demanded civic service from his subjects as unconditionally as did the classical *res publica* in the times of their ancestors." On Stoic dissidence, see Brunt 1973: 7–39.

13. See Morford 1967: 8–9; Schönberger 1961: 187–94; Saylor 1990: 291–300; Leigh 1997: 259ff.; Hershkowitz 1998: 212–214.

14. Ahl 1976: 119; cf. his extensive bibliography on the topic; see also Bayet 1951; McGuire 1990: 41–42; Rutz 1960: 466–68; Thompson and Bruère 1970: 164–67; Henderson 1987: 139; Saylor 1990.

15. *o terque quaterque beati, / quis ante ora patrum Troiae sub moenibus altis / contigit oppetere*, "three and four times blessed those who died under the high walls of Troy under their father's eyes," *Aen.*1.94–96.

16. In the *Aeneid* even Priam underlines the cruelty and wickedness of Pyrrhus, who obliged him to witness the death of his son Polites: *"at tibi pro scelere"* exclamat, *"pro talibus ausis / di, si qua est caelo pietas, quae talia curet, / persolvant grates dignas et praemia reddant / debita, qui nati coram me cernere letum / fecisti et patrios foedasti funere voltus,* "For what you have done, for what you've dared," he said, / "if there is care in heaven for atrocity, / may the gods render fitting thanks, reward you / as you deserve. You forced me to look on / at the destruction of my son: defiled / a father's eyes with death" (*Aen.* 2.535–39, tr. Fitzgerald).

17. Cf. Liv. 22.14.3–4 where all Saguntines are condemned to death by Hannibal.

18. Cf. Liv. 21.13: even though Hannibal's terms of peace are "more necessary than equitable" (*pacem . . . necessariam quam equam,* 21.13.4), Alorco tries to convince the Saguntines to accept them and to have their life spared (*corpora vestra coniugum ac liberorum vestrorum servat inviolate, si . . . ,* "your persons, with those of your wives and children, he preserves inviolate if . . . ," 21.13.7). At *BC* 4.507–8 Vulteius warns his companions against the enemies' attempt to come to terms with them: *temptare parabunt / foederibus turpique volent corrumpere vita,* "they will try to tempt us with terms of peace, they will want to corrupt us with the offer of a worthless life."

19. On death as a spectacle, see Leigh 1997: 243–64.

20. Rosenmeyer 1989: 37–62; Solimano 1991; for the theatricality of Pompey's behavior in Lucan's poem, see especially Syndikus 1958.

21. For Seneca's text I have used that of R. M. Gummere in the Loeb Classical library or a slightly modified version of it.

22. Leigh 1997: 263: "He turns his death into a spectacle and himself into a ludicrous *prima donna* who finds her only satisfaction under the spotlight." Leigh also connects Vulteius' attitude and the vocabulary employed by Lucan in this episode with those of

Seneca's *Medea*, especially at 976–77: *non in occulto tibi est / perdenda virtus; approba populo manum,* "Virtue should not go lost in hiding; my handywork will be admired by the people."

23. "Soltanto quelli toccati dall'imminenza del fato possono riconoscere quanto è dolce morire!" Badalí 1996.

24. Thomas 1988: 261–75.

25. Esposito 2001: 47.

26. Rist 1978: 239.

27. Esposito 2001: 55.

28. Rist 1978: 248; Barton 2001: 123–30.

29. Leigh 1997, esp. in chapter 5, illustrates the relationship between *exemplum* and *spectaculum* and inserts it in the wider frame of the Roman educational system. For a recent discussion of *exemplum* in Livy, see Chaplin 2000.

30. Cf. *Aen.* 9.184–85: *dine hunc ardorem mentibus addunt, / Euryale, an sua cuique deus fit dira cupido?* ("Do the gods cause this ardor in our minds, Euryalus. Or does each man's fierce desire become a god to him?"). Nisus describes his daring desire to help Aeneas, resulting in his solo surprise attack to the Rutilians, with the word *cupido*.

31. Polarization between reason and madness is for instance already used by Cicero (*Parad.* 4.1.27) to condemn the enemies of the Roman state; see Gill 1997b: 232–34.

32. Yet there are several instances in the *Bellum Civile* when the word *furor* seems to be qualified as a positive attribute (cf. chap. 4). This is in keeping with the poem's linguistic ambiguity and the similarity in behavior between positive and negative characters. Cf. the description of the instability of meaning in the *Bellum Civile* and the characterization of "Cato *furens*" in Hershkowitz 1998: 231–46. While she argues for a slippage of *pietas* into *furor*, I will be arguing for the opposite.

33. Fitzgerald's translation of *Aen.* 2.316–17 renders well the consolatory force of a glorious death in the epic world: "So fury drove me, and it came to me that meeting death was beautiful in arms."

34. Anchises, Creusa, and Ascanius are mentioned right after this at *Aen.* 2.596–98.

35. Illuminating on this point is Esposito 2001: 55–63.

36. Leigh 1997: 240–42.

37. Esposito 2001: 59; Cavajoni 1979: 252.

38. Esposito 2001: 62; Ahl 1976: 120: "Thus Vulteius, who is not fighting for the cause of liberty, can become an example to those who think they are fighting for the cause of liberty but who do not understand, as Vulteius does, that death is a means of gaining freedom" (contra Berhold 1977). Indirectly the presence of the narrator in the final comment is identified also by Hershkowitz 1998: 212, who notices that while, perversely, the word *virtus* describes the mass suicide of the soldiers, in the narrator's apostrophe at *BC* 4.580–81 it has a conventional connotation.

39. Marti 1975: 88; Quint 1992: 147–51; Bartsch 1997: 140–41; Leigh 1997: 304–306.

40. Quint 1992: 151.

41. Especially *Ep.* 70 and 77; see Griffin 1986.

42. Williams 1978: 179. Statius will explore these issues in the suicide of Maeon. On suicide, see McGuire 1990: 21–46.

43. On similarities and differences between Vulteius and Scaeva, see Esposito 2001: 42ff. Negative judgments on Scaeva's *virtus* are given by Rutz 1960: 474; Deratani 1970, esp.145; Metger 1957: 176; Conte 1974b: 257–62; Ahl 1976: 118; Marti 1966: 254. Emphasizing Scaeva's inhuman and divine features is Hardie 1993: 68–69. The best and most sophisticated treatment is in Leigh 1997: 158–90.

44. After the Romans threw out their monarchy in 509 BCE, the Etruscan king Lars Porsenna attacked Rome and might have succeeded in taking the city if not for Horatius Cocles ("Horatius the one-eyed"). The Romans had fled their farms and gathered inside the city walls. They felt protected by the Servian walls and the Tiber River. The only vulnerable spot was the wooden Sublician bridge over the Tiber. Horatius Cocles guarded the bridge when the enemy's army appeared. Most of the Roman soldiers panicked and retreated, but Horatius stopped them as they ran across the bridge and urged them not to desert. He persuaded them that their only hope was to demolish the wooden bridge with axes or fire while he himself would stand alone and delay the enemy's crossing as far as he was able. For Liv. 2.9–13 as relevant source, see Marti 1966: 238ff. and Lucifora 1991: 253–57. On Virgil's influence on the Scaeva episode, see Conte 1974b.

45. On Scaeva as a wall, cf. Leigh 1997: 185–90; Marti 1966: 247; Saylor 1978.

46. Mezentius is like a boar (*Aen.* 10.707ff.) and like a lion (*Aen.* 10.723ff.). We should remember that at the beginning of the *Bellum Civile*, Caesar is described as an angered lion careless of wounds (*BC* 1.205–207 . . . 210–12: *sicut squalentibus arvis / aestiferae Libyes viso leo communis hoste / subsedit dubius, totam dum colligit iram . . . / si lancea Mauri / haereat aut latum subeant venabula pectus, / per ferrum tanti securus volneris exit*, "Just so in torrid Libya's barren fields the lion, on seeing his enemy at hand, crouches in hesitation till he has concentrated all his anger . . . if a lance hurled by a Moor, or hunting spears pierce and stick in his broad chest; ignoring such a terrible wound he rushes onward, driving the weapon deeper." The comparison to a lion had already been applied by Virgil to Mezentius and Turnus; see Schiesaro 2003: 124–26. On Mezentius' *aristeia* see Glenn 1971a; Glenn 1971 and 1972; Burke 1974; Nethercut 1975; Sullivan 1969; Thome 1979; and Gotoff 1984.

47. According to Leigh 1997: 181, the behavior and voice of Scaeva only produce in his men excitement and a passive desire to watch (*movit tantum vox illa furorem / quantum non primo succendunt classica cantu*, "His voice excited such fury as never was kindled by bugle's first brassy blare," *BC* 6.165–66). The effect of Scaeva's words on his men is reminiscent of the effect of Cato's spurning of Brutus (*excitat in nimios belli civilis amores*, "he roused the young man's choler to passion for civil war," *BC* 2.325) and of his army before the desert march (*BC* 9.292–93: *sic voce Catonis / inculcata viris iusti patientia Martis*, "Thus, Cato with his voice drummed into his men courage to face a just war"). Cato's discourse provokes in his audiences not a passive stare but a genuine desire to fight.

48. La Penna 1979–80: 23–24 quotes all the evidence that brings the Senecan *sapiens* to the level of god, making the relationship between the two almost antagonistic. The equality between god and wise man, according to the Italian scholar, is supported by the Old Stoa, esp. SVF 3.245 to 254 with Chrysippus' words, "in virtue Zeus does not rise above Dion" ("per la virtù Zeus non supera Dione").

49. Virgil's dependence on the *Aithiopis* is very likely; for such an interpretation, see Fraenkel 1932: 242ff.

50. Aeneas says about Lausus, *fallit te incautum pietas tua* ("your piety tricked you, imprudent," *Aen.* 10.812). Mezentius himself, attacked by Aeneas, confesses to have been made vulnerable by his son's death (*Aen.* 10.878–79).

51. Mezentius' appeal to the piety of the enemy can be compared to Euryalus' mother's plea to her enemies (*Aen.* 9.493–94): *Figite me, si qua est pietas* ("kill me if there is any piety in you"). Killing someone can be a generous gesture.

52. Gotoff 1984: 202.

53. Nugent 1999: 258–60, without acknowledging the Stoic pattern that frames her interpretation. Cf. Gotoff 1984 and recently Mazzocchini 2000.

54. Nugent 1999: 259; Gotoff 1984 believes that in the end Mezentius does not gain an awareness of his responsibilities toward the world and society but only the understanding that responsibility to his son interferes with heroic invulnerability. I am not convinced by this determination, and I tend to agree with Nugent's conclusions.

55. It is the same gesture employed by Caesar in front of the dead Pompey (*BC* 9.1035ff.); see my comments below.

56. Paratore 1990, *ad loc.*; Putnam 1981: 145ff.

57. Compare this phenomenon with the bewilderment which Ovid's *Metamorphoses* produce in the reader. Ovid's extreme exploitation of epic's structural freedom and techniques (*mise en abîme*, narrators, flashbacks, etc.) neutralizes the audience's ability to judge the action. The Ovidian reader—unable to keep track of the plot, lost in the subtales—forgets the "big picture" and focuses unreflectively on individual characters; see Schiesaro 2003: 250.

58. Conte 1974b: 77.

59. On the nature of the grotesque I have found Harpham 1982 particularly helpful.

60. Conte 1974b: 78

61. Usener 1967: 198.

62. In the same way Scaeva is characterized at the beginning of his *aristeia*: *pronus ad omne nefas et qui nesciret, in armis / quam magnam virtus crimen civilibus esset* (*BC* 6.147–8), during the civil war *virtus* is a great crime!

63. For instance, it is used in Lucan at *BC* 3.39, 5.760, 8.749, 9.739 and only in the last example does the idea of perception/feeling seem to be predominant.

64. Interpretations of the speech are offered by Ahl 1976: 192–97 and Masters 1992: 78–90. In the finest reading of the episode Leigh 1997: 51–68 argues that Caesar's contention (in his account of Ilerda, at *BC* 1.74–75) that the fraternization is a Pompeian betrayal of their camp becomes in Lucan's rendition Petreius' wrong interpretation of the truce: "the Caesarian account enters Lucan only from the perspective of the general Petreius, who infers from what he hears and sees that he has been betrayed, but whose perceptions are entirely in conflict with those of the narrator" (51).

65. Leigh 1997: 65–66: in Lucan's mind, Augustus did not restore freedom but took it away (*BC* 1.670 *cum domino pax ista venit*).

66. Leigh 1997: 57–62 demonstrates that Lucan's Caesar (like Nero and Domitian in subsequent times) sees himself as an absolute ruler with the right to punish or spare opponent Republican citizens. Leigh also gathers relevant evidence to contextualize *clementia* with the theory of absolutism. He connects Petreius' speech to Seneca's *Ben.* 1.1.2–4, 1.5.7, and 1.8.5; Seneca's *De clementia* is also relevant for an evaluation of *BC* 4.337ff.

since in his disquisition Seneca realistically accepts and praises Nero's absolute power but tries to neutralize it by convincing the emperor to embrace clemency. Underscoring Nero's earthly omnipotence, Seneca flatters him into believing that being a god on earth (*Clem.* 1.1.2; 3.17.8), he should behave like a benevolent one. I believe that Afranius (at *BC* 4.344–52) is ironically flattering Caesar and using Seneca's strategy to convince him to let his men go.

67. Von Albrecht 1970: 260–301.

68. Leigh 1997: 48. cf. *BC* 7.212–13: *omnes veluti venientia fata, / non transmissa.* I will discuss this statement more extensively in chapter 3.

69. In this apostrophe the emphasis given to the war trumpets (*classica*, *BC* 4.186) might be a direct allusion to Caesar's reflection in his commentaries on men's desire to fight (esp. at 3.92, which I have quoted above).

70.

> Man's first attachment is to the things in accordance with nature. But as soon as he acquires understanding [*intelligentia*] or rather, perhaps the capacity to form concepts [*notio*], i.e. what the Stoics call *ennoia,* and sees the order [*ordo*] and as it were harmony [*concordia*] of acts, and he concludes by rational argument [*cognitione et ratione colligit*] that man's end, that highest something which is praiseworthy and desirable for its own sake—the good, lies in this [i.e. in this order and harmony]; this [good], since it consists in what the Stoics call *homologia* and we may call conformity [i.e., with the order and harmony mentioned]—since in this resides that good to which everything must be referred, noble acts and the noble itself, which alone is counted among things good.

Quoted by Engberg-Pedersen 1986: 156–57; see also Striker 1983: 153–71 and Morford 2002: 54–55, who stresses that in his definition of *oikeiôsis* Cicero develops that of Chrysippus, Diogenes of Babylon, and Antipater of Tyre; White 1995 underlines that the Stoics' view has interesting affiliations with Aristotle's ethical doctrine since it focuses on the importance of realizing that we are rational creatures and as such must live in a certain way to preserve and develop our true selves (White 1995: 320). A similar view prevails in *Off.* 3: when discussing cases of conflict between what is good and what is expedient, Cicero, despising corrupted political leaders who act according to personal interests (e.g., Marius, Pompey, and Caesar, *Off.* 3.1–3 and 3.79–85), affirms that the good must prevail over the expedient since to act otherwise is contrary to nature and destroys the social fabric of a nation and even humanity itself (*Off.* 3.20–28). Leigh 1997: 72 notes that the theme of *concordia* is important for Lucan's Book 4 as a whole; Moretti 1984: 46–47 observes that Lucan's *concordia discors* (*BC* 1.98–100) derives from the Hymn of Cleanthes (SVF 1.537 lines 14–15); Lapidge 1979: 365–67 links Lucan's language of "cosmic harmony" to Chrysippus.

71. The notion of *oikeiôsis* as "a process of taking something to oneself, or accepting or appropriating it or making it one's own" (the definition is in Pembroke 1971: 115–16) will be central to understanding Cato's decision to participate in the civil war. On Stoic *oikeiôsis*, see also Kerferd 1972 and Long 1996b: 172–77

72. Casali 1999: 235.
73. Hershkowitz 1998: 222; Rosner-Siegel 1983; Newmyer 1983; Ahl 1976: 198–200, defining Caesar as "energy incarnate"; Johnson 1987: 74–75.
74. E.g., Hershkowitz 1998: 246: "Cato's extreme behaviour resembles Caesar"; according to Malamud 1995: 179, Lucan's attraction toward the leader would be revealed at *BC* 9.984 when the narrator, addressing his poetical enterprise and Caesar, calls his work *Pharsalia nostra*.
75. The threats of Caesar's clemency are already disclosed by Cic. *Att.* 9.16.2; 10.4.8; 8.9a.2: *metuo ne omnis haec clementia ad Cinneam illam crudelitatem conligatur* (" I fear that all this clemency is gathered for a Cinna-like massacre." Good observations about Cicero's description of Caesar's *clementia* are in Roller 2001: 184–85:

> For even as Cicero observes the effectiveness of Caesar's *clementia* in gaining good will, he nevertheless describes it as "treacherous" (*insidiosa*, literally "full of traps/ambushes," *Att.* 8.16.2), where the negative connotations of the adjective overwhelm the generally positive connotation of the noun. Moreover, since the noun *insidiosa* often occurs in military contexts, referring to soldiers lying in ambush, and since military matters are among the subjects of this letter, it seems likely that *insidiosa* here could be felt as carrying its military associations in particular. If so, Cicero too suggests that Caesar's clemency is symbolic violence: but in this characterization it is axiologically identical to the violence it displaces, rather than axiologically opposite, as Caesar presents it. An ambush is still an ambush. In Cicero's presentation, then, Caesar's clemency does not terminate hostile reciprocity, but perpetuates it through nonviolent means.

76. Hershkowitz 1998: 217, quoting Henderson 1987; italics are Henderson's.
77. See chapter 1, apostrophe to Turnus.
78. On *clementia* see Jal 1963: 464–72; Cizek 1972: 96–105; Griffin 1976: 148–71; Earl 1967: 60.
79. Plass 1995: 163; Roller 2001: 176–82 quotes Velleius Paterculus 2.56–57, which presents *clementia* and gift-offering by Caesar as a tie that should bind the recipients into subordinate relationships to Caesar and which should preclude them (if they are duly grateful) from attacking him. Velleius' panegyrical history itself can be viewed as a gift offered to Tiberius for the benefits provided to him and his family; for this interpretation, see Woodman 1975: 287–96. Roller 2001: 186 also quotes Sen. *Clem.* 1.9, where the philosopher describes Augustus' *clementia* and urges Nero to adopt it. On this topic see also Warren 1996: 11–14; Mortureaux 1989: 1680; Charlesworth 1937: 112–13; Borgo 1985: 63.
80. Roller 2001: 183.
81. On Pompey's final hours see Esposito 1986a; Esposito 1996; Scarcia 1996; and Crevatin 1996.
82. Pompey's wife, children, colleagues, and enemies all differently lament his death; in Book 9 Lucan explores their different reactions. On lamentation in Roman epic see chapters 1 and 4.
83. Johnson 1987: 185.

84. This is, according to some recent criticism, the way in which Sappho would use apostrophe; see Greene 1994: 124ff. Johnson's qualification of apostrophe is fit for some of Virgil's apostrophes in the *Aeneid* (e.g., to Dido at *Aen.* 4.401–405).

85. *Rh.* 1378b–1379b. A different evaluation of irony is given by Aristotle in his ethical treatises; see *E.N.* 1108a and 1127b and *E.E.* 1233b–1234a.

86. Goebel 1981: 90: in the absence of true *pietas*, clemency is a mockery. Caesar's first pardoning of Domitius is mentioned at *Clem.* 1.10.1. On Domitius' death in the *Bellum Civile*, see Lounsbury 1975; Lounsbury 1986; Lounsbury 1976. According to Leigh, the word *venia* substituted for *clementia* is important because Seneca had carefully distinguished the two concepts. For Seneca *venia*, "remission of proper punishment," as a form of forgiveness, is constantly refused by the sage. At *De clementia* 2.7.1–2 he clearly states that the wise man does not remit the punishment that he ought to exact (Leigh 1997: 54–67).

87. Barchiesi 1984: especially his last chapter.

88. On *par* in the *Bellum Civile*, Jal 1963: 322–26, 415–16; Hardie 1993: 19–56; Ahl 1976: 86–88; Masters 1992: 35, 44, 109–10; Feeney 1991: 297, quoting the words of Caesar's soldiers at *BC* 5.290 (*facinus quos inquinat aequat*, "crime makes equal those whom it pollutes"); Henderson 1987: 150. For the use of *par* in connection with the gladiatorial games, see Haskins 1887 and Leigh 1997: 235–36, 244.

89. Lucan reveals in one of his most quoted lines that freedom is impossible as long as a Caesar is alive (*sed par quod semper habemus / Libertas et Caesaris erit*).

90. Quoted in Rorty 1989: 177–78.

91. Malamud 2003: 38 has some interesting observations on the passage: "As Caesar takes possession on the Gorgonic head of Pompey, he reveals the control over speech and gesture that gives him his terrifying power. Like Ovid's Perseus, who uses Medusa's head to turn his enemies into statues that monumentalize his power, Caesar's acquisition of Pompey's head gives him a symbolic command of the process of signification." Yet Caesar's soldiers in this episode are not persuaded by Caesar's power of signification.

92. Marti 1958: 494.

93. Williams 1978: 223.

94. Walker 1996: 74–75.

95. Another important passage in which Caesar is shown without the support of his troops is the mutiny at *BC* 5.237–373.

96. Milosz 1981: 54.

97. Ibid., 58.

98. Ibid., 80.

99. The concept of transvaluation, in a different context, is famously employed by Friedrich Nietzsche in his *The Genealogy of Morals*.

100. Besides Scaeva and Caesar, Valerius Maximus also praises Curio; see Esposito 2000; Ahl 1976: 84–115; Saylor 1982; Offermann 1977; Potz 1998.

101. Leigh 1997: 170–71.

102. Masters 1994: 167, characterizing the description of Domitius' death (*BC* 7.597–616), suggests that Lucan wants his readers to become aware of how different his treatment is from that of other historical sources: "nowadays few scholars would deny that Lucan wrote his poem as an 'answer' to Caesar's own *De Bello Civili*—which is to admit that the

poem's readers might well have had access to Caesar's version of the story." Cf. Grottanelli 1993. Cocles and Scaevola appear separately in Valerius Maximus (3.2.1 and 3.3.1) and linked in Livy. Grottanelli points out that even Caesar (*B.C.* 3.53) associates details from the two episodes (e.g., the name Scaeva, the loss of an eye, the defensive heroism evident in the peculiarity of the shield pierced by innumerable arrows). Important observations on the ideological construction of parallelism between Caesar's time and the Roman origins are in Fraschetti 1990. Finally, even Virgil in his Book 6 portrays the history of Rome in terms of continuity and triumph.

103. The expression "*mise en scène* of spectatorship" is from Stam 1992: 29.

104. E.g., at *BC* 5.70–23 and 6.413–830 the narrator responds in direct apostrophe to the response of the gods received by Appius and Sextus.

105. Narducci 2002: 92 correctly identifies these apostrophes as invectives, in which the narrator's perspective "prevails *from the inside* on the psychology of the characters, with the only goal to highlight the perversity of their actions" (emphasis in the original).

106. In Aristotle's view (*Po.* 1449b24–28) drama, with its peculiar strategies of communication, affects the reader much more intensely than narrative. In agreement with Aristotle, Schiller observes that while narrative does not bind the reader completely, the effects of dramatic representations on the audience are rather drastic: "When the event moves in front of me [i.e., in the case of dramatic action], I am firmly shackled to the present as I apprehend it through my senses, my phantasy loses all freedom, a constant restlessness rises in me and stays in me, I must always remain by the object, all looking back, all reflections is forbidden, because I am following an external force." Schiller is quoted by Schiesaro 2003: 246. Schiesaro tries to ascertain whether Seneca's theater can be illuminated by Brecht's aesthetics.

107. Willet 1964: 70–71.

108. Ibid., 71.

109. Leigh 1997: 305, discussing how "the prominence in the *Pharsalia* of the disengaged and aesthetically satisfied spectator poses problems which are richly political."

110. Bartsch 1997: 39.

111. Willet 1964: 248.

112. Ibid., 100–101.

113. On Brecht and Aristotle, see Curran 1998: 291; Willet 1964, especially the section "Theater for Pleasure or Theater for Instruction"; Boal 1985. Cf. the soldiers' reactions to Caesar's tears (*BC* 9.1104–1108).

114. Sherman 1998: 90. Her consideration refers to Adam Smith's concept of empathy in his *Theory of Moral Sentiments*.

115. O'Connor 2000: 255, reproduced from Adorno's *Aesthetic Theory* (tr. C. Lenhardt).

Chapter Three

1. Leigh 1997: 6–10 mentions a similar definition of *phantasia* in Quint. 12.2.29. On these passages see also Nisbet 1992: 1–17; for *phantasia* and prophetic utterance,

Plutarch, *De Pythiae oraculis* 397ff. For Quintilian's emphasis on the connection between listener and speaker, see Kirby 1990; for the importance of *ekplêxis* in drama, Lada 1996: 399–402.

2. Like Longinus' sublime, Lucan's style creates "a mode of intersubjectivity" through which "it becomes impossible to distinguish between the author and the audience" (Too 1998: 199).

3. Halliwell 2002: 310 stresses the contiguity between *mimesis* and *phantasia*, comparing Quintilian's definition of *phantasia* (Quint. 6.2.29) with Aristotle's definition of *enargeia* at *Po.* 17.1455a22–6 and also considering Demetrius' broad conceptualization of *mimesis* as the strong evocation of reality as virtually synonymous with his characterization of *enargeia* as "vividness" (Halliwell 2002: 293 n23 with loci: J. *B.J.* 7.142; Plu. *Glor. Ath.* 347a). Halliwell 2002: 330 also quotes the philosopher Proclus (c. 410–485 CE), who praises Homer and Plato for their "vividness" (*enargeia*) in the following way: "Their use of mimesis moves our imagination [*phantasia*] in every way, changes our beliefs, and molds us to the events they present, so that many readers weep with the wailing Apollodorus [of *Phaedo* 59a and 117d], and many share the grief of Achilles as he laments his friend [. . .]. We seem to be present at the events represented, thanks to the vivid impression [*phantasia*] arising from the *mimesis*" (Procl. *In R.* 1.163.19–164.7). On *enargeia* see also Manieri 1998: 97–192. On the evolution of the semantic sphere pertaining to *phantasia*, see Rispoli 1985.

4. Quoted by Leigh 1997: 11–12.

5. Leigh 1997: 14, mentioning Longinus, *Subl.* 15.2 and clarifying that *enargeia* and *phantasia* are not always distinguishable since at times ancient writers discuss *enargeia* as a rhetorical figure in its own right, in other instances as the effect of the employment of a rhetorical figure. For *enargeia* and the passions, see Walker 1993 and Rispoli 1985: 90. According to Plutarch, *enargeia* and *ekplêxis* are fundamental for tragic historiography, in which battles and events are described as if they were not past but unraveling under our eyes (Plu. *Art.* 8.1). Duris (*FGrH* 76F1) complains that Ephorus and Theopompus produce historical treatments that lack "*mimesis* and pleasure," that is, dramatic qualities. According to Halliwell 2002: 290–91, Duris uses the idea of *mimesis* "to mean not representation *tout court* [. . .] but a certain kind of representation, one that exhibits the objects of representation with imaginative directness or immediacy." On "representation" in tragic history, see Gray 1987; Leigh 1997: 33–37; Kebric 1977: 15–19; Walbank 1960. On *enargeia* in classical and late antiquity, see also Preminger and Brogan 1993: 284 and 1037–38.

6. De Lacy 1958: 249.

7. This categorization is also found in Cic. *Tusc.* 4.11–12: "The different classes of emotions, they say, arise from two kinds of things thought to be good and two thought to be evil [. . .]. For the things that we fear when they are in prospect are the very things that bring distress when they are upon us. Gladness and desire, on the other hand, are concerned with belief about what things are good: desire catches fire from its attraction toward what seems good, while gladness is wildly excited at having obtained some longed-for object." At *Tusc.* 4.18 Cicero's defines pity as "distress over the misery of another who is suffering unjustly—for no one is moved to pity by the punishment of a parricide or a traitor" (tr. Graver 2002: 43, 45).

8. Even though Aristotle's *Poetics* was probably not available during the Hellenistic Age or even antiquity, some of his now lost works (*On Poets* and *Homeric Problems*) presented the ideas that he had exposed in the *Poetics*. Aristotle's Peripatetic successors also played a role in promulgating and developing the founder's most important aesthetic conceits: see Halliwell 2002: 263–44 n3 (with bibliography on the topic), Guthrie 1962–81, vol. 6: 59–65, and Lord 1986. Even if it is not possible to demonstrate Horace's direct knowledge of Aristotle's *Poetics*, Horace's *Ars Poetica* (e.g., 101–105, 97–113, 128–152, etc.) shows acquaintance with some of Aristotle' ideas in the *Poetics* as well as with some of those formulated by Neoptolemus of Parium; see Hardison and Golden 1995: 38–41. Brink 1971, vol. 1: 182f. *ad A.P.* 99–113 highlights the connections between Horace's stylistic doctrine of sympathy and Aristotle's: "Aristotle's second point in *Rhet.* III 7 is emotion, pathos, 1408 a16–25. I have argued, *Prol.* 98f., that this is the fundamental theory underlying this section. Aristotle lays down that style should be *pathetike*, and that it should be apt, *oikeia*, by which he means appropriate to the emotions involved—angry language when there is a feeling of outrage, etc. Then reaction will be right; the listener sympathizes with the emotions thus expressed: *sunomopathei* a23." On Aristotle's influence on late Republican stylistic theory and Horace's satire, see Freudenburg 1993:119–32.

9. Gorgias too, in his *Encomium of Helen*, grants to speech the ability to stir emotions: "it can stop fear and banish grief and create joy and nurture pity . . . fearful shuddering and tearful pity and grievous longing come upon its hearers, and at the actions and physical suffering of others in good fortunes and in evil fortunes, through the agency of words, the soul is wont to experience a suffering of its own" (8).

10. Leigh 1997: 15 with ancient *loci*. At *BC* 8.590–91 Cornelia, apprehensive because of the premonition of Pompey's imminent death, is described as "anxious with a numbing fear" (*anxia . . . attonitoque metu*).

11. Halliwell 2002: 190, indicating passages in Aristotle's work with metaphors that "place things before the eyes," *Rh.* 3.10, 1410b33, 1411a27–28, 35, 1411b4–22, 25 and *Po.* 17.1455a22–30; for *enargeia* as *mimesis*, cf. *Rh.* 1412a9.

12. Parry 1966: 122.

13. Ibid.

14. On Pompey as a negative character, see Bartsch 1997: 97; Leigh 1997: 110–57, with very acute observations on Pompey's shortcomings; Esposito 1986a. Masters 1994: 168 highlights the incongruity of Lucan's descriptions of several Pompeians (e.g., Domitius). On Pompey's (positive) characterization in apostrophe, Bartsch 1997: 73–100 elaborates on some of the ideas in Narducci 1979, where the Italian scholar notices Lucan's willingness to console Pompey by reminding him of Aeneas' labors in the final days of Troy. Thus in the *Bellum Civile* Lucan's apostrophes to Pompey do not follow the pattern of harsh criticism I have highlighted in apostrophes directed to other characters. They express instead a "Virgilian sympathy"; see Narducci 1979: 118.

15. Marti 1979: 182; Marti 1975: 89; Leigh 1997: 38.

16. The theme of civil war is felt by Aristotle as eminently tragic (*Po.* 1453b20). On the centrality of *peripeteia* and *anagnôrisis* in tragedy, Halliwell 2002: 221 states: "*Peripeteia* marks a direct contradiction of intentions and expectations, an ironic rupture of the normal consequentiality of action. *Anagnôrisis* by definition occasions an increase in knowledge or understanding, but this knowledge is often irremediably negative." Cf. Leigh 1997: 38

n61: "While *eleos* may find some reflection in the sympathy which future readers will feel for Pompey, it is not clear what relation it bears to Lucan's *spes*. Similarly Aristotelian fear, generally regarded as the product of seeing something dreadful happen to someone 'like us,' is considerably different from the altruistic, anticipatory emotion which Lucan suggests."

17. Lada 1996: 403. Aristotle inherited from Plato a deep sense of apprehension toward emotional appeal; in order to make drama acceptable he had to come to grips with the traditional objection that dramatic poets incite irrational pleasures. To do this, Aristotle introduced the possibility of a rational emotional response. In fact, he proposes a philosophical model in which emotions are not eradicated but properly educated. See primarily Fortenbaugh 1975; Halliwell 1992; Lear 1992; Belfiore 1992, esp. chap. 7. Even if Lucan did not have direct access to the *Poetics*, he must have been aware of other works in which these ideas were expressed.

18. The characterization of Pompey as a tragic figure "buffeted between the powers of good and evil, his life determined by Fate, yet free to choose his course and to determine himself," was first given by Marti 1945b: 358, who mentions its Aristotelian derivation on pages 352 and 354. In Marti's opinion, Lucan knew Aristotle's statement according to which the unity of a plot consists in having not simply one hero but an organically unified action. He also agreed with Aristotle's understanding that poetry is more philosophical than history. With a higher degree of precision, Marti 1945b: 368 connects Pompey to the figure of the Stoic *proficiens*, an average man who struggles toward goodness trying to perfect himself: "while the early Stoics had been unwilling to accept any intermediate steps between the two extremes of goodness and evil, a graded scale of achievements was soon developed, according to which moral improvement and a progressive march toward the ideal were possible. Cleanthes' description of humanity strikingly applies to Pompey: 'man lives in wickedness all his life or, if not all the time, at least most of the time. If he ever does so late and toward the setting of his days' (fr. 429 Von Armin)." George 1991 has expanded on Pompey as a *proficiens*. Recently Marti's thesis of Pompey as a Stoic *proficiens* has been revisited by Sklenár 2003: 106–107. Conserva 1997: 69–80 describes Pompey as a "weak hero" and connects him with characters (like Thyestes, Jason and Agamemnon) whose "weakness" is featured in Seneca's tragedies.

19. *Proficiens* (Gr. προκόπτον) is the man who is not yet wise nor perfect but progresses toward virtue; see Rist 1969: 90–91. Seneca's *Ep.* 75 discusses the notion.

20. On Pompey's desire to comply with his soldiers and the Senate, thus bowing to the dictates of Republican constitutionalism, see Rambaud 1955: 262–66 and Lounsbury 1976: 213–17. The expression *hoc placet, o superi* is reminiscent of *Aen.* 12.503–504: *tanton placuit . . . Iuppiter.*

21. He is certainly helped in this strategy by Appian's treatment; see Gabba 1956: 121–51; Bartsch 1997: 78–79; Rambaud 1955.

22. The conflicting logic of *pietas* is well captured by Roller 2001: 33. For the ironies of Virgilian *pietas*, see Eagan 1980: 165–67; Johnson 1965: 172; Di Cesare 1974: 172–97; Segal 1965a: 143.

23. Narducci 1979: 112–29. Pompey's assimilation to Aeneas is quite strong in Lucan's description of the general's escape from Rome qualified as a second Troy (*BC* 2.719–31; cf. *Aen.* 2.801–804 and 3.12–13); Menz 1952: 80; Marti 1964: 182; Brugnoli and Stok 1996.

24. Quint 1992: 360.
25. On Pompey's *amor*, see Ahl 1976: 173–89.
26. Zyroff 1971: 248.
27. The idea that winning in civil war is worse than losing is present also at *BC* 7.123 and 4.258–59. Cf. Seneca, *Prov.* 3.14: *prosperae res et in plebem ac vilia ingenia deveniunt; at calamitates terroresque mortalium sub iugum mittere proprium magni viri est* ("Success comes to the common man, and even to average ability; but to triumph over the calamities and terrors of mortal life is characteristic of a great man only").
28. Irwin 2003: 348: "Each virtue, according to the Stoics, includes some conviction about the value of the actions it prescribes. The just person, for instance, not only does just actions, but also does them for their own sake, in the conviction that they are worth doing simply because they are just, and not because of some further causal result. Conceptions of the final good that leave out rightness [. . .] demote the virtues to a purely instrumental status that conflicts with the outlook of the virtuous person (Cic. *Fin.* II 35)." Cf. Plutarch, *De Stoicorum repugnantiis* 26.1046 = SVF 3.54.5–14.
29. For Lentulus as a living exemplar of Republican institutions and traditional *virtus*, see Sklenár 2003: 121–23. On Pompey's oscillation between fear and desire to preserve a dignified compartment, see Dilke 1979; on his negative traits, Esposito 1986a and George 1986: 368–73. Narducci 2002: 325–28 highlights how at the beginning of Book 8 Lucan, by echoing several historical sources, describes Pompey as physically and psychologically devastated, not at all stoically ready to tolerate his personal misfortune. For a detailed analysis of episodes in which Pompey is described in a negative light, cf. Bartsch 1997: 77–85.
30. Marti 1945b: 371. Cf. the depiction of Cato at *BC* 2.239–41: *insomni volventem publica cura / fata virumque casusque urbis cunctisque timentem / securumque sui* ("brooding in sleepless anxiety over public affairs—human destinies, the City's future—fearful for all, unconcerned for himself").
31. *Res mihi Romanas dederas, fortuna, regendas / accipe maiores et caeco in Marte tuere* ("Fortune, you gave me the Roman state to rule, take it back now, greater than before, and protect it from blind Mars" (*BC* 7.110ff.); and *quid opus victo populis aut urbibus?* ("What need has a conquered man of troops and towns?"), *BC* 7.720.
32. . . . *quantum scelerum quantumque malorum / in populos lux ista feret!* ("How much evil, how much hurt today's light brings the people!") *BC* 7.114–15ff.; and *BC* 7.659–66: *Parcite—ait—superi, cunctas prosternere gentes. / Stante potest mundo Romaque superstite Magnus / esse miser. Si plura iuvant mea volnera, coniunx / est mihi, sunt nati; dedimus tot pignora fatis. / Civiline parum est bello, si meque meosque / obruit? Exiguae clades sumus orbe remoto? / Omnia quid laceras? Quid perdere cuncta laboras? / Iam nihil est, Fortuna, meum* ("Pity them, gods above, and do not erase all nations! Though the world stands and Rome survives, Magnus can still be made miserable! Should you want to wound me more, I have a wife, I have sons: all these are Fortune's hostages. Isn't it enough for civil war to overthrow me and mine? Is our death too trifling without the world's? Why wreak havoc on all, why work for total destruction? Fortune, I have nothing left as it is")
33. Narducci 2002: 309–24 has analyzed with sophistication Pompey's behavior at Pharsalus and his *devotio*. More skeptical about Pompey's final redemption and *devotio* are Leigh 1997: 108ff. and Sklenár 2003: 120ff.

34. Bartsch 1997: 87 and 91.

35. Narducci 2002: 330.

36. Another sign of Pompey's idealization can be found in the transmigration of his soul to the lunar orbit (*BC* 9.5–9), the eschatological dwelling place of the virtuous. On this point see Schotes 1969: 74–75; Marti 1945b: 373; Narducci 2002: 340–48. For an ironic characterization, cf. Johnson 1987: 70.

37. Narducci 2002: 330–31 and 134–37.

38. With artistic acuity, Lucan does not put Cato at the center of his narration. The Stoic sage, according to Conte, is so composed in his Stoic understanding of human existence that he would have not made a good tragic model. For Cato's "*purezza prototipica*" see Conte 1968: 230. For a more nuanced picture see my characterization of Cato in chapter 4.

39. Halliwell 2002: 198. Cf. Marti 1945b: 358: "Thus the Stoic practice of depriving individuals of personal characteristics, of turning them into models to be admired or abhorred, influenced Lucan more when he introduced philosophical types into his epic than the Aristotelian theory of the Universal." Cf. Sikes 1923: 201: "Lucan, however, whether consciously or unconsciously, pushed the Aristotelian theory of the Universal to an extreme from which Aristotle himself might well have recoiled."

40. Lada 1996: 399 quoting S. *Tr.* 385–86; cf. Eur. *Alc.* 115, Th. 2.65.9, and Gorg. *Hel.* 16.

41. "But we have not yet brought our chief accusation (μέγιστον κατηγορήκαμεν αὐτῆς) against it [poetry]. Its power to corrupt (λωβᾶσθαι), with rare exceptions, even the better sort of men is surely the chief cause of alarm" (*R.* 10.605c–d).

42. Halliwell 2002: 93.

43. 215c: ὁ μέν γε δι' ὀργάνων ἐκήλει τοὺς ἀνθρώπους τῇ ἀπὸ τοῦ στόματος δυνάμει, καὶ ἔτι νυνὶ ὃς ἂν τὰ ἐκείνου αὐλῇ —ἃ γὰρ Ὄλυμπος ηὔλει, Μαρσύου λέγω, τούτου διδάξαντος—τὰ οὖν ἐκείνου ἐάντε ἀγαθὸς αὐλητὴς ἐάντε αὐλῇ φαύλη αὐλητρίς, μόνα κατέχεσθαι ποιεῖ καὶ δηλοῖ τοὺς τῶν θεῶν τε καὶ τελετῶν δεομένους διὰ τὸ θεῖα εἶναι. σὺ δ' ἐκείνου τοσοῦτον μόνον διαφέρεις, ὅτι ἄνευ ὀργάνων ψιλοῖς λόγοις ταὐτὸν ("Why, yes, and a far more marvelous one than the satyr. His lips indeed had power to entrance mankind by means of instruments; a thing still possible today for anyone who can pipe his tunes: for the music of Olympus' flute belonged, I may tell you, to Marsyas his teacher. So that if anyone, whether a fine flute-player or paltry flute-girl, can but flute his tunes, they have no equal for exciting a ravishment, and will indicate by the divinity that is in them who are apt recipients of the deities and their sanctifications. You differ from him in one point only—that you produce the same effect with simple prose unaided by instruments"). (tr. H. N. Fowler)

44. Lada 1996: 399–400.

45. Cleanthes recognized that poetry was equipped to express sublimity better than was philosophy (SVF 1.486); Most 1989: 2026.

46. Tieleman 1996.

47. Nussbaum 1993: 99. Before discussing the relationship between the Stoic view(s) of poetry and its effects on the soul, she acknowledges the existence of a paradox in Stoic thought: its belief in the extirpation of all passions and its acceptance of poetry, which encourages the passions. In general, my treatment of Stoic views of poetry is strongly dependent on her thesis.

48. Steinmetz 1986: 26–27.

49. On Stoic poetics and aesthetics, see Zagdoun 2000; on semantics in Stoic philosophy, Graeser 1978. Graeser summarizes the issue in the following way: "The Stoics, then, held a fundamentally nonreferential or rather intensional theory of meaning, one in which meanings in general are viewed as linguistic contents isomorphically related to the respective thing on the level of expression." The general term for such linguistic contents was *lekton*. On Stoic epistemology, see Hankinson 2003. Laird 1999: 46–78 contains a very interesting discussion about the difficulty of isolating *logos* from *lexis* in Plato's *Republic*: "what Plato's discussion here [*Republic* 396e4–7] seems to show is that it is impossible to isolate the notion of narrative anyway. Plato's terms are smudgy at the edges because the notions behind them overlap. Distinctions between the terms *logoi, lexis,* and *diegesis* cannot be made easily, even if Socrates exhibits a sense of difference between *logoi* and *lexis*. For him, the point of acquiring this sense of the differences is not for literary theoretical purposes but for practical moral and political ends" (Laird 1999: 61).

50. De Lacy 1958.

51. On Philodemus' account, see Jensen 1923; Greenberg 1990; Mangoni 1993; Dorandi, 1990; Asmis 1990; and the chapter by the same author in Obbink 1995: 148–77.

52. De Lacy 1958: 252–53; on the discussion between Aristo and Crates, see Jensen 1923: 146–74; Setaioli 1985: 833. A similar view about the relationship between poetry and moral precepts is in Seneca, *Ep.* 108.9–10, where Cleanthes' metaphor is mentioned.

53. The Greek term *lexis* is generally translated into Latin as *elocutio* defined at *Rhetorica ad Herennium* 1.3 as "the adaptation of suitable words and sentences to the matter devised" (*elocutio est idoneorum verborum et sententiarum ad inventionem accommodatio*).

54. Nussbaum 1993: 105.

55. Quoted by De Lacy 1958: 254; similar conclusions in Setaioli 1985: 834. On Crates, see Asmis 1992.

56. Nussbaum 1993: 100.

57. *G.*1.1.10 and 1.2.3–5.

58. Cicero translates the Stoic term *phantasia* sometimes as *visio* or *visum* (e.g., *Ac.* 1.11.40; 2.6,18, etc.), in other cases as *species* (e.g, *De fato* 43).

59. Nussbaum 1993: 100. Since the seventies the emotions have been intensely studied and attention has been directed to the fact that anger, pity, grief, etc., are not merely irrational feelings or passive psychophysical reaction. Emotions are not only intentional but tightly connected to the representational and evaluative acts of those undergoing them. Involving cognition, evaluation and judgment, the emotions can be understood as a function of reason. For an overview of the scholarship on the emotions, see Knuttila and Sihvola 1998; on *pathe* in Greco-Roman philosophy, Gill 1997a; Gill 1998a; Sorabji 2000, esp. 29–55.

60. This psychological model is also employed by Aristotle. A useful account of Platonic and Aristotelian psychology can be found in Harris 2001: 88–128.

61. Imbert 1980, esp. 182, containing Longinus' quote, "the term *phantasia* is used generally for anything which in any way suggests a thought productive of speech" (*Sub.* 15.1). Imbert also reminds us that the connection between this definition of "vision" and

Stoicism was drawn by Russell 1964: 120; Long 1996a: 270 explains that "the Stoics treat *phantasia* as the mental faculty encompassing all objects of awareness" and that in Stoic thought from Zeno to Marcus Aurelius *phantasia* as the representation of "an affection in the soul which reveals itself and its cause" (Aetius 4.12.1) has a centrality that is not present in Plato or Aristotle: "how things appear to a rational animal depend upon the kind of language user that it is" (Long 1996a: 273). In Stoic speculation, every external reality must be interiorized by the single individual: representation is tightly connected with the individual who produces it; Rispoli 1985: 58–61 with sources. For primary evidence of the concept in early Stoicism, see also Long and Sedley 1987 section 39; for the correspondences between Stoic and Saussurean theory, Manetti 1993: 92–94.

62. Rist 1978: 241. A similar idea is formulated by Most 1989: 2026: "For the Stoics literary texts were an important source of evidence about theology (hence about physics), and allegoresis was one way to make them yield this evidence; but the interpretation of poetry did not offer problems that were in principle different from those connected with the interpretation of other kinds of monuments." For Aristotle visualization (*phantasia*) is a necessary precursor of desire and movement since when one fears or hopes for something, there is in his mind an impression similar to the one that was there when something fearful or pleasant was actually taking place. In the *Rhetoric* (2.1378a19–22), *phantasiai* are analyzed not as motivating factors for real actions but in reference to the orator and how through emotions (*pathe*) he can influence his audience's judgment. For *enargeia* in Aristotle and Demetrius, see Salomone 1988.

63. Long 1996a: 272; he also clarifies on page 271 that the Stoics and Aristotle as well maintain that "all our concepts (*ennoiai*) are *phantasiai*, that memory is a 'store' of them, and that they enter into the causal account of everything we do." He gives sources for these concepts in note 18; Imbert 1980, esp. 182.

64. Taylor 1989: 137: "The [Stoics'] singling out of . . . assent is one source of the developing notion of the will, and there is already an important change in moral outlook in making this the central human faculty. What is morally crucial about us is not just the universal nature or rational principle which we share with others, as with Plato and Aristotle, but now also this power of assent, which is essentially mine." On the complex relationship between Stoic speculations on *horme* (*impetus*) and Seneca's development of the notion of will (*voluntas*), see Grimal 1992: 16; Reale 2000: xcv–xcix; Donini 1982: 203ff.

65. Long 1996a: 282.

66. According to *R*. 387–388a, Achilles' excessive grieving for Patroklos persuades the audience that it is right to become desperate for the death of a friend. Instead of considering that the self-sufficient person would not behave like Achilles, the audience tends to accept passively Achilles' opinion and behavior. Considering this problem in *Republic* 2–3, Socrates suggests that the identification process, and with it the transmission of the false belief, can be disrupted if the false belief and reproachable behavior are put in the mouth of an inferior character (387e9–388a1); see Nussbaum 1993: 106–107 and Nadaff 2002: 92–120.

67. Nussbaum 1993: 137.

68. Lada 1998: 390. For the role of audiences in ancient writing, see Pucci 1998.

69. Nussbaum 1993: 138.

70. Halliwell 2002: 297–302 is uncertain as to how much Stoic influence can be detected in Plutarch's treatise. More positive about Chrysippus' presence in *De audiendis poetis* are Nussbaum 1993: 122–49 and Babut 1969: 87–93. Platonic and Aristotelian echoes in the treatise are examined by Flashar 1979a: 109 and Sicking 1998: 101–11. Ideas similar to some found in *De audiendis poetis* can be found in the *Essay on the Life and Poetry of Homer*, traditionally attributed to Plutarch but more probably the work of a pedagogue of the second century CE. For instance, according to Lamberton and Keaney 1996: 14–15, in chapter 4 and 218, he views "the experience of literature, or at least of Homer, as a participational act, in which the reader is brought into unusual and morally ambiguous situations, and is expected to make value judgments [. . .]. The task of the author is to mix good and evil in order to cause his readers to use and so develop their own moral sense by coming to terms with extraordinary (*paradoxoi*) situations. Our author posits for the poet a goal of poetic effectiveness that justifies the means of 'extraordinary and mythical treatment' of his material and of saying 'some things that are highly improbable' (ch. 6). It is his task to capture the imagination, and these techniques are the most direct path to that end." If the form and style of the *Essay* are un-Plutarchean, "much of the content seems to echo passages in preserved authentic work of Plutarch" (Lamberton and Keaney 1996: 7).

71. Nussbaum 1993: 139.

72. Nussbaum 1993: 140: "for example, when they listen to Odysseus' rebuke to Achilles, as he sits idly amusing himself with the maidens of Scyrus, they are to think how this rebuke applies to other profligate and wasteful people (*De aud. poet.* 34bff.)."

73. "Stop wanting your husband, and there is not one of the things you want that will fail to happen. Stop wanting him to live with you at any cost. Stop wanting to remain in Corinth. And in general, stop wanting anything else but what the gods wants. And who will prevent you? Who will compel you?" (*Diss.* 2.17.21–22). According to Nussbaum, Epictetus is following Chrysippus. Cicero in *Off.* 1.136 (which probably has Panaetius as main source) explains that sometimes a philosopher must reproach his listener and use harsh words: *obiurgationes etiam non numquam incidunt necessariae, in quibus utendum est fortasse et vocis contentione maiore et verborum gravitate acriore, id agendum etiam ut ea facere videamur irati. Sed, ut ad urendum et secandum, sic ad hoc genus castigandi raro invitique veniemus, nec umquam nisi necessario, si nulla reperietur alia medicina: sed tamen ira procul absit, cum qua nihil recte fieri, nihil considerari potest* ("It may sometimes happen that there is need of administering reproof. On such occasions we should perhaps use a more emphatic tone of voice and more forcible and severe terms and even assume an appearance of being angry. But we shall have recourse to this sort of reproof, as we do to cautery and amputation, rarely and reluctantly—never at all, unless it is unavoidable and no other remedy can be discovered. We may seem angry, but anger should be far from us; for in anger nothing right or judicious can be done," tr. Miller). Epictetus was Musonius' most famous student and, together with all philosophers, was expelled from Rome in 93 CE by Domitian. See Dobbin 1998: xi–xiv and Barnes 1997: 24–125. On Cicero and Panaetius, see Lefèvre 2001; Dyck 1996.

74. Nussbaum 1993: 143–44.

75. Ibid., 141.

76. Halliwell 2002: 78.

77. Ibid., 77.

78. Ibid., 80. A similar conclusion is reached in Lada 1996. On the topic of poetry in the *Republic* see also Nadaff 2002. On page 78 Halliwell observes that sympathy and identification are often used as practically synonymous in English (e.g., Ferrari 1989: 98 and 134 and Halliwell 1988: 147–49), but he keeps these two concepts carefully apart in his most recent study. My study, too, maintains a distinction between "empathy" and "sympathy," in Virgil as well as in Lucan. On these two notions, besides the citations already offered in chapter 1, see Feagin 1996: 83–142; Sherman 1998; and Tan 1996: 189–190 in relationship to films. For a view of Plato in the *Republic* as legitimately praising (inspired) literature for its valuable truths and positive moral influence, as well as the idea that the inspired poet remains a thinking individual, see Büttner 2000: 255–365 and Too 1998: 51–82.

79. The narrator's attitude toward these characters has been discussed in chapter 2.

80. Morford 2002: 39.

81. Long 1986: 231.

82. Setaioli 1985; cf. Mazzoli 1970; Traina 1974; Hadot 1969; Maguinness, 1956. On Seneca's tragedy as a negation of poetry's didactic power, see Dingel 1974. Important observations about poetry and theater are in Rosenmeyer 1989: 39–43; Fantham 1982: 19–34; Russell 1974.

83. Even Plutarch in *De audiendis poetis* 16d–e observes: "Whenever, therefore, in the poems of a man of note and repute some strange and disconcerting statement either about gods or lesser deities or about virtue is made by the author, he who accepts the statement as true is carried off his feet and has his opinion perverted; whereas he who always remembers and keeps clearly in mind the sorcery of the poetic art in dealing with falsehood [. . .] will not suffer any dire effects or even acquire any base belief." (tr. F. C. Babbitt) Echoing *Republic* 2–3, Plutarch asserts that poetry is dangerous not only because it harbors wrong opinions but also because these opinions are voiced by characters portrayed as admirable or divine.

84. Gill 2003: 49: "Is Seneca offering his own innovative view of the formation of a passion? One of the unfamiliar elements, the idea of a 'pre-passion' (i.e., an instinctive or impulsive reaction not yet rationally adopted) may go back to Posidonius, and has some parallels elsewhere in Stoic sources. Also, as Inwood (1993) suggests, other factors may be at work. Seneca seems to be taking the essence of the orthodox Stoic view of emotions—that they depend on the rational assent of the person involved but that, once formed, they can outrun rational control—and to be recasting it in his own vivid, non technical terms." On Seneca's "orthodoxy" or innovation in this matter, see Rist 1989; Sorabji 2000, chs. 3–4; Rispoli 1985: 81–85.

85. De Lacy 1958: 252 mentions Crates, who considered a poem bad if it has a bad *synthesis*.

86. Theophrastus, *Peri Lexeos*, ed. A. Mayer; cf. Hendrickson 1905: 255; Kennedy 1957.

87. Leeman 1963, vol. 1: 277 emphasizes that in Greek Stoic theories (chiefly formulated by Diocles) "to speak well is to speak the truth and the aim of speaking is only *docere*. Still, the speaker is bound by the usual categories of the *elocutio*, *ellenismos* [*Latinitas*], *saphêneia* [*explanatio*, later called *perspicuitas* or *planitas*], *prepon* [*decorum*], *cataskeuê* [*ornatus*] (*St. Vet.* 3, 214). But the last is reduced to its minimum" and figures of speech

are reluctantly admitted. Leeman (ibid.) adds that a schema (figure of speech) is defined as "a fault committed on rational grounds (*Rhet. Gr.* 3.171.3)," and the *prepon* is restricted to "a style adapted to the subject" (*St. Vet.* 3, 214). Neither the personality of the speaker nor the character of the audience is taken into account in that Stoic formulation. Interestingly, on the same page Leeman underscores the importance of *saphêneia*, which is strengthened into *enargeia*. Not simply clarity but "concentrated evidence" is needed in a discourse: *expressa verba et, ut vult Zeno, sensu tincta esse debent* ("the words must be clear and, as Zeno says, steeped in meaning"), Quint. 4.2.117; cf. Sklenár 2003: 10. Freudenburg 1993: 137 quotes and comments on Dionysius' description of Stoic style: "'Well, it seemed to me that we should follow nature as much as possible, and to fit together the parts of speech as she demands [*On Word Arrangement* 5].' Nature herself [*phusis*] determines arrangement, that is, a natural word order [*ordo naturalis*] taught not by art but by a life attuned to the unseen logical structures at work in the cosmos. The thinking is entirely Stoic." In harmony with a "Stoic style," compression and directness are employed by Seneca, who does not limit himself to them but exploits in full all kinds of stylistic means.

88. Seneca echoes Cicero's complaints about the dryness and ineffectiveness of Stoic syllogisms at *Ep.* 82.9.

89. Cato excuses his simple style but also admits that a grander matter would call for a more sublime diction: *Haec dicuntur fortasse ieiunius; sunt enim quasi prima elementa naturae, quibus ubertas orationis adhiberi vix potest; nec equidem eam cogito consectari. Verumtamen cum de rebus grandioris dicas, ipsae res verba rapiunt: ita fit gravior tum etiam splendidior oratio*, "All this is perhaps somewhat simply expressed; for it deals with what may be called the primary elements of nature, to which any stylistic elaboration can scarcely be applied. Nor am I concerned to attempt it. On the other hand, when one is treating of more majestic topics, the style instinctively rises with the subject and the brilliance of the language increases with the dignity of the theme" (*Fin.* 3.5.19; tr. H. Rackham).

90. On this passage and in general on Cato's innovations in Stoic oratorical practice, see Stem 2005.

91. Setaioli 1985: 796–98.

92. Cited by Setaioli 1985: 799.

93. The reference is to Euripides' *Phoenissae* 469.

94. Freudenburg 1993: 160. On Seneca's alleged conformity to Stoic stylistic doctrine, see Smiley 1919.

95. Setaioli 1985: 794–801. If the will to discover the truth is essential, the operation of "tuning" in to the *logos* depends on the mind of each individual poet. Seneca, like Panaetius, is revolutionarily aware of poetry's dependence on the poet's personality and is convinced that the poet's greatness is determined by his nature, i.e., that his vices and virtues are tightly twined together (*Ep.* 114.12). The connections between Seneca and Panaetius are highlighted also by Grilli 1953: 115, 270; Dyck 1996.

96. According to Mueller 1910: 70–100, Seneca also accepts Diogenes of Babylon's five virtues of speech: σαφήνεια (clarity), συτομία (brevity), πρέπον (propriety), κατασκευή (ornamentation), and *Latinitas* (grammatical correctness).

97. This realization seems to be characteristic of all Hellenistic philosophies; cf. Nussbaum 1994: 34–36.

98. Traina 1974: 25ff. observes that the "stylistic cell" of Seneca's prose is not the

compound sentence (as it was for Cicero) nor the word (as it will be in Fronto) but the simple clause. Quintilian accuses Seneca of having broken up weighty concepts (*rerum pondera*) into *minutissimae sententiae* (Quint. 10.1.130). Seneca's appreciation of the *sententiae* comes to him through the schools of declamation but also through rhetoric, which, being characterized by a certain conciseness and subtlety, can be defined as Stoic. On the topic see Moretti 1995.

99. Guillemin 1952 and Guillemin 1957.
100. On this proximity, see Schiesaro 1997.
101. See also Sen. *Ben.* 4.12.1 and *Ep.* 94.46, in which *admonitio* is connected to *magni animi*.
102. Seneca is commenting on the style of Lucilius' letter: *invenio tamen translationem verborum ut non temerarias ita quae periculum sui fecerint; invenio imagines, quibus si quis nos uti vetat et poetis illas solis iudicat esse concessas*, "I find some metaphors which without being too daring are a bit dangerous; I also find some images which some people would like to ban from us [philosophers] considering them a privilege to grant only to poets" (*Ep.* 59.5-7). Casamante 1999: 128 discusses Seneca's use of *sententiae* in his tragedies: "pochi sono i momenti in cui una o più sentenze non compaiono a scandire, muovere, sollecitare o sintetizzare l'*actio* tragica. Un'analisi delle tragedie, in tal senso orientata, rivela un uso sistematico e coerente di tali poetiche 'frecce,' che sono le sentenze, che corrisponde con tutta evidenza a una scelta stilistica e a un programma compositivo" ("Few are the instances [in the text] in which one or more *sententiae* do not appear to explicate, move, hurry, or synthetize the tragic action. When we sistematically analyze the tragedies with this purpose, we see a methodical and coherent employment of these poetic 'arrows' [the *sententiae*], a usage which obviously corresponds to a deliberate stylistic choice and program"). Thus for Casamante *Ep.* 108.10 can be read as an almost programmatic statement for Seneca's theater. Moretti 1995: 168ff. links the metaphor of *Ep.* 108.10—poetry as a straight arrow hitting its target—to Stoic oratory.
103. Brink 1971, vol. 2: 184–85.
104. Tate 1928: 67–68. He connects several of Horace's ideas with those of Philodemus in his *On Poetry*.
105. Tate 1928: 69
106. Anderson 1982: 14–15.
107. Setaioli 1985: 806.
108. See also *Symp.* 215e, quoted above. Mazzoli 1970: 55–56 believes that Seneca (following Posidonius and against Chrysippus' theory of *apatheia*) embraced the Peripatetic tradition endorsing the idea of a controlled and moderate excitement.
109. On the contiguity between goodness and beauty, see Kristeller 1951: 498:

> Beauty, does not appear in ancient thought or literature with its specific modern connotations. The Greek term *kalón* and its Latin equivalent (*pulchrum*) were never neatly or consistently distinguished from the moral good. When Plato discusses beauty in the *Symposium* and the *Phaedrus,* he is speaking not merely of the physical beauty of human persons, but also of beautiful habits of the soul and of beautiful cognitions, whereas he fails completely to mention works of art in this connection. An incidental remark made in

the *Phaedrus* and elaborated by Proclus was certainly not meant to express the modern triad of Truth, Goodness and Beauty. When the Stoics in one of their famous statements connected Beauty and Goodness (*Stoicorum Veterum Fragmenta* III, p. 9ff.), the context as well as Cicero's Latin (*De finibus* III, 26, *quod honestum sit id solum bonum*) rendering suggest that they meant by "Beauty" nothing but moral "goodness," and in turn understood by "good" nothing but the useful. Only in later thinkers does the speculation about "beauty" assume an increasingly "aesthetic" significance, but without ever leading to a separate system of aesthetics in the modern sense.

110. Here I have chosen *sopita* (Reynolds 1965) rather than *soluta*.
111. Setaioli agrees with Mazzoli's idea of an influence of the Middle Stoa on Seneca (especially in his employment of emotions in *admonitio*), but he rejects Mazzoli's recourse to artistic *enthusiasmos* as an irrational impulse; see Setaioli 1985: 802; Mazzoli 1970: 46–59. Recently Mazzoli's ideas have been adopted by Schiesaro 2003, esp. 21–25. Schiesaro is right to underline the ambiguity of Senecan terminology in discussing the passions and poetry: Seneca seems aware that, for instance, inspiration is dangerous because it can trigger the elaboration of great philosophical truth or misguiding and powerful lies (p. 24).
112. Seneca's "sparks of virtue" might be drawn from Panaetius' "drives" (*aphormai*). On these Rist 1969: 189 writes: "There is no need to regard the *aphormai* as essentially rational or irrational. They are rather to be thought of as instincts, though they are admittedly directed by nature to rational ends, and thus potentially rational. They will only become rational when they are recognized for what they are by reason and 'rationalized.'" The kinship between philosophy and poetry is also affirmed by Strabo 1.2.3. In the Roman world philosophy becomes ancillary to rhetoric; see Manetti 1993: 140: "Rhetoric in fact is the highest accomplishment of philosophy—from which it cannot be dissociated (cf. *De oratore*, III, 59–61)—and should not be considered simply the technical ability to add an elegant expression to an already-formed thought. As Baratin and Desbordes (1981, p. 50) point out, Cicero is working on a somewhat ill-defined but frequently reiterated view that if you speak well, you also think well, or, to put it another way, that you can think well only when you can speak well."
113. Husner has shown that there are in Seneca's prose elements deriving from Hellenistic stylistic doctrines distinctive of Demetrius, namely *mimeticon, enarges, meta megalophrosunes nouthetikon;* cf. Dem. *Peri Ermeneias* 298, discussed by Husner 1924.
114. Leeman 1963: 277 and 282: "We have seen that Stoic theories on style do not seem to have had a decisive influence. At most Seneca seems to have felt and stressed that he is not at variance with the Stoic principles." Contra Smiley 1919.
115. Mazzoli 1970: 26–27. According to Mazzoli, all *technai* in Seneca are evaluated in relation to philosophy not as a science of the universal but as an ethical enterprise: *artes ministrae sunt, praestare debent quod promittunt, sapientia domina rectrixque est: artes serviunt vitae, sapientia imperat* ("The arts are the handmaids; they must accomplish what they promise to do. But wisdom is mistress and ruler. The arts render a slave's service to life; wisdom issues the commands"), *Ep.* 85.32; cf. Aristo on the role of liberal arts (SVF 1.350). A servant is good only if she follows the master's order; so *technai* are good if they help men's moral elevation (Lana 1961: 384). In a sense even "wisdom is an art" (*sapientia*

ars est, Ep. 29.3) because "the archer ought not to hit the mark only sometimes; he ought to miss it only sometimes. That which takes effect by chance is not an art. Now wisdom is an art; it should have a definite aim, choosing only those who will make progress, but withdrawing from those whom it has come to regard as hopeless—yet not abandoning them too soon, and just when the case is becoming hopeless trying drastic remedies" (*Ep.* 29.3; tr. R. M. Gummere).

116. Nussbaum 1993: 148.

117. Ibid., 148–49; for a more nuanced view of the dangers posed by literature to philosophy, see also ibid., 439–83.

118. On Seneca's drama as Stoic poetry, see Rogenbogen 1927–8; Marti 1945a: 216–45; Marti 1974: 1–16; Cacciaglia 1974; Bäumer 1982: 130–36; Pratt 1983: 73–131; Pratt 1948; defending Seneca's Stoicism more on the ground of cosmology than ethics, Rosenmayer 1989, contra Dingel 1974. For the history of interpretation of Seneca's tragedies, especially in the Renaissance, see Mayer 1994. A nice overview of several different critical tendencies through which Seneca's plays have been interpreted and a good bibliography on the role of the chorus in Seneca's plays up to 1989 are in Blandsdorf 1996. On Seneca's tragedies, see also Hilt-Brunner 1985; more recently on Seneca's chorus: Davies 1993; Mazzoli 1996; and Caviglia 1996.

119. Schiesaro 1997: 109–110, discussed at the beginning of chapter 2.

120. Due 1970: 214; Schotes 1969: 174; Dick 1967; Narducci 1979: 35; Narducci 1985: 1541ff.; Lapidge 1979: 367; and Lapidge 1989: 1405–1409.

121. An important modern critical approach that sanctions Stoic allegorism in the *Aeneid* is Heinze 1993: 235–50. The bibliography on religion and philosophy in the *Aeneid* is quite massive; see Feeney 1991: 150–55 and Braund 1997, who remarks: "When we consider 'religion' and 'philosophy' in Virgil, we are always talking about how Virgil grapples with and articulates the origins, working and telos (purpose) of the world and the way in which human beings fit into that world, particularly in their behaviour as individuals and as members of communities toward other individuals and communities. In other words, gods and morality are inextricably linked" (204–205). For a more specific discussion on Aeneas' behavior in connection with ancient ethics, see Galinsky 1988; Galinsky 1994; and Putnam 1990.

122. Hardie 1989: 91,103ff., and 362: "the simultaneous presentation of cosmic setting and history . . . are to be traced to the ideological equation of *cosmos* and *imperium;* the separate presentation of an account of the universe, apart from the sketch of Roman history, is otiose when the history of the city itself is viewed as a cosmogony."

123. Nussbaum 1993: 131.

124.

> Hic subit etiam inter ludicra scaenae spectacula et lectiones rerum vetustarum. . . . Cantus nos nonnumquam et citata modulatio instigat Martiusque ille tubarum sonus; movet mentes et atrox pictura et iustissimorum suppliciorum tristis adspectus; inde est quod adridemus ridentibus et contristat nos turba maerentium et effervescimus ad aliena certamina. Quae non sunt irae, non magis quam tristitia est quae ad conspectum mimici naufragii contrahit frontem, non magis quam timor qui Annibale post Cannas moenia

circumsidente lectorum percurrit animos, sed omnia ista motus sunt animorum moveri nolentium nec adfectus sed principia proludentia adfectibus. Sic enim militaris viri in media pace iam togati aures tuba suscitat equosque castrenses erigit crepitus armorum. (*Ira* 2.2.5–6)

125. Leigh 1997: 39.
126. Ibid.: "Lucan moves beyond tragic history, beyond *enargeia*"; and Narducci 2002: 104: "Così l'*enargeia* della narrazione resta praticamente sommersa sotto la soggettività del narratore [. . .] a una reale oggettivazione drammatica la Pharsalia preferisce una esposizione il cui fuoco principale è incentrato sulle passioni che albergano nell'animo del poeta" ("In this way the narration's *enargeia* remains buried under the subjectivity of the narrator [. . .] to dramatic realism the *Pharsalia* prefers an exposition centered on the emotions living in the soul of the poet"). What Narducci 2002: 89 says about Ovid's narrator can also describe Lucan's: Ovid uses apostrophe to defuse the reader's empathetic reaction rather than to promote it and to inhibit excessive identification with the fiction. In other words, he employs it to dissipate the enchantment created by his verses and to foster ironic detachment. See Rosati 1983: 42, and cf. my observations on Apollonius' narrator in chapter 1.
127. Johnson 1987; Leigh 1997: 275–82; Henderson 1987; Putnam 1995a; Eldred 2000; Bartsch 1997: 48–72. This tendency is denounced in Narducci 2001: 368 and 1999.
128. Bartsch 1997: 49.
129. Leigh 1997: 4; my emphasis.
130. The choice of the word *otium* has a strong philosophical resonance. The word has obviously a negative connotation on the lips of a Caesarian but it will assume a negative nuance even in Cato's speech at *BC* 2.295. On *otium*, André 1962: 125–28. On the elaboration of the meaning of *otium* as "passivity" at the end of the Republic, Barton 2001: 88–130 is particularly enlightening.
131. Cf. *Metamorphoses* 14.568–72, describing the final duel between Turnus and Aeneas as motivated by the sheer desire to win. Quint 1992: 82 and Hardie 1993: 25 emphasize the similarity between the opposing parties.
132. The idea that victory *a posteriori* determines the legitimacy of a conflict is underscored by Caesar in his apostrophe to the troops at *BC* 7.259ff.: "This is the day that will prove, with Fate as witness, who took up arms with more justice [*qui iustius arma sumpserit*]; this battle will make the defeated into the guilty party [*haec acies victum factura nocentem*]."
133. Feeney 1991: 273 and 263, where he reports the comments of Isidore (*Etym.* 7.7) and Lactantius (*Inst.* 1.11.25). For an important and well-documented discussion of ancient attitudes toward history and myth, see Feeney 1991: 250–69.
134. Ahl 1993: 141.
135. Whitman 1987: 3 and n1, with bibliography on allegorical interpretation.
136. De Lacy 1958: 259; Nussbaum 1993: 133, though she believes that allegorical interpretation was not Chrysippus' favorite avenue of interpretation (p. 135). At *Republic* 2.378d Plato uses the term *hyponoi* when he says that young people should not be exposed to poetical tales even if they have "allegorical" meanings; see Rollinson 1981: 4–7 and Nussbaum 1993:

135. According to Ford 1999: 38, Plutarch, writing in the first century CE, explains that the term *allēgoria* is relatively recent and that earlier the word *huponoia* was used (*Moralia* 19e). Ford discusses early allegorical exegesis of Homer. On the history of term allegory, see Whitman 1987, Appendix I. On Stoic *allegoresis* of Homer, see Long 1992: 41–66; on allegorical or symbolic mimesis, Halliwell 2002: 273–75 and Kardaun 1993.

137. For the Stoic idea that the relationship between words and meaning is natural, see Frede 1978: 68–74. De Lacy 1958: 258 remarks: "In his work *On Anomaly* Chrysippus pointed out that 'similar things are denoted by dissimilar words, and dissimilar things by similar words' (Varro, *Ling. Lat.* IX. 1 = SVF II.45.21 cf. D.L. VII.192)." Chrysippus' quoted statement seems very important to me because even if, as Sklenár 2003: 10 suggests, the Stoics in their rationalism "cannot admit the doctrine of the floating signifiers" and link the ambiguity of the sign to the inadequate understanding of the subject, they seriously come to terms with the difficulty of describing reality through imperfect linguistic means. On Stoic ambiguity see Atherton 1993.

138. Another instance of the ambiguity of poetical speech is given by Quintilian at 8.634f., where he says that catachresis—the application of the name of a thing to another which has no name of its own—is used by poets even if the thing so designated has a proper name.

139. Whitman 1987: 38.

140. De Lacy 1958: 257: "[s]ometimes a poem does not copy that which it signifies but rather presents a situation in which the relations of the elements correspond to those found in the thing signified, though the elements themselves are different." Plutarch explains that we should not consider myth as true accounts (*logoi*) but "should adopt that which is appropriate in each legend in accordance with its verisimilitude" (*Moralia* 374e). In other words, as Rollinson 1981: 6 suggests, "the practice of symbolic interpretation involves not the understanding of new meanings but the appropriate adjustment of mythic details to truths already known—leaving literal what is consonant with truth and symbolically constructing what is not."

141. Tate 1929: 44 and 41, interpreting Cornutus' *Theologiae Graecae Compendium* and citing c.17 and c.35 (ed. C. Lang). On Strabo's employment of Zeno and Crates to defend poetry against the opinion of Erathostenes and Aristarchus, see Rispoli 1985: 86–87.

142. Rispoli 1985: 56–57, discussing the Stoic conception of *phantasiai logikai*: "La logikê phantasia risulta dunque definita dalla potenzialità in essa implicita di essere organizzata discorsivamente e comunicata mediante parole. Essa è pertanto un'immagine che ha come sua caratteristica, a differenza delle rappresentazioni puramente reattive che si compongono e si scompongono senza che ad esse si accompagni un moto di autocoscienza, la potenzialità discorsiva, e quindi il dispiegarsi nel tempo" ("The *logikê phantasia* is defined by the potentiality implicit within it to be organized discursively and communicated by words. This is therefore an image that has as its characteristic—distinct from purely reactive representations that combine and dissolve unconsciously—discursive potentiality, and thus is unraveled in time").

143. Cf. Manetti 1993: 108: "Sextus Empiricus (*Adversus Mathematicos*, VIII, 275–76, 287) informs us that the Stoics believed that humans differed from animals because of their capacity for 'internal speech' (*lógos endiáthetos*) and their ability to combine concepts and to pass from one concept to another. Humankind possesses the notion of consequen-

tiality or 'following' (*akolouthía*) and concomitant with this is the notion of the sign in the form 'If this, then this other.' The existence of the sign is a direct result of the nature of human thought."
144. De Lacy 1978: 262.
145. Long 1996b: 276.
146. Whitman 1987: 43 and 37; on the history of allegorism, see Tate 1934.
147. De Lacy 1978: 268 and 266: the condemnation of poetry typically involves the "assumption of a simple relation between the *phone* of a poem and its meaning. Poems are interpreted literally, as if each word were used with the precision and clarity of a philosophical writing. The more usual Stoic view is that the poet does not mean literally what he says, but rather disguises his meaning by giving it poetic elaboration."
148. The quote about Prodicus' allegory is from Whitman 1987: 22; on the allegorical meaning of the desert march, see chapter 4.
149. Malamud 2003: 39.
150. Most 1989: 2057.
151. Most 1989: 2047–2048; Setaioli 1985: 839–43; Tate 1929: 41.
152. Lucan must have known well the ideas of his teacher Cornutus. Lapidge 1979: 360–62 finds that some ideas of Lucan's *Bellum Civile* parallel some *loci* in Cornutus' *Epidrome*. Most 1989: 2056 observes that Lucan does not necessarily depend on Cornutus but might be using Cornutus' same Stoic sources.
153. Cf. Liebeschuetz 1979: 149: "The gods are only introduced to show that in fact the world order does not follow the moral principles men have come to associate with gods—even to the extent that plain sacrilege, the offence that concerns the gods most closely, is rewarded rather than punished."
154. Malamud 2003: 39: "There are too many allusions to too many events, myths, and texts that would need to be explained or excluded in such a purely allegorical reading." A similar opinion is expressed in Leigh 2000. The objection is not completely tenable since in all interpretative allegory there is a tension between divergence and correspondence. Cf. Whitman 1987: 2: "The more allegory exploits the divergence between corresponding levels of meaning, the less tenable the correspondence becomes. Alternatively, the more it closes ranks and emphasizes the correspondence, the less oblique, and thus less allegorical, the divergence becomes."
155. Fantham 1992a.
156. Malamud 2003: 43. On Lucretius' belief that myth can be used to reinforce rational truths, see Gale 1994: 139; on Virgil's employment of myth in the *Georgics,* Gale 2000, esp.141–42: "Lucretius hopes with the help of the light of philosophy to dispel the darkness of the mythological world-view; for the poet of the *Georgics,* the real world—like the world of the myths—is a much more mysterious and, perhaps, finally inexplicable place."

Chapter Four

1. Johnson 1987: 55. Narducci 2002: 416 acutely responds to Johnson's criticism, explaining that while Cato's attitude might stir the antipathy of the modern reader, we

cannot know for sure if a Neronian reader would feel in the same way. Narducci's critical approach to some recent theoretical trends can be found in Narducci 1999: 37–81. On "Lucan the nihilist," see also Sklenár 2003: 1–12.

2. Marti 1945b: 361; Hemmen 1954: 125.

3. Marti 1945b: 361. Despite this characterization Marti concedes that at *BC* 2.296ff. Cato seems less indifferent.

4. Leigh 1997: 274–82.

5. ... *Catonem iam partibus non semel fractis stantem nihilo minus inter ruinas publicas rectum* (" ... Cato, after more than once his cause had been shattered, nevertheless standing erect amid the ruins of the republic," *Prov.* 2.9); *liquet mihi cum magno spectasse gaudio deos* ("I am sure that the gods looked on with exceeding joy ... ," *Prov.* 2.11). Seneca's image recalls Horace's *Ode* 3.3.78. As we will see, it is possible that in Book 2 Lucan is subtly criticizing Horace's image.

6. Bartsch 1997.

7. Among them are Ahl 1976: 231–74; George 1991; Viarre 1982; Due 1962; Morford 1967; Shoaf 1978. Arnaldi 1956: 498–99 writes, "non sai se il protagonista sia più un eroe o un santo" ("you do not know if the protagonist is more a hero than a saint"); on page 157 he describes Cato as "uguale agli dei e persino ad essi superiore" ("similar and even superior to the gods").

8. Bartsch 1997: 35.

9. I am thinking especially of Virgil's depiction of Cato on Aeneas' shield as *dantem iura* (*Aen.* 8.670). According to Narducci 2002: 403, Lucan's *BC* 2.314–16 underscores Virgil's hypocritical attempt to attribute to the imperial regime the values (law and right) that only Cato tried to defend. Cato's attachment to the law also emerges at *BC* 2.314–16: *solum invadite ... / me frustra leges et inania iura tuentem* ("attack me / while alone I am protecting in vain the law and right").

10. Bartsch 1997: 35. The expression "vile bodies" is taken from Waugh's novel of that name, via the title of Malamud (ed.) 1998.

11. Bartsch 1997: 117ff.

12. Ibid., 117. Building on Bartsch's observations, Debra Hershkowitz (Hershkowitz 1998: 231–46) points out how dangerously in the milieu of civil war words tend to shift and positive notions to mutate into their opposite. According to Hershkowitz, Cato's desire for *devotio* "moves beyond a 'healthy' Stoic attitude toward suicide into a sort of *amor mortis* worthy of Scaeva and Lucan's Stoic saint displays a sort of rashness characteristic more of Caesar than of the Stoic *sapiens*" (236). Like Caesar, Cato strives to become the absolute protagonist of the war when he wants to fight alone against all armies (*BC* 2.315–18). Cato's *virtus* does not seem different from Caesar's *furor* when both result in men's slaughter.

13. Fantham 1992b: 134; her judgment is echoed by Hershkowitz 1998: 236: "the picture of excessive grief with which Cato chooses to illustrate it [*oikeiôsis*] is inconsistent with the Stoic doctrine of *apatheia*."

14. To Lucan's Cato Bartsch opposes Seneca's Cato of *Ep.* 95.70 and *Ep.* 104. 29–31: the latter is confident to fight for a restorable "party of liberty." Yet Seneca seems quite aware of the practical futility of Cato's stance in *Ep.* 14.13: *Quid tibi vis, Marce Cato? Iam non agitur de libertate; olim pessumdata est. Quaeritur, utrum Caesar an Pompeius possideat*

rempublicam; quid tibi cum ista contentione? Nullae partes tuae sunt; dominus eligitur. Quid tua, uter vincat? Potest melior vincere, non potest non peior esse, qui vicerit. Potest melior vincere, non potest non peior esse, qui vicerit" ("What do you mean, Marcus Cato? It is not now a question of freedom; freedom disappeared long ago. The question is whether it is Caesar or Pompey who runs the state. What do you have at stake in that dispute? Nothing, because a tyrant is being chosen. What does it concern you who conquers? The better man may win, but who won is bound to be the worse man"). Seneca's last reflection becomes almost programmatic for Lucan's characterization of Cato at *BC* 1.128: *victrix causa deis placuit, sed victa Catoni*. In turn, the idea is repeated by Tacitus, *Hist.* 1.50: *inter duos quorum bello solum id scires, deteriorem fore qui vicisset.*

15. Bartsch 1997: 122–23.
16. Ibid., 106 and Pavan 1970: 414–15.
17. Bartsch 1007: 129. Cato's awareness of the importance of living among free men is presented in Seneca's *Ep.* 24.7: *non pro mea adhuc sed pro patriae libertate pugnavi, nec agebam tanta pertinacia, ut liber, sed ut inter liberos, viverem* ("So far I fought not for my freedom but for my fatherland's freedom, nor I was I acting with such steadfastness to live free but to live among free men").
18. Bartsch is perfectly aware of the contradictory nature of her characterization; she deals with this problem in the last chapter of her book, in which she frames the dilemma of "detachment" and "engagement" in a wider context. Here she writes:

> The *Bellum Civile* cannot therefore be seen as the work of a pure ironist, as recent critics have understood him. Lucan is more than a man composing "a dream of freedom which became and remained the nightmare of ruined Rome," to quote Ralph Johnson's eloquent account (1987: 69). The epic is instead the quintessential product of the composite figure I have termed a political ironist: whereas the ironist pure and simple practices cultural criticism at a cynical distance from his subject, our author presents himself as both detached from and implicated in his project; the political Lucan and the ironist Lucan draw their doubled existence from the twin perspectives I have examined in this book. As an ironist critic interested in effecting change in those who read him, therefore, our author is no mere mirror to senselessness; amid the horror of collapse, he somehow preserves "a clearing in which [his] readers can reconnect to a project of political action" (Roth 1995:149). (Bartsch 1997: 140–41)

Overall, Bartsch's treatment is fundamental to understanding Lucan's narrator in all his complexity.

19. As Cicero saw, the attempt to separate political reasons from philosophical motivations in Cato's project was practically impossible: *sed vere laudari ille vir non potest nisi haec ornata sint, quod ille ea quae nunc sunt et futura viderit et ne fierent contenderit et facta ne videret vitam reliquerit* ("But he is a man who cannot be properly praised, unless these points are discussed: how he foresaw the present state of affairs and tried to prevent it; and how he terminated his life to avoid seeing what actually happened," *Att.* 12.4.2; tr. E. Winstedt, adapted).

20. Goar 1987: 66–67.

21. The prophetic revelation is submerged and undermined by what, at the level of the plot, comes before and after it, that is the Pythia's excuses for not wanting to prophesy, the description of her frenzy, the digressions on the nature of the oracle, and the various apostrophes. On prophecy in epic see Dick 1963. On this episode, Bayet 1946; Dick 1965: 460–66; Ahl 1976: 121–30; Feeney 1991: 286–95. In his seminal contribution, Masters 1992 views Appius' encounter with the Pythia as an antiphrastic rendition of that between Aeneas and the Sibyl (91–147). He also reviews (127) the scholarship on the two episodes: Pichon 1912: 228–29; Bayet 1946: 57; Amandry 1950: 21; Schrempp 1964: 22; Ahl 1976: 127; Barratt 1979: 24 and 27; Parke and McGing 1988: 147. According to Narducci 2002: 137–41, by countering the silence of the Pythia, the voice of the narrator constructs a picture of Rome's tragic destiny dominated by a malignant power that is willing to give obscure premonitions of a tragic future but not to indicate how to exorcize that future.

22. Morford 2002: 201: "Lucan is a Stoic with a difference, a Stoic who cannot accept the injustice of the Roman republic destroyed and liberty removed, except by seeing in these disasters the dismantling of the ordered cosmos. His wise man, Cato, points out the difference between the Stoic ideal (which Seneca taught was possibly attainable) and the cruel reality of the world of the *Bellum Civile.*"

23. Sklenár 2003: 95.

24. Joyce 1993: 287 suggests that, though Acoreus is not an historical figure, his old age, moderation (*placidus senio, BC* 8.476), counseling activity, respect for pledges, and knowledge of the universe remind us of Lucan's uncle Seneca, appointed to be the advisor of the young Nero. At *BC* 10 Acoreus' explanation about the causes of Nile's flooding follows that given by Seneca at *Quaestiones naturales* 3.22. The serene Acoreus appears at first in the council of Book 8. Here he recommends that the Egyptian king show Pompey "the trust, gratitude, the sacred pledge of the king's departed father." In vain he opposes his will to that of the wicked Pothinus, who dares to recommend that the king kill Pompey (*ausus Pompeium letum damnare, BC* 8.485) and to side with the victorious Caesar: "Bow to fate and the gods, honor the lucky and avoid the wretched" (*fatis accede deisque / et cole felices, miseros fuge, BC* 8.486–87).

25. The episode concludes strangely with the statement, "with these speeches they were safe and, in peace, they lingered beyond midnight" (*sic velut in tuta securi pace trahebant / noctis iter mediae, BC* 10.332–33). As night advances we are left with the impression that Acoreus's *fabulae* have protected him and cheated the demanding tyrant.

26. Cf. Ahl 1976: 265: "Though Cato doubts the possibility that the oracle has any truth to communicate, his prime attack is directed against the *kind* of knowledge to be gained from such a consultation" (emphasis in original).

27. Liebeschuetz 1979: 153.

28. Cf. "This battle will make the defeated guilty" (*haec acies victum factura nocentem*), *BC* 7.260.

29. Sklenár 2003: 94.

30. *Fortunati ambo! Si quid mea carmina possunt, / nulla dies umquam memori vos eximet aevo, / dum domus Aeneae Capitoli immobile saxum / accolet, imperiumque pater Romanus habebit.* About this address, see chapter 1.

31. O'Higgins 1988: 221 connects the power of the *vatis* to that of the witch Erichtho, who is called by Sextus to prophesy about the future in *BC* 6.413–830. According to Gordon 1987: 234, in Lucan's poem "the role of magic is to emblematize the consequent demolition of norms and rules which make ordered social life possible." I believe that the power of magic shares something with poetical *ekplêxis* as well as with counterfactual history. Witchcraft interferes with social and natural order (*BC* 6.830). It can alter the flow of water, the natural succession of night and day; it reverses the typical sequence of things. Similarly, poetry can change history, not its plots but men's understanding of them. On Erichtho, see Baldini-Moscaldi 1976; Paoletti 1963. Samse 1942: 330ff. reads the passage as a Hellenistic *periegesis*.

32. Like Seneca, Lucan uses the language of mystic frenzy without fully accepting the doctrine of poetic *enthusiasmos*. See Setaioli 1985: 805–806 n176: "*Psicagogia* non vuol dire affatto produrre l'invasamento né in chi legge né in chi scrive, neppure in chi non ha gli scopi filosofici di Seneca [. . .] se ne rende conto anche il Mazzoli (p. 58), che giustamente osserva che Seneca 'non potrebbe mai acconsentire ad un divorzio dal logos irreversibile, fine a se stesso'" ("*Psychagogia* does not mean producing intoxication in those who read or write, not even in those who are not led by Seneca's same philosophical aims [. . .] Mazzoli too is aware of it (p. 58) when he observes that Seneca 'could never endorse the irreversible divorce of logos, its separation as an end in itself'").

33. See my chapter 3; Leigh 1997, esp. ch. 1, with a very helpful discussion of *phantasia*. A list of primary sources dealing with the phenomenon is also in Webb 1997.

34. D'Agostino 1954; Galinsky 1972: 101ff. and 160ff. Prodicus' allegory is also discussed by Nestle 1936. Leigh 2000: 102–103 describes the symbolic conception of the two paths as already visible in Hesiod's *Works and Days* 287–92 and in Simonides *PMG* 579.

35. Cato is described as "unconquered" at *BC* 9.18 (*invicti . . . Catonis*). The presence of Prodicus' intertext has been discussed by Moretti 1999: 238–41. Moretti cites as a possible source of the passage Cornelius Severus' fr. 2, which is mentioned in the *Scholia Bernensia* at *BC* 9.402. She also suggestively points out that during the Civil war, while the Republican side adopted *Hercules invictus* as its symbol, Caesar employed "*Venus victrix*" (246 n33). Recently, Leigh 2000: 95–109 has gathered all the sources that may have influenced Lucan in his description of the desert and has pronounced it to be a unique "conceptual space" in which heroes are challenged by the temptations of pleasure and concupiscence. I do not think that he has indisputably shown the defeat of Cato's "desiccated morality" if in fact it allows him to "pass through this land unscathed" (Leigh 2000: 109).

36. The difficulties of the soldiers' journey bear resemblance to those faced by the Trojans in *Aeneid* 3 when they are unable to find their way because of bad weather: *continuo venti volvunt mare magnaque surgunt / aequora, dispersi iactamur gurgite vasto; / involvere diem nimbi et nox umida caelum / abstulit, ingeminant abruptis nubibus ignes. / Executimur cursu et caecis erramus in undis. / Ipse diem noctemque negat discernere caelo / nec meminisse viae media Palinurus in unda* ("And we are scattered, tossed upon the vast / abyss; clouds cloak the day; damp night annuls / the heavens; frequently lightning fires / flash through the tattered clouds; cast from our course, we wander / across the blind waves. Even Palinurus / cannot tell day from night upon the heavens, / cannot recall our way among the waters," *Aen.* 3.196–202; tr. Mandelbaum). Cf. *BC* 9.493–97 and *BC* 9.866–67.

37. For a comparison of Cato and Hercules, see Anderson 1928: 31–37; on Hercules as a contradictory embodiment of spiritual and physical strength, Feeney 1986: 52–54 and Leigh 2000: 106–107. For connections with Lucretius' *De rerum natura,* see Esposito 1986b: 288–93.

38. The Hercules-Cato figure will be used by Silius Italicus to describe Scipio when he must choose between *virtus* and *voluptas* at *Punica* 15.102ff, Attilius Regulus fighting a giant snake, and even Hannibal crossing the Alps (3.496–502). The association between Hercules, Regulus, and Cato is also in Seneca, *Tranq.* 16.4: *ego Herculem fleam, quod vivus uritur, aut Regulum, quod tot clavis confingitur, aut Catonem, quod vulnera vulnerat sua* ("I will cry for Hercules burned alive, for Regulus crossed by nails, for Cato who wounds his own wounds"). Cf. Ahl 1976: 270–71; Bassett 1966: 258–73; Anderson 1928; on the snakes, Ahl 1976: 260–74; Shoaf 1968: 150; Aumont 1968b: 103–119; Kebric 1976; Thomas 1982: 103–123; Cazzaniga 1957; Batinski 1992; Biffi 2000; Malamud 2003; Eldred 2000. For Cato as an overachiever, see Fantham 1992a.

39. Viarre 1982: 103–110; Ahl 1976; 91ff.; Morford 1967: 123–29; Moretti 1999: 250; Paratore 1992: 85–115; Leigh 2000. The contrast between practical defeat and moral triumph is highlighted by Pfligersdorfer 1959: 344.

40. Leigh 1997: 275 seems to acknowledge his harshness.

41. Cf. Sen. *Ep.* 30.3: *hoc philosophia praestat, in conspectu mortis hilarem et in quocumque corporis habitu fortem laetumque nec deficientem, quamvis deficiatur* ("Philosophy bestows this boon upon us; it makes us joyful in the very sight of death, strong and brave no matter in what state the body may be, cheerful and never failing though the body fail us," tr. R. M. Gummere). The idea that the spirit can deal with and circumscribe bodily pain is also highlighted in Marcus Aurelius: "Let not the command center and governing part of your soul [. . .] mix with the smooth and rough movement in the body. Instead let it circumscribe itself and limit those sufferings with the [bodily] parts" (5.26.1). Quoted and discussed by Engberg-Pedersen 1996: 318.

42. Roller 2001: 77–88 explains that in Seneca human conscience is considered our judge and God is compared to a censor who scrutinizes human deeds and words (*De vita beata* 20.5). On the importance of "looking" in Seneca, see also Solimano 1991.

43. On Lucan's Stoicism and his "orthodoxy," see Guillemin 1951: 217; Gagliardi 1968: 80–81; Jal 1962; Brisset 1964: 57ff.

44. For the selflessness paradigmatically attributed by the Romans to their best leaders, see Gill 1997b: 232–33. Cf. Leigh 2000: 100: "When Cato leads his army out on the march he warns them that they face snakes, thirst, and the heat of the sand but promises that he will never bid them do anything which he is not willing to do himself. This is the characteristic manner of the good general in ancient literature." Conte 1968: 230 points out that Cato is so untouched by the web of freedom and necessity, so perfectly composed in his Stoic understanding of human existence, that he would not have made a good tragic model. Yet Lucan's insistence on Cato's sorrow and desire to make a difference in the world brings him closer to humanity and makes him vulnerable to Fortune.

45. Hardie 1993: 7.

46. Lucan's mockery of the custom of conferring divine status on emperors is visible in his ironic *elogium Neronis* (*BC* 1.33–66) and in his invitation to trample the ghosts of Rome's gods (*BC* 6.805–809). See Feeney 1991: 294–301.

47. Greene 1966: 93.

48. Lucan implicitly condemns all the emperors who have illegitimately been granted that designation. Caesar began to be called *pater patriae* in the 40s, and Nero between 55 and 56; see Narducci 2002: 414. Alföldi 1971 has shown that the title was linked to the idea of "preserver of life." According to Seneca, through the title *pater patriae* the father-son relationship was institutionalized as paradigmatic for the emperor and his subjects because what "must be done by a parent must also be done by the *princeps,* whom we have called 'father of the fatherland' with no empty flattery in view [. . .] we have called him this that he might know that *patria potestas* has been granted him, which is as moderate as can be, taking consideration for the children and subordinating his needs to theirs. Only after much delay would a father cut off his own limbs; even when he had cut them off, he would wish to replace them, and in the cutting he would groan, hesitating a great deal" (*hoc, quod parenti, etiam principi faciendum est, quem appellavimus patrem patriae non adulatione vana addducti. . . . patrem patriae appellavimus, ut sciret datam sibi potestatem patriam, quae est temperantissima liberis consulens suaque post illos reponens. Tarde sibi pater membra sua abscidat; etiam cum absciderit, reponere cupiat, et in abscidendo gemat cunctatus multum diuque*), Sen. *Clem.* 1.14.2–3 quoted by Roller 2001: 244, whose discussion (233–72) contains interesting observations on the father-son relationship as a positive model for the ruler's relationship with his subjects.

49. For a discussion of most important passages in Plutarch's *De fortuna Romanorum* and *Vitae Parallelae,* see Swain 1989a and Swain 1989b.

50. Luce 1977. On *virtus* and *fortuna* as complementary or contrasting qualities present in the makeup of a successful man, see Wistrand 1987 and Kajanto 1981, discussing the dichotomy between moral effort and random chance in the literature of the early Empire. The idea that virtue can overcome fortune morally if not physically appears in Cic. *Tusc.* 2.30, 3.36, 5.2, 5.17, etc. The Stoics obviously denied the relevance of fortune and gave priority to virtue in the establishment of the flourishing of the individual; cf. Cic. *Fin.* 5.71,78, 81ff. and Colish 1985: 42–46.

51. Beagon 2002: 111–133.

52. Ibid., 122.

53. Beagon 2002: 124 and Roller 2001: 64–77. Beagon 1992: 17–18 also notices that through Sergius' defeat and physical deformity Pliny might be indirectly praising the *virtus* of the maimed Claudius against its lack in his able-bodied successor, Nero.

54. The passage alludes to Lucretius' description of the peaceful abodes of the gods at *De rerum natura* 5.146–55.

55. A fine discussion on "indifferents" is in Roller 2001: 66–70: while "good" and "bad" are predicated by the Stoics only of an agent's mental disposition (e.g., D.L. 7.101–103), they cannot be applied to a person's actions or to the consequences of her actions, nor to physical circumstances of a person's life. These contingencies are labeled "indifferents" in relationship to the acquiring of happiness. Cf. Ormsby 1970: 25 (quoting Zeller 1962: 289): "The only absolute standard for the *sapiens* is that of virtuous intent. The absolute standard of praiseworthiness in the effects of an action is modified, so that: "every action is proper or according with duty which consists in the choice of a thing to be preferred (*proegmenon*) and in avoiding a thing to be eschewed." In order to support his argument, Ormsby also cites Cicero's definition of *media officia.* On indifferents, as well

as the importance of duty, see my appendix "Stoic Inhumanity? (A Philosophical Appraisal of Passions and Pursuits)."

56. Stephens 1996: 204.
57. Fantham 1992b: 125.
58. All these instances will be analyzed in the course of this chapter.
59. Cf. Narducci 2002: 418: "[Catone] è tutt'altro che sadicamente autoritario ("Cato is everything but sadistically authoritarian"): *monstrat tolerare labores, / non iubet* (*Phars.* 9.588)"; and at 409: "*concitus ira* . . . lo allontana nuovamente da un'immagine di stoica imperturbabilità" ("separates him from an image of Stoic imperturbability").
60. Cavajoni 1999: 78. For the meaning of the episode and ancient parallels, see Ahl 1976: 257ff.; Rutz 1970: 242ff.; Aumont 1968: 304ff.; Viarre 1982: 103–110; Brouwers 1989; Narducci 2002: 405–422 (esp. 221 and 419) for sources on the activism of the good military leader (e.g., Liv. 8.36.4).
61. The expression *suffecit unda* is found in Arrian with reference to Alexander, *Anabasis* 6.26.3, and in Plutarch, *De tuenda sanitate praecepta* 123f–124a, with reference to Philip II. On this point see Cavajoni 1999: 79–80.
62. Similarly in Plutarch *orgê* is a disease when it is not under the guidance of reason (fr. 148, ed. F. H. Sandbach 1969), but in *De cohibenda ira* 457c the *orgai* approached in the proper way offer a good spectacle; passions when accompanied by reason can intensify the vigor of virtue (*De virtute morali* 451c); cf. Laurenti 1988: 40–42; Babut 1969: 362–66.
63. Hershkowitz 1998: 246.
64. Another example of positive versus negative "burning" in Book 7 is given by George 1986: 380: "While Pompey's troops burn (*flagrant* 7.383) and *Romana virtus* arises, Caesar and his men have been inflamed by lust for tyranny (*flagrantque cupidine regni, BC* 7.240)." George (1986: 381) notices that the reactions of the two armies are triggered respectively by the speeches of Pompey and Caesar. While Pompey concludes his talk by exhorting his men to remember their families, Caesar does not hesitate to spur his soldiers to kill their relatives if they try to stand in the way.
65. Cf. Sen. *Ep.* 107.9: *optimum est pati, quod emendare non possis* ("It is best to endure what you cannot change").
66. *olim vera fides Sulla Marioque receptis / libertatis obit: Pompeio rebus adempto / nunc et ficta perit* ("Once when Sulla and Marius were admittted / actual faith in liberty died: now with Pompey's death / even its fiction perishes," *BC* 9.204–206). Notice in the passage "*libertatis obit*" echoing "*libertate perit*" of *BC* 3.146.
67. Narducci 2002: 438–42.
68. Turnus' resentment toward the gods is not Servius' only explanation; see Paratore 1990, *ad loc*. On Turnus as a tragic character, see Duckworth 1940 and more recently Panoussi 2002, with extended bibliography.
69. Hardie 1993: 38 notices the similarity between Turnus' and Pompey's death.
70. Narducci 2002: 442. Even Pompey's son Sextus condemns the gods for his father's death (*BC* 9.143–45).
71. The Stoic idea according to which the world is a stage on which men act out the good life for the gods to observe is fully developed by Seneca in epistles (e.g., *Ep.* 74.7; 76.31; 108.6–8;115.14ff.) and plays. As Rosenmeyer 1989: 47–48 points out, "Seneca compares the students who look for philosophical instruction to spectators in the stalls.

The world is an amphitheater in which an audience of immortals watches Cato struggle with Fortune (*Prov.* ch. 2). In the plays Seneca comes close, on a number of occasions, to making it appear as if attending an exhibition or a performance defined the agents appropriately and constituted their principal fulfillment as human beings." Rosenmeyer 1989: 50 observes that Marcus Aurelius and Epictetus "slip into the theatrical trope particularly when they highlight the alienation of the responsible man from his fellows and the loneliness that makes him see himself imprisoned at the center of a watchful universe. The central Stoic dogma that the self is under obligation of attempting to assimilate itself to nature produces a degree of reflection and argumentation that, paradoxically problematizes the dimension of the self." Cf. Leigh 1997: 280–83.

72. Cf. Sen. *Brev. Vit.* 10.2: *hoc [quod fuit] est enim, in quod fortuna ius perdidit, quod in nullius arbitrium reduci potest* ("On it [the past], fortune has lost his power, on what cannot be made to conform to anybody's will"); *Ep.* 98.2: *valentior enim omni fortuna animus est* ("a strong soul is stronger than fortune").

73. Narducci 2002: 444 and Jal 1962: 188; cf. Mayer 1981, *ad loc.* and Haskins 1971, with *loci*.

74. Malamud 2003: 34. She further notes that even Pompey's attempt to check his voice (*ne quas effundere voces, BC* 8.616) reminds us of two crucial episodes of the *Bellum Civile*: Cato's refusal to consult the oracle at *BC* 9.564 (*effudit dignas adytis e pectore voces*) and the speech in which he reveals his decision to join the fight against Caesar (*arcano sacras reddit Cato pectore voces, BC* 2.285).

75. Contra Herschkowitz 1998: 236–38, who talks about Brutus' "demonic zeal." More balanced is Fantham 1992b: 138, where she observes that the passage is modeled on Hector's encounter with Paris at *Il.* 6.325–68 and especially on Allecto's goading of Turnus to war (at *Aen.* 7.419–62). Lucan uses his Virgilian model antiphrastically. Lucan's "supreme *sapiens* finds a higher necessity that justifies war, even makes it a duty," yet the word *nimios* also betrays Lucan's condemnation of the civil war. The adjective *nimius* typically means "excessive in degree," "too great," "immoderate," "transgressing the limits," yet as it can be verified in the *OCD* (1996), more rarely is also used without the idea of excess to mean "very great," "extraordinary," as in Plautus, *Am.* 616 or in Cic. *Att.* 9.7.6.

76. Fantham 1992b, *ad loc.*

77. Paratore 1990, *ad loc.* considers some ancient *loci* (Dio Cassius 53.30; Servius *ad Aen.* 1.712; Sen. *Cons. Marc.* 2.3–4) and observes that Virgil was possibly inspired by the *oratio funebris* recited by Augustus for Marcellus. Of the same opinion is Brenk 1999: 76–86, who also notices that lamentation of the unfulfilled aspirations of noble youths does not seem to be part of the Greek sepulchral epigram tradition (p.79); cf. Norden 1916: 341–45 and Austin 1977: 272–73. Anchises' *miseratio* anticipates those pronounced by the narrator for the Trojans and Italians who will die in Books 11 and 12.

78. Hardie 1993: 94.

79. Von Albrecht 1999: 115. Associations with the Roman funeral ceremonies in which the masks of illustrious ancestors are paraded are proposed by Habinek 1989: 236–38 and Bettini 1991: 142–50. Bettini explains that in Virgil's parade of heroes the model of the funeral "has been expanded into a meditation on the whole Roman history and also becomes a meditation on the future" (p.146).

80. Skard 1965: 51ff.; Bettini 1991: 290nn3 and 12 points out that Skard's thesis

should be reversed since it was not the funeral of Marcellus that inspired Virgil's "Review of Heroes," but the "Review of Heroes" that inspired Augustus' funeral.

81. Brenk 1999: 83.

82. cf. Hardie 1993: 29. Leach 1999: 12 notes that as he looks at Caesar and Pompey as well as at Marcellus, "Anchises' authority falters, or rather it becomes the subject of regret. The interventions impose a model of hindsight upon this past-become-future as he recognizes that he too is an enforced spectator of prospects he would like to change."

83. Narducci 2002: 388. In Stoic thought "[t]he name of unfolding events is fate, which is described as an eternal movement that is contiguous and well-ordered. Fate is a power of the material *pneuma* which directs everything in an orderly way. It is a single series of causes, it is providence and God's will. It is Zeus (God) and Zeus' mind. It is the single soul of the universe, of the single, all-containing "nature" (*physis*), "common nature" (*koine physis*). It determines what happens in advance. Right from the start God knows in advance everything that happens and hence, as Cicero says, if there were a human being who could grasp in his mind the connection of all causes, he would know everything" (Engberg-Pedersen 1990: 208).

84. Narducci 2002: 152–66. In Lucan and in Seneca "nature," "fortune," and "fate" can all be names for god: "call it nature, fate or fortune, these are all names of an identical god which uses his power in different ways" (Sen. *Ben.* 4.8.3). Narducci collects the most significant ancient passages in which the idea of "provvidenza crudele" is already implicit. The notion of a "cruel providence" is also present in a study by Pier Luigi Donini (Donini and Giannotti 1979: 209–43) on Seneca's *Naturales quaestiones*. Even if the destruction of the world is considered unavoidable in Stoic physics and everywhere there are signs of the imminent ending of it (e.g., the waves constantly trying to conquer the shore, water waiting everywhere ready to destroy the world, *Q.N.* 3.30.1–4), Seneca describes this observable fact as a siege conducted by nature with "malignant constancy. . . . Without ever mentioning the goodness of the whole or divine providence, suddenly he depicts in a sinister light the fatal decrees; he presents as prodromes of death and exercises in destruction those things which should be considered normal, prearranged and, in principle, beneficial phenomena of natural order" (258). Seneca would denounce the absurdity of a cosmic order that ties humanity to a cyclical regeneration but eternally denies it a way out.

85. Haskins 1971, *ad loc.*

86. Long 1996b: 178. Diogenes Laertius' passage (7.85–89) is extremely important for the Stoic idea of "following nature." The popular image of a Stoic sage dispassionately acquiescent to all external events, which he knows to be determined by a cosmic reason identical to god, was the target of John Stuart Mill's famous accusation against the Stoic ethical principle of "following nature." On this charge Long 1996b: 175 remarks, "Mill took nature in Stoic ethics to refer univocally to an externally observable criterion of good—the providential course of everything that happens."

87. Long 1996b: 174. To the extent that Long gives priority to nature as an internal criterion and as a teleological principle that exists inside us in order to structure human life in the best way possible, Engberg-Pedersen agrees with him. He writes: "it is because human beings see certain things as valuable that these things are valuable." (Engberg-Pedersen 1990: 40–41 is responding to Long 1996b: 134–56 = ch. 6, "The logical basis

of Stoic ethics," and 1996: 156–79 = ch. 7, "Greek Ethics after McIntyre and the Stoic Community of Reason").

88. For a more problematic interpretation of *BC* 9.573–80, see the last section of this chapter.

89. Cf. *BC* 2.44: *effundunt iustas in numina saeva querellas* ("they raise to the cruel gods just lamentations") and *BC* 2.59–60: *saeve parens, utrasque simul partesque ducesque, / dum nondum meruere, feri* ("Oh savage parent, destroy both factions and both leaders before they have earned it!").

90. Narducci 2002: 157–62.

91. The soldiers summoned by Cato to face the hardships of Libya are described in similar terms at *BC* 9.406–408: *sic ille paventes / incendit virtute animos et amore laborum, / inreducemque viam deserto limite carpit* ("Thus he fired their fearful spirits with virtue and love of toil and continued along the desert path, the road from which there is no turning back"). Note the occurrence of the vocabulary employed in the description of Brutus, *BC* 2.323–25.

92. The entire speech flows from Cato's mouth as an oracular utterance (*erupere ducis sacro de pectore voce, BC* 9.255).

93. Ormsby 1970: 54.

94. Important studies of the bees in *Georgics* 4 are: Dahlmann 1954; Griffin 1979; Johnston 1980; Leach, 1977; Thomas 1982: 70–92; Bettini 1991: 198–219. In a paper read in Leeds (April 2004) for the Annual Conference of the Classical Association of England and Wales, Martin Brady has noticed the similarity of *BC* 9.283–93 to *Iliad* 2.84–93: Homer's passage contains a simile that compares the Achean army with a swarm of bees as it makes its way to the assembly to hear the speech of Agamemnon, "shepherd of men" (2.85).

95. Thomas 1982: 79 and n41.

96. The incoherence between Virgil's first and second image of the bees is caught by Miles 1980: 241.

97. Miles 1980: 250; Barton 2001: 113: "Virgil's bees, conceived under Augustus, understood that the health of the hive depended on the health of their 'king.' With him, they were of one mind; if anything should happen to the 'king,' the bees would 'break their faith' and tear the hive to pieces. Moreover, it was for the 'king' bee—and not for the hive—that the bees exposed their bodies to the risks of battle and sought a glorious death (*Georgica* 210–218)."

98. Ormsby 1970: 58.

99. Ormsby 1970: 57 reminds us that *aeris sonus* can also be the sound of a horn.

100. The episode of the Corycian old man is hard to interpret: cf. Miles 1980: 236–40; Perkell 1981; Thomas 1982: 56–60; Kenney 1984: xxxvi–xxxix; Ross 1987: 201–206.

101. Thomas 1982: 87.

102. Hershkowitz 1998: 231–46.

103. In chapter 3 I have discussed the importance of "the Phrygian bronze" in connection with philosophical *logos*, which propels auditors toward the pursuit of a better life. It is possible that at *BC* 9.283–93 Lucan is also alluding to *Ep.* 84, where Seneca develops the *topos* of the bees' production of honey.

104. On the importance of *oikeiôsis* in the *Bellum Civile*, see George 1988.

105. [*P*]*ertinere autem ad rem arbitrantur* [*sc. Stoici*] *intellegi natura fieri ut liberi a parentibus amentur, a quo initio profectam communem humani generis societatem persequimur.*

106. Quoted in Long 2003: 385–86. The compelling power of the social *oikeiôsis* that parents felt toward their children is emphasized by Epictetus at *Diss.* 1.23.5: it is not possible not to love your children (cf. SVF 3.179; 2.724).

107. Rorty 1998: 244–59; Engberg-Pedersen 1990; Striker 1983; Long 1991.

108. Haskins 1971: 58; cf. Tacitus *Ann.* 1.1.3: *sine ira et studio.*

109. On the *laudatio* as a way of highlighting Cato's Stoic traits, see Fantham 1992b and Haskins 1971 *ad loci;* Nutting 1932: 43.

110. Describing Cato's intervention against the conspirators, Velleius Paterculus represents him as "incarnating virtue" and "closer to the gods than to the rest of men" (*homo virtuti simillimus* and *diis quam hominibus propior,* 2.35.1ff). Cf. Goar 1987: 42: "Cato is as mighty and just a judge of causes as the gods themselves; perhaps he is even morally superior to them." According to the scholar, Cato's legend reached its acme with Lucan's *Bellum Civile.* Seneca praises him for his stability: *nemo mutatum Catonem totiens mutata republica vidit: eundem se in omni statu praestitit, in praetura, in repulsa, in accusatione, in provincia, in concione, in exercitu, in morte* ("No one ever saw Cato change, no matter how often the state changed; he kept himself the same in all circumstances: in the praetorship, in defeat, under accusation, in his province, on the platform, in the army, in death," *Ep.* 104.30). At any rate, sometimes Seneca underscores Cato's emotional involvement; for instance, at *Ep.* 24.8 he describes the dying Cato as *iratus* at Caesar as well as at himself.

111. Tandoi 1966: 68; Goar 1987: 72. Fehrle 1983: 277 calls attention to Cato's *exit* as that of a hopeless Roman noble. Plutarch is critical of the Stoics; thus he appreciates Cato particularly when he seems to go against the School's prescription. As Babut remarks, "Il est frappant que les seules réserves enregistrées sur la conduite de Caton portent précisément sur des actes parfaitement conformes aux préceptes et à l'enseignement stoïciens, plutôt que sur les rares manquements du héros à l' idéal de son école" ("It is shocking that the only reservations registered on the conduct of Cato pertain precisely to acts perfectly conforming to Stoic precepts and teachings, rather than referring to the hero's shortcomings from the School's ideal"), Babut 1969 quoted by Goar 1987: 66. Thus Cato's "passionate behavior" is for Plutarch a positive element not a negative one.

112. Yet Ormsby 1970: 27 finds the attire odd considering that Hortensius had died months before Caesar's crossing of the Rubicon; cf. George 1986: 383.

113. Ahl 1976: 251.

114. I follow in this case Fantham 1992b, who prints *persequar* instead of the weaker *prosequar.*

115. Ahl 1976: 244: "This passage [2.297–303] should warn us that we will severely misconstrue Lucan's Cato if we regard him solely as a Stoic hero, more dedicated to pure philosophy than to political ideals."

116. Lucan might also have in mind Seneca's description of Scaevola at *Ep.* 24.5 (*Mucius ignibus manum imposuit*). For a negative characterization of Lucan's scene, see Fantham 1992b: 134, suggesting that Cato's ritual action "is made to seem passionate and hazardous by the unexpected *ignibus atris inseruisse manum.* If "black torches" evoke the Furies and their frenzy, the allusion to Scaevola's brave *exemplum* contributes to Cato's positive allure.

117. Keith 2000: 68–69.

118. Dido is presented as a victim also at *Aen.* 4.60–66. About these lines Spence 1999: 85 writes: "The verses are strikingly ambiguous. Line 65 reintroduces the image of the inner fire that is destroying Dido (*mollis flamma*, "a supple flame") as if to suggest that the fire is also that of the sacrifice she is performing. It is not until the end of the next line that the reader can be sure that the fire is metaphoric, not literal. This ambiguity suggests that Dido is, herself, the sacrificial victim."

119. Hardie 1993: 29 and 41.

120. Ahl 1976: 83 quotes the passages of the *Bellum Civile* that ground his reading, *BC* 4.789–90—"Let bloody Hannibal and the Carthaginians have this as a terrible placatory offering (*piacula dira*)"—and *BC* 6.309–311: "Nor would Juba have lain heavy and naked upon the sands of Africa, nor would Scipio have placated the ghosts of Carthage with the shedding of his blood, nor would holy Cato have been lost to life" (*nec Iuba Marmaricas nudus pressisset harenas / Poenorumque umbras placasset sanguine fuso / Scipio, nec sancto caruisset vita Catone*). According to Ahl 1976: 86–67, the influence of the gladiatorial combats on Lucan's poem would be particularly evident in his use of the word *par* in the sense of "matched" rather than "equal" and almost programmatically employed to describe the struggle between liberty and tyranny (*par quod semper habemus, / libertas et Caesar, erit,* 7.695–96).

121. Verbal echoes link Cleopatra's death with that of Dido; see Keith 2000: 119; Parry 1966: 115 and 120.

122. The snakes here and elsewhere in the poem are heralds of death (e.g., *Aen.* 2.203; 7.450; 8.289). Timbres, the instruments typically used in the cult of Isis, and twin snakes also appear in Horace, *Carmen* 1.37.7 and in Propertius 3.2.43: *Romamque tubam crepitanti pellere sistro;* cf. Paratore 1990, *ad loc.*

123. Although a sistrum is different from a cymbal, both instruments are often mentioned together in connection with the worship of Cybele. According to Smith's dictionary (1875: 382), sistrum is sometimes referred to the class of cymbala and Bessaraboff 1941: 10 and 17–18 classifies them as "idiophones," instruments that produce sounds from the substance of the instrument itself.

124. Keith 2000: 119.

125. Ahl 1976: 319 n27 and most recently Radicke 2004, ch. 3.

126. This is Courtney's text as cited and translated by Keith 2000: 120. As Courtney 1993: 338–39 explains, Cleopatra collected criminals to test different methods of death. Eventually she chose the cobra; at line 47 the basilisk seems envisaged. About the *Carmen de bello Actiaco*, see Benario 1983 and Cozzolino 1975.

127. On the snakes as an incarnation of Caesar, see Eldred 2000: 70–71 and Ormsby 1970: 110.

128. Leigh 1997: 273–91.

129. Line 9.483 echoes Nisus' concerns for Euryalus at *Aen.* 9.20 (*solum te in tanta pericula mittam?*). On the importance of Euryalus' mother in the *Aeneid,* and on her similarities to Penelope and Dido, see Wiltshire 1999: 172–77. On Euryalus' mother and Mezentius, see Eagan 1980: 159–63; on the tendency of men longing for honor to fail to mention its costs to women, Heilbrun 1979: 135. The lamentations of Virgil's women counteract this bias without really offering an alternative vision.

130. Eagan 1980: 161–63 compiles a long list of similarities between the story of Lausus and Mezentius and that of Euryalus and Euryalus' mother.

131. Cf. Cato's final prayer to his enemy (*me, me . . . in me convertite ferrum, BC.* 9.437).

132. Nugent 1999: 263.

133. Narducci 2002: 400–401.

134. Ahl 1976: 240. He also notes that Lucan's dilemma in dealing with Cato's entry in Book 2 is reminiscent of the problem faced by Virgil in Book 2. Here Aeneas, like Cato, is endowed with the appropriate instinct to perish with Troy, but Venus convinces him not to do it by pointing out that the inclemency of the gods (*divum inclementia, divum, Aen.* 2.602) not any human action is to blame for Troy's destruction.

135. Ahl 1993 emphasizes the importance of Neronian Rome "as one of the great (if neglected) crossroads of western intellectual history . . . [T]he Julio-Claudian principate, through Lucan and St. Paul, yields our first canonical definitions of Cato and Christ and confirms the divinity of those prepared to make a ritual offering of themselves, a *devotio*, for the community at large. . . . As hopes of political *libertas* vanished, those who, like Lucan, idealized Cato gradually shifted allegiance to Christ and regenerated Rome as the *civitas dei*" (136–37).

136. Hardie 1997: 93.

137. Rorty 1998: 251. For a reevaluation of the emotions in the sage, see also Irwin 1998b and Sorabji 2000. I discuss their approach in my Appendix.

138. Sorabji 2000: 175, commenting on Epictetus 2.22. This kind of detachment is in fact what allows Cato to be above all factions.

139. Rorty 1998: 244 and 250.

Conclusion

1. Barton 2001: 34.
2. Ibid., 88.
3. Fears 1981: 824
4. Barton 2001: 116.
5. Ibid., 118.
6. Barton 2001: 119, quoting Seneca, *Ep.*104.30.
7. Ibid., 123.
8. Ibid., 125
9. Ibid., 129–30 mentions Ajax's fight against divine bolts as a symbol of Seneca's inability to pursue his philosophy to its ultimate consequences.
10. "The Serpent and the Flame: the Imagery of the Second Book of the *Aeneid*" is the title of Knox's famous article (Knox 1950).
11. On Seneca's employment of attractive snake imagery in *Medea* and on the aesthetic consequences of this representation on the reader, see Nussbaum 1994: 439–83.
12. Too 1998: 199.
13. Ibid., 211.
14. Ibid., 205–206.

15. Ibid.
16. Lada 1996: 403.
17. Cf. *fatum* at *BC* 9.980.
18. Eldred 2000: 68.
19. Ibid., 70.
20. Mazzoli 1970: 39: "*Carmen* è la formula dell' incantatore e del legislatore, l'oracolo del profeta, il verso del poeta, la ricetta del medico: è la parola che agisce e costruisce."
21. Naddaff 2002: 133; cf. Halliwell 2002: 77ff.
22. Clay 2003: 103.
23. Pucci 1977: 105.
24. Ibid., 28 and 64.

Appendix

1. Irwin 1998a: 219. He deals with the topic again, and at greater length, in 1998b:151–92. My comments on Stoic attitudes toward indifferents and emotions are strongly influenced by his discussion, which is accessible even to an audience of nonexperts.
2. Nussbaum 1994, chapters 7 and 8. Perhaps the first to accuse the Stoics of inhumanity was Lactantius in *Divinae Institutiones* 6.10.2 (= SVF 3.450). An important modern criticism of Stoic *apatheia* is in Striker 1991:1–75. Striker believes that "the Stoic misdescribed virtue in order to guarantee its unwavering stability" and make it dependent upon nothing but ourselves.
3. Irwin 1998a: 228.
4. Irwin 1998b: 165ff. Only the good is worth choosing per se; all the other supposed goods are really only preferred indifferents. On this topic see Stob. *Eclogues* 2.46.5–10 (= SVF 3.2); 2.77.16–19 (= SVF 3.16).
5. Quoted by Irwin 1998b: 175–76.
6. Quoted by Irwin 1998b: 176.
7. Irwin 1998a: 232.
8. The Stoics claimed that the judgment of good and evil implicit in emotional reactions is always unwarranted since Providence never allows anything truly grievous to befall you, though you might wrongly judge that it has. Therefore, according to Stoic consideration no fellow human or event is truly hateful of worthy of anger. The debate about emotions can be easily transformed into a debate about values.
9. See Sauvé Meyer 1998: 221–40.
10. Besides the classical treatment in Rist 1978: 239ff., see Annas 1993 and Cooper 1989a: 9–38. On Cato's suicide as a Stoic act, Rist 1969: 244–46; Griffin 1976: 190–91 and 380–81; Grisé 1982: 201–204; Delarue 1996: 212–30.
11. Brennan 2003: 287.
12. This seems to be Seneca's suggestion at *Ep.* 14.12. According to Griffin 1976: 192, Cato's decision to participate in the war is not endorsed by Seneca. Narducci 2002: 423 n22 notes that in other instances Seneca seems to be of a different opinion. For instance, in *Ep.* 95 Seneca compares Cato fighting in the civil war to a fiery horse (95.69). He observes

that Cato was the only one to fight for the integrity of the state, that facing foreign and Roman legions he was not afraid to raise his free voice for the sake of the Republic, and that he risked everything for the cause of freedom. Here we obviously have Seneca's praise of a sage actively engaged to confront his political environment. In the school of rhetoric the debate between Brutus and Cato must have become a *topos;* see Narducci 2002: 370–74.

13. Inwood 1985: 127 warns the reader that the word *pathos* is used rather narrowly by the Stoics and it is not really clear what the Stoics meant with the term *pathê*, which is generally translated as "passions" or "emotions." One of the first authors to record the difficulty of translating the Greek word *pathê* is Cicero in *Tusculanae Disputationes* 3.7. In Aristotle the term covers a set of phenomena that we would qualify as "emotions" and consider in certain instances positive. Instead, for the Stoics *pathê* are wrong by definition and this is why the term is perhaps better rendered by "passions," which suggests exaggerated and extreme behavior. Brennan 1998: 34 maintains that in connection with Stoic theory *pathê* should be translated not simply as emotions and not even as "excessive passions," but as "vicious motivations." This should not be forgotten since, when we think about a passionate person today, we tend to emphasize the way in which she carries out an action and not about her intentions while she is carrying it out. Once we know that the Stoics were rightly opposed to vicious motivations, we still wonder whether they were opposed to emotions in the familiar sense and if or how the Stoic sage, who is obviously free from wicked motivations and excessive feelings, might still have some emotions (Brennan 1998: 21–70; cf. Irwin 1998a: 223). Stoic sources do mention some positive emotions like joy (*chara*), volition (*boulesis*), and caution (*eulabeia*): "They say that there are three ways of being well affected (*eupatheiai*)—joy, caution, and wish. Joy is opposed to pleasure, being reasonable elation. Caution is opposed to fear, being reasonable avoidance; for the sage will not fear at all, but will be cautious. And wish is opposed to appetite, being reasonable desire . . . and they say that the sage is also unaffected because he is not carried away. But another sort of unaffected person is the bad person, where 'unaffected' is equivalent to 'insensitive' and 'relentless'" (D.L. 7.115–116; SVF 3.432). Rorty 1998: 243 lists the ancient sources that document these benign affections (*eupatheiai*). On *eupatheia* or "good passion," see Inwood 1985: 173–75. Pain is not given as a possible positive emotional available to the sage since according to Chrysippus it can only be triggered by the recognition that a true evil is present, but since vice is the only evil the sage is not exposed to it. At any rate, later Stoics (Seneca included) seem to have a different opinion. On this, see below.

14. *Ep.* 11.1–3 contains very important information about Seneca's ideas on "automatic reactions," esp. paragraphs 1–2: *nulla enim sapientia naturalia corporis aut animi vitia ponuntur: quidquid infixum et ingenitum est, lenitur arte, non vincitur. Quibusdam etiam constantissimis in conspectu populi sudor erumpit non aliter quam fatigatis et aestuantibus solet, quibusdam tremunt genua dicturis, quorundam dentes colliduntur, lingua titubat, labra concurrunt. Haec nec disciplina nec usus umquam excutit, sed natura vim suam exercet et illo vitio sui etiam robustissimos admonet* ("Wisdom cannot completely extirpate the natural reactions [*vitia*] of soul and body: whatever is radicated and congenital can be attenuated with training [*arte*] not defeated. There are men, even extremely stable men, who, facing a multitude, sweat as if they were working or were hot; there are others whose knees

tremble when they are about to talk, whose teeth chatter, whose tongue freezes and whole lips become sealed. Neither discipline nor habit can eliminate these reactions, but nature displays her strength and through that reaction admonishes even the strongest men to be aware of her presence").

15. *Ep.* 9 is also extremely important for establishing that even the sage is subject to pain. In this letter Seneca underlines the inappropriateness of rendering the Greek word *apatheia* simply as *impatientia* (*Ep.* 9.2), and he distinguishes between an "invulnerable soul" and "a soul incapable of suffering" (*invulnerabile animum . . . aut animum extra omnem patientiam*, 9.3). The sage "feels" all hardships but can overcome them (*noster sapiens vincit quidem incommodum omne, sed sentit*, 9.3). The fact that if he loses an eye or a limb he does not regret his lost physical wholeness does not mean that he prefers his mutilation (*erit inminuto corpore et amputato tam laetus quam [in] integro fuit; sed si quae sibi desunt non desiderant, non deesse mavult*, 9.5). Finally, Seneca acknowledges the self-sufficiency of the sage (*se contentus est sapiens*, 9.13), but he also explains that his self-sufficiency is often misunderstood (*hoc, mi Lucili, plerique perperam interpretantur*, 9.13): "they withdraw the wise man from the world and force him to dwell within his own skin" (*sapientem mundique submovent et intra cutem suam cogunt*, 9.13). He corroborates his idea with the words of Chrysippus, according to whom "the wise man is in want of nothing and yet needs many things" (*Volo tibi Chrysippi quoque distinctionem indicare. Ait sapientem nulla re egere, et tamen multis illi rebus opus esse*, 9.14).

16. Pain in the sage's psyche appears to be possible in the view of Posidonius, according to whom affective movements (παθητικαί κινήσεις) are determined partly by natural constitution, partly by environment. They are necessarily present, and they cannot really be removed from the self: "Indeed, given that for Posidonius it is the affective movement that gives rise to the impulsive impression, one can assume that for him the virtuous agent could not in fact simply set aside or get rid of that impression [. . .] it would seem then that the virtuous agent would be in conflict with himself, after all, and in a state of disharmony that should be counted as detracting from his happiness" (Cooper 1998: 96–97). Thus grief according to Posidonius can problematically affect even the best person.

17. Rorty 1998: 251; cf. White 1990: 42–58. Lucan's description of Cato suggests the same point: Cato's concerns never become inappropriate and never turn into unreasonable and unhealthy passions (*BC* 2.390–91).

18. Inwood 1985: 176 and 177, quoting Aulus Gellius' *testimonia*:

> Presentations in the mind [. . .] with which the intellect of man is struck as soon as the appearance of something which happens reaches the mind are not voluntary or subject to one's control; but by a force of their own they press themselves on men to be acknowledged. But the assents [. . .] by which the same presentations are acknowledged are voluntary and occur subject to human control. Therefore, when some frightening sound from the sky or a collapsing building or the sudden announcement of some danger, or something else of the sort, occurs it is inevitable that even a sage's soul be moved for a short while and be contracted and grow pale, not because he has formed an opinion of anything evil but because of certain rapid and unreflective movements which forestall the proper function of the intellect

and reason [. . .]. And they say that the difference between the mind of the
sage and the fool is that the fool thinks that the violent and harsh presenta-
tions which first strike his mind really are as they seem; and he also confirms
with his own assent these initial reactions [. . .] whereas the sage [. . .] does
not assent. (*Noctes Atticae* 19.1.14–20)

Inwood (ibid.) finds the same notion in Seneca, *De ira* 1.16–17 (= SVF 1.215) and in Cicero, *Tusculanae Disputationes* 3.83: *morsus tamen et contractiuncula quedam animi relinquetur* ("nevertheless, a 'bite' and a certain small contraction of the mind will remain"). On this topic, see also *Ep.* 57.1–6.

19. It is generally accepted that Chrysippus' theory assumed a monistic model of the soul since he did not recognize that human action can be governed by more than one power. Later Stoics like Posidonius rejected this monism "for a more complex analysis of human psychology which granted considerable importance to the sort of non-rational powers of the soul which Plato and Aristotle had both recognized" (Inwood 1985: 131). See also Cooper 1989b: 25–42 and Cooper 1998: 71–111, explaining that while Chrysippus understood emotions as functions of the adult human being's reasoning power, according to Galen "Posidonius adopted the rival, tripartite psychology of reason, spirit and appetite, that is most familiar to us from Plato's republic but was accepted also, as Galen correctly notes, by Aristotle" (p. 71). Cf. Gilbert-Thirry 1977: 345–93; Kidd 1988; Kidd 1971: 200–215; Rist 1969: 182–84.

20. Irwin 1998b: 189.

21. Ibid., 190.

22. Rorty 1998: 243–44. Similarly Marcus Aurelius 6.39 and 7.13, of which Engberg-Pedersen 1998: 333 says, "Marcus' idea is clearly that loving *others* and doing good to *them*, and moreover doing it from one's heart and *not* as a mere duty, is the only proper content of the joy that goes with benefiting oneself, that is, with leading a happy life."

23. Quoted in Long 2002: 115 and 232, where nevertheless he suggests that the explicit linkage between "what is appropriate" (*kathekon*) and "not being unmoved" is absent from earlier Stoic texts.

24. *E.N.* 1101a5: "If activities are, as we said, what gives life its character, no happy man can become miserable; for he will never do the acts that are hateful and mean. For the man who is truly good and wise, we think, bears all the chances of life becomingly and always makes the best of circumstances, as a good general makes the best military use of the army at his command and a good shoemaker makes the best shoes out of the hides that are given him; and so with all other craftsmen. And if this is the case, the happy man can never become miserable; though he will not reach blessedness, if he meet with fortunes like those of Priam" (tr. D. Ross).

25. Irwin in Everson 1998: 190–91.

26. Engberg-Pedersen 1998: 306: "In the last resort the general view appears to be that [*apatheia*] should be rejected." For rejection of *apatheia* as "impassivity," see Nussbaum 1994, chs. 10–12; for a humane kind of Stoic sage, Engberg-Pedersen 1990.

27. Sorabji 2000: 8 and 170–71, in which the primary sources are given: Stobaeus 2.76.9–15 (= SVF 3 Diogenes 44; Antipater 57); Clement of Alexandria *Stromateis* 2.21 (= SVF 3 Diogenes 46; Antipater 58); D.L. 7.88 (SVF 3 Diogenes 45); Cicero *Fin.*

3.22 (= SVF 3.18); 5.20 (=SVF 3.44); Plutarch, *De communibus notitiis adversus Stoicos* 1079F–1071E (SVF 3.195); 1072E–F (= SVF 3 Antipater 59).

28. Zanker 1995: 90–108, quoted by Sorabji 2000: 8 and 186.

29. Sorabij 2000: 186; on page 106 he suggests that even Posidonius, perhaps following Zeno, did not recommend being emotionless but simply free from excessive emotions.

30. E.g., Seneca, *Ep.* 116.1: "It has often been asked whether it is better to have moderate passions or no passions. We Stoics expel them, whereas the Peripatetics temper them. I do not see how any moderate condition of a disease could be healthy or useful."

31. Gill 1998a: 124; see also the bibliography given above.

32. See Cic. *Off.* 1.101: "Souls have a dual power and nature. One part resided in impulse (*appetitus*), which drives a human being in different directions, and the other in reason (*ratio*), which teaches and explains what should be done and what should be avoided. Thus it comes about that reason leads, impulse obeys." Cf. *Off.* 1.132 and 2.18. Sorabji 2000: 106 reminds us that the Latin *perturbatio* is Cicero's translation of the Greek *pathos*.

33. Alesse 1994: 156–62; Morford 2002: 26.

34. Morford 2002: 24–25, pointing out that although Panaetius' moderation was pleasing to Cicero and Seneca, his precepts, if we are to believe *Pro Murena* 66, were also accepted by Cato. Sedley 2003: 24 is skeptical about attributing to Panaetius a shift of ethical focus from the sage to the non-sage.

35. Graver 2002: xxiv.

36. Sorabji 2000: 202, commenting on Philodemus, *De ira,* col. 37–41 (ed. Indelli).

37. On Roman eclecticism, see Cambiano 1992: 323–25 and Cambiano 1987: 118–24.

38. Sedley 2003: 32 points out that Arius Didymus was maintained by Augustus and is "widely if controversially" identified with the Arius whose *Epitome* is copiously excerpted by Stobaeus. Gill 2003: 44–45 judges "eclecticism" positively and cautions the reader that even if "most philosophically committed thinkers saw themselves as having a determinate intellectual position," they were also ready to "interpret what it meant to be a Stoic or Academic . . . in broader terms than was normal . . . incorporat[ing] within the school's theory ideas drawn from other sources" or "redescribing the position of one's own school in terms drawn from another position." On eclectism see also Dillon and Long 1988, esp. Introduction and ch. 1.

Bibliography

Ahl, F.M. 1976. *Lucan. An Introduction.* Ithaca, NY: Cornell University Press.
_____. 1993. "Form Empowered: Lucan's *Pharsalia.*" In Boyle (ed.) 1993: 124–43.
Alesse, F. 1994. *Panezio di Rodi e la tradizione stoica.* Napoli: Bibliopolis.
Alexiou, M. 1974. *The Ritual Lament in Greek Tradition.* Cambridge: Cambridge University Press.
Alföldi, A. 1971. *Der Vater des Vaterlandes im römischen Denken.* Darmstadt: Wissenschaftliche Buchgesellschaft.
_____. 1985. *Caesar in 44 v. Chr.* Bonn: Habelt.
Allen, W. 1940. "The Epyllion. A Chapter in the History of Literary Criticism." *TAPhA* 71: 1–26.
Amandry, P. 1950. *La Mantique apollinienne à Delphes.* Paris: E. de Boccard.
Anderson, A. R. 1928. "Heracles and His Successors." *HSCP* 39: 31–42.
Anderson, W. S. 1982. *Essays on Roman Satire.* Princeton, NJ: Princeton University Press.
André, J. M. 1962. "*Otium* et vie contemplative dans le 'Lettres à Lucilius." *REL* 40: 125–28.
Annas, J. 1993. *The Morality of Happiness.* Oxford: Oxford University Press.
_____. 1980. "Truth and Knowledge." In Barnes, Burnyeat, and Schofield (eds.) 1980: 84–104.
Aristotle. 1905–1952. *The Works of Aristotle, translated into English under the editorship of W. D. Ross.* Oxford: Clarendon Press.
Arnaldi, F. 1956. *Antologia della poesia latina.* Vol. II. Napoli.
Asmis, E. 1990. "The Poetic Theory of the Stoic 'Aristo.'" *Apeiron* 23.3: 147–201.
_____. 1992. "Crates on Poetic Criticism." *Phoenix* 45.2: 138–69.
_____. 1995. "Philodemus on Censorship, Moral Utility and Formalism in Poetry." In Obbink (ed.) 1995: 148–77.
Atherton, C. 1993. *The Stoics on Ambiguity.* Cambridge: Cambridge University Press.
Aumont, J. 1968a. "Cato en Libye (Lucain, *Pharsale,* 9.294–949)." *Revues des Etudes Anciennes* 70: 304–20.
_____. 1968b. "Sur l'épisode des reptiles dans la *Pharsale* de Lucain (9.587–937)." *Bulletin de l'association Guillaume Budé* 1: 103–119.
Austin, R.G. (ed.) 1977. *P. Vergili Maronis Aeneidos Liber Sextus.* Oxford: Clarendon Press.
Babbit, F. C. (tr.) 1960. *Plutarch's Moralia.* Cambridge, MA: Harvard University Press.
Babut, D. 1969. *Plutarque et le Stoïcisme.* Paris: Presses Universitaires de France.
Badalí, R. (ed.) 1996. *Marco Anneo Lucano, La Guerra civile o Farsaglia.* (Introduzione e traduzione di L. Canali). Milan: Biblioteca Universale Rizzoli.
Bakhtin, M., 1981. *The Dialogic Imagination. Four Essays by M. M. Bakhtin,* ed. M. Holquist, tr. C. Emerson and M. Holquist. Austin: University of Texas Press.
Bal, M. 1985. *Narratology. Introduction to the Theory of Narrative.* Toronto: University of Toronto Press.

Baldini-Moscaldi, L. 1976. "Osservazioni sull'episodio magico del VI libro della 'Farsaglia' di Lucano." *Studi Italiani di Filologia Classica* 48: 140–99.

Baratin, M., and F. Desbordes. 1981. *L'Analyse linguistique dans l'antiquité classique.* Paris: Klinscksieck.

Barchiesi, A. 1984. *La traccia del modello: effetti omerici nella narrazione virgiliana.* Pisa: Giardini.

———. 1999. "Suffering and Interpretation in the *Aeneid.*" in Hardie (ed.) 1999: 324–44.

———, and G. B. Conte. 1989. "Imitazione e arte allusiva. Modi e funzioni dell'intertestualità." In Cavallo, Fedeli, and Giardina (eds.) 1989. Vol. 2: 81–141.

Barnes, J. 1997. *Logic and the Imperial Stoa.* Leiden: Brill.

Barnes, J., M. Burnyeat, and M. Schofield (eds.) 1980. *Doubt and Dogmatism.* Oxford: Oxford University Press.

Barratt, P. 1979. *Belli Civilis Liber V: A Commentary.* Amsterdam: Adolf M. Hakkert.

Barton, C. 1993. *The Sorrows of the Ancient Romans.* Princeton, NJ: Princeton

———. 2001. *Roman Honor.* Berkeley: University of California Press.

Bartsch, S. 1997. *Ideology in Cold Blood. A Reading of Lucan's Civil War.* Cambridge, MA.: Cambridge University Press.

Basore, J. W. 1904. "Direct Speech in Lucan as an Element of Epic Technique." *TAPhA* 35: 94–96.

Bassett, E. 1966. "Hercules and the Hero of the Punica." in Wallach (ed.) 1966: 258–73.

Bastiaensen, A. A. R., A. Hilhorst, and C. H. Kneepkens, (eds.) 1989. *Fructus centesimus —Mélanges offertes à Gerard J. M. Bartelink à l'occasion de son soixante-cinquième anniversaire* [in the series "Instrumenta Patristica" XIX]. Turnhout: Brepols.

Batinski, E. E. 1992. "Cato and the Battle with the Serpents." *Syllecta Classica.* 3: 71–80.

Bayet, J. 1946. "La Mort de la Pythie: Lucain, Plutarque et La Chronologie Deophique." In *Mélanges dédiés à la mémoire de Félix Grat,* I.53–76. Paris: Pecqueur-Grat.

———. 1951. "Le suicide mutuel dans la mentalité des Romains." *L'Année sociologique,* (3 ser.) 1: 35–89.

Beagon, M. 1992. *Roman Nature: The Thought of Pliny the Elder.* Oxford: Oxford University Press.

———. 2002. "M. Sergius, *Fortunae Victor.*" In Clark and Rajak (eds.) 2002: 111–133.

Beissinger, M., J. Tylus, and S. Wofford (eds.). 1999. *Epic Traditions in the Contemporary World: the Poetics of Community.* Berkeley: University of California Press.

Belfiore, E. 1992. *Tragic Pleasures: Aristotle on Plot and Emotion.* Princeton, NJ: Princeton University Press.

Benario, H.W. 1983. "The 'Carmen de bello Actiaco' and Early Imperial Epic." *ANRW* 2.30.3: 1656–62.

Berhold, H. 1977. "Beobachtungen zu den Epilogen Lucans (spez. IV, 402–581; 575–581)." *Helikon* 17: 218–25.

Bessaraboff, N. 1941. *Ancient European Musical Instruments: An Organological Study of the Musical Instruments in the Leslie Lindsey Mason Collection at the Museum of Fine Arts, Boston.* Cambridge, MA: Harvard University Press.

Bettini, M. 1991. *Anthropology and Roman Culture: Kinship, Time, Images of the Soul.* (tr.

J. van Sickle). Baltimore: Johns Hopkins University Press.
Beye, C. 1982. *Apollonius' Argonauatica: Epic and Romance.* Carbondale, IL: University of Southern Illinois Press.
_____. 1993. *Ancient Epic Poetry. Homer, Apollonius, Virgil.* Ithaca: Cornell University Press.
_____. 1999. "Vergil and Apollonius." In Perkell (ed.) 1999: 271–85.
Biffi, N. 2000. "La Marcia di Catone nel deserto libico (Luc. 9, 498–510)." *Invigilata Lucernis* 22: 13–21.
Bing, P. 1988. *The Well-Read Muse: Present and Past in Callimachus and the Hellenistic Poets* (Hypomnemata 90). Göttingen: Vandenhoeck & Ruprecht.
Blandsdorf, J. 1996. "Stoici a teatro? La Medea di Seneca nell'ambito della teoria della tragedia." *Rendiconti dell'Istituto Lombardo* 130: 217–36.
Block, E. 1982. "The Narrator Speaks. Apostrophe in Homer and Virgil." *TAPhA* 112: 7–22.
Boal, A. 1985. *Theatre of the Oppressed.* New York: Urizen Books.
Borgo, A. 1985. "*Clementia:* studio di un campo semantico." *Vichiana* 14: 25–73.
Boyle, A. J. (ed.) 1995. *Roman Literature and Ideology. Ramus. Essays for J. P. Sullivan.* Bendigo, Victoria: Aureal Publications.
_____. (ed.) 1990. *The Imperial Muse. Essays on Roman Literature of the Empire. Flavian Epicist to Claudian.* Bendingo, Vic.: Aureal Publications.
_____. (ed.) 1993. *Roman Epic.* London and New York: Routledge.
Braund, M. S. 1997. "Virgil and the Cosmos: Religious and Philosophical Ideas." In Martindale (ed.) 1997: 204–222.
_____, and C. Gill (eds.) 1997. *The Passions in Roman Thought and Literature.* Cambridge: Cambridge University Press.
Brenk, E. Frederick. 1999. *Clothed in Purple Light: Studies in Vergil and in Latin Literature, Including Aspects of Philosophy, Religion, Magic, Judaism, and the New Testament Background.* Stuttgart: Franz Steiner Verlag.
Brennan, T. 1998. "The Old Stoic Theory of the Emotions." in Sihvola and Engberg-Pedersen (eds.) 1998: 21–70.
_____. 2003. "Stoic Moral Psychology." In Inwood (ed.) 2003: 257–97.
Briggs, W. 1981. "Vergil and the Hellenistic Epic." *ANRW* 2.31.2: 948–84.
Brilli, A. 1973. *Retorica della satira.* Bologna: Il Mulino.
Brink, C. O. 1971. *Horace on Poetry.* 2 vols. Cambridge: Cambridge University Press.
Brisset, J. 1964. *Les idées politiques de Lucain.* Paris: Les Belles Lettres.
Brody, B. (ed.) 1992. *Suicide and Euthanasia.* Dordrecht: Kluwer Academic.
Brouwers, J. H. 1989. "Lucan über Cato Uticensis als *exemplar virtutis.*" In Bastiaensen, Hilhorst, and Kneepkens (eds.) 1989: 49–60.
Brugnoli, G., and F. Stok (eds.) 1996. *Pompei exitus. Variazioni sul tema dall' Antichità alla Controriforma.* Pisa: Edizioni ETS.
Brunschwig, J., and M. Nussbaum (eds.) 1993. *Passions and Perceptions. Studies in Hellenistic Philosophies of Mind.* Cambridge: Cambridge University Press.
Brunt, P. 1973. "Stoicism and the Principate." *Papers of the British School at Rome* 43: 7–39.
Bulloch, E. A. 1985. "Hellenistic Poetry," In P. E. Easterling and B. M. W. Knox (eds) 1985. Vol. 1: 543–621.

Burke, J. F. 1974. "The Role of Mezentius in the *Aeneid.*" *Classical Journal* 19: 202–209.
Büttner, Stefan. 2000. *Die Literaturtheorie bei Platon und ihre anthropologische Begründung.* Tübingen and Basel: A. Francke Verlag.
Cacciaglia, M. 1974. "L'etica stoica nei drammi di Seneca." *Rendiconti dell'istituto lombardo* 108: 78–104.
Cambiano, G. 1987. *La filosofia in Grecia e a Roma.* Rome–Bari: Laterza.
———. 1992. "Le filosofie tra l'impero e il cielo." In Schiavone (ed.) 1992: 321–69.
Cartledge, P., G. Peter, and E. Gruen (eds.). 1997. *Hellenistic Constructs. Essays in Culture, History and Historiography.* Berkeley: University of California Press.
Casali, Sergio. 1999. "Mercurio a Ilerda: *Pharsalia* 4 ed *Eneide* 4." In Esposito e Nicastri (eds.) 1999: 223–36.
Casamante, A. 1999. "*Lumina Orationis:* l'uso delle *sententiae* nelle tragedie di Seneca." *Studi Italiani di Filologia Classica* 17.1: 123–32.
Castagna, L. (ed.) 1996. *Nove studi sui cori tragici di Seneca.* Milan: Vita e pensiero. Pubblicazioni dell'Università Cattolica.
Cavajoni, G. A. 1999. "Catone in Lucano 9, 509 s. *Sic concitus ira / excussit galea suffecitque omnibus unda.*" in Conca (ed.) 1999: 71–82.
——— (ed.) 1979. *Supplementum Adnotationum super Lucanum Libri I–V.* Milan: Cisalpino-Goliardica.
Cavallo, G., P. Fedeli, and A. Giardina (eds.) 1989. *Lo Spazio Letterario di Roma antica.* 5 vols. Rome–Bari: Laterza.
Caviglia, F. 1996. "I cori dell' *Oedipus* di Seneca e l'interpretazione della tragedia." In Castagna (ed.) 1996: 87–103.
Cazzaniga, I. 1957. "L'Episodio dei serpi libici in Lucano e la tradizione dei 'Theriaca' Nicandrei." *Acme: Annali della Facoltà di Lettere e Filosofia dell'Università di Milano* 10: 27–41.
Chaplin, J. 2000. *Livy's Exemplary History.* Oxford: Oxford University Press.
Charlesworth, M. 1937. "The Virtues of a Roman Emperor: Propaganda and the Creation of Belief." *Proceedings of the British Academy* 23: 105–138.
Citroni, M. 1980. "Musa pedestre." in Cavallo, Fedeli, and Giardina (eds.) 1989. Vol. 1: 311–43.
Cizek, E. 1972. *L'époque de Néron et ses controverses idéologique.* Leiden: Brill.
Clay, J. S. 1994. "The Education of Perses: From 'Mega Nepios' to 'Dion Genos' and Back." In Schiesaro, Mitsis, and Clay (eds.) 1994: 23–35.
———. 2002. *Philosophy and Power in the Graeco-Roman World. Essays in Honour of Miriam Griffin.* Oxford: Oxford University Press.
———. 2003. *Hesiod's Cosmos.* Cambridge: Cambridge University Press.
Colish, M. C. 1985. *The Stoic Tradition from Antiquity to the Early Middle Ages.* 2 vols. Leiden: Brill.
Commager, S. (ed.) 1966. *Virgil: A Collection of Critical Essays.* Englewood Cliffs, NJ: Prentice-Hall.
Conca, F. (ed.) 1999. *Ricordando Raffaele Cantarella. Miscellanea di Studi.* Bologna: Cisalpino.
Conserva, M. 1997. *L'eroe debole. L'evoluzione di Pompeo nella* Pharsalia. Palermo: Brotto.

Conte, G. B. 1968. "La guerra civile nella rievocazione del popolo: Lucano II.67–233. Stile e forma della *Pharsalia.*" *Maia* 20: 224–53.

———. 1974a. *Memoria dei poeti e sistema letterario. Catullo, Virgilio, Ovidio, Lucano.* Torino: Einaudi.

———. 1974b. *Saggio di commento a Lucano. Pharsalia VI 118–260: l'Aristia di Sceva.* Pisa: Giardini.

———. 1986. *The Rhetoric of Imitation. Genre and Poetic Memory in Virgil and other Latin Poets.* Ithaca: Cornell University Press.

Cooper, J. M. 1989a. "Greek Philosophers on Euthanasia and Suicide." In Brody (ed.) 1989: 9–38.

———. 1989b. "Some Remarks on Aristotle's Moral Psychology." *The Southern Journal of Philosophy* 27: 25–42.

———. 1998. "Posidonius on Emotions." In Sihvola and Egberg-Pedersen (eds.) 1998: 71–111.

Corbett, E. 1971. *Classical Rhetoric for the Modern Student.* New York: Oxford University Press.

Costa, C. D. N. (ed.) 1974. *Seneca. [Greek and Latin Studies. Classical Literature and Its Influence].* London: Routledge.

Courtney, E. 1993. *Fragmentary Latin Poets.* Oxford: Oxford University Press.

Cox Brinton, A. 2002. *Maphaeus Vegius and His Thirteenth Book of the* Aeneid. London: Duckworth.

Cozzolino, A. 1975. "Il *Bellum Actiacum* e Lucano." *Bollettino del Centro Internazionale per lo Studio dei Papiri Ercolanesi* 5: 81–86.

Crevatin, G. 1996. "L' empio dono." In Brugnoli and Stok (eds.) 1996: 161–81.

Curran, A. 1998. "Feminism and the Narrative Structures of the *Poetics.*" In Freeland (ed.) 1998: 289–327.

D'Agostino, V. 1954. "La favola del Bivio in Senofonte, in Luciano e in Silio Italico." *Rivista di Studi Classici* 2: 172–84.

D'Alessandro Behr, F. 2005. "The Narrator's Voice: A Narratological Reappraisal of Apostrophe in Virgil's *Aeneid.*" *Arethusa* 38.2: 189–221.

Dahlmann, H. 1954. "Die Bienenstaat in Vergils *Georgica.*" *Abhandlungen der Akademie der Wissenschaften und der Literatur in Mainz* 10: 547–62.

Davis, P. J. 1993. *Shifting Song: The Chorus in Seneca's Tragedies.* Hildesheim–Zurich: Olms-Weidmann.

DeForest, M. 1994. *Apollonius' Argonautica: A Callimachean Epic.* Leiden: Brill.

De Jong, I. 1987. *Narrators and Focalizers: The Presentation of the Story in the Iliad.* Amsterdam: B. R. Grüner.

———. 2001. *A Narratological Commentary on the Odyssey.* Cambridge: Cambridge University Press.

De Lacy, P. 1958. "Stoic Views of Poetry." *American Journal of Philology* 69: 241–71.

Delarue, F. 1996 "La Guerre Civile de Lucain: une épopée plus que pathétique." *REL* 74: 212–30.

Deratani, N. F. 1970. "Der Kampf für Freiheit, Patriotismus und Heldentum im Gedicht Lucans 'Über den Bürgerkrieg.'" In Rutz (ed.) 1970: 133–48.

Deroux, C. (ed.) 1980. *Studies in Latin Literature and Roman History.* Brussels: Collection Latomus.

———. (ed.) 1983. *Studies in Latin Literature and Roman History.* Brussels: Collection Latomus.

———. (ed.) 1986. *Studies in Latin Literature. and Roman History.* Brussels: Collection Latomus.

De Sousa, R. 1987. *The Rationality of Emotions.* Cambridge, MA: The MIT Press.

Di Cesare, A. 1974. *The Altar and the City: A Reading of Vergil's* Aeneid. New York and London: Columbia University Press.

Dick, B. F. 1963. "The Technique of Prophecy in Lucan." *TAPhA* 94: 37–49.

———. 1965. "The Role of the Oracle in Lucan's *De Bello Civili.*" *Hermes* 93: 460–66.

———. 1967. "*Fatum* and *Fortuna* in Lucan's *Bellum Civile.*" *CP* 62: 235–42.

Dilke, O. A. W. 1979. "Lucan's account of the Fall of Pompey." In *Studi in onore di B. Riposati. Studi su Varrone, sulla retorica, storiografia e poesia latina.* Vol. 1: 171–84. Rieti.

Dillon, J., and A. A. Long (eds.) 1988. *The Question of 'Eclecticism.'* Berkeley: University of California Press.

Dingel, Joachim.1974. *Seneca und die Dichtung.* Heidelberg: C. Winter.

Dobbin, R. 1998. *Epictetus. Discourses: Book 1.* Oxford: Clarendon Press.

Donini, P. L. 1982. *Le scuole, l'anima, l'impero: la filosofia antica da Antioco a Plotino.* Torino: Rosenberg & Sellier.

———, and G. F. Giannotti, 1979. *Modelli filosofici e letterari: Lucrezio, Orazio, Seneca.* Bologna: Pitagora editrice.

Dorandi, Tiziano, 1990. "Filodemo: orientamenti della ricerca attuale." *ANRW* 2.36.4: 2328–68.

Duckworth, G. E. 1940. "Turnus as a Tragic Character." *Vergilius* 4: 5–17.

Due, O. S. 1962. "An Essay on Lucan." *C&M* 23: 68–136.

———. 1970. "Lucani et la philosophie." In Durry (ed.) 1970: 203–232.

Duff, J. D. 1928. *Lucan with an English Translation.* Cambridge, MA: Harvard University Press.

Durry, M. (ed.) 1970. *Lucain.* (Entretiens sur l'antiquité classique 15). Vandoeuvres–Genève.

Dyck, A. R. 1996. *A Commentary on Cicero, De Officiis.* Ann Arbor, MI: The University of Michigan Press.

Eagan, R. B. 1980. "Euryalus's mother and *Aeneid* 9–12." In Deroux (ed.) 1980. Vol. 2: 157–76.

Earl, D. 1967. *The Moral and Political Tradition of Rome.* London: Thames & Hudson.

Easterling, P. E., and B. M. W. Knox (eds.) 1989. *Cambridge History of Classical Literature.* 4 vols. Cambridge: Cambridge University Press.

Edelstein, L., and I. K. Kidd (eds.) 1972. *Posidonius: The Fragments.* Vol.1. Cambridge: Cambridge University Press.

Eldred, K. O. 2000. "Poetry in Motion: the Snakes of Lucan." *Helios* 27: 63–74.

Elsner, J., and J. Masters (eds.) 1994. *Reflections on Nero: Culture, History and Representation.* Chapel Hill and London: The University of North Carolina.

Engberg-Pedersen, T. 1984. "Beyond Egoism and Altruism." *International Philosophical Quarterly* 24: 327–29.

———. 1986. *Aristotle's Theory of Moral Insight.* Oxford: Clarendon Press.

———. 1990. *The Stoic Theory of Oikeiôsis. Moral Development and Social Interaction in Early Stoic Philosophy.* Aarhus: Aarhus University Press.

———. 1996. "Marcus Aurelius on the Emotions." In Sihvola and Engberg-Pedersen (eds.) 1996: 305–337.

Esposito, P. 1986a. "L'Accettazione della sconfitta (Pompeo e Scipione in Livio, V. Massimo, Seneca e Luciano)." *Vichiana* 15: 294–99.

———. 1986b. "Le Esperidi e le mele d'oro (da Lucrezio a Lucano)." *Vichiana* 15: 288–93.

———. 1996. "La Morte di Pompeo." In Brugnoli and Stok (eds.) 1996: 75–125.

———. 2000. "La fine di Curione in Lucano (*Phars.* IV 581–824)." *Vichiana* 4.2: 39–54.

———. 2001. "Paradosso ed esemplarità nell'episodio di Vulteio (*B.C.* IV 402–581)." *Vichiana* 4.3: 39–65.

———, and L. Nicastri (eds.) 1999. *Interpretare Lucano. Miscellanea di Studi.* Università degli Studi di Salerno. Napoli: L'arte Tipografica.

Everson, S. (ed.) 1991. *Psychology. Companion to Ancient Thought: 2.* Cambridge: Cambridge University Press.

———. (ed.) 1998. *Ethics. Companions to Ancient Thought: 4.* Cambridge: Cambridge University Press.

Faedo, L. 1970. "L' inversione del rapporto poeta—Musa nella cultura ellenistica." *Ann. Sc. Norm. Sup. Pisa* 39: 377–96.

Fantham, E. 1982. *Seneca's Troades. A Literary Introduction with text, translation and commentary.* Princeton, NJ: Princeton University Press.

———. 1992a. "Lucan's Medusa Excursus: Its Design and Purpose." *Materiali e discussioni per l'analisi dei testi classici* 29: 95–119.

———. (ed.) 1992b. *Lucan. De Bello Civili. Book II.* Cambridge: Cambridge University Press.

———. 1999. "The Role of Lament in the Growth and Death of Roman Epic." In Beissinger, Tylus, and Wofford (eds.) 1999: 221–35.

Feagin, S. L. 1983. "The Pleasures of Tragedy." *American Philosophical Quarterly* 20: 95–104.

———. 1996. *Reading with Feeling.* Ithaca: Cornell University Press.

Fears, J. R. 1981. "The Teology of Victory at Rome: Approaches and Problems." *ANRW* 2.17.2: 736–826.

Feeney, D. C. 1986. "Following after Hercules in Virgil and Apollonius." *Proceedings of the Vergilian Society* 18: 47–83.

———. 1991. *The Gods in Epic. Poets and Critics of the Classical Tradition.* Oxford: Oxford University Press.

Fehrle, R. 1983. *Cato Uticensis.* Darmstadt: Wissenschaftliche Buchgesellschaft.

Ferrari, G. R. F. 1989. "Plato and Poetry." In Kennedy (ed.) 1989: 92–148.

Ferroni, G. (ed.) 1985. *Il dialogo. Scambi e passaggi della parola.* Palermo: Sellerio.

Fitzgerald, R. 1981. *The Aeneid. Virgil.* New York: Random House.

Fitzgerald, W. 1984. "Aeneas, Daedalus and the Labyrinth." *Arethusa* 17: 51–65.

———. 1995. *Catullan Provocations. Lyric Poetry and the Drama of Position.* Berkeley: University of California Press.

Flashar, H. 1979a. "Die klassizische Theorie der Mimesis." In Flashar (ed.) 1979: 79–111

_____. (ed.) 1979b. *Le Classicisme à Rome*. Geneva: Fondation Hardt.
Foley, H. 2001. *Female Acts in Greek Tragedy*. Princeton and Oxford: Princeton University Press.
Ford, A. 1999. "Performing Interpretation: Early Allegorical Exegesis of Homer." In Beissinger, Tylus, and Wofford (eds.) 1999: 33–53.
Fortenbaugh, W. W. 1975. *Aristotle on Emotions*. London: Duckworth.
Fowler, D. 1990. "Deviant Focalization in Virgil's *Aeneid*." *PCPS* 36: 42–63.
_____. 1997a. "Virgilian Narrative: Story Telling." In Martindale (ed.) 1997: 259–71.
_____. 1997b. "Second Thoughts on Closure." In Roberts, Dunn, and Fowler (eds.) 1997: 3–22.
Fraenkel, E. 1932. "Virgil und die *Aithiopis*." *Philologus* 87: 242–48.
Fraschetti, A. 1990. *Roma e il principe*. Rome–Bari: Laterza.
Frede, Michael. 1978. "Principles of Stoic Grammar." in Rist (ed.) 1978: 68–74.
Freeland, C. (ed.) 1998. *Feminist Interpretations of Aristotle*. University Park: The Pennsylvania State University Press.
Freudenburg, K. 1993. *The Walking Muse: Horace on the Theory of Satire*. Princeton, NJ: Princeton University Press.
Fusillo, M. 1985. *Il tempo delle Argonautiche: Un'analisi del racconto in Apollonio Rodio*. Rome: Istituti Editoriali e Poligrafici Internazionali.
Gabba, E. 1956. *Appiano e la storia delle guerre civili*. Firenze: La nuova Italia.
Gagé, J. 1933. "La théologie de la Victoire impériale." *Revue historique* 171: 1–43.
Gagliardi, D. 1968. *Lucano poeta della libertà*. Naples: Loffredo.
_____. 1975. *Annaei Lucani Belli civilis, Belli Civilis. Liber Septimus. Introduzione, testo critico e commento*. Firenze: La Nuova Italia.
Gale, M. 1994. *Myth and Poetry in Lucretius*. Cambridge: Cambridge University Press.
_____. 2000. *Virgil on the Nature of Things*. Cambridge: Cambridge University Press.
_____. 2003. "Poetry and the Backward Glance in Virgil's *Georgics* and *Aeneid*." *TAPhA* 133: 323–52.
Galinsky, K. 1972. *The Herakles Theme. The Adaptations of the Hero in Literature from Homer to the Twentieth Century*. Oxford: Oxford University Press.
_____. 1988. "The Anger of Aeneas." *AJP* 109: 321–48.
_____. 1994. "How to Be Philosophical about the End of the *Aeneid*." *Illinois Classical Studies* 19: 191–201.
_____. 1996. *Augustan Culture: An Interpretative Introduction*. Princeton. NJ: Princeton University Press.
Gallo, I. (ed.) 1988. *Aspetti dello Stoicismo e dell'Epicureismo in Plutarco*. (Atti del II Convegno di Studi su Plutarco, Ferrara 2–3 Aprile 1987). Ferrara.
Genette, G. 1980. *Narrative Discourse: An Essay in Method*. Ithaca, NY: Cornell University Press.
George, D. B. 1986. "The Meaning of the *Pharsalia* Revisited." *Studies in Latin Literature and Roman History* 6: 362–89.
_____. 1988. "Lucan's Caesar and οἰκείωσις Theory: The Stoic Fool." *TAPhA* 118: 331–41.
_____. 1991. "Lucan's Cato and Stoic Attitudes to the Republic." *CA* 10.2: 237–58.
Geymonat, M. 1984. "Cornuto." *Enciclopedia Virgiliana* 1: 897–98. Rome: Istituto dell'Enciclopedia Virgiliana.

Gilbert-Thirry, A. 1977. La théorie stoïcienne de la passion chez Chrysippus et son évolution chez Posidonius." *Revue Philosophique de Louvain* 75: 393–45.
Gill, C. 1996. *Personality in Greek Epic, Tragedy and Philosophy: The Self in Dialogue.* Oxford: Oxford University Press.
———. 1997a. "The Emotions in Greco-Roman Philosophy." In Braund and Gill (eds.) 1997: 5–16.
———. 1997b. "Passion as Madness in Roman Poetry." In Braund and Gill (eds.) 1997: 213–42.
———. 1998a. "Did Galen Understand Platonic and Stoic Thinking on Emotions?" In Sihvola and Engberg-Pedersen (eds.) 1998: 113–48.
———. 1998b. "Altruism or Reciprocity in Greek Ethical Philosophy?" in Gill, Postlethwaite, and Seaford (eds.) 1998: 303–28.
———. 2003. "The School in the Roman Imperial Period." In Inwood (ed.) 2003: 33–59.
———, N. Postlethwaite, and R. Seaford (eds.) 1998. *Reciprocity in Ancient Greece.* Oxford: Oxford University Press.
Glare, P. G. W. (ed.) 1983. *Oxford Latin Dictionary.* Oxford: Clarendon Press.
Glenn, J. M. 1971. "Mezentius and Polyphemus." *AJP* 92: 129–55.
———. 1972. "The Fall of Mezentius." *Vergilius* 18: 10–15.
Goar, Robert. 1987. *The Legend of Cato Uticensis from the first Century.* [Vol. 197]. Bruxelles: Latomus
Goebel, G. H. 1981. "Rhetorical and Poetical Thinking in Lucan's Harangues (7.250–382)." *TAPhA* 111: 79–94.
Goldberg, S. 1995. *Epic in Republican Rome.* Oxford: Oxford University Press.
Gordon, R. 1987. "Lucan's Erictho." In Whitby and Hardie (eds.) 1987: 231–41.
Gotoff, H. C. 1984. "The Transformation of Mezentius." *TAPhA* 114: 191–218.
Graeser, A. 1978. "The Stoic Theory of Meaning." In Rist (ed.) 1978: 77–100.
Grandsen, K.W. 1984. *Virgil's Iliad: An Essay on Epic Narrative.* Cambridge: Cambridge University Press.
Graver, M. 2002. *Cicero on the Emotions. Tusculan Disputations 3 and 4.* Chicago and London: The University of Chicago Press.
Gray, V. 1987. "*Mimesis* in Greek Historical Theory." *AJP* 108: 467–86.
Greenberg, Nathan. 1990. *The Poetic Theory of Philodemus.* New York: Garland.
Greene, E. 1994. "Apostrophe and Women's Erotics in the Poetry of Sappho." *TAPhA* 124: 41–56.
———. 1999. "The Natural Tears of Epic." In Beissinger, Tylus, and Wofford (eds.) 1999: 189–203.
Greene, T. M. 1966. *The Descent from Heaven: A Study in Epic Continuity.* New Haven: Yale University Press.
Griffin, J. 1979. "The Fourth *Georgic*, Virgil and Rome." *Greece and Rome* 26: 61–80.
Griffin, M. T. 1976. *Seneca: A Philosopher in Politics.* Oxford: Oxford University Press.
———. 1986. "Philosophy, Cato and Roman Suicide." *Greece and Rome* 33: 64–77.
Grilli, A. 1953. *Il Problema della Vita Contemplativa nel Mondo Greco-romano.* Milan: Fratelli Bocca Editori.
———. 1965. *Studi Enniani.* Brescia: Paideia.

Grillo, A. 1988. *Fra Filologia e narratologia: dai poemi omerià ad Apollonio Rodio, Ilias Latina, Dittio Settimo, Darete Frigio, Draconzio*. Rome: Edizioni dell'Ateneo.
Grimal, P. 1992. *Seneca*. [tr. by T. Capra of Grimal 1978 *Sénèque*. Paris: Belles Lettres] Milan: Garzanti.
Grisé, Y. 1982. *Le Suicide dans la Rome Antique*. Paris: Bellarmin et les Belles Lettres.
Grottanelli, C. 1993. "Evento e Modello nella storia antica: due eroi Cesariani." In Poli (ed.) 1993: 427–45.
Guillemin, A. 1951. "L'inspiration virgilienne dans la *Pharsale*." *REL* 29: 214–217.
_____. 1952. "Sénèque, Directeur d Âmes." *REL* 30: 202–219.
_____. 1957. "Sénèque, Second Fondateur de la Prose Latine." *REL* 35: 265–84.
Gummere, R. M. (ed. and tr.) 1934. *Seneca. Ad Lucilium Epistulae Morales*. London and Cambridge: Harvard University Press.
Guthrie, W. K. C. 1962–1981. *A History of Greek Philosophy*. 6 vols. Cambridge: Cambridge University Press.
Guy-Bray, S. 2002. *Homoerotic Space. The Poetics of Loss in Renaissance Literature*. Toronto: University of Toronto Press.
Habinek, T. 1989. "Science and Tradition in *Aeneid* 6." *HSCP* 92: 223–54.
Hadot, I. 1969. *Seneca und die griechisch-römische Tradition der Seelenleitung*. (Quellen u. Studien zur Geschichte d. Philos. 13.) Berlin: De Gruyter.
Halliwell, S. 1988. *Plato Republic* 10. Warminster: Artis & Phillips.
_____. 1992. "Pleasure, Understanding, and Emotion in Aristotle's *Poetics*." In A. O. Rorty (ed.) 1992: 241–60.
_____. 2002. *The Aesthetics of Mimesis. Ancient Text and Modern Problems*. Princeton: Princeton University Press.
Hampel, E. 1908. "De Apostrophae apud Romanorum Poetas Usu." Diss. Jena.
Hankinson, R. J. 2003. "Stoic Epistemology." in Inwood (ed.) 2003: 59–85.
Hardie, P. 1989. *Virgil's Aeneid: Cosmos and Imperium*. Oxford: Oxford University Press.
_____. 1993. *The Epic Successors of Virgil: A Study in Epic Continuity*. Cambridge: Cambridge University Press.
_____. 1997."Virgil and Tragedy." In Martindale (ed.) 1997: 312–27.
_____. 1999a. "Vergil's Epic Technique." In Hardie (ed.) 1999. Vol. 3: 1–13.
_____. (ed.) 1999b. *Virgil. Critical Assessments of Classical Authors*. 4 vols. London: Routledge.
Hardison, O. B., and L. Golden. 1995. *Horace for Students of Literature*. Gainesville: University Press of Florida.
Harpham, G. G. 1982. *On the Grotesque: Strategies of Contradiction in Art and Literature*. Princeton: Princeton University Press.
Harris, W. 2001. 88–128. *Restraining Rage. The Ideology of Anger Control in Classical Antiquity*. Cambridge, Mass.: Harvard University Press.
Haskins, C. E. 1971 [reprint of 1887 ed.] *M. Annaei Lucani Pharsalia*, edited with English Notes. Hildesheim and New York: Georg Olms Verlag.
Havelock, E. 1963. *Preface to Plato*. Cambridge, Mass.: Harvard University Press.
Heilbrun, C. 1979. *Reinventing Womanhood*. New York: Norton.
Heinze, R. 1965. *Virgils Epische Technik*. Stuttgart: Teubner.
_____. 1993.*Virgil's Epic Technique* [trs. H. D. Harvey and F. Robertson of Heinze 1965]. Berkeley: The University of California Press.

Hemmen, W. 1954. "Das Bild des M. Porcius Cato in der antiken Literatur." Diss. Göttingen.
Henderson, C. (ed.) 1964. *Classical, Medieval and Renaissance Studies in Honor of Berthold Louis Ullman.* Rome: Edizioni di Storia e Letteratura.
Henderson, J. 1987. "Lucan /the Word at War." *Ramus* 16: 122–64.
Hendrickson, G. L. 1905. "The Origin and Meaning of Characters of Style." *AJP* 26: 249–90.
Hershkowitz, D. 1998. *The Madness of Epic. Reading Insanity from Homer to Statius.* Oxford: Clarendon Press.
Hilt-Brunner, O. 1985. Seneca als Tragödiendichter." *ANRW* 2.32: 909–911.
Holst-Warhaft, G. 1992. *Dangerous Voices: Women's Laments and Greek Literature.* New York: Routledge.
Horsfall, N. 1995a. "*Aeneid.*" In Horsfall (ed.) 1995: 192–216.
_____. 1995b. *A Companion to the Study of Virgil.* Leiden: Brill.
Huby, P., and G. Neal (eds.) 1989. *The Criterion of Truth.* Liverpool: Liverpool University Press.
Hunter, R. 2001. "The Poetics of Narrative in the *Argonautica.*" In Papanghelis and Rengakos (eds.) 2001: 93–127.
Husner, F. 1924. *Leib und Seele in der Sprache Senecas. Ein Betrag zur sprachlichen Formulierung der moralischen Adhortatio.* Leipzig: Dieterich.
Imbert, C. 1980. "Stoic Logic and Alexandrian Poetics." In Schofield, Burnyeat, and Barnes (eds.) 1980: 182–216.
Inwood, B. 1985. *Ethics and Human Action in Early Stoicism.* Oxford: Oxford University Press.
_____. 1993. "Seneca and Psychological Dualism." In Brunschwig and Nussbaum (eds.) 1993: 150–84.
_____. (ed.) 2003. *The Cambridge Companion to the Stoics.* Cambridge: Cambridge University Press.
Irwin, T. H. 1977. *Plato's Moral Theory: The Early and Middle Dialogues.* Oxford: Clarendon Press.
_____. (ed.) 1995. *Classical Philosophy. Collected Papers.* Vols. 1–8. New York and London: Garland Publishing.
_____. 1998a. "Stoic Inhumanity." In Sihvola and Engberg-Pedersen (eds.) 1998: 219–43.
_____. 1998b. "Socratic Paradox and Stoic Theory." In Everson (ed.) 1998: 151–92.
_____. 2003. "Stoic Naturalism and Its Critics." In Inwood (ed.) 2003: 345–64.
Jackson, C. 1913. "The Latin Epyllion." *HSCP* 24: 37–59.
Jal, P. 1962. "Les dieux et les guerres civiles dans la Rome de la fin de la République." *REL* 40: 170–200.
_____. 1963. *La guerre civile à Rome: Étude littéraire et morale.* Paris: Publications de la Faculté des Lettres et Sciences humaines de Paris.
Jensen, C. 1923. *Philodemos. Über die Gedichte. Fünftes Buch. Griechischer text mit Übersetzung und Erläuterungen von Ch.* Berlin: Weidmann.
Johnson, B. 1987. "Apostrophe, Animation, and Abortion." In Johnson (ed.) 1987: 184–200.

———. (ed.) 1987. *A World of Difference*. Baltimore: Johns Hopkins University Press.
Johnson, W. R. 1965. "Aeneas and the Ironies of *Pietas*." *CJ* 60: 359–64.
———. 1976. *Darkness Visible: A Study of Vergil's Aeneid*. Berkeley: Harvard University Press.
———. 1987. *Momentary Monsters: Lucan and his Heroes*. Ithaca: Cornell University Press.
Johnston, P. 1980. *Vergil's Agricultural Golden Age: A Study of the Georgics*. (*Mnemosyne Suppl.* 60.) Leiden: E. J. Brill.
Kallendorf, Craig. 1999. "Historicizing the 'Harvard School': Pessimistic Readings of the *Aeneid* in Italian Renaissance Scholarship." *HSCP* 99: 391–403.
Kardaun, M. 1993. *Der Mimesisbegriff in der griechischen Antike*. Amsterdam: Koninklijke Nederlandse Akademie van Wetenschappen.
Keaney, J. J., and R. Lamberton (eds.) 1992. *Homer's Ancient Readers*. Princeton: Princeton University Press.
———. (eds.) 1996. *[Plutarch] Essay on the Life and Poetry of Homer*. Atlanta: Scholar Press.
Kebric, R. B. 1976. "Lucan's Snake Episode: A Historical Model." *Latomus* 35: 380–82.
———. 1977. *In the Shadow of Macedonia: Duris of Samos*. Wiesbaden: Franz Steiner Verlag.
Keith, A. 2000. *Engendering Rome. Women in Latin Epic*. Cambridge: Cambridge University Press.
Kelly, M. (ed.) 1998. *Encyclopedia of Aesthetics*. New York: Oxford University Press.
Kennedy, G. A. 1957. "Theophrastos and Stylistic Distinction." *HSCP* 62: 93–104.
———. (ed.). 1989. *The Cambridge History of Literary Criticism*. Cambridge: Cambridge University Press.
Kenney, E. J. (ed.) 1984. *The Ploughman's Lunch. Moretum. A Poem ascribed to Virgil*. Bristol: Bristol Classical Press.
Kerferd, G. B. 1972. "The Search for Personal Identity in Stoic Thought." *Bulletin of the John Rylands Library*. University of Manchester 55: 177–96.
Kidd, I. G. 1971. "Posidonius on Emotions." In Long (ed.) 1971: 200–215.
———. 1989. "*Orthos Logos* as a Criterion of Truth." In Huby and Neal (eds.) 1989: 137–50.
Kirby, J. T. 1990. *The Rhetoric of Cicero's 'Pro Cluentio.'* Amsterdam: Gieben.
Knauer, N. G. 1999. "Vergil's *Aeneid* and Homer." In Hardie (ed.) 1999. Vol. 3: 93–114.
Knox, B. 1950. "The Serpent and the Flame: The Imagery of the Second Book of the *Aeneid*." *AJP* 71: 379–400.
Knuttila, S., and J. Sihvola 1998. "How the Philosophical Analysis of Emotions Was Introduced." In Sihvola and Engberg-Pedersen (eds.) 1998: 1–17.
Konstan, D. 1994. "Forward to the Reader." In Schiesaro, Mitsis, and Clay (eds.) 1994: 11–23.
Kristeller, Oskar, 1951. "The Modern System of the Arts: A Study in the History of Aesthetics." *Journal of the History of Ideas* 12.4: 496–527.
Kristeva, J. 1982. *Powers of Horror: An Essay in Abjection*. New York: Columbia University Press.

Lada, I. 1996. "Emotion and Meaning in Tragic Performance." in Silk (ed.) 1996: 397–414.

———. 1998. "Hellenistic Aesthetic: Philosophers and Literary Critics." In Kelly (ed.) 1998: 389–91.

Laird, A. 1999. *Powers of Expression, Expressions of Power: Speech Presentation and Latin Literature.* Oxford: Oxford University Press.

Lang, C. (ed.) 1881. *Cornuti Theologiae Craecae Compendium.* Leipzig: Teubner.

La Penna, A. 1967. "Sul cosidetto stile soggettivo e sul cosidetto simbolismo di Virgilio." *Dialoghi di Archeologia* 1: 220–44.

———. 1979. *Fra teatro, poesia e politica romana: politica e cultura in Roma antica e nella tradizione classica moderna.* II serie. Torino: Einaudi.

Lapidge, M. 1979. "Lucan's Imagery of Cosmic Dissolution." *Hermes* 107: 344–70.

———. 1989. "Stoic Cosmology and Roman Literature, First to Third Century A.D." *ANRW* 2.36.3: 1379–1429.

Laurenti, R. 1988. "Lo Stoicismo Romano e Plutarco di fronte al tema dell'ira." In Gallo (ed.) 1988: 33–58.

Leach, E.W. 1977. "*Sedes Apibus:* From the *Georgics* to the *Aeneid.*" *Vergilius* 22: 2–16.

———. 1988. *The Rhetoric of Space: Literary and Artistic Representations of Landscape in Republican Augustan Rome.* Princeton, NJ: Princeton University Press.

———. 1999. "Viewing the *Spectacula* of *Aeneid* 6." in Perkell (ed.) 1999: 111–228.

Lear, J. 1992. "Katharsis." in Rorty (ed.) 1992: 315–40.

Lebek, W. D. 1976. *Lucans* Pharsalia: *Dichtungstruktur und Zeitbzung.* Göttingen: Vandenhoeck & Ruprecht.

Leeman, A. D. 1963. Orationis Ratio. *The Stylistic Theories and Practice of the Roman Orators, Historians and Philosophers.* 2 vols. Amsterdam: A. Hakkert Publisher.

Lefèvre, Eckard. 2001. *Panaitios und Ciceros Pflichtenlehre: Vom philosophischen Traktat zum politischen Lehrbuch.* Historia Einzelschriften 150. Stuttgart: Franz Steiner Verlag.

Leigh, M. 1997. *Lucan. Spectacle and Engagemement.* Oxford: Oxford University Press.

———. 2000. "Lucan and the Libyan Tale." *The Journal of Roman Studies* 90: 95–109.

Liebeschuetz, J. H. W. G. 1979. *Continuity and Change in Roman Religion.* Oxford: Oxford University Press.

Long, A. A. (ed.). 1971. *Problems in Stoicism.* London: Athlone Press.

———. 1986. *Hellenistic Philosophy.* Berkeley: University of California Press.

———. 1991. "Representation and the Self in Stoicism." in Everson (ed.) 1991: 102–120.

———. 1992. "Stoic Readings of Homer." In Keaney and Lamberton (eds.) 1992: 41–66.

———. 1996a. "Representation and the Self in Stoic Studies." In Long 1996: 264–86.

———. 1996b. *Stoic Studies.* Cambridge: Cambridge University Press.

———. 2002. *Epictetus. A Stoic and Socratic Guide to Life.* Oxford: Oxford University Press.

———. 2003. "Stoicism in the Philosophical Tradition." in Inwood (ed.) 2003: 365–93.

———, and D. N. Sedley. 1987. *The Hellenistic Philosophers.* 2 vols. Cambridge: Cambridge University Press.

Loraux, N. 1986. *The Invention of Athens: the Funeral Oration in the Classical City* [tr. A. Sheridan]. Cambridge, MA: Harvard University Press.
_____. 2002. *The Mourning Voice: An Essay in Greek Tragedy* [tr. E. Rawlinson]. Ithaca: Cornell University Press.
Lord, C. 1986. "On the Early History of the Aristotelian Corpus." *AJP* 107: 137–61.
Lounsbury, R. 1975. "The Death of Domitius in the *Pharsalia*." *TAPhA* 105: 209–12.
_____. 1976. "History and Motive in Book Seven of Lucan's *Pharsalia*." *Hermes* 104: 210–39.
_____. 1986. "Lucan, the *Octavia* and Domitius Nero." In Deroux (ed.) 1986. 4: 499–520.
Luce, T. J. 1977. *Livy: The Composition of His History*. Princeton: Princeton University Press.
Lucifora, Rosa Maria. 1991. "Un centurione valoroso. (Lucan. *Phars.*, VI 140–262)." *Vichiana: Rassegna di Studi Classici* 3.2: 253–57.
Maguinness, W. S. 1956. "Seneca and the Poets." *Hermathena* 88: 81–90.
Malamud, M. 1995. "Happy Birthday Dead Lucan: (P)raising the dead in *Silvae* 2.7." In Boyle (ed.) 1995: 169–98.
_____. (ed.) 1998. *Vile Bodies. Roman Satire and Corporeal Discourse*. Arethusa 31.
_____. 2003. "Pompey's Head and Cato's Snakes." *CP* 98: 31–44.
Malcovati, Enrica. 1940. *M. Anneo Lucano*. Milan: U. Hoepli.
Mandelbaum, A. (tr.) 1971. *The Aeneid of Virgil*. New York: Bantam.
Manetti, G. 1993. *Theories of the Sign in Classical Antiquity* [tr. C. Richardson]. Bloomington: Indiana University.
Mangoni, C. 1993. *Philodemos. Il quinto libro della Poetica: (PHerc. 1425 e 1538)*. Napoli: Bibliopolis.
Manieri, A.1998. *L'immaginazione poetica nella teoria degli antichi*. Pisa: Istituti editoriali e poligrafici Internazionali. This reference does not appear in the notes.
Marti, B. M. 1945a. "Seneca's Tragedies: A New Interpretation." *TAPhA* 76: 216–45.
_____. 1945b. "The Meaning of the *Pharsalia*." *AJP* 66: 352–76.
_____. 1958. *Arnulfi Aurelianensis Glosule super Lucanum*. Rome: American Academy in Rome.
_____.1964. "Tragic History and Lucan's *Pharsalia*." In Henderson (ed.) 1964: 1164–204.
_____. 1966. "Cassius Scaeva and Lucan's Inventio." in Wallach (ed.) 1966: 239–57.
_____. 1974. "The Prototypes of Seneca's Tragedies." *CP* 42: 1–16.
_____.1975. "Lucan's Narrative Technique." *Parola del Passato* 30: 74–90.
Martindale, C. 1976. "Paradox, Hyperbole and Literary Novelty in Lucan's *De Bello Civile*." *Bulletin of the Institute of Classical Studies of the University of London* 23: 45–54.
_____. 1993. *Redeeming the Text*. Cambridge: Cambridge University Press.
_____. (ed.) 1997. *The Cambridge Companion to Virgil*. Cambridge: Cambridge University Press.
Masters, J. 1992. *Poetry and Civil War in Lucan's Bellum Civile*. Cambridge: Cambridge University Press.

———. 1994. "Deceiving the Reader: The Political Mission of Lucan's *Bellum Civile.*" In Elsner and Masters (eds.) 1994: 151–78.
Mayer, A. (ed.) 1910. *Theophrasti. Peri Lexeos Libri Fragmenta.* Leipzig: Teubner.
Mayer, R. 1981. Lucan: *Civil War VIII.* Warminster, Wilts.: Aris & Phillips.
———. 1994. "*Personata Stoa:* Neostoicism and Senecan Tragedy." *Journal of the Warburg and Courtauld Institutes* 57: 151–74.
Mazzocchini, P. 2000. *Forme e significati della narrazione bellica nell'epos virgiliano. I cataloghi degli uccisi e le morti minori dell'Eneide.* Fasano: Schena Editore.
Mazzoli, G. 1970. *Seneca e la poesia.* Milan: Ceschina.
———. 1996. "Tipologie e strutture dei cori senecani." In Castagna (ed.) 1996: 3–17.
McGuire, D. 1990. "Textual Strategies and political Suicide in Flavian Epic." In Boyle (ed.) 1990: 21–46.
Menz, W. 1952. "Caesar und Pompeius im Epos Lucans." Diss. Berlin.
Merriam, C. 2001. *The Development of the Epyllion Genre through the Hellenistic and Roman Period.* Lewiston, NY.: Edwin Mellen Press.
Metger, W. 1957. "Kampf und Tod in Lucans *Pharsalia.*" Diss. Kiel.
Miles, G. 1980. *Virgil's Georgics. A New Interpretation.* Berkeley: University of California Press.
Miller, W. (ed. and intro.) 1913. *Cicero. De Officiis.* Cambridge, MA: Harvard University Press.
Milosz, C. 1981. *The Captive Mind.* New York: Vintage Books.
Moretti, G. 1984. "Formularità e tecniche del paradossale in Lucano." *Maia* 36: 37–49.
———. 1995. *Acutum dicendi genus. Brevità, oscurità, sottigliezze e paradossi nelle tradizioni retoriche degli Stoici.* Bologna: Pàtron.
———. 1999. "Catone al bivio. Via della virtù, lotta contro i mostri e viaggio ai confini del mondo: il modello di Eracle nel IX del *Bellum Civile.*" In Esposito and Nicastri (eds.) 1999: 238–41.
Morford, M. 1967. *The Poet Lucan. Studies in Rhetorical Epic.* Oxford: Oxford University Press.
———. 2002. *The Roman Philosophers. From the Time of Cato the Censor to the Death of Marcus Aurelius.* London and New York: Routledge.
Mortureaux, B. 1989. "Les Idéaux Stoïciens et les premières responsabilités politiques: Le 'De Clementia.'" *ANRW* 2.36.3: 1639–95.
Most, G. W. 1989. "Cornutus and Stoic Allegoresis." *ANRW* 2.36.3: 2014–2065.
Mueller, G. H. 1910. "Animadversiones ad L. Annaei Senecae epistulas quae sunt de oratione spectantes." Diss. Weida.
Murnaghan, S. 1999. "The Poetics of Loss in Greek Epic." In Beissinger et al. (eds.) 1999: 203–221.
Naddaff, R. A. 2002. *Exiling the Poets: the Production of Censorship in Plato's Republic.* Chicago and London: The University of Chicago Press.
Nagy, G. 1979. *The Best of the Acheans. Concepts of the Hero in Archaic Greek Poetry.* Baltimore: The Johns Hopkins University Press.
Narducci, E. 1979. *La Provvidenza crudele. Lucano e la distruzione dei miti Augustei.* Pisa: Giardini.
———. 1985. "Ideologia e tecnica allusiva nella *Pharsalia.*" *ANRW* 2.32.3: 1538–64.
———. 1999. "Deconstructing Lucan, ovvero Le nozze (coi fichi secchi) di Ermete Trismegisto e di Filologia." In Esposito and Nicastri (eds.) 1999: 37–81.

———. 2001 "Catone in Lucano (e alcune interpretazioni recenti)." *Athenaeum* 89.1: 171–86
———. 2002. *Lucano. Un' epica contro l'impero.* Rome–Bari: Laterza.
Nestle, W. 1936. "Die Horen des Prodikos." *Hermes* 71: 151–70
Nethercut, W. R. 1975. "The Characterization of Mezentius: *Aen.* 10.843–845." *Classical Bulletin* 51.3: 33–36.
Newmyer, S. 1983. "Imagery as a Means of Character Portrayal in Lucan." In Deroux (ed.) 1983: 226–52.
Nietzsch, G. W. 1860. "The Apostrophe in *Ilias* und *Odyssee.*" *Philologus* 16: 151–54.
Nietzsche, F. 1956. *The Birth of Tragedy and The Genealogy of Morals.* Garden City, NY: Doubleday.
Nisbet, R. B. 1992. "The Orator and the Reader: Manipulation and Response in Cicero's "Fifth *Verrine.*" In Woodman and Powell (eds.) 1992: 1–17.
Nock, A. D. 1931. "Kornutos." *RE Suppl.* 5: 995–1005.
Norden, E. 1916. *P. Vergilius Maro. Aeneis Buch VI.* Leipzig: Teubner.
Nugent 1999. "The Women of the *Aeneid:* Vanishing Bodies, Lingering Voices." In Perkell (ed). 1999: 251–85.
Nussbaum, M. 1986. *The Fragility of Goodness: Luck and Ethics in Greek Tragedy and Philosophy.* Cambridge: Cambridge University Press.
———. 1993. "Poetry and the Passions: Two Stoic Views." In Brunschwig and Nussbaum (eds.) 1993: 97–149.
———. 1994. *The Therapy of Desire: Theory and Practice in Hellenistic Ethics.* Princeton, NJ: Princeton University Press.
Nutting, H. C. 1932. "The Hero of the *Pharsalia.*" *AJP* 53: 41–52.
Obbink, D. (ed.) 1995. *Philodemus and Poetry: Poetic Theory and Practice in Lucretius, Philodemus, and Horace.* New York: Oxford University Press.
O'Connor, B. (ed.) 2000. *The Adorno Reader.* Oxford: Blackwell Publishers.
Offermann, H. 1977. "*Curio-miles Caesaris?* Caesars Urteil über Curio BC 2, 42." *Hermes* 105: 351–68.
O'Gorman, E. 2000. *Irony and Misreading in the Annals of Tacitus.* Cambridge: Cambridge University Press.
O'Hara, J. 1997. "Virgil's Style." In Martindale (ed.) 1997: 249–51.
O'Higgins, D. 1988. "Lucan as *Vates.*" *CA* 7.2: 208–26.
Ormsby, Robert. 1970. "The Literary Portrait of Cato Uticensis in Lucan's *Bellum Civile.*" Diss. University of Washington.
Otis, B. 1964. *Virgil, a Study in Civilized Poetry.* Oxford: Oxford University Press.
Paduano, G. 1972. *Studi su Apollonio.* Rome: Edizioni dell'Ateneo.
———. 1985. "Il cuore diviso a metà. La comunicazione dell'io nella poesia ellenistica." In Ferroni (ed.) 1985: 33–46.
———. 1986. *Apollonio Rodio. Le Argonautiche.* Milan: Biblioteca Universale Rizzoli.
Panoussi, V. 2002. "Vergil's Ajax: Allusion, Tragedy, and Heroic Identity in the *Aeneid.*" *Classical Antiquity* 21.1: 95–134.
Paoletti, L. 1963. "Lucano magico e Virgilio." *Atene e Roma* 8: 11–26.
Papanghelis, T. D., and A. Rengakos (eds.) 2001. *A Companion to Apollonius Rhodius.* Leiden: Brill.
Paratore, E. 1992. *Lucano.* Rome: Ateneo.

———— (ed.) 1990 . *Eneide*. 6 vols. Milan: Fondazione Lorenzo Valla, Arnoldo Mondadori Editore (II edizione).
Paratore, E. 1943. "Virgilio Georgico e Lucano." *Annali della Scuola normale superiore di Pisa* 12: 40–69.
Parke, H. W., and B. C. McGing. 1988. *Sibyls and Sibylline Prophecy in Classical Antiquity*. London and New York: Routledge.
Parry, A. 1966. "The Two Voices of Virgil's *Aeneid*." In Commager (ed.) 1966: 107–24.
————. 1972. "Language and Characterization in Homer." *HSCP* 76: 1–22.
Paschalis, M. 1986. "The Unifying Theme of Daedalus' Sculptures on the Temple of Apollo Cumanus (*Aen.* 6.20–33)." *Vergilius* 32: 33–43.
Pavan, M. 1970. "Das politische Ideal Lucans." In Rutz (ed.) 1970: 407–422.
Pembroke, S. G. 1971. "Oikeiosis." In A. A. Long (ed.) 1971: 114–49.
Perkell, C. 1981. "On the Corycian farmer of Virgil's *Fourth Georgic*." *TAPhA* 111: 167–77.
————. (ed.). 1999. *Reading Vergil's Aeneid. An Interpretative Guide*. Norman: University of Oklahoma Press.
Perutelli, A. 1972. "Similitudini e stile 'soggettivo' in Virgilio." *Maia* 24: 42–60.
————. 1973. "Genesi e significato della *Vergils Epische Technik*." *Maia* 25: 293–316.
————. 1979. "Registri narrativi e stile indiretto libero in Virgilio (a proposito di *Aen.* 4.279 sgg.)." *Materiali e Discussioni per lo studio dei testi classici* 3: 69–82.
Pfligersdorfer, G. 1959. "Lucan als Dichter des geistigen Widerstandes." *Hermes* 87: 344–77.
Pichon, R. 1912. *Le Sources de Lucain*. Paris: E. Leroux.
Plass, P. 1995. *The Game of Death in Ancient Rome: Arena Sport and Political Suicide.* Madison: University of Wisconsin Press.
Plato. 1925. *Plato in Twelve Volumes*. Vol. 9. Tr. H. N. Fowler. London: W. Heinemann.
Pohlenz, M. 1938. "Zenon und Chrysipp." *Nachrichten der Akademie der Wissenschaft in Göttingen* (phil.-hist. Kl.). 1.2.9: 173–210.
Poli, D. (ed.) 1993. *La cultura in Cesare*. (Atti del convegno Internazionale di Studi Macerata-Matelica, 30 Aprile–4 Maggio.) Rome: Editrice 'Il Calamo.'
Pöschl, V. 1962. *Art of Vergil: Image and Symbol in the Aeneid* [tr. G. Seligson]. Ann Arbor: University of Michigan Press (= 1950. *Die Dichtkunst Virgils*. Berlin: De Gruyter).
————. 1975. "Die Tempeltüren des Dädalus in der *Aeneis* (VI 14–33)." *Würzburger Jahrbücher* 1: 119–23.
Potz, E. 1998. "Appians Klio dichtet. Die Curio-Episode bei Appian (E 2,44, 175–245, 185) und Caesar (B.C. II 23–44)." *Philologus* 142: 293–99.
Pratt, N. T. 1948. "The Stoic Base of Senecan Drama." *TAPhA* 79: 1–11.
————. 1983. *Seneca's Drama*. Chapel Hill and London: University of North Carolina.
Preminger, A., and T. V. F. Brogan. 1993. *The New Princeton Encyclopedia of Poetry and Poetics*. Princeton, NJ: Princeton University Press.
Pucci, P. 1977. *Hesiod and the Language of Poetry*. Baltimore and London: The Johns Hopkins University Press.
————. 1998. *The Full Knowing Reader: Allusion and the Power of the Reader in the Western Literary Tradition*. New Haven: Yale University Press.
————. 2002. "Theology and Poetics in the *Iliad*." *Arethusa* 35: 17–34.

Pugliatti, P. 1985. *Lo Sguardo nel Racconto. Teorie e prassi del punto di vista*. Bologna: Zanichelli.

Putnam, M. 1981. "*Pius* Aeneas and the Metamorphosis of Lausus." *Arethusa* 14: 137–54.

———. 1990. "Anger, Blindness, and Insight in Virgil's *Aeneid.*" *Apeiron* 23: 7–40.

———. 1995a. "Deceiving the Reader: the Political Mission of Lucan's *Bellum Civile* 7." in Elsner and Masters (eds.) 1995: 151–77.

———. 1995b. *Virgil's "Aeneid": Interpretation and Influence*. Chapel Hill: University of North Carolina Press.

———. 1998. *Virgil's Epic Design. Ekphrasis in the* Aeneid. New Haven and London: Yale University Press.

———. 1999. "*Aeneid* 12. Unity in Closure." In Perkell (ed.) 1999: 210–30.

Quinn, K. 1968. *Virgil's* Aeneid. *A Critical Description*. Ann Arbor: University of Michigan Press.

Quint, D. 1993. *Epic and Empire: Politics and Generic From from Virgil to Milton*. Princeton, NJ: Princeton University Press.

Rackham, H. (ed. and intro.) 1931. *De Finibus Bonorum et Malorum*. London: W. Heinemann.

Radicke, J. 2004. *Lucans poetische Technik. Studien zum historischen Epos*. Mnemosyne Supplement 249. Leiden: Brill.

Rambaud, M. 1955. "L'apologie de Pompée par Lucain au livre VII de la *Pharsale*." *REL* 33: 258–96.

Reale, G. (ed.) 2000. *Lucio Anneo Seneca. Tutte le opere*. Milan: Bompiani.

Reggiani, R. 1979. *I proemi degli Annales di Ennio: programma letterario e polemica letteraria*. Rome: Ateneo e Bizzarri.

Reynolds, L. D. (ed.) 1965. *Lucius Annaeus Seneca: Ad Lucilium Epistulae Morales*. Oxford: Clarendon Press.

Rispoli, G. M. 1985. *L'artista sapiente. Per una storia della fantasia*. Naples: Liguori.

Rist, J. M. 1969. *Stoic Philosophy*. Cambridge: Cambridge University Press.

———. (ed.) 1978. *The Stoics*. Berkeley: University of California Press.

———. 1989. "Seneca and Stoic Orthodoxy." *ANRW* 2.36.3: 1993–2012.

Roberts, D. H., F. M. Dunn, and D. Fowler (eds.) 1997. *Classical Closure. Reading in Greek and Latin Literature*. Princeton, NJ: Princeton University Press.

Rogenbogen, O. 1927–8. "Schmerz und Tod in den Tragödien Senecas." *Vorträge der Bibliothek Warburg* 7: 167–219.

Roller, M. 2001. *Constructing Autocracy. Aristocrats and Emperors in Julio-Claudian Rome*. Princeton, NJ: Princeton University Press.

Rollinson, Philip. 1981. *Classical Theories of Allegory and Christian Culture*. Pittsburgh: Duquesne University Press.

Rorty, A. O. (ed.) 1980. *Explaining Emotions*. Berkeley: University of California Press.

———. 1989. *Contingency, Irony and Solidarity*. Cambridge: Cambridge University Press.

———. (ed.) 1992. *Essays on Aristotle's Poetics*. Princeton, NJ: Princeton University Press.

———. 1998. "The Two Faces of Stoicism: Rousseau and Freud." In Sihvola and Engberg-Pedersen (eds.) 1998: 243–70.

Rosati, G. 1979. "Punto di vista narrativo ed antichi esegeti." *Annali della Scuola Superiore di Pisa* 9: 539–62.
_____. 1983. *Narciso e Pigmalione. Illusione e spettacolo nelle* Metamorfosi *di Ovidio*. Firenze: Sansoni.
Rosenmeyer, T. 1989. *Senecan Drama and Stoic Cosmology*. Berkeley: University of California Press.
Rosner-Siegel, J. A. 1983. "The Oak and the Lightning: Lucan, *Bellum Ciuile* I.135–157." *Athenaeum* 61: 165–77.
Ross, D. O. 1987. *Virgil's Elements. Physics and Poetry in the* Georgics. Princeton, NJ: Princeton University Press.
Rudich, V. 1993. *Political Dissidence under Nero: The Price of Dissimulation*. London: Routledge.
_____. 1997. *Dissidence and Literature under Nero. The Price of Rhetoricization*. London: Routledge.
Russell, D. A. (ed.) 1964. *On the Sublime*. Oxford: Oxford University Press.
_____. 1974. "Letters to Lucilius." In Costa (ed.) 1974: 70–96.
Rutz, W. 1960. "*Amor Mortis* bei Lucan." *Hermes* 88: 462–75.
_____. (ed.) 1970. *Lucan*. Darmstadt: Wissenschaftsliche Buchgesellschaft.
Salomone, S. 1998. "Una chiarezza ben poco chiara (*saphêneia, emphasis, enargeia* nel De Elocutione di Demetrio)." *Maia* 50: 81–87.
Samse, R. 1942. "Lukans Exkurs über Thessalien VI 333–412." *Rheinisches Museum* 91: 259–68.
Sandbach, F. H. (ed. and trans.) 1969. *Plutarch. Moralia XV. Fragments*. Cambridge, MA: Harvard University Press.
Sauvé Meyer, S. 1998. "Moral Responsibility: Aristotle and After." In Everson (ed.) 1998: 221–40.
Saylor, C. 1978. "*Belli spes improba:* The Theme of Walls in Lucan, *Pharsalia* 6." *TAPhA* 108: 243–57.
_____. 1982. "Curio and Anteus: the African Episode of Lucan *Pharsalia* IV." *TAPhA* 112: 169–77.
_____. 1990. "*Lux extrema:* Lucan, *Pharsalia* 4, 402–581." *TAPhA* 120: 291–300.
Scarcia, R. 1996. "Morte e (in)sepoltura di Pompeo." In Brugnoli and Stok (eds.) 1996: 125–49.
Schiavone, A. (ed.) 1992. *Storia di Roma*. Torino: Giulio Einaudi Editore.
Schiesaro, A. 1994. "Il destinatario discreto. Funzioni didascaliche e progetto culturale nelle *Georgiche*." In Schiesaro, Mitsis, and Clay (eds.) 1994: 129–47.
_____. 1997. "Passion, Reason and Knowledge in Seneca." In Braund and Gill (eds.) 1997: 89–111.
_____. 2003. *The Passions in Play. Thyestes and the Dynamics of Senecan Drama*. Cambridge: Cambridge University Press.
_____, P. Mitsis, and J. S. Clay (eds.) 1994. *Mega Nepios: Il destinatario nell'epos antico*. Pisa: Giardini.
Schofield, M., M. Burnyeat, and J. Barnes (eds.) 1980. *Doubt and Dogmatism. Studies in Hellenistic Epistemology*. Oxford: Clarendon Press.
Schönberger, O. 1961. "Untersuchungen zur Widerholungstechnic Lucans." Diss. Heidelberg.

Schotes, H.A. 1969. *Stoische Physik. Psychologie und Theologie bei Lucan.* Bonn: R. Habelt.

Schrempp, O. 1964. "Prophezeiung und Rückschau in Lucans *Bellum Civile.*" Diss. Winterthur.

Sedley, D. 2003. "The School, from Zeno to Arius Didymus." In Inwood (ed.) 2003: 7–35.

Segal, C. P. 1965a. "The Achievement of Vergil." *Arion* 4: 126–49.

———. 1965b. "*Aeternum per saecula nomen:* The Golden Bough and the Tragedy of History." *Arion* 4: 615–45.

———. 1999. "Art and the Hero: Participation, Detachment, and Narrative Point of View in the *Aeneid.*" in Hardie (ed.) 1999. Vol. 4: 42–59.

Seidel, M. 1979. *Satiric Inheritance: Rabelais to Sterne.* Princeton, NJ: Princeton University Press.

Seitz, K. 1965. "Der pathetische Erzählstil Lukans." *Hermes* 93: 204–32.

Setaioli, Aldo. 1985. "Seneca e la poesia." *ANRW* 2.32.2: 776–857.

Sherman, N. 1998. "Empathy and Imagination." *Midwest Studies in Philosophy* 22: 82–119.

Shoaf, R. A. 1978. "'*Certius Exemplar sapientis viri*': Rhetorical Subversion and Subversive Rhetoric in *Pharsalia.*" *Phililogical Quarterly* 9: 143–54.

Sicking, C. M. J. 1998. *Distant Companions: Selected Papers.* Leiden: E. J. Brill.

Sihvola, J., and T. Engberg-Pedersen (ed.) 1998. *The Emotions in Hellenistic Philosophy.* Dordrecth and Boston: Kluwer Academic Publishers.

Sikes, E. E. 1923. *Roman Poetry.* New York: E. P. Dutton.

Silk, M. S. (ed.) 1996. *Tragedy and the Tragic. Greek Theatre and Beyond.* Oxford: Clarendon Press.

Skard, E. 1965. "Die Heldenschau in Virgils *Aeneis.*" *Symbolum* (Oslo) 40: 53–65.

Sklenár, R. 1998. "La République des Signes: Caesar, Cato, and the Language of Sallustian Morality." *TAPhA* 128: 205–220.

———. 2003. *The Taste for Nothingness. A Study of* Virtus *and Related Themes in Lucan's* Bellum Civile. Ann Arbor: The University of Michigan Press.

Smiley, C. N. 1919. "Seneca and the Stoic Theory of Literary Style." *University of Wisconsin Studies in Language and Literature* 3: 50–61.

Smith. C. F. 1953–59. *Thucydides, with an English Translation.* Cambridge, MA: Harvard University Press.

Smith, W. 1875. *A Dictionary of Greek and Roman Antiquities.* London: Murray.

Solimano, G. 1991. *La prepotenza dell'occhio. Riflessioni sull' opera di Seneca.* Genova: D.AR.FI.CL.ET.

Sorabji, R. 2000. *Emotions and Peace of Mind. From Stoic Agitation to Christian Temptation.* Oxford: Oxford University Press.

Southern, P. 1998. *Augustus.* London and New York: Routledge.

Spence, S. 1999. "*Varium et Mutabile:* Voices of Authority in *Aeneid* 4." In Perkell (ed.) 1999: 80–96.

Stam, R. 1992. *Reflexivity in Film and Literature. From Don Quixote to Jean-Luc Godard.* New York: Columbia University Press.

Stem, R. 2005. "The First Eloquent Stoic: Cicero on Cato the Younger." *CJ* 101: 37–49.

Steinmetz, P. 1986. "Allegorische Deutung und allegorische Dichtung in der alten Stoa." *Rheinische Museum* 129:18–30.
Stephens, W. O. 1996. "Epictetus on How the Stoic Sage Loves." *Oxford Studies in Ancient Philosophy* 14: 193–210.
Strawson, P. 1962. "Freedom and Resentment." *Proceedings of the British Academy* 48: 187–211.
Striker, G. 1983. "The Role of *Oikeiôsis* in Stoic Ethics." *Oxford Studies in Ancient Philosophy* 1: 145–67.
———. 1991. "Following Nature: A Study in Stoic Ethics." *Oxford Studies in Ancient Philosophy* 9: 1–75.
Sullivan, F. A. 1969. "Mezentius, a Virgilian Creation." *CP* 64: 219–25.
Suzuki, M. 1989. *Metamorphoses of Helen. Authority, Difference, and the Epic.* Ithaca: Cornell University Press.
Swain, S. 1989a. "Plutarch: Chance, Providence, and History." *AJP* 110: 272–302
———. 1989b. "Plutarch's *De Fortuna Romanorum.*" *CQ* 39: 504–516.
Syme, R. 1939. *The Roman Revolution.* Oxford: Clarendon Press.
Syndikus, H. P. 1958. "Lucans Gedicht Vom Bürgerkrieg. Untersuchungen zur epischen Technik und zu den Grundlagen des Werkes." Diss. Munchen.
Tan, E. S. 1996. *Emotion and the Structure of Narrative Film.* [Tr. B. Fasting.] Mahwah, NJ: Lawrence Erlbaum Associates.
Tandoi, V. 1966. "*Morituri Verba Catoni.*" *Maia* 68: 34–64.
Tate, J. 1928. "Horace and the Moral Function of Poetry." *Classical Quarterly* 22: 65–71.
———. 1929. "Cornutus and the Poets." *Classical Quarterly* 23: 41–45.
———. 1934. "On the History of Allegorism." *Classical Quarterly* 28: 105–114.
Taylor, C. 1989. *Sources of the Self.* Cambridge, MA: Harvard University Press.
Thomas, R. F. 1982. *Lands and Peoples in Roman Poetry: The Ethnographical Tradition.* Cambridge: Cambridge University Press.
———. 1988. "Tree Violation and Ambivalence in Virgil." *TAPhA* 118: 261–75.
Thompson, L., and R. Bruère. 1970. "The Virgilian Background of Virgil's Fourth Book." *CP* 65: 152–72.
Thome, G. 1979. *Gestalt und Funktion des Mezentius bei Vergil—mit einem Ausblick auf die Schlußszene der Aeneis.* Frankfurt am Main: Lang.
Tieleman, T. L. 1996. *Galen and Chrysippus: Argument and Refutation in the 'De Placitis' Books II–III.* Leiden: E.J. Brill.
Timpanaro, S. 1986. *Per la storia della filologia virgiliana antica.* Rome: Salerno Editrice.
Too, Y. L. 1998. *The Idea of Ancient Literary Criticism.* Oxford: Clarendon Press.
Traina, A.1974. *Lo stile 'drammatico' del filosofo Seneca.* Bologna: Pàtron.
Usener, H. (ed.) 1967. *M. Annaei Lucani Commenta Bernensia.* Hildesheim: G. Olms.
Van Straaten, M. 1962. *Panaetii Rhodii Fragmenta.* Leiden: Brill.
Viansino, G. 1974. *Studi sul Bellum Civile di Lucano.* Salerno: Società editrice Salernitana.
Viarre, S. 1982. "Caton en Libye: L'Histoire et la métaphore (Lucain, *Pharsale,* 9.294–949)." In J.-M. Croisille and P.-M. Fauchère, (eds.) *Neronia. Actes du Colloque de Clermont-Ferrand* 1977: 103–110.
———. 1970. "Der Dichter Lucan und die epische Tradition." In Durry (ed.) 1970: 267–308.

———. 1999. *Roman Epic. An Interpretative Introduction*. Leiden: Brill.
Walbank, F. W. 1960. "History and Tragedy." *Historia* 9: 216–34.
Walker, A. 1993. "*Enargeia* and the Spectator in Greek Historiography." *TAPhA* 123: 353–77.
———. 1996. "Lucan's Legends of the Fall." *Ramus* 25.1: 65–87.
Wallach, L. (ed.) 1966. *The Classical Tradition: Literary and Historical Studies in Honor of Harry Caplan*. Ithaca, NY: Cornell University Press.
Warren, B. 1996. "Authority, Gift-Exchange, and Senecan *Clementia*." Unpublished MS. Baltimore.
Watson, G. 1966. *The Stoic Theory of Knowledge*. Belfast: Queen's University.
Webb, R. 1997. "Imagination and the Arousal of Emotions in Graeco-Roman Rhetoric." In Braund and Gill (eds.) 1997: 112–27.
Wehrle, W. T. 1992. *The Satiric Voice. Program, Form and Meaning in Persius and Juvenal*. Hildesheim–New York: Olms-Weidmann.
Weinstock, S. 1957. "*Victor* and *Invictus*." *Harvard Theological Review* 50: 211–47.
———. 1971. *Divus Julius*. Oxford: Clarendon Press.
Whitby, M., and P. R. Hardie (eds.) 1987. *Homo Viator: Classical Essays for John Bramble*. Bristol: Bristol Classical Press.
White, N. P. 1990. "Stoic Values." *Monist* 73: 42–58.
———.1995. "The Basis of Stoic Ethics." In Irwin (ed.) 1995, vol. 8: 317–52.
Whitman, J. 1987. *Allegory: The Dynamics of an Ancient and Medieval Technique*. Cambridge, MA.: Harvard University Press.
Willet, J. (ed. and tr.) 1964. *Brecht on Theatre. The Development of an Aesthetic*. New York: Hill and Wang.
Williams, G. 1978. *Change and Decline. Roman Literature in the Early Empire*. Berkeley: University of California Press.
———. 1983. *Technique and Ideas in the* Aeneid. New Haven and London: Yale University Press.
Wilson, J. (trans.) 1993. *Lucan: Pharsalia*. Ithaca: Cornell University Press.
Wiltshire, S. F. 1999. "The Man Who Was Not There: Aeneas and Absence." In Perkell (ed.) 1999: 162–78.
Winstedt, E. O. (ed. and trans.) 1967. *Cicero. Letters to Atticus*. Cambridge, MA: Harvard University Press.
Wistrand, E. 1987. *Felicitas Imperatoria*. Göteborg : Acta Universitatis Gothoburgensis.
Wofford, S. 1992. *The Choice of Achilles: The Ideology of Figure in the Epic*. Stanford: Stanford University Press.
Woodman, A. J. 1975. "Questions of Date, Genre and Style in Velleius: Some Literary Answers." *Classical Quarterly* 25: 272–306.
Woodman, T., and J. Powell (eds.) 1992. *Author and Audience in Latin Literature*. Cambridge: Cambridge University Press.
Yamagata, B. N. 1989. "The Apostrophe in Homer as Part of the Oral Technique." *BICS* 36: 91–103.
Zagdoun, M.-A. 2000. *La philosophie stoïcienne de l'art*. Paris: CNRS editions.
Zanker, P. 1995. *The Mask of Socrates* [tr. by A. Shapiro]. Oxford: Oxford University Press.

Zeller, E. 1962. *The Stoics, Epicureans and Sceptics* [tr. O. Reichel]. New York: Russel and Russel.
———. 1980. *Outlines of the History of Greek Philosophy.* [Tr. L. R. Palmer of 1923. *Die Philosophie der Griechen*, 5th ed. Leipzig.] Dover: Dover Publications.
Zetzel, J. 1981. *Latin Textual Criticism in Antiquity.* New York: Arno Press.
Zyroff, E. S. 1971. "The Author's Apostrophe in Epic from Homer through Lucan." Ph.D. Diss. The Johns Hopkins University.

Index Locorum

[I am indexing only the most important discussed passages]

Aristotle, *Po.* 1453a, **75**; 1449b25–29, **78**; 1450–1453b10, **82, 110**; 1454a4, **78**; 1460a5–11, **87, 105**; 16.1455a17, **78**
Caesar, *B.C.* 3.92, **54**
Carmen de Bello Actiaco v.36–43 and vi.45–52, **154–55**
Cicero, *Att.* 9.7c, **62**
D.L. 7.130, **173**
Epictetus, *Diss.* 1.6.10, **109**
Horace, *A.P.* 99–100, **99**; 309–11, **99**
Longinus, *Subl.* 16.2, **1–2**
Lucan, *BC* 1.168–71, **61**; 1.522–25, **80**; 2.15, **9, 170**; 2.38–42, **69, 150**; 2.251–56, **139**; 2.289–98, **115, 126, 133**; 2.297–305, **71, 141, 148, 151–53, 155, 163**; 2.304–18, **158**; 2.309–11, **48**; 2.323–25, **115, 138**; 2.295–96, **138**; 2.377–78, **149, 163**; 2.390–91, **149**; 3.112–114, **134**; 3.145–47, **135**; 4.189–91, **58–59**; 4.212–35, **57, 57–58**; 4.497–504, **37**; 4.516–20, **39, 45**; 4.548–56, **42–43**; 4.573–79, **43–44**; 4.703–10, **107**; 5.224–31, **117**; 5.385–86, **34**; 6.155–56, **46**; 6.165–69, **46**; 6.189–92, **47**; 6.250–62, **51–52**; 6.299–313, **83–84**; 7.6–25, **82**; 7.37–44, **69, 80**; 7.210–13, **76–78, 80, 165–66, 170**; 7.445–55, **143**; 7.457–59, **35**; 7.460–69, **54**; 7.470–75, **55**; 7.617–43, **41**; 7.680–86, **86**; 7.703–8, **84**; 8.605–6, **108**; 8.629–31, **137**; 8.663–67, **136**; 9.283–93, **122, 145, 147, 164**; 9.359–60, **108**; 9.378–94, **125, 126**; 9.509–10, **133–34**; 9.564–84, **119, 120**; 9.587–604, **129, 163**; 9.606–18, **111–112**; 9.593–603, **14**; 9.619–23, **110**; 9.735–36, **155**; 9.909–36, **168–69**; 9.984–89, **15, 127**; 9.1045–1062, **60, 63–65**; 9.1097–1102, **66**; 9.1104–1108, **68, 70**; 10.189–298, **119–20**
Ovid, *Met.* 4.312, **111**
Plato
 R. 377b7, **92**; 604b9–c3, **169**; 605c–d, **88, 93–94**
 Symp. 215c–e, **88, 123**
Pliny, *Natural History* 7.106, **131**
Plutarch
 De Audiendis Poetis 15d–16a, **92, 104**
 Life of Cato Minor 67 and 68.3, **150**
Polybius, *Universal History* 6.54, **151**
Quintilian, 6.2.29, **77**
Sallust, *C.* 52.11–12, **34**
Seneca
 Ajax 532–33, **164**
 Brev. Vit. 22.4, **172**
 Const. 3.5, **164**
 Ep. 7.115, **95**; 9.2–5, **175, 227n15**; 11.1–3, **174**; 34.1–2, **147**; 49.12, **97**; 59.5–7,

98–99; 59.9, **116, 121;** 71.27–29, **174;** 75.3–6, **102, 198n19;** 90.20, **96–97;** 92.11, **172;** 94.27–30, **101;** 94.72–74, **127;** 95.52, **148;** 100.1–2, **97;** 107.11, **159;** 107.9–12, **38–39;** 108.7–8, **98–103, 106n202, 123;** 108.9–10, **98–99, 201n52**
Ira 2.3.1, **91, 95, 174;** 2.2–6, **105;** 2.3.4, **134**
Med. 681–739, **166–67**
Prov. 2.7–17, **114**
Strabo, 1.2.5–8, **90**
Virgil
Aen. 1.1–11, **17, 27;** 1.430–37, **145;** 1.450–52, **79;** 4.384–86, **153;** 4.401–5, **29;** 4.449, **60;** 4.490–97, **38;** 4.607–610, **153;** 6.30–33, **25–26, 159;** 6.882–86, **140;** 8.696–97, **153, 164;** 9.446–49, **22, 121–22;** 9.481–99, **156;** 10.460–465, **27, 159, 60;** 10.501–5, **25;** 10.507–9, **23;** 10.821–26, **50, 67;** 12.500–4, **27;** 12.872–81, **19, 164**
G. 4.103–105, **146;** 4.153–218, **146**

General Index

Ahl, F. 36, 108, 153,193n73, 223n120
Acoreus, 119–20, 214
Ajax, 164, 224n9,
Alcibiades, 88
alienation (*Verfremdungseffek*), 8, 71, 73–75
allegoresis, 10, 181, 202n62, 210n135
allegory, 110, 124, 165, 210n135; as defined by the Stoics 108–9. See also *allegoresis; fabula*
Ammon, 116, 118, 120
Anchises, 50, 139–40, 150–51
anger, 42, 46, 134–37, 149, 176, 178, 201n59; of the gods, 17–18, 27
Antiochus of Ascalon, 177–78
apatheia, 11, 13, 115, 149–50, 160, 163, 227n15
Aristotle, 9, 97–98, 110, 166, 171–72, 176–78; and emotional involvement, 73–74, 78
assent, 5, 9, 12, 90–94, 104, 174–76
autarkeia, 48, 127

Barton, C., 162–63, 187–87
Bartsch, S., 73, 86, 106, 114–15
Beagon, M., 131
bees, 123, 144–47
Brecht. B., 8, 73–75
Brennan, T., 173
Brutus, 47, 80, 114–17, 138–39, 159

Caesar: and Acoreus, 119–20; apostrophe to, 60, 64–68, 83–84; facing Pompey's head, 63–65; and *furor,* 42, 139; and *ira,* 134; and manipulation of Roman ethical vocabulary, 7, 33–34, 36, 57, 61–71, 74; and snakes, 130, 155; and victory, 14, 41, 104, 127, 142
Carmen de Bello Actiaco, 154

Cato, 4; affecting audiences, 89, 139, 144–46; as anti-Aeneas, 32, 60, 131, 150, 159; and *autarkeia,* 48; and the emotions, 12, 133–34, 138–39, 149, 171–78 ; and the *fons* of poetry, 109–111; as Hercules, 125; as husband of the Republic, 150; inspiring hope, 80; as mourner, 71, 138, 141, 148–60; and the narrator, 116–119, 121–23, 130–31, 162–69; as negative character, 10–11, 113–116, 147; as *pater patriae,* 150, 152; as perfect general, 128–29; in Plutarch, 115–16, 149–50; to his soldiers, 125–28, 144–45; and political intervention, 14, 47, 131, 147; and snakes, 154–55, 162–69; as Stoic sage, 8, 13, 96, 120, 131, 133, 171–78; as a Titan, 142–43, 152–53, 155–58
Chrysippus, 112, 193; as advocate of allegorical interpretations, 108–9; and criterion of truth, 51; and poetry, 89–91
Cleanthes, 89, 100, 123, 159
clementia: at *BC* 1045–1066, 60–63, 66–67; in Caesar's first pardoning of Domitius, 65–66; as gift, 62; as *insidiosa,* 193n75; as a tool to break ideological resistance to the Caesars, 61; in Virgil's *Aeneid,* 25
Cleopatra, 13, 152–54, 164
Commenta Berniensia, 52, 68
Conte, G. B., 3, 19–22, 51–52
Cornutus, 100, 108, 110, 211n151
Cotta, 122, 135, 145
Crastinus, 53–55
Crates of Mallus, 90
Curio 69, 106–7

death as a spectacle, 38, 188n19

Dido, 13, 24, 57–58, 152–53; apostrophe to, 21, 28–30

ekplêxis, 11, 77–78, 104; as able to alter the reader's emotional disposition, 88; as the soul's response to philosophical *logos*, 116, 123, 177
enargeia, 60; as making the readers emotionally involved, 116, 123, 165; as style which conveys a vision, 77–78, 105
empathy, 3, 18–20, 73–74, 94
Euryalus' mother, 155–58

Fantham, E., 24, 115, 133, 139
fabula, 11, 107–8, 111, 120–21, 125, 160
fear: aroused by a poem, 78–80, 105; in Aristotle's *Poetics*, 78, 82; and Cato, 115, 126, 133, 139, 160, 165; in connection to hope, 9, 75, 79–80, 166, 170; and Stoic sage, 175
focalization, 3, 50, 57, 72
furor, 29, 37, 42, 115, 134, 138–39, 164
future, 9, 16, 21–25, 24–25, 41, 44–45, 52–53, 59, 61, 85, 121–23, 139, 158–59, 170

gladiatorial contest, 106, 153; and audience, 59
Glosule super Lucanum, 68
Halliwell, S., 88, 93, 197n8 and n16
Heraclitus, 100, 108
Hershkowitz, D., 134, 147, 212n12
hope, 9, 44–45, 57–58, 79–80, 82, 103, 144, 157–60, 162, 165–66, 170 (*see also* fear); at *Aen.* 1.208–9, 126
Homer, 3, 35, 90, 108, 110, 121–22

imperium, 19, 21–23, 79, 104, 122, 131
indifferents, 133, 160, 171–77, 217n55; as preferred, 31
instability of meaning, 7–8, 106; 125; during times of internal strife, 33, 35. *See also* Caesar and manipulation of Roman ethical vocabulary
Inwood, B., 12, 174, 226n13
Irwin, T., 171–72, 175–76

Johnson, W. R., 113
Juturna, 18–19, 27, 153, 158, 164

Keith, A., 152
Ketman, 70–71

Labienus, 118–19
Lada, I., 88, 92
lamentation, 23–24, 27, 30–31, 68, 84–85, 148, 151, 186n44
Leigh, M., 42–43, 73, 76, 78, 114, 127
Libyan march, 109–11, 124–26, 129, 134, 153; and snakes, 167
Long, A., 35, 91, 142

Malamud, M., 110–11, 137–38
Marti, B., 82, 113–14
Mazzoli, G. C., 100, 102, 169
mental lethargy, 13, 103, 163
Metellus, 12, 134–35
Mezentius, 46–50, 64, 157
Milosz, C., 70–71
Mucius Scaevola, 46–47, 151–52, 174

Narducci, E., 86, 136, 141, 143, 152, 160
narrator, 1–14; in *Aeneid*, 17–30; condemning the gods, 140–43; in connection with Cato and poetry, 116–33, 147–48, 150–60, 165–66, 169–70; in connection with Pompey 77–87, 137; and *fabula*, 107–11; and negative characters, 40–45, 50–55, 58–72
Nugent, G., 49, 158
Nussbaum, M., 9, 90, 92, 100, 103, 187, 201n47

oikeiôsis, 59, 148, 160, 193n71

passions (or emotions), 9, 12–13, 77–78,

88–91, 104–105, 108, 111, 160, 171, 174–76, 178, 226n13
phantasia: as mental picture conducive to shock, 77, 165; as object of assent, 90–92; as subject to interpretation, 35
Phrygian bronze, 122–23, 144–45, 153, 164
Panaetius, 10, 12, 96–97, 102, 177, 203n73, 205n95
Petreius, 53, 55, 57–59
pietas, 30, 36–37, 53, 61–62; and Aeneas, 50; and Caesar, 64–65, 67; and Euryalus' mother, 156; and Mezentius, 48–49; and Pompey, 83–84, 86; and Scaeva, 46
piety, 54, 84, 106
pity, 114, 169, 197n8; in Aristotle's *Poetics,* 74, 78, 82; of the reader, 37, 86
Plutarch, 5, 9, 82, 92, 104, 115–16, 131, 149–50, 167, 175
poetry: in connection with the passions and *ekplêxis,* 77–78, 87–88; in Horace, 97, 99; and philosophy 98–102; and Plato, 73, 88–94, 100, 169; in Seneca, 10, 89–91, 94–105, 112, 123; Stoic approaches to, 9, 11, 90–96
point of view, 7, 184n15; of the character, 18–21, 107; of the narrator, 40, 42–43. *See also* empathy
Pompey, death of, 64, 69–70, 135–38; described in an unfavorable light, 80, 85; as favored by the narrator, 11, 80, 82–87; as a Stoic *proficiens,* 82, 84–85, 137; as a tragic character, 8–9, 82, 166

Posidonius, 9, 89, 90, 102, 174, 177–78
Prodicus, 109, 125
Providence, 11, 13, 103, 172; as cruel, 142–43
Psylli, 166–69

Roller, M., 34, 128, 193n75

Scaeva, 36, 45–53, 104, 158
Schiesaro, A., 5, 103
Sklenár, R., 120
Socrates, 89, 123, 169
Sorabji, R., 176–77
spectatorship, 72, 106, 161; techniques useful to the formation of a detached spectatorship, 10, 92–93, 165
Stoic inhumanity, 171–77
"subjective style," 18, 31
suicide, of Cato, 150, 154, 164; imposed on Lucan, 14; as rational act of the *sapiens,* 173; and the Stoics, 40; of Vulteius' men, 36–37, 40, 45; and women, 19, 153–54, 159
sympathy, Virgilian, 3, 9, 18, 20–21, 29, 31, 84; toward Pompey, 82, 87

Tandoi, V., 149–50
tragedy, 9, 24, 48, 130, 184n31; described by Aristotle, 78, 82; as interpreted by I. Lada, 88; and Plato, 88, 94
Turnus, 3, 18, 21, 24–25, 27, 37, 136

Vulteius, 36–45, 53, 74

Wofford, S., 27–28

www.ingramcontent.com/pod-product-compliance
Lightning Source LLC
Chambersburg PA
CBHW020944230426
43666CB00005B/162